Praise for *Spring in Action*

This is an excellent book. It is very well written. Examples are very concise and easy to follow.

—Sunil Parikh, DZone

5 out of 5 stars ... a great instructive book.

—Nicola Pedot, Java User Group Trento

You will learn how to use Spring to write simpler, easier-to-maintain code so that you can focus on what really matters—your critical business needs.

—Springframework.org

Encyclopedic and eminently readable. Five stars all around!

—JavaLobby.org

Superbly organized and fluently written.

—Internet Bookwatch

Easy to read ... with just enough humor mixed in.

—Books-On-Line

A rare book.

—Computing Reviews

Best overall introduction to Spring.

—Taruvai Subramaniam, Amazon reader

"Really pushes Spring into Action."

—Patrick Steger, Zühlke Engineering

"Tremendous focus and fun to read ... zooms in on things developers need to know."

—Doug Warren, Java Web Services

Spring in Action

THIRD EDITION

CRAIG WALLS

MANNING
SHELTER ISLAND

For online information and ordering of this and other Manning books, please visit www.manning.com. The publisher offers discounts on this book when ordered in quantity. For more information, please contact

Special Sales Department
Manning Publications Co.
20 Baldwin Road
PO Box 261
Shelter Island, NY 11964
Email: orders@manning.com

Manning Publications Co.
20 Baldwin Road
PO Box 261
Shelter Island, NY 11964

Development editors: Sebastian Stirling
Copyeditor: Benjamin Berg
Proofreader: Katie Tennant
Typesetter: Dottie Marsico
Cover designer: Marija Tudor

ISBN 9781935182351
Printed in the United States of America
1 2 3 4 5 6 7 8 9 10 – MAL – 16 15 14 13 12 11

brief contents

PART 1 CORE SPRING 1

1 ■ Springing into action 3
2 ■ Wiring beans 30
3 ■ Minimizing XML configuration in Spring 64
4 ■ Aspect-oriented Spring 84

PART 2 SPRING APPLICATION ESSENTIALS 111

5 ■ Hitting the database 113
6 ■ Managing transactions 146
7 ■ Building web applications with Spring MVC 164
8 ■ Working with Spring Web Flow 199
9 ■ Securing Spring 224

PART 3 INTEGRATING SPRING 253

10 ■ Working with remote services 255
11 ■ Giving Spring some REST 277
12 ■ Messaging in Spring 310
13 ■ Managing Spring beans with JMX 333
14 ■ Odds and ends 350

contents

preface *xv*
acknowledgments *xvii*
about this book *xix*
about the cover illustration *xxiii*

PART 1 CORE SPRING 1

1 ***Springing into action 3***

1.1 Simplifying Java development 4

Unleashing the power of POJOs 5 ▪ Injecting dependencies 6
Applying aspects 10 ▪ Eliminating boilerplate code with templates 15

1.2 Containing your beans 17

Working with an application context 18 ▪ A bean's life 19

1.3 Surveying the Spring landscape 20

Spring modules 20 ▪ The Spring portfolio 23

1.4 What's new in Spring 27

What's new in Spring 2.5? 27 ▪ What's new in Spring 3.0? 28
What's new in the Spring portfolio? 28

1.5 Summary 29

2 *Wiring beans 30*

2.1 Declaring beans 31

Setting up Spring configuration 32 ▪ Declaring a simple bean 33 ▪ Injecting through constructors 34 ▪ Bean scoping 38 ▪ Initializing and destroying beans 39

2.2 Injecting into bean properties 41

Injecting simple values 42 ▪ Referencing other beans 43 Wiring properties with Spring's p namespace 46 ▪ Wiring collections 47 ▪ Wiring nothing (null) 52

2.3 Wiring with expressions 52

Expressing SpEL fundamentals 53 ▪ Performing operations on SpEL values 56 ▪ Sifting through collections in SpEL 59

2.4 Summary 63

3 *Minimizing XML configuration in Spring 64*

3.1 Automatically wiring bean properties 65

The four kinds of autowiring 65 ▪ Default autowiring 68 Mixing auto with explicit wiring 69

3.2 Wiring with annotations 70

Using @Autowired 71 ▪ Applying standards-based autowiring with @Inject 74 ▪ Using expressions with annotation injection 76

3.3 Automatically discovering beans 77

Annotating beans for autodiscovery 78 Filtering component-scans 79

3.4 Using Spring's Java-based configuration 80

Setting up for Java-based configuration 80 ▪ Defining a configuration class 81 ▪ Declaring a simple bean 81 Injecting with Spring's Java-based configuration 82

3.5 Summary 83

4 *Aspect-oriented Spring 84*

4.1 What's aspect-oriented programming? 85

Defining AOP terminology 86 ▪ Spring's AOP support 88

4.2 Selecting join points with pointcuts 91

Writing pointcuts 92 ▪ Using Spring's bean() designator 93

4.3 Declaring aspects in XML 93

Declaring before and after advice 95 ▪ Declaring around advice 97 ▪ Passing parameters to advice 98 ▪ Introducing new functionality with aspects 100

4.4 Annotating aspects 102

Annotating around advice 104 ▪ Passing arguments to annotated advice 105 ▪ Annotating introductions 106

4.5 Injecting AspectJ aspects 107

4.6 Summary 110

PART 2 SPRING APPLICATION ESSENTIALS 111

5 *Hitting the database 113*

5.1 Learning Spring's data access philosophy 114

Getting to know Spring's data access exception hierarchy 115 Templating data access 117 ▪ Using DAO support classes 119

5.2 Configuring a data sourcc 121

Using JNDI data sources 121 ▪ Using a pooled data source 122 ▪ JDBC driver-based data source 123

5.3 Using JDBC with Spring 124

Tackling runaway JDBC code 124 ▪ Working with JDBC templates 127

5.4 Integrating Hibernate with Spring 132

A Hibernate overview 134 ▪ Declaring a Hibernate session factory 134 ▪ Building Spring-free Hibernate 137

5.5 Spring and the Java Persistence API 138

Configuring an entity manager factory 139 ▪ Writing a JPA-based DAO 143

5.6 Summary 144

6 *Managing transactions 146*

6.1 Understanding transactions 147

Explaining transactions in only four words 148 Understanding Spring's transaction management support 149

6.2 Choosing a transaction manager 150

JDBC transactions 151 ▪ Hibernate transactions 151 ▪ Java Persistence API transactions 152 ▪ Java transaction API transactions 153

6.3 Programming transactions in Spring 153

6.4 Declaring transactions 155

Defining transaction attributes 156 ▪ Declaring transactions in XML 160 ▪ Defining annotation-driven transactions 162

6.5 Summary 163

7 *Building web applications with Spring MVC 164*

7.1 Getting started with Spring MVC 165

Following a request through Spring MVC 165 ▪ Setting up Spring MVC 167

7.2 Writing a basic controller 169

Configuring an annotation-driven Spring MVC 170 ▪ Defining the home page controller 170 ▪ Resolving views 173 ▪ Defining the home page view 177 ▪ Rounding out the Spring application context 179

7.3 Handling controller input 181

Writing a controller that processes input 181 ▪ Rendering the view 183

7.4 Processing forms 185

Displaying the registration form 185 ▪ Processing form input 187 ▪ Validating input 189

7.5 Handling file uploads 193

Adding a file upload field to the form 193 ▪ Receiving uploaded files 194 ▪ Configuring Spring for file uploads 197

7.6 Summary 197

8 *Working with Spring Web Flow 199*

8.1 Installing Spring Web Flow 200

Configuring Web Flow in Spring 200

8.2 The components of a flow 203

States 203 ▪ Transitions 206 ▪ Flow data 207

8.3 Putting it all together: the pizza flow 209

Defining the base flow 209 ▪ Collecting customer information 213 ▪ Building an order 218 ▪ Taking payment 221

8.4 Securing web flows 222

8.5 Summary 223

9 *Securing Spring 224*

9.1 Introducing Spring Security 225

Getting started with Spring Security 226 ▪ Using the Spring Security configuration namespace 226

9.2 Securing web requests 227

Proxying servlet filters 228 ▪ Configuring minimal web security 228 ▪ Intercepting requests 232

9.3 Securing view-level elements 235

Accessing authentication details 235 ▪ Rendering with authorities 236

9.4 Authenticating users 238

Configuring an in-memory user repository 239 Authenticating against a database 240 ▪ Authenticating against LDAP 241 ▪ Enabling remember-me functionality 245

9.5 Securing methods 246

Securing methods with @Secured 246 ▪ Using JSR-250's @RolesAllowed 247 ▪ Pre-/Post-invocation security with SpEL 247 ▪ Declaring method-level security pointcuts 252

9.6 Summary 252

PART 3 INTEGRATING SPRING 253

10 *Working with remote services 255*

10.1 An overview of Spring remoting 256

10.2 Working with RMI 258

Exporting an RMI service 259 ▪ Wiring an RMI service 261

10.3 Exposing remote services with Hessian and Burlap 263

Exposing bean functionality with Hessian/Burlap 264 Accessing Hessian/Burlap services 266

10.4 Using Spring's HttpInvoker 268

Exposing beans as HTTP services 268 ▪ Accessing services via HTTP 269

10.5 Publishing and consuming web services 270

Creating Spring-enabled JAX-WS endpoints 271
Proxying JAX-WS services on the client side 274

10.6 Summary 276

11 *Giving Spring some REST 277*

11.1 Getting REST 278

The fundamentals of REST 278 ▪ How Spring supports REST 279

11.2 Writing resource-oriented controllers 279

Dissecting a RESTless controller 280 ▪ Handling RESTful URLs 281 ▪ Performing the REST verbs 284

11.3 Representing resources 287

Negotiating resource representation 288 ▪ Working with HTTP message converters 291

11.4 Writing REST clients 294

Exploring RestTemplate's operations 295 ▪ GETting resources 296 ▪ PUTting resources 299 ▪ DELETE-ing resources 301 ▪ POSTing resource data 301 ▪ Exchanging resources 304

11.5 Submitting RESTful forms 306

Rendering hidden method fields in JSP 306 ▪ Unmasking the real request 307

11.6 Summary 309

12 *Messaging in Spring 310*

12.1 A brief introduction to JMS 311

Architecting JMS 312 ▪ Assessing the benefits of JMS 314

12.2 Setting up a message broker in Spring 316

Creating a connection factory 316 ▪ Declaring an ActiveMQ message destination 317

12.3 Using Spring's JMS template 318

Tackling runaway JMS code 318 ▪ Working with JMS templates 319

12.4 Creating message-driven POJOs 325

Creating a message listener 326 ▪ Configuring message listeners 327

12.5 Using message-based RPC 327

Working with Spring message-based RPC 328 ▪ Asynchronous RPC with Lingo 330

12.6 Summary 332

13 *Managing Spring beans with JMX 333*

13.1 Exporting Spring beans as MBeans 334

Exposing methods by name 337 ▪ Using interfaces to define MBean operations and attributes 339 ▪ Working with annotation-driven MBeans 340 ▪ Handing MBean collisions 342

13.2 Remoting MBeans 343

Exposing remote MBeans 343 ▪ Accessing remote MBeans 344 Proxying MBeans 345

13.3 Handling notifications 346

Listening for notifications 348

13.4 Summary 349

14 *Odds and ends 350*

14.1 Externalizing configuration 351

Replacing property placeholders 352 ▪ Overriding properties 354 ▪ Encrypting external properties 355

14.2 Wiring JNDI objects 357

Working with conventional JNDI 357 ▪ Injecting JNDI objects 359 ▪ Wiring EJBs in Spring 362

14.3 Sending email 363

Configuring a mail sender 363 ▪ Constructing the email 365

14.4 Scheduling and background tasks 370

Declaring scheduled methods 371 ▪ Declaring asynchronous methods 373

14.5 Summary 374

14.6 The end...? 374

index 377

preface

Wow! As I write this, it's been almost seven years since Spring 1.0 was released and Ryan Breidenbach and I started work on the first edition of *Spring in Action*. Back then, who would have guessed that Spring would transform Java development as much as it has?

In that first edition, Ryan and I tried to cover every corner of the Spring Framework. For the most part, we were successful. Back then the entire Spring story could easily be told in 11 chapters with dependency injection, AOP, persistence, transactions, Spring MVC, and Acegi Security as the main characters. Of course, back then that story had to be told with a lot of XML. (Does anybody remember what it was like declaring transactions with `TransactionProxyFactoryBean`?)

By the time I got around to writing the second edition, Spring had grown quite a bit. Again, I tried to squeeze everything I could into a single book. I found out it wasn't possible. Spring had expanded well beyond what could be discussed in a 700- to 800-page book. In fact, entire, completely written chapters were cut out of the second edition because there wasn't room.

More than three years and two major versions of Spring have passed since the second edition was printed. Spring covers more ground than ever before and it would take several volumes to comprehensively cover the entire Spring portfolio. It's not possible to cram everything there is to know about Spring into a single book.

So I'm not going to even try.

Often books get thicker with each successive edition. But you've probably noticed by now that this third edition of *Spring in Action* has fewer pages than the second edition. That's possible for a couple of reasons.

Since I couldn't fit everything into one volume, I was choosy about what topics made it into this edition. I decided to focus on what I believe are the core Spring topics that most Spring developers should know. That's not to say that the other topics aren't important, but these are the essentials of Spring development.

The other reason this edition is smaller is due to the fact that while Spring's reach has continued to expand, it has continued to become simpler with each release. Spring's rich set of configuration namespaces, adoption of annotation-driven programming models, and application of sensible conventions and defaults have reduced Spring configuration from page upon page of XML down to only a handful of elements.

But make no mistake: though there are fewer pages, I've still managed to pack a lot of new Spring goodness into them. Along with the dependency injection, AOP, and declarative transactions Spring has long provided, here's a sampling of the stuff you'll learn in this edition that's new or changed since the second edition:

- Annotation-based bean wiring that dramatically reduces the amount of Spring XML configuration
- A new expression language for evaluating values wired into bean properties dynamically at runtime
- Spring's all-new annotation-driven Spring MVC framework, which is far more flexible than the former hierarchical controller framework
- Securing Spring applications with Spring Security, much simpler now with a new configuration namespace, convenient defaults, and support for expression-oriented security rules
- First-class support for building and consuming REST resources, based on Spring MVC

Whether you're new to Spring or a Spring veteran, I hope that you'll find this book to be an indispensable guide as you use Spring in your projects.

acknowledgments

Before you put your hands on this book, it was touched by many other hands—hands that edited it, reviewed it, proofread it, and managed the whole publishing process. You wouldn't be reading this book if it weren't for all those hands.

First, I'd like to thank everyone at Manning for working hard, pressuring me to get this darn thing done, and for doing their part to make sure that this book is the best it could be: Marjan Bace, Michael Stephens, Christina Rudloff, Karen Tegtmeyer, Maureen Spencer, Mary Piergies, Sebastian Stirling, Benjamin Berg, Katie Tennant, Janet Vail, and Dottie Marsico.

Along the way, a handful of other people were given the opportunity to read the manuscript in its roughest form and provide feedback, telling me what I got right and (gasp) where I missed the mark. Many thanks to all of those reviewers for their valuable feedback: Valentin Crettaz, Jeff Addison, John Ryan, Olivier Nouguier, Joshua White, Deiveehan Nallazhagappan, Adam Taft, Peter Pavlovich, Mykel Alvis, Rick Wagner, Patrick Steger, Josh Devins, Dan Alford, Alberto Lagna, Dan Dobrin, Robert Hanson, Chad Davis, Carol McDonald, Deepak Vohra, and Robert O'Connor. And a special thanks to Doug Warren for taking on the role of technical reviewer and going over the technical details of the book with a fine-toothed comb.

My gratitude is also due to those who played no direct part in producing the book, but were there providing support, friendship, good conversation, and making sure that I had adequate breaks from writing to do other things.

First and foremost, thanks to my wife Raymie. You're my best friend, the love of my life, and the reason for everything I do. I love you very much. Thank you for putting up with another writing project and for supporting me.

To Maisy and Madi, my little princesses, thank you for your hugs, laughs, imagination, and the occasional Mario Kart breaks.

To my colleagues at SpringSource, thank you for continuing to revolutionize how we develop software and for giving me the opportunity to be a part of what you do. Special thanks to the two SpringSourcers I work with every day, Keith Donald and Roy Clarkson—we've done some awesome stuff in the past year and I look forward to the amazing things that lie ahead.

Many thanks to my No Fluff/Just Stuff cohorts for reminding me every few weekends that I'm not nearly as smart as you guys: Ted Neward, Venkat Subramaniam, Tim Berglund, Matthew McCullough, Matt Stine, Brian Goetz, Jeff Brown, Dave Klein, Ken Sipe, Nathaniel Schutta, Neal Ford, Pratik Patel, Rohit Bhardwaj, Scott Davis, Mark Richards, and of course, Jay Zimmerman.

Finally, there are *many* other folks out there that I'd like to send a shout out to for their part in shaping me, my career, and this book: Ryan Breidenbach, Ben Rady, Mike Nash, Matt Smith, John Woodward, Greg Vaughn, Barry Rogers, Paul Holser, Derek Lane, Erik Weibust, and Andrew Rubalcaba.

about this book

The Spring Framework was created with a very specific goal in mind—to make developing Java EE applications easier. Along the same lines, *Spring in Action, Third Edition* was written to make learning how to use Spring easier. My goal is not to give you a blow-by-blow listing of Spring APIs. Instead, I hope to present the Spring Framework in a way that is most relevant to a Java EE developer by providing practical code examples from real-world experiences. Since Spring is a modular framework, this book was written in the same way. I recognize that not all developers have the same needs. Some may want to learn the Spring Framework from the ground up, while others may want to pick and choose different topics and go at their own pace. That way, the book can act as a tool for learning Spring for the first time as well as a guide and reference for those wanting to dig deeper into specific features.

Who should read this book

Spring in Action, Third Edition, is for all Java developers, but enterprise Java developers will find it particularly useful. While I will guide you along gently through code examples that build in complexity throughout each chapter, the true power of Spring lies in its ability to make enterprise applications easier to develop. Therefore, enterprise developers will most fully appreciate the examples presented in this book.

Because a vast portion of Spring is devoted to providing enterprise services, many parallels can be drawn between Spring and EJB. Therefore, any experience you have will be useful in making comparisons between these two frameworks. A portion of this book is dedicated to this topic. In fact, the final five chapters demonstrate how Spring can support enterprise integration of web applications. If you are an enterprise application developer, you will find the last part of this book especially valuable.

Roadmap

Spring in Action, Third Edition, is divided into three parts. The first part introduces you to the essentials of the Spring Framework. Part 2 goes beyond that by delving into the common elements of a Spring application. The final part shows how Spring can be used to integrate with other applications and services.

In part 1, you'll explore dependency injection (DI) and aspect-oriented programming (AOP), two essential features of the Spring Framework. This will give you a good understanding of Spring's fundamentals that will be utilized throughout the book.

In chapter 1, you'll be introduced to DI and AOP and how they lend themselves to developing loosely coupled Java applications.

Chapter 2 takes a more detailed look at how to configure and associate your application objects using dependency injection. You'll learn how to write loosely coupled components and wire their dependencies and properties within the Spring container using XML.

Once you have the basics of Spring XML configuration down, chapter 3 will present annotation-oriented alternatives to XML configuration.

Chapter 4 explores how to use Spring's AOP to decouple cross-cutting concerns from the objects that they service. This chapter also sets the stage for later chapters, where you'll use Spring AOP to provide declarative services such as transactions, security, and caching.

Part 2 builds on the DI and AOP features introduced in part 1, and shows you how to apply these concepts to build the common elements of an application.

Chapter 5 covers Spring's support for data persistence. You'll be introduced to Spring's JDBC support, which helps you remove much of the boilerplate code associated with JDBC. You'll also see how Spring integrates with persistence frameworks such as Hibernate and the Java Persistence API (JPA).

Chapter 6 complements chapter 5, showing you how to ensure integrity in your database using Spring's transaction support. You'll see how Spring uses AOP to give simple application objects the power of declarative transactions.

Chapter 7 introduces you to Spring's MVC web framework. You'll discover how Spring can transparently bind web parameters to your business objects and provide validation and error handling at the same time. You'll also see how easy it is to add functionality to your web applications using Spring MVC controllers.

Chapter 8 explores Spring Web Flow, an extension to Spring MVC that enables development of conversational web applications. In this chapter you'll learn how to build web applications that guide the user through a specific flow.

In chapter 9 you'll learn how to apply security to your application using Spring Security. You'll see how Spring Security secures applications both at the web request level using servlet filters and at the method level using Spring AOP.

After building an application with what you've learned from part 2, you may want to integrate it with other applications or services. In part 3 you'll learn how to do that.

Chapter 10 explores how to expose your application objects as remote services. You'll also learn how to seamlessly access remote services as though they were any other object in your application. Remoting technologies explored will include RMI, Hessian/Burlap, SOAP-based web services, and Spring's own `HttpInvoker`.

Chapter 11 revisits Spring MVC, showing how to use it to expose your application data as RESTful resources. In addition, you'll learn how to develop REST clients with Spring's RestTemplate.

Chapter 12 looks at using Spring to send and receive asynchronous messages with JMS. In addition to basic JMS operations with Spring, you'll also learn how to use the open source Lingo project to expose and consume asynchronous remote services over JMS.

Chapter 13 will show you how to use Spring to schedule jobs, send emails, access JNDI-configured resources, and manage your application objects with JMX.

Wrapping up our exploration of Spring, chapter 14 will show you how to use Spring to schedule jobs, send emails, and access JNDI-configured resources.

Code conventions

There are many code examples throughout this book. These examples will always appear in a `fixed-width code font`. If there is a part of an example I want you to pay extra attention to, it will appear in a bolded code font. Any class name, method name or XML fragment within the normal text of the book will appear in code font as well.

Many of Spring's classes and packages have exceptionally long (but expressive) names. Because of this, line-continuation markers (➥) may be included when necessary.

Not all code examples in this book will be complete. Often I only show a method or two from a class to focus on a particular topic. Complete source code for the applications found throughout the book can be downloaded from the publisher's website at www.manning.com/SpringinActionThirdEdition.

About the author

Craig Walls is a software developer with more than 13 years of experience and is the coauthor of *XDoclet in Action* (Manning, 2003) and two earlier editions of *Spring in Action* (Manning, 2005 and 2007). He's a zealous promoter of the Spring Framework, speaking frequently at local user groups and conferences and writing about Spring on his blog. When he's not slinging code, Craig spends as much time as he can with his wife, two daughters, six birds, four dogs, two cats, and an ever-fluctuating number of tropical fish. Craig lives in Plano, Texas.

Author Online

Purchase of *Spring in Action, Third Edition* includes free access to a private web forum run by Manning Publications where you can make comments about the book, ask technical questions, and receive help from the author and from other users. To access the forum and subscribe to it, point your web browser to www.manning.com/SpringinActionThirdEdition. This page provides information on how to get on the forum once you are registered, what kind of help is available, and the rules of conduct on the forum.

Manning's commitment to our readers is to provide a venue where a meaningful dialogue between individual readers and between readers and the author can take place. It is not a commitment to any specific amount of participation on the part of the author, whose contribution to the book's forum remains voluntary (and unpaid). We suggest you try asking the author some challenging questions, lest his interest stray!

The Author Online forum and the archives of previous discussions will be accessible from the publisher's website as long as the book is in print.

About the title

By combining introductions, overviews, and how-to examples, the *In Action* books are designed to help learning and remembering. According to research in cognitive science, the things people remember are things they discover during self-motivated exploration.

Although no one at Manning is a cognitive scientist, we are convinced that for learning to become permanent it must pass through stages of exploration, play, and, interestingly, retelling of what is being learned. People understand and remember new things, which is to say they master them, only after actively exploring them. Humans learn in action. An essential part of an *In Action* guide is that it is example-driven. It encourages the reader to try things out, to play with new code, and explore new ideas.

There is another, more mundane, reason for the title of this book: our readers are busy. They use books to do a job or to solve a problem. They need books that allow them to jump in and jump out easily and learn just what they want just when they want it. They need books that aid them in action. The books in this series are designed for such readers.

about the cover illustration

The figure on the cover of *Spring in Action, Third Edition,* is a "Le Caraco," or an inhabitant of the province of Karak in southwest Jordan. Its capital is the city of Al-Karak, which boasts an ancient hilltop castle with magnificent views of the Dead Sea and surrounding plains.

The illustration is taken from a French travel book, *Encyclopédie des Voyages* by J. G. St. Sauveur, published in 1796. Travel for pleasure was a relatively new phenomenon at the time and travel guides such as this one were popular, introducing both the tourist as well as the armchair traveler to the inhabitants of other regions of France and abroad.

The diversity of the drawings in the *Encyclopédie des Voyages* speaks vividly of the uniqueness and individuality of the world's towns and provinces just 200 years ago. This was a time when the dress codes of two regions separated by a few dozen miles identified people uniquely as belonging to one or the other. The travel guide brings to life a sense of isolation and distance of that period and of every other historic period except our own hyperkinetic present.

Dress codes have changed since then and the diversity by region, so rich at the time, has faded away. It is now often hard to tell the inhabitant of one continent from another. Perhaps, trying to view it optimistically, we have traded a cultural and visual diversity for a more varied personal life. Or a more varied and interesting intellectual and technical life.

We at Manning celebrate the inventiveness, the initiative, and the fun of the computer business with book covers based on the rich diversity of regional life two centuries ago brought back to life by the pictures from this travel guide.

Part 1

Core Spring

Spring does a lot of things. But when you break it down to its core parts, Spring's primary features are dependency injection (DI) and aspect-oriented programming (AOP). Starting in chapter 1, "Springing into action," I'll give you a quick overview of DI and AOP in Spring and see how they can help you decouple application objects.

In chapter 2, "Wiring beans," we'll dive deeper into how to use Spring's XML-based configuration to keep application objects loosely coupled with dependency injection. You'll learn how to define application objects and then wire them with their dependencies.

XML isn't the only way that Spring can be configured. Picking up where the previous chapter left off, chapter 3, "Minimizing XML configuration in Spring," explores some new features in Spring that make it possible to wire application objects with minimal or (in some cases, no) XML.

Chapter 4, "Aspect-oriented Spring," explores how to use Spring's AOP features to decouple systemwide services (such as security and auditing) from the objects they service. This chapter sets the stage for chapters 6 and 9, where you'll learn how to use Spring AOP to provide declarative transaction and security.

1 Springing into action

This chapter covers

- Exploring Spring's core modules
- Decoupling application objects
- Managing cross-cutting concerns with AOP
- Spring's bean container

It all started with a bean.

In 1996, the Java programming language was still a young, exciting, up-and-coming platform. Many developers flocked to the language because they'd seen how to create rich and dynamic web applications using applets. They soon learned that there was more to this strange new language than animated juggling cartoon characters. Unlike any language before it, Java made it possible to write complex applications made up of discrete parts. They came for the applets, but they stayed for the components.

In December of that year, Sun Microsystems published the JavaBeans 1.00-A specification. JavaBeans defined a software component model for Java. This specification defined a set of coding policies that enabled simple Java objects to be reusable and easily composed into more complex applications. Although JavaBeans were intended as a general-purpose means of defining reusable application components, they were primarily used as a model for building user interface widgets. They seemed too simple to be capable of any "real" work. Enterprise developers wanted more.

Sophisticated applications often require services such as transaction support, security, and distributed computing—services not directly provided by the JavaBeans specification. So in March 1998, Sun published version 1.0 of the Enterprise JavaBeans (EJB) specification. This specification extended the notion of Java components to the server side, providing much-needed enterprise services, but failed to continue the simplicity of the original JavaBeans specification. Except in name, EJB bears little resemblance to the original JavaBeans specification.

Despite the fact that many successful applications have been built based on EJB, EJB never achieved its intended purpose: to simplify enterprise application development. It's true that EJB's declarative programming model simplifies many infrastructural aspects of development, such as transactions and security. But in a different way, EJBs complicate development by mandating deployment descriptors and plumbing code (home and remote/local interfaces). Over time, many developers became disenchanted with EJB. As a result, its popularity has waned in recent years, leaving many developers looking for an easier way.

Today, Java component development has returned to its roots. New programming techniques, including aspect-oriented programming (AOP) and dependency injection (DI), are giving JavaBeans much of the power previously reserved for EJBs. These techniques furnish plain-old Java objects (POJOs) with a declarative programming model reminiscent of EJB, but without all of EJB's complexity. No longer must you resort to writing an unwieldy EJB component when a simple JavaBean will suffice.

In fairness, even EJBs have evolved to promote a POJO-based programming model. Employing ideas such as DI and AOP, the latest EJB specification is significantly simpler than its predecessors. But for many developers, this move is too little, too late. By the time the EJB 3 specification had entered the scene, other POJO-based development frameworks had already established themselves as de facto standards in the Java community.

Leading the charge for lightweight POJO-based development is the Spring Framework, which we'll explore throughout this book. In this chapter, we'll explore the Spring Framework at a high level, giving you a taste of what Spring is about. This chapter will give you a good idea of the types of problems Spring solves, and will set the stage for the rest of the book. First things first—let's find out what Spring is all about.

1.1 Simplifying Java development

Spring is an open source framework, originally created by Rod Johnson and described in his book *Expert One-on-One: J2EE Design and Development*. Spring was created to address the complexity of enterprise application development, and makes it possible to use plain-vanilla JavaBeans to achieve things that were previously only possible with EJBs. But Spring's usefulness isn't limited to server-side development. Any Java application can benefit from Spring in terms of simplicity, testability, and loose coupling.

A BEAN BY ANY OTHER NAME... Although Spring uses the words *bean* and *JavaBean* liberally when referring to application components, this doesn't mean that a Spring component must follow the JavaBeans specification to the letter. A Spring component can be any type of POJO. In this book, I assume the loose definition of JavaBean, which is synonymous with POJO.

As you'll see throughout this book, Spring does many things. But at the root of almost everything Spring provides are a few foundational ideas, all focused on Spring's fundamental mission: *Spring simplifies Java development.*

That's a bold statement! A lot of frameworks claim to simplify something or other. But Spring aims to simplify the broad subject of Java development. This begs for more explanation. How does Spring simplify Java development?

To back up its attack on Java complexity, Spring employs four key strategies:

- Lightweight and minimally invasive development with plain old Java objects (POJOs)
- Loose coupling through dependency injection and interface orientation
- Declarative programming through aspects and common conventions
- Boilerplate reduction through aspects and templates

Almost everything Spring does can be traced back to one or more of these four strategies. Throughout the rest of this chapter, I'll expand on each of these ideas, showing concrete examples of how Spring makes good on its promise to simplify Java development. Let's start with seeing how Spring remains minimally invasive by encouraging POJO-oriented development.

1.1.1 Unleashing the power of POJOs

If you've been doing Java development for long, you've probably seen (and may have even worked with) frameworks that lock you in by forcing you to extend one of their classes or implement one of their interfaces. The classic example is that of an EJB 2–era stateless session bean. As you can see from this trivial `HelloWorldBean`, the EJB 2 specification made some rather heavy demands:

Listing 1.1 EJB 2.1 forced you to implement methods that weren't needed.

```
package com.habuma.ejb.session;

import javax.ejb.SessionBean;
import javax.ejb.SessionContext;

public class HelloWorldBean implements SessionBean {
  public void ejbActivate() {
  }

  public void ejbPassivate() {
  }

  public void ejbRemove() {
  }
```

Why are these methods needed?

```
  public void setSessionContext(SessionContext ctx) {
  }

  public String sayHello() {
    return "Hello World";
  }

  public void ejbCreate() {
  }
}
```

EJB core business logic

The SessionBean interface would let you hook into the EJB's lifecycle by implementing several lifecycle callback methods (those methods that start with *ejb*). Or I should rephrase that to say that the SessionBean interface would *force* you to hook into the EJB's lifecycle, even if you didn't need to. The bulk of the code in HelloWorldBean is there solely for the sake of the framework. This raises the question: who's working for whom?

EJB 2 wasn't alone when it came to being invasive. Other popular frameworks such as the earlier versions of Struts, WebWork, and Tapestry imposed themselves upon otherwise simple Java classes. These heavyweight frameworks forced developers to write classes that were littered with unnecessary code, locked into their framework, and were often difficult to write tests against.

Spring avoids (as much as possible) littering your application code with its API. Spring almost never forces you to implement a Spring-specific interface or extend a Spring-specific class. Instead, the classes in a Spring-based application often have no indication that they're being used by Spring. At worst, a class may be annotated with one of Spring's annotations, but is otherwise a POJO.

To illustrate, if the HelloWorldBean class shown in listing 1.1 were to be rewritten to function as a Spring managed bean, it might look like this.

Listing 1.2 Spring doesn't make any unreasonable demands on HelloWorldBean.

```
package com.habuma.spring;

public class HelloWorldBean {
  public String sayHello() {
    return "Hello World";
  }
}
```

This is all you needed

Isn't that better? Gone are all of those noisy lifecycle methods. HelloWorldBean doesn't implement, extend, or even import anything from the Spring API. HelloWorldBean is lean, mean, and in every sense of the phrase, a plain-old Java object.

Despite their simple form, POJOs can be powerful. One of the ways Spring empowers POJOs is by assembling them using dependency injection. Let's see how dependency injection can help keep application objects decoupled from each other.

1.1.2 Injecting dependencies

The phrase *dependency injection* may sound intimidating, conjuring up notions of a complex programming technique or design pattern. But as it turns out, DI isn't nearly as complex as it sounds. By applying DI in your projects, you'll find that your code will become significantly simpler, easier to understand, and easier to test.

Any nontrivial application (pretty much anything more complex than a Hello World example) is made up of two or more classes that collaborate with each other to perform some business logic. Traditionally, each object is responsible for obtaining its own references to the objects it collaborates with (its dependencies). This can lead to highly coupled and hard-to-test code.

For example, consider the `Knight` class shown next.

Listing 1.3 A `DamselRescuingKnight` can only embark on RescueDamselQuests.

```
package com.springinaction.knights;

public class DamselRescuingKnight implements Knight {
  private RescueDamselQuest quest;

  public DamselRescuingKnight() {
    quest = new RescueDamselQuest();          <-- Tightly coupled to RescueDamselQuest
  }

  public void embarkOnQuest() throws QuestException {
    quest.embark();
  }
}
```

As you can see, `DamselRescuingKnight` creates its own quest, a `RescueDamselQuest`, within the constructor. This makes a `DamselRescuingKnight` tightly coupled to a `RescueDamselQuest` and severely limits the knight's quest-embarking repertoire. If a damsel needs rescuing, this knight's there. But if a dragon needs slaying or a round table needs... well...rounding, then this knight's going to have to sit it out.

What's more, it'd be terribly difficult to write a unit test for `DamselRescuingKnight`. In such a test, you'd like to be able to assert that the quest's `embark()` method is called when the knight's `embarkOnQuest()` is called. But there's no clear way to accomplish that here. Unfortunately, `DamselRescuingKnight` will remain untested.

Coupling is a two-headed beast. On one hand, tightly coupled code is difficult to test, difficult to reuse, difficult to understand, and typically exhibits "whack-a-mole" bug behavior (fixing one bug results in the creation of one or more new bugs). On the other hand, a certain amount of coupling is necessary—completely uncoupled code doesn't do anything. In order to do anything useful, classes need to know about each other somehow. Coupling is necessary, but should be carefully managed.

With DI, on the other hand, objects are given their dependencies at creation time by some third party that coordinates each object in the system. Objects aren't expected to create or obtain their dependencies—dependencies are injected into the objects that need them.

To illustrate this point, let's look at `BraveKnight` in the following listing, a knight that's not only brave, but is capable of embarking on any kind of quest that comes along.

Listing 1.4 A BraveKnight is flexible enough to take on any Quest he's given

```
package com.springinaction.knights;

public class BraveKnight implements Knight {
  private Quest quest;

  public BraveKnight(Quest quest) {
    this.quest = quest;                    <-- Quest is injected
  }

  public void embarkOnQuest() throws QuestException {
    quest.embark();
  }
}
```

As you can see, unlike `DamselRescuingKnight`, `BraveKnight` doesn't create his own quest. Instead, he's given a quest at construction time as a constructor argument. This is a type of dependency injection known as *constructor injection*.

What's more, the quest he's given is typed as `Quest`, an interface that all quests implement. So `BraveKnight` could embark on a `RescueDamselQuest`, a `SlayDragonQuest`, a `MakeRoundTableRounderQuest`, or any other `Quest` implementation he's given.

The point here is that `BraveKnight` isn't coupled to any specific implementation of `Quest`. It doesn't matter to him what kind of quest he's asked to embark upon, so long as it implements the `Quest` interface. That's the key benefit of DI—loose coupling. If an object only knows about its dependencies by their interface (not by their implementation or how they're instantiated), then the dependency can be swapped out with a different implementation without the depending object knowing the difference.

One of the most common ways that a dependency will be swapped out is with a mock implementation during testing. You were unable to adequately test `DamselRescuingKnight` due to tight coupling, but you can easily test `BraveKnight` by giving it a mock implementation of `Quest`, as shown next.

Listing 1.5 To test BraveKnight, you'll inject it with a mock Quest.

```
package com.springinaction.knights;

import static org.mockito.Mockito.*;

import org.junit.Test;

public class BraveKnightTest {
  @Test
  public void knightShouldEmbarkOnQuest() throws QuestException {
    Quest mockQuest = mock(Quest.class);                <-- Create mock Quest

    BraveKnight knight = new BraveKnight(mockQuest);     <-- Inject mock Quest
    knight.embarkOnQuest();

    verify(mockQuest, times(1)).embark();
  }
}
```

Here you're using a mock object framework known as *Mockito* to create a mock implementation of the `Quest` interface. With the mock object in hand, you create a new instance of `BraveKnight`, injecting the mock `Quest` via the constructor. After calling the `embarkOnQuest()` method, you ask Mockito to verify that the mock `Quest`'s `embark()` method was called exactly once.

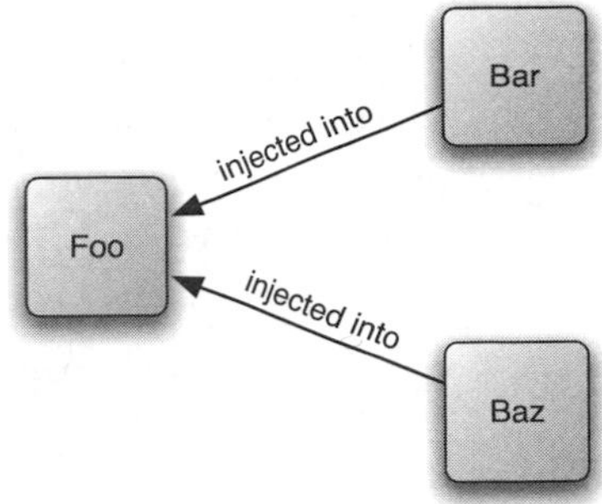

Figure 1.1 Dependency injection involves giving an object its dependencies as opposed to an object having to acquire those dependencies on its own.

INJECTING A QUEST INTO A KNIGHT

Now that your `BraveKnight` class is written in such a way that you can give him any quest you want, how can you specify which `Quest` to give him?

The act of creating associations between application components is commonly referred to as *wiring*. In Spring, there are many ways to wire components together, but a common approach has always been via XML. The following listing shows a simple Spring configuration file, knights.xml, that gives a `BraveKnight` a `SlayDragonQuest`.

Listing 1.6 Injecting a `SlayDragonQuest` into a `BraveKnight` with Spring

```
<?xml version="1.0" encoding="UTF-8"?>
<beans xmlns="http://www.springframework.org/schema/beans"
    xmlns:xsi="http://www.w3.org/2001/XMLSchema-instance"
    xsi:schemaLocation="http://www.springframework.org/schema/beans
     http://www.springframework.org/schema/beans/spring-beans-3.0.xsd">

  <bean id="knight" class="com.springinaction.knights.BraveKnight">
    <constructor-arg ref="quest" />                    <-- Inject quest bean
  </bean>

  <bean id="quest"
        class="com.springinaction.knights.SlayDragonQuest" />   <-- Create SlayDragonQuest
</beans>
```

This is a simple approach to wiring beans in Spring. Don't concern yourself too much with the details right now. We'll dig more into Spring configuration and see what's going on when we get to chapter 2. We'll also look at other ways that we can wire beans in Spring.

Now that you've declared the relationship between `BraveKnight` and a `Quest`, you need to load up the XML configuration file and kick off the application.

SEEING IT WORK

In a Spring application, an *application context* loads bean definitions and wires them together. The Spring application context is fully responsible for the creation of and wiring of the objects that make up the application. Spring comes with several implementations of its application context, each primarily differing only in how they load their configuration.

Because the beans in knights.xml are declared in an XML file, an appropriate choice for application context might be `ClassPathXmlApplicationContext`. This Spring context implementation loads the Spring context from one or more XML files located in the application's classpath. The `main()` method in the following listing uses `ClassPathXmlApplicationContext` to load knights.xml and to get a reference to the `Knight` object.

Listing 1.7 KnightMain.java loads the Spring context containing a knight.

```
package com.springinaction.knights;

import org.springframework.context.ApplicationContext;
import org.springframework.context.support.ClassPathXmlApplicationContext;

public class KnightMain {
  public static void main(String[] args) {
    ApplicationContext context =
        new ClassPathXmlApplicationContext("knights.xml");      <-- Load Spring context

    Knight knight = (Knight) context.getBean("knight");         <-- Get knight bean

    knight.embarkOnQuest();            <-- Use knight
  }
}
```

Here the `main()` method creates the Spring application context based on the knights.xml file. Then it uses the application context as a factory to retrieve the bean whose ID is *knight*. With a reference to the `Knight` object, it calls the `embarkOnQuest()` method to have the knight embark on the quest that it was given. Note that this class knows nothing about which type of `Quest` our hero has. For that matter, it's blissfully unaware of the fact that it's dealing with `BraveKnight`. Only the knights.xml file knows for sure what the implementations are.

And with that you have a quick introduction to dependency injection. You'll see a lot more DI throughout this book. But if you want even more dependency injection, I encourage you to have a look at Dhanji R. Prasanna's *Dependency Injection*, which covers DI in fine detail.

But now let's have a look at another of Spring's Java-simplifying strategies: declarative programming through aspects.

1.1.3 Applying aspects

Although DI makes it possible to tie software components together loosely, aspect-oriented programming enables you to capture functionality that's used throughout your application in reusable components.

Aspect-oriented programming is often defined as a technique that promotes separation of concerns within a software system. Systems are composed of several components, each responsible for a specific piece of functionality. Often these components also carry additional responsibility beyond their core functionality. System services such as logging, transaction management, and security often find their way into components whose core responsibility is something else. These system services are commonly referred to as *cross-cutting concerns* because they tend to cut across multiple components in a system.

By spreading these concerns across multiple components, you introduce two levels of complexity to your code:

- The code that implements the systemwide concerns is duplicated across multiple components. This means that if you need to change how those concerns work, you'll need to visit multiple components. Even if you've abstracted the concern to a separate module so that the impact to your components is a single method call, that method call is duplicated in multiple places.
- Your components are littered with code that isn't aligned with their core functionality. A method to add an entry to an address book should only be concerned with how to add the address and not with whether it's secure or transactional.

Figure 1.2 illustrates this complexity. The business objects on the left are too intimately involved with the system services. Not only does each object know that it's being logged, secured, and involved in a transactional context, but also each object is responsible for performing those services for itself.

AOP makes it possible to modularize these services and then apply them declaratively to the components that they should affect. This results in components that are more cohesive and that focus on their own specific concerns, completely ignorant of any system services that may be involved. In short, aspects ensure that POJOs remain plain.

It may help to think of aspects as blankets that cover many components of an application, as illustrated in figure 1.3. At its core, an application consists of modules that implement business functionality. With AOP, you can then cover your core application with layers of functionality. These layers can be applied declaratively throughout your application in a flexible manner without your core application even knowing they

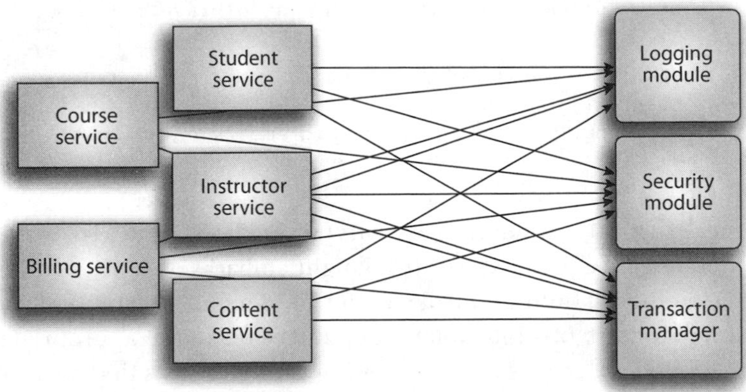

Figure 1.2 Calls to systemwide concerns such as logging and security are often scattered about in modules where those concerns are not their primary concern.

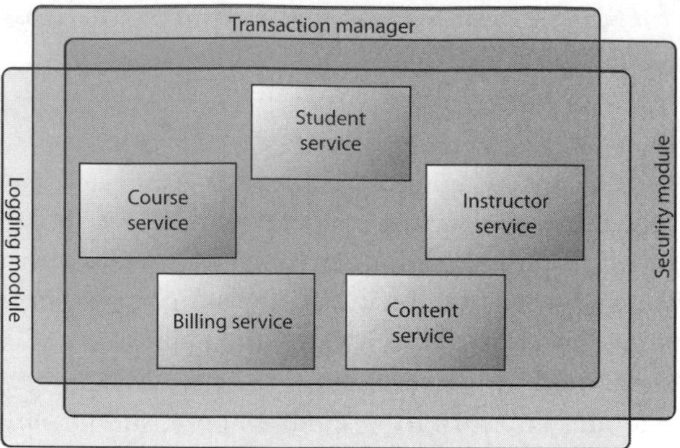

Figure 1.3 Using AOP, systemwide concerns blanket the components that they impact. This leaves the application components to focus on their specific business functionality.

exist. This is a powerful concept, as it keeps the security, transaction, and logging concerns from littering the application's core business logic.

To demonstrate how aspects can be applied in Spring, let's revisit the knight example, adding a basic Spring aspect to the mix.

AOP IN ACTION

Anyone who knows anything about knights only knows about them because their deeds were chronicled in song by the musically inclined storytellers known as minstrels. Let's suppose that you want to record the comings and goings of your `BraveKnight` using the services of a minstrel. The following shows the `Minstrel` class you might use.

Listing 1.8 A `Minstrel` is a musically inclined logging system of medieval times

```
package com.springinaction.knights;

public class Minstrel {
  public void singBeforeQuest() {                          <-- Called before quest
    System.out.println("Fa la la; The knight is so brave!");
  }

  public void singAfterQuest() {                           <-- Called after quest
    System.out.println(
            "Tee hee he; The brave knight did embark on a quest!");
  }
}
```

As you can see, `Minstrel` is a simple class with two methods. The `singBeforeQuest()` method is intended to be invoked before a knight embarks on a quest, and the `singAfterQuest()` method should be invoked after the knight has completed a quest. It should be simple to work this into your code, so let's make the appropriate tweaks to `BraveKnight` to use the `Minstrel`. The following listing shows a first attempt.

Listing 1.9 A `BraveKnight` that must call `Minstrel` methods

```
package com.springinaction.knights;

public class BraveKnight implements Knight {
  private Quest quest;
  private Minstrel minstrel;

  public BraveKnight(Quest quest, Minstrel minstrel) {
    this.quest = quest;
    this.minstrel = minstrel;
  }

  public void embarkOnQuest() throws QuestException {
    minstrel.singBeforeQuest();              <-- Should knight
    quest.embark();                              manage its own
    minstrel.singAfterQuest();                   Minstrel?
  }
}
```

That should do the trick. But something doesn't seem right here. Is it really within the knight's range of concern to manage his minstrel? It seems to me that a minstrel should just do his job without the knight asking him to do so. After all, that's the minstrel's job—to sing about the knight's endeavors. Why should the knight have to keep reminding the minstrel to do his job?

Furthermore, because the knight needs to know about the minstrel, you're forced to inject the `Minstrel` into the `BraveKnight`. This not only complicates the `BraveKnight`'s code, but also makes me wonder if you'd ever want a knight who didn't have a minstrel. What if the `Minstrel` is `null`? Should we introduce some `null`-checking logic to cover that case?

Your simple `BraveKnight` class is starting to get more complicated and would become more so if you were to handle the `nullMinstrel` scenario. But using AOP, you can declare that the minstrel should sing about a knight's quests and free the knight from having to deal with the `Minstrel` methods directly.

To turn `Minstrel` into an aspect, all you need to do is declare it as one in the Spring configuration file. Here's the updated knights.xml file, revised to declare `Minstrel` as an aspect.

Listing 1.10 Declaring the `Minstrel` as an aspect

```
<?xml version="1.0" encoding="UTF-8"?>
<beans xmlns="http://www.springframework.org/schema/beans"
 xmlns:xsi="http://www.w3.org/2001/XMLSchema-instance"
 xmlns:aop="http://www.springframework.org/schema/aop"
 xsi:schemaLocation="http://www.springframework.org/schema/beans
    http://www.springframework.org/schema/beans/spring-beans-3.0.xsd
    http://www.springframework.org/schema/aop
    http://www.springframework.org/schema/aop/spring-aop-3.0.xsd">

  <bean id="knight" class="com.springinaction.knights.BraveKnight">
    <constructor-arg ref="quest" />
  </bean>
```

```
<bean id="quest"
      class="com.springinaction.knights.SlayDragonQuest" />

<bean id="minstrel"
   class="com.springinaction.knights.Minstrel" />          Declare Minstrel bean

<aop:config>
  <aop:aspect ref="minstrel">

    <aop:pointcut id="embark"
        expression="execution(* *.embarkOnQuest(..))" />    Define pointcut

    <aop:before pointcut-ref="embark"
            method="singBeforeQuest"/>          Declare before advice

    <aop:after pointcut-ref="embark"
            method="singAfterQuest"/>           Declare after advice

  </aop:aspect>
</aop:config>
</beans>
```

Here you're using Spring's aop configuration namespace to declare that the Minstrel bean is an aspect. First, you had to declare the Minstrel as a bean. Then you refer to that bean in the <aop:aspect> element. Defining the aspect further, you declare (using <aop:before>) that before the embarkOnQuest() method is executed, the Minstrel's singBeforeQuest() should be called. This is called *before advice*. And you (using <aop:after>) declare that the singAfterQuest() method should be called after embarkOnQuest() has executed. This is known as *after advice*.

In both cases, the pointcut-ref attribute refers to a pointcut named *embark*. This pointcut is defined in the preceding <pointcut> element with an expression attribute set to select where the advice should be applied. The expression syntax is AspectJ's pointcut expression language.

Don't worry if you don't know AspectJ or the details of how AspectJ pointcut expressions are written. We'll talk more about Spring AOP later in chapter 4. For now it's enough to know that you've asked Spring to call the Minstrel's singBeforeQuest() and singAfterQuest() methods before and after the BraveKnight embarks on a quest.

That's all there is to it! With a tiny bit of XML, you've just turned Minstrel into a Spring aspect. Don't worry if this doesn't make complete sense yet—you'll see plenty more examples of Spring AOP in chapter 4 that should help clear this up. For now, there are two important points to take away from this example.

First, Minstrel is still a POJO—nothing about it indicates that it's to be used as an aspect. Instead Minstrel became an aspect when we declared it as such in the Spring context.

Second, and most important, Minstrel can be applied to the BraveKnight without the BraveKnight needing to explicitly call on it. In fact, BraveKnight remains completely unaware of the Minstrel's existence.

I should also point out that although you used some Spring magic to turn Minstrel into an aspect, it was declared as a Spring <bean> first. The point here is that you can do anything with Spring aspects that you can do with other Spring beans, such as injecting them with dependencies.

Using aspects to sing about knights can be fun. But Spring's AOP can be used for even more practical things. As you'll see later, Spring AOP can be employed to provide services such as declarative transactions (chapter 6) and security (chapter 9).

But for now, let's look at one more way that Spring simplifies Java development.

1.1.4 Eliminating boilerplate code with templates

Have you ever written some code and then felt like you'd already written the same code before? That's not déjà vu, my friend. That's boilerplate code—the code that you often have to write over and over again to accomplish common and otherwise simple tasks.

Unfortunately, there are a lot of places where Java APIs involve a bunch of boilerplate code. A common example of boilerplate code can be seen when working with JDBC to query data from a database. For example, if you've ever worked with JDBC before, then you've probably written something similar to the following.

Listing 1.11 Many Java APIs, such as JDBC, involve writing a lot of boilerplate code.

```
public Employee getEmployeeById(long id) {
  Connection conn = null;
  PreparedStatement stmt = null;
  ResultSet rs = null;
  try {
    conn = dataSource.getConnection();
    stmt = conn.prepareStatement(
          "select id, firstname, lastname, salary from " +
          "employee where id=?");                          <-- Select employee
    stmt.setLong(1, id);
    rs = stmt.executeQuery();
    Employee employee = null;
    if (rs.next()) {                                        Create object
      employee = new Employee();                         <-- from data
      employee.setId(rs.getLong("id"));
      employee.setFirstName(rs.getString("firstname"));
      employee.setLastName(rs.getString("lastname"));
      employee.setSalary(rs.getBigDecimal("salary"));
    }
    return employee;                                      What should
  } catch (SQLException e) {                           <-- be done here?

  } finally {
      if(rs != null) {                               <-- Clean up mess
        try {
          rs.close();
        } catch(SQLException e) {}
      }

      if(stmt != null) {
        try {
        stmt.close();
```

```
        } catch(SQLException e) {}
      }

      if(conn != null) {
        try {
          conn.close();
        } catch(SQLException e) {}
      }
    }

    return null;
  }
```

As you can see, this JDBC code queries the database for an employee's name and salary. But I'll bet you had to look hard to see that. That's because the small bit of code that's specific to querying for an employee is buried in a heap of JDBC ceremony. You first have to create a connection, then a statement, and then finally you can query for the results. And, to appease JDBC's anger, you must catch `SQLException`, a checked exception, even though there's not a lot you can do if it's thrown.

Finally, after all is said and done, you have to clean up the mess, closing down the connection, statement, and result set. This could also stir JDBC's anger. Therefore you must catch `SQLException` here as well.

What's most notable about listing 1.11 is that much of it is the exact same code that you'd write for pretty much any JDBC operation. Little of it has anything to do with querying for an employee, and much of it is JDBC boilerplate.

JDBC's not alone in the boilerplate code business. Many activities often require similar boilerplate code. JMS, JNDI, and the consumption of REST services often involve a lot of commonly repeated code.

Spring seeks to eliminate boilerplate code by encapsulating it in templates. Spring's `JdbcTemplate` makes it possible to perform database operations without all of the ceremony required by traditional JDBC.

For example, using Spring's `SimpleJdbcTemplate` (a specialization of `JdbcTemplate` that takes advantage of Java 5 features), the `getEmployeeById()` method can be rewritten so that its focus is on the task of retrieving employee data and not catering to the demands of the JDBC API. The following shows what such an updated `getEmployeeById()` method might look like.

Listing 1.12 Templates let your code focus on the task at hand.

```
public Employee getEmployeeById(long id) {
  return jdbcTemplate.queryForObject(
          "select id, firstname, lastname, salary " +        <-- SQL query
          "from employee where id=?",
          new RowMapper<Employee>() {
            public Employee mapRow(ResultSet rs,
                    int rowNum) throws SQLException {        <-- Map results to object
              Employee employee = new Employee();
              employee.setId(rs.getLong("id"));
              employee.setFirstName(rs.getString("firstname"));
```

```
            employee.setLastName(rs.getString("lastname"));
            employee.setSalary(rs.getBigDecimal("salary"));
            return employee;
          }
        },
        id);                                          <-- Specify query parameter
}
```

As you can see, this new version of `getEmployeeById()` is much simpler and acutely focused on selecting an employee from the database. The template's `queryForObject()` method is given the SQL query, a `RowMapper` (for mapping result set data to a domain object), and zero or more query parameters. What you don't see in `getEmployeeById()` is any of the JDBC boilerplate from before. It's all handled internal to the template.

I've shown you how Spring attacks complexity in Java development using POJO-oriented development, dependency injection, AOP, and templates. Along the way I showed you how to configure beans and aspects in XML-based configuration files. But how do those files get loaded? And what are they loaded into? Let's look at the Spring container, the place where your application's beans will reside.

1.2 Containing your beans

In a Spring-based application, your application objects will live within the Spring container. As illustrated in figure 1.4, the container will create the objects, wire them together, configure them, and manage their complete lifecycle from cradle to grave (or `new` to `finalize()`, as the case may be).

In the next chapter, you'll see how to configure Spring to know what objects it should create, configure, and wire together. First, it's important to get to know the container where your objects will be hanging out. Understanding the container helps you grasp how your objects will be managed.

The container is at the core of the Spring Framework. Spring's container uses dependency injection (DI) to manage the components that make up an application. This includes creating associations between collaborating components. As such, these objects are cleaner and easier to understand, support reuse, and are easy to unit test.

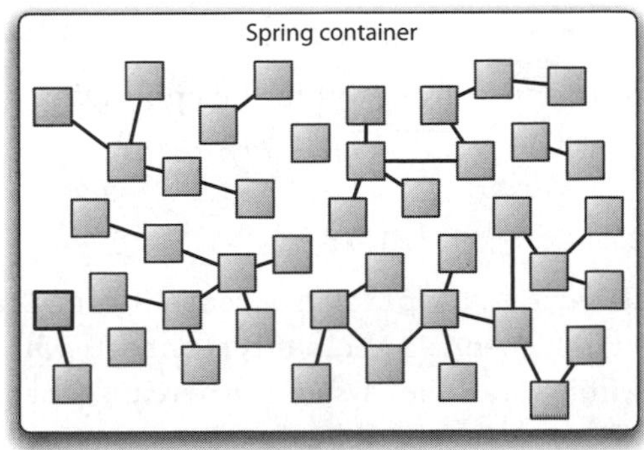

Figure 1.4 In a Spring application, objects are created, wired together, and live within the Spring container.

There's no single Spring container. Spring comes with several container implementations that can be categorized into two distinct types. *Bean factories* (defined by the `org.springframework.beans.factory.BeanFactory` interface) are the simplest of containers, providing basic support for DI. *Application contexts* (defined by the `org.springframework.context.ApplicationContext` interface) build on the notion of a bean factory by providing application framework services, such as the ability to resolve textual messages from a properties file and the ability to publish application events to interested event listeners.

Although it's possible to work with Spring using either bean factories or application contexts, bean factories are often too low-level for most applications. Therefore, application contexts are preferred over bean factories. We'll focus on working with application contexts and not spend any more time talking about bean factories.

1.2.1 Working with an application context

Spring comes with several flavors of application context. The three that you'll most likely encounter are

- `ClassPathXmlApplicationContext`—Loads a context definition from an XML file located in the classpath, treating context definition files as classpath resources.
- `FileSystemXmlApplicationContext`—Loads a context definition from an XML file in the file system.
- `XmlWebApplicationContext`—Loads context definitions from an XML file contained within a web application.

We'll talk more about `XmlWebApplicationContext` in chapter 7 when we discuss web-based Spring applications. For now, let's simply load the application context from the file system using `FileSystemXmlApplicationContext` or from the classpath using `ClassPathXmlApplicationContext`.

Loading an application context from the file system or from the classpath is similar to how you load beans into a bean factory. For example, here's how you'd load a `FileSystemXmlApplicationContext`:

```
ApplicationContext context = new
        FileSystemXmlApplicationContext("c:/foo.xml");
```

Similarly, you can load an application context from within the application's classpath using `ClassPathXmlApplicationContext`:

```
ApplicationContext context = new
        ClassPathXmlApplicationContext("foo.xml");
```

The difference between using `FileSystemXmlApplicationContext` and `ClassPathXmlApplicationContext` is that `FileSystemXmlApplicationContext` will look for foo.xml in a specific location within the file system, whereas `ClassPathXmlApplicationContext` will look for foo.xml anywhere in the classpath (including JAR files).

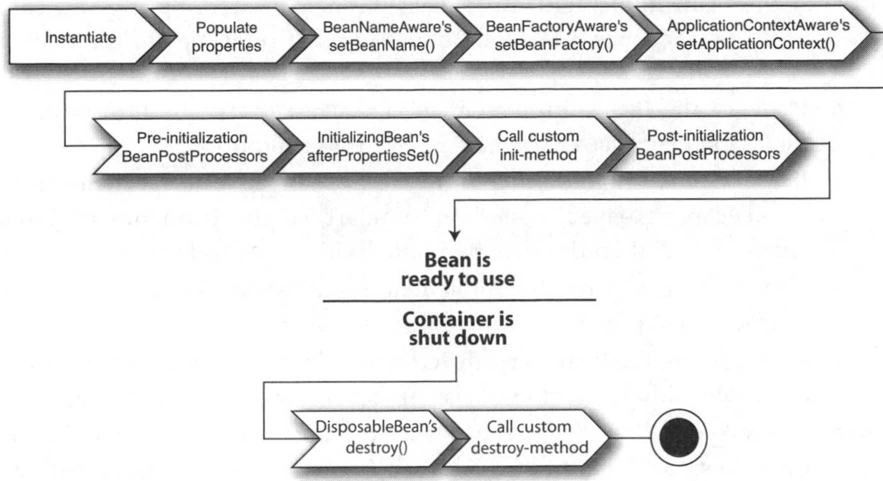

Figure 1.5 A bean goes through several steps between creation and destruction in the Spring container. Each step is an opportunity to customize how the bean is managed in Spring.

With an application context in hand, you can retrieve beans from the Spring container by calling the context's `getBean()` method.

Now that you know the basics of how to create a Spring container, let's take a closer look at the lifecycle of a bean in the bean container.

1.2.2 A bean's life

In a traditional Java application, the lifecycle of a bean is simple. Java's `new` keyword is used to instantiate the bean (or perhaps it's deserialized) and it's ready to use. Once the bean is no longer in use, it's eligible for garbage collection and eventually goes to the big bit bucket in the sky.

In contrast, the lifecycle of a bean within a Spring container is more elaborate. It's important to understand the lifecycle of a Spring bean, because you may want to take advantage of some of the opportunities that Spring offers to customize how a bean is created. Figure 1.5 shows the startup lifecycle of a typical bean as it's loaded into a Spring application context.

As you can see, a bean factory performs several setup steps before a bean is ready to use. Breaking down figure 1.5 in more detail:

1. Spring instantiates the bean.
2. Spring injects values and bean references into the bean's properties.
3. If the bean implements `BeanNameAware`, Spring passes the bean's ID to the `setBeanName()` method.
4. If the bean implements `BeanFactoryAware`, Spring calls the `setBeanFactory()` method, passing in the bean factory itself.

5. If the bean implements `ApplicationContextAware`, Spring will call the `setApplicationContext()` method, passing in a reference to the enclosing application context.
6. If any of the beans implement the `BeanPostProcessor` interface, Spring calls their `postProcessBeforeInitialization()` method.
7. If any beans implement the `InitializingBean` interface, Spring calls their `afterPropertiesSet()` method. Similarly, if the bean was declared with an `init-method`, then the specified initialization method will be called.
8. If there are any beans that implement `BeanPostProcessor`, Spring will call their `postProcessAfterInitialization()` method.
9. At this point, the bean is ready to be used by the application and will remain in the application context until the application context is destroyed.
10. If any beans implement the `DisposableBean` interface, then Spring will call their `destroy()` methods. Likewise, if any bean was declared with a `destroy-method`, then the specified method will be called.

Now you know how to create and load a Spring container. But an empty container isn't much good by itself; it doesn't contain anything unless you put something in it. To achieve the benefits of Spring DI, we must wire our application objects into the Spring container. We'll go into bean wiring in more detail in chapter 2.

But first, let's survey the modern Spring landscape to see what the Spring Framework is made up of and to see what the latest versions of Spring have to offer.

1.3 Surveying the Spring landscape

As you've seen, the Spring Framework is focused on simplifying enterprise Java development through dependency injection, aspect-oriented programming, and boilerplate reduction. Even if that were all that Spring did, it'd be worth using. But there's more to Spring than meets the eye.

Within the Spring Framework proper, you'll find several ways that Spring can ease Java development. But beyond the Spring Framework itself is a greater ecosystem of projects that build upon the core framework, extending Spring into areas such as web services, OSGi, Flash, and even .NET.

Let's first break down the core Spring Framework to see what it brings to the table. Then we'll expand our sights to review the other members of the greater Spring portfolio.

1.3.1 Spring modules

The Spring Framework is composed of several distinct modules. When you download and unzip the Spring Framework distribution, you'll find 20 different JAR files in the dist directory, as shown in figure 1.6.

The 20 JAR files that make up Spring can be arranged in one of six different categories of functionality, as illustrated in figure 1.7.

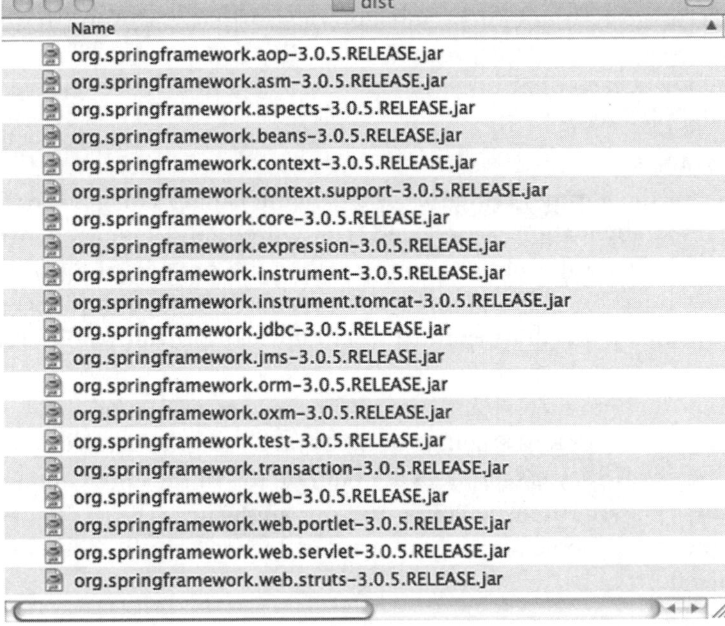

Figure 1.6 The JAR files that come with the Spring Framework distribution

When taken as a whole, these modules give you everything you need to develop enterprise-ready applications. But you don't have to base your application fully on the Spring Framework. You're free to choose the modules that suit your application and

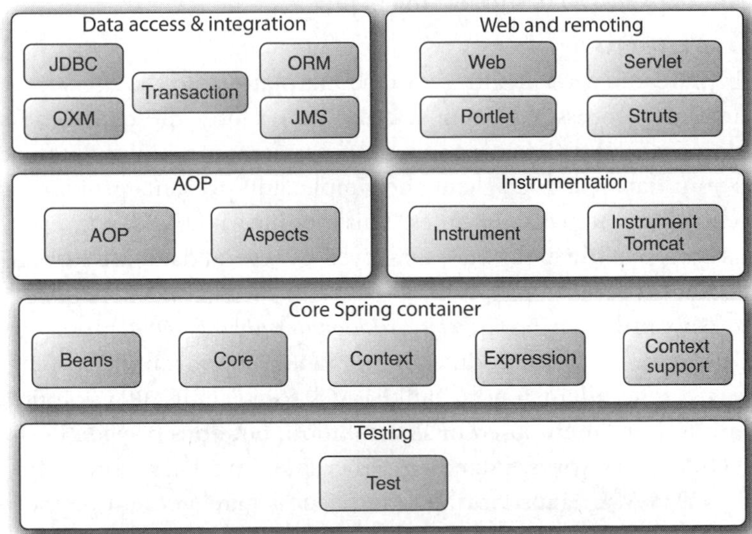

Figure 1.7 The Spring Framework is made up of six well-defined modules.

look to other options when Spring doesn't fit the bill. Spring even offers integration points with several other frameworks and libraries so that you won't have to write them yourself.

Let's take a look at each of Spring's modules, one at a time, to see how each fits in the overall Spring picture.

CORE SPRING CONTAINER

The centerpiece of the Spring Framework is a container that manages how the beans in a Spring-enabled application are created, configured, and managed. Within this module you'll find the Spring bean factory, which is the portion of Spring that provides dependency injection. Building upon the bean factory, you'll find several implementations of Spring's application context, each of which provides a different way to configure Spring.

In addition to the bean factory and application context, this module also supplies many enterprise services such as email, JNDI access, EJB integration, and scheduling.

As you can see, all of Spring's modules are built on top of the core container. You'll implicitly use these classes when you configure your application. We'll discuss the core module throughout this book, starting in chapter 2 where we dig deep into Spring dependency injection.

SPRING'S AOP MODULE

Spring provides rich support for aspect-oriented programming in its AOP module. This module serves as the basis for developing your own aspects for your Spring-enabled application. Like DI, AOP supports loose coupling of application objects. But with AOP, application-wide concerns (such as transactions and security) are decoupled from the objects to which they're applied.

We'll dig into Spring's AOP support in chapter 4.

DATA ACCESS AND INTEGRATION

Working with JDBC often results in a lot of boilerplate code that gets a connection, creates a statement, processes a result set, and then closes the connection. Spring's JDBC and *data access objects (DAO)* module abstracts away the boilerplate code so that you can keep your database code clean and simple, and prevents problems that result from a failure to close database resources. This module also builds a layer of meaningful exceptions on top of the error messages given by several database servers. No more trying to decipher cryptic and proprietary SQL error messages!

For those who prefer using an *object-relational mapping (ORM)* tool over straight JDBC, Spring provides the ORM module. Spring's ORM support builds on the DAO support, providing a convenient way to build DAOs for several ORM solutions. Spring doesn't attempt to implement its own ORM solution, but does provide hooks into several popular ORM frameworks, including Hibernate, Java Persistence API, Java Data Objects, and iBATIS SQL Maps. Spring's transaction management supports each of these ORM frameworks as well as JDBC.

We'll see how Spring's template-based JDBC abstraction can greatly simplify JDBC code when we look at Spring data access in chapter 5.

This module also includes a Spring abstraction over the Java Message Service (JMS) for asynchronous integration with other applications through messaging. And, as of Spring 3.0, this module includes the object-to-XML mapping features that were originally part of the Spring Web Services project.

In addition, this module uses Spring's AOP module to provide transaction management services for objects in a Spring application. We'll look at Spring's transaction support in detail in chapter 6.

WEB AND REMOTING

The *Model-View-Controller (MVC)* paradigm is a commonly accepted approach to building web applications such that the user interface is separate from the application logic. Java has no shortage of MVC frameworks, with Apache Struts, JSF, WebWork, and Tapestry among the most popular MVC choices.

Even though Spring integrates with several popular MVC frameworks, its web and remoting module comes with a capable MVC framework that promotes Spring's loosely coupled techniques in the web layer of an application. This framework comes in two forms: a servlet-based framework for conventional web applications and a portlet-based application for developing against the Java portlet API.

In addition to user-facing web applications, this module also provides several remoting options for building applications that interact with other applications. Spring's remoting capabilities include *Remote Method Invocation (RMI)*, Hessian, Burlap, JAX-WS, and Spring's own HTTP invoker.

We'll look at Spring's MVC framework in chapter 7. Then, in chapter 10, we'll check out Spring remoting.

TESTING

Recognizing the importance of developer-written tests, Spring provides a module dedicated to testing Spring applications.

Within this module you'll find a collection of mock object implementations for writing unit tests against code that works with JNDI, servlets, and portlets. For integration-level testing, this module provides support for loading a collection of beans in a Spring application context and working with the beans in that context.

We'll get our first taste of Spring's testing module in chapter 4. Then in chapters 5 and 6, we'll expand on what we've learned by seeing how to test Spring data access and transactions.

1.3.2 The Spring portfolio

When it comes to Spring, there's more than meets the eye. In fact, there's more than what comes in the Spring Framework download. If we stopped at just the core Spring Framework, we'd miss out on a wealth of potential afforded by the larger Spring portfolio. The whole Spring portfolio includes several frameworks and libraries that build upon the core Spring Framework and upon each other. All together, the entire Spring portfolio brings the Spring programming model to almost every facet of Java development.

It would take several volumes to cover everything that the Spring portfolio has to offer, and much of it's outside the scope of this book. But we'll look at some of the elements of the Spring portfolio. Meanwhile, here's a taste of what lies beyond the core Spring Framework.

SPRING WEB FLOW

Spring Web Flow builds upon Spring's core MVC framework to provide support for building conversational, flow-based web applications that guide users toward a goal (think wizards or shopping carts). We'll talk more about Spring Web Flow in chapter 8, and you can learn more about Spring Web Flow from its home page at http://www.springsource.org/webflow.

SPRING WEB SERVICES

Although the core Spring Framework provides for declaratively publishing Spring beans as web services, those services are based on an arguably architecturally inferior contract-last model. The contract for the service is determined from the bean's interface. Spring Web Services offers a contract-first web services model where service implementations are written to satisfy the service contract.

I won't be talking about Spring-WS in this book, but you can read more about it from its home page at http://static.springsource.org/spring-ws/sites/2.0.

SPRING SECURITY

Security is a critical aspect of many applications. Implemented using Spring AOP, Spring Security offers a declarative security mechanism for Spring-based applications. We'll see how add Spring Security to applications in chapter 9. For further exploration, Spring Security's home page is at http://static.springsource.org/spring-security/site.

SPRING INTEGRATION

Many enterprise applications must interact with other enterprise applications. Spring Integration offers implementations of several common integration patterns in Spring's declarative style.

We won't cover Spring Integration in this book. But if you want more information on Spring Integration, have a look at *Spring Integration in Action* by Mark Fisher, Jonas Partner, Marius Bogoevici, and Iwein Fuld. Or you can visit the Spring Integration home page at http://www.springsource.org/spring-integration.

SPRING BATCH

When it's necessary to perform bulk operations on data, nothing beats batch processing. If you're going to be developing a batch application, you can leverage Spring's robust, POJO-oriented development model to do it using Spring Batch.

Spring Batch is outside of the scope of this book. But Thierry Templier and Arnaud Cogoluègnes will enlighten you in their book, *Spring Batch in Action*. You can also learn about Spring Batch from its home page at http://static.springsource.org/spring-batch.

SPRING SOCIAL

Social networking is a rising trend on the internet, and more and more applications are being outfitted with integration into social networking sites such as Facebook and Twitter. If this is the kind of thing that interests you, then you'll want to look at Spring Social, a social networking extension to Spring.

Spring Social is relatively new and didn't make it into this book. But you can find out more about it at http://www.springsource.org/spring-social.

SPRING MOBILE

Mobile applications are another significant area of software development. Smartphones and tablet devices are taking over as the preferred client for many users. Spring Mobile is a new extension to Spring to support development of mobile web applications.

Related to Spring Mobile is the Spring Android project. This new project, less than a month old as I write this, aims to bring some of the simplicity afforded by the Spring Framework to development of native applications for Android-based devices. Initially, this project is offering a version of Spring's `RestTemplate` (see chapter 11 to learn about `RestTemplate`) that can be used within an Android application.

Again, these projects are new and are outside of the scope of *Spring in Action*. But you can learn more about them at http://www.springsource.org/spring-mobile and http://www.springsource.org/spring-android.

SPRING DYNAMIC MODULES

Spring Dynamic Modules (Spring-DM) blends Spring's declarative dependency injection with OSGi's dynamic modularity. Using Spring-DM, you can build applications that are composed of several distinct, highly cohesive, loosely coupled modules that publish and consume services declaratively within the OSGi framework.

It should be noted that due to its tremendous impact in the world of OSGi, the Spring-DM model for declarative OSGi services has been formalized into the OSGi specification itself as the *OSGi Blueprint Container.* In addition, SpringSource has transitioned Spring-DM to the Eclipse project as a part of the Gemini family of OSGi projects and is now known as Gemini Blueprint.

SPRING LDAP

In addition to dependency injection and AOP, another common technique applied throughout the Spring Framework is to create template-based abstractions around unnecessarily complex operations such as JDBC queries or JMS messaging. Spring LDAP brings Spring-style template-based access to LDAP, eliminating the boilerplate code that's commonly involved in LDAP operations.

More information on Spring LDAP can be found at http://www.springsource.org/ldap.

SPRING RICH CLIENT

Web-based applications seem to have stolen the spotlight from traditional desktop applications. But if you're one of the few still developing Swing applications, you'll want to check out Spring Rich Client, a rich application toolkit that brings the power of Spring to Swing.

SPRING.NET

You don't have to abandon dependency injection and AOP if you're put on a .NET project. Spring.NET offers the same loose-coupling and aspect-oriented features of Spring, but for the .NET platform.

In addition to the core DI and AOP functionality, Spring.NET comes with several modules for simplifying .NET development, including modules for working with ADO.NET, NHibernate, ASP.NET, and MSMQ.

To learn more about Spring .NET, visit http://www.springframework.net.

SPRING-FLEX

Adobe's Flex and AIR offer one of the most powerful options for rich internet application development. When those rich user interfaces need to interact with Java code on the server side, they can use a remoting and messaging technology known as *BlazeDS*. The Spring-Flex integration package enables Flex and AIR applications to communicate with server-side Spring beans using BlazeDS. It also includes an addon for Spring Roo to enable rapid application development of Flex applications.

You may begin your exploration of Spring Flex at http://www.springsource.org/spring-flex. You may also want to check out Spring ActionScript at http://www.springactionscript.org, which offers many benefits of the Spring Framework in ActionScript.

SPRING ROO

As more and more developers are basing their work on Spring, a set of common idioms and best practices has emerged around Spring and its related frameworks. At the same time, frameworks such as Ruby on Rails and Grails have arisen with a script-driven development model that makes simple work of building applications.

Spring Roo provides an interactive tooling environment that enables rapid development of Spring applications, pulling together the best practices that have been identified over the past few years.

What differentiates Roo from these other rapid application development frameworks is that it produces Java code using the Spring Framework. The outcome is an honest-to-goodness Spring application, not a separate framework coded in a language that's foreign to many corporate development organizations.

More information about Spring Roo can be found at http://www.springsource.org/roo.

SPRING EXTENSIONS

In addition to all of the projects described up to this point, there's also a community-driven collection of Spring extensions at http://www.springsource.org/extensions. A few of the goodies you'll find there include

- An implementation of Spring for the Python language
- Blob storage

- db4o and CouchDB persistence
- A Spring-based workflow management library
- Kerberos and SAML extensions for Spring Security

1.4 What's new in Spring

It's been almost three years since I wrote the second edition of this book, and a lot has happened in the intervening time. The Spring Framework has seen two significant releases, each bringing new features and improvements to ease application development. And several of the other members of the Spring portfolio have undergone major changes.

We'll cover many of these changes throughout this book. But for now, let's briefly size up what's new in Spring.

1.4.1 What's new in Spring 2.5?

In November 2007, the Spring team released version 2.5 of the Spring Framework. The significance of Spring 2.5 was that it marked Spring's embrace of annotation-driven development. Prior to Spring 2.5, XML-based configuration was the norm. But Spring 2.5 introduced several ways of using annotations to greatly reduce the amount of XML needed to configure Spring:

- Annotation-driven dependency injection through the `@Autowired` annotation and fine-grained auto-wiring control with `@Qualifier`.
- Support for JSR-250 annotations, including `@Resource` for dependency injection of a named resource, as well as `@PostConstruct` and `@PreDestroy` for life-cycle methods.
- Auto-detection of Spring components that are annotated with `@Component` (or one of several stereotype annotations).
- An all-new annotation-driven Spring MVC programming model that greatly simplifies Spring web development.
- A new integration test framework that's based on JUnit 4 and annotations.

Even though annotations were the big story of Spring 2.5, there's more:

- Full Java 6 and Java EE 5 support, including JDBC 4.0, JTA 1.1, JavaMail 1.4, and JAX-WS 2.0.
- A new bean-name pointcut expression for weaving aspects into Spring beans by their name.
- Built-in support for AspectJ load-time weaving.
- New XML configuration namespaces, including the `context` namespace for configuring application context details and a `jms` namespace for configuring message-driven beans.
- Support for named parameters in `SqlJdbcTemplate`.

We'll explore many of these new Spring features as we progress through this book.

1.4.2 What's new in Spring 3.0?

With all of the good stuff in Spring 2.5, it's hard to imagine what could possibly follow in Spring 3.0. But with the 3.0 release, Spring one-upped itself with the continuation of the annotation-driven theme and several new features:

- Full-scale REST support in Spring MVC, including Spring MVC controllers that respond to REST-style URLs with XML, JSON, RSS, or any other appropriate response. We'll look into Spring 3's new REST support in chapter 11.
- A new expression language that brings Spring dependency injection to a new level by enabling injection of values from a variety of sources, including other beans and system properties. We'll dig into Spring's expression language in the next chapter.
- New annotations for Spring MVC, including `@CookieValue` and `@RequestHeader`, to pull values from cookies and request headers, respectively. We'll see how to use these annotations as we look at Spring MVC in chapter 7.
- A new XML namespace for easing configuration of Spring MVC.
- Support for declarative validation with JSR-303 (Bean Validation) annotations.
- Support for the new JSR-330 dependency injection specification.
- Annotation-oriented declaration of asynchronous and scheduled methods.
- A new annotation-based configuration model that allows for nearly XML-free Spring configuration. We'll see this new configuration style in the next chapter.
- The Object-to-XML (OXM) mapping functionality from the Spring Web Services project has been moved into the core Spring Framework.

Just as important as what's new in Spring 3.0 is what's not in Spring 3.0. Specifically, starting with Spring 3.0, Java 5 is now required, as Java 1.4 has reached end-of-life and will no longer be supported in Spring.

1.4.3 What's new in the Spring portfolio?

Aside from the core Spring Framework, there's also been exciting new activity in the projects that are based on Spring. I don't have enough space to cover every detail of what's changed, but there are a few items that I think are significant enough to mention:

- *Spring Web Flow 2.0* was released with a simplified flow definition schema, making it even easier to create conversational web applications.
- With Spring Web Flow 2.0 came *Spring JavaScript* and *Spring Faces*. Spring JavaScript is a JavaScript library that enables progressive enhancement of web pages with dynamic behavior. Spring Faces allows use of JSF as a view technology within Spring MVC and Spring Web Flow.
- The old Acegi Security framework was completely overhauled and released as *Spring Security 2.0*. In this new incarnation, Spring Security offers a new configuration schema that dramatically reduces the amount of XML required to configure application security.

Even as I was writing this book, Spring Security continued to evolve. Spring Security 3.0 was recently released, further simplifying declarative security by taking advantage of Spring's new expression language to declare security constraints.

As you can see, Spring is an active, continuously evolving project. There's always something new that aims to make developing enterprise Java applications easier.

1.5 Summary

You should now have a good idea of what Spring brings to the table. Spring aims to make enterprise Java development easier and to promote loosely coupled code. Vital to this is dependency injection and AOP.

In this chapter, we got a taste of dependency injection in Spring. DI is a way of associating application objects such that the objects don't need to know where their dependencies come from or how they're implemented. Rather than acquiring dependencies on their own, dependent objects are given the objects that they depend on. Because dependent objects often only know about their injected objects through interfaces, coupling is kept low.

In addition to dependency injection, we also saw a glimpse of Spring's AOP support. AOP enables you to centralize logic that would normally be scattered throughout an application in one place—an aspect. When Spring wires your beans together, these aspects can be woven in at runtime, effectively giving the beans new behavior.

Dependency injection and AOP are central to everything in Spring. Thus you must understand how to use these principal functions of Spring to be able to use the rest of the framework. In this chapter, we've just scratched the surface of Spring's DI and AOP features. Over the next few chapters, we'll dig deeper into DI and AOP. Without further ado, let's move on to chapter 2 to learn how to wire objects together in Spring using dependency injection.

2 Wiring beans

This chapter covers

- Declaring beans
- Injecting constructors and setters
- Wiring beans
- Controlling bean creation and destruction

Have you ever stuck around after a movie long enough to watch the credits? It's incredible how many different people it takes to pull together a major motion picture. In addition to the obvious participants—the actors, scriptwriters, directors, and producers—there are the not-so-obvious—the musicians, special effects crew, and art directors. And that's not to mention the key grip, sound mixer, costumers, makeup artists, stunt coordinators, publicists, first assistant to the cameraperson, second assistant to the cameraperson, set designers, gaffer, and (perhaps most importantly) the caterers.

Now imagine what your favorite movie would've been like had none of these people talked to one another. Let's say that they all showed up at the studio and started doing their own thing without any coordination of any kind. If the director keeps to himself and doesn't say "roll 'em," then the cameraperson won't start shooting. It probably wouldn't matter anyway, because the lead actress would still be in her trailer and the lighting wouldn't work because the gaffer wouldn't have been hired. Maybe you've seen a movie where it looks like this is what happened. But most movies (the good ones anyway) are the product of thousands of people working together toward the common goal of making a blockbuster movie.

In this respect, a great piece of software isn't much different. Any nontrivial application is made up of several objects that must work together to meet some business goal. These objects must be aware of one another and communicate with one another to get their jobs done. In an online shopping application, for instance, an order manager component may need to work with a product manager component and a credit card authorization component. All of these will likely need to work with a data access component to read from and write to a database.

But as we saw in chapter 1, the traditional approach to creating associations between application objects (via construction or lookup) leads to complicated code that's difficult to reuse and unit test. At best, these objects do more work than they should. At worst, they're highly coupled to one another, making them hard to reuse and hard to test.

In Spring, objects aren't responsible for finding or creating the other objects that they need to do their jobs. Instead, they're given references to the objects that they collaborate with by the container. An order manager component, for example, may need a credit card authorizer—but it doesn't need to create the credit card authorizer. It just needs to show up empty-handed and it'll be given a credit card authorizer to work with.

The act of creating these associations between application objects is the essence of dependency injection (DI) and is commonly referred to as *wiring*. In this chapter we'll explore the basics of bean wiring using Spring. As DI is the most elemental thing Spring does, these are techniques you'll use almost every time you develop Spring-based applications.

2.1 Declaring beans

At this point, I'd like to welcome you to the first (and likely the last) annual JavaBean talent competition. I've searched the nation (actually, just our IDE's workspace) for the most talented JavaBeans to perform and in the next few chapters, we'll set up the competition and our judges will weigh in. Spring programmers, this is your *Spring Idol*.

In our competition, we're going to need some performers, which are defined by the `Performer` interface:

```
package com.springinaction.springidol;

public interface Performer {
  void perform() throws PerformanceException;
}
```

In the *Spring Idol* talent competition, you'll meet several contestants, all of which implement the `Performer` interface. To get started, let's set the stage for the competition by looking at the essentials of a Spring configuration.

2.1.1 *Setting up Spring configuration*

As has been said already, Spring is a container-based framework. But if you don't configure Spring, then it's an empty container and doesn't serve much purpose. We need to configure Spring to tell it what beans it should contain and how to wire those beans so that they can work together.

As of Spring 3.0, there are two ways to configure beans in the Spring container. Traditionally, Spring configuration is defined in one or more XML files. But Spring 3.0 also offers a Java-based configuration option. We'll focus on the traditional XML option for now, but we'll look at Spring's Java-based configuration later in section 3.4.

When declaring beans in XML, the root element of the Spring configuration file is the <beans> element from Spring's beans schema. A typical Spring configuration XML file looks like this:

```
<?xml version="1.0" encoding="UTF-8"?>
<beans xmlns="http://www.springframework.org/schema/beans"
       xmlns:xsi="http://www.w3.org/2001/XMLSchema-instance"
       xsi:schemaLocation="http://www.springframework.org/schema/beans
           http://www.springframework.org/schema/beans/spring-beans-3.0.xsd">

  <!-- Bean declarations go here -->

</beans>
```

Within the <beans> you can place all of your Spring configuration, including <bean> declarations. But the `beans` namespace isn't the only Spring namespace you'll encounter. All together, the core Spring Framework comes with ten configuration namespaces, as described in table 2.1.

Table 2.1 Spring comes with several XML namespaces through which you can configure the Spring container

Namespace	Purpose
`aop`	Provides elements for declaring aspects and for automatically proxying `@AspectJ`-annotated classes as Spring aspects.
`beans`	The core primitive Spring namespace, enabling declaration of beans and how they should be wired.
`context`	Comes with elements for configuring the Spring application context, including the ability to autodetect and autowire beans and injection of objects not directly managed by Spring.
`jee`	Offers integration with Java EE APIs such as JNDI and EJB.
`jms`	Provides configuration elements for declaring message-driven POJOs.
`lang`	Enables declaration of beans that are implemented as Groovy, JRuby, or BeanShell scripts.
`mvc`	Enables Spring MVC capabilities such as annotation-oriented controllers, view controllers, and interceptors.

Table 2.1 Spring comes with several XML namespaces through which you can configure the Spring container *(continued)*

Namespace	Purpose
oxm	Supports configuration of Spring's object-to-XML mapping facilities.
tx	Provides for declarative transaction configuration.
util	A miscellaneous selection of utility elements. Includes the ability to declare collections as beans and support for property placeholder elements.

In addition to the namespaces that come with the Spring Framework, many of the members of the Spring portfolio, such as Spring Security, Spring Web Flow, and Spring Dynamic Modules, also provide their own Spring configuration namespace.

We'll see more of Spring's namespaces as this book progresses. But for now, let's fill in that conspicuously empty space in the middle of the XML configuration by adding some <bean> elements within <beans>.

2.1.2 Declaring a simple bean

Unlike some similarly named talent competitions that you may have heard of, *Spring Idol* doesn't cater to only singers. Many of the performers can't carry a tune at all. For example, one of the performers is a Juggler.

Listing 2.1 A juggling bean

```
package com.springinaction.springidol;

public class Juggler implements Performer {
  private int beanBags = 3;

  public Juggler() {
  }

  public Juggler(int beanBags) {
    this.beanBags = beanBags;
  }

  public void perform() throws PerformanceException {
    System.out.println("JUGGLING " + beanBags + " BEANBAGS");
  }
}
```

As you can see, this Juggler class does little more than implement the Performer interface to report that it's juggling some beanbags. By default, the Juggler juggles three beanbags, but can be given some other number of beanbags through its constructor.

With the Juggler class defined, please welcome our first performer, Duke, to the stage. Duke is defined as a Spring bean. Here's how Duke is declared in the Spring configuration file (spring-idol.xml):

```
<bean id="duke"
      class="com.springinaction.springidol.Juggler" />
```

The <bean> element is the most basic configuration unit in Spring. It tells Spring to create an object for you. Here you've declared Duke as a Spring-managed bean using what's nearly the simplest <bean> declaration possible. The id attribute gives the bean a name by which it'll be referred to in the Spring container. This bean will be known as duke. And, as you can see from the class attribute, Duke is a Juggler.

When the Spring container loads its beans, it'll instantiate the duke bean using the default constructor. In essence, duke will be created using the following Java code:[1]

```
new com.springinaction.springidol.Juggler();
```

To give Duke a try, you can load the Spring application context using the following code:

```
ApplicationContext ctx = new ClassPathXmlApplicationContext(
    "com/springinaction/springidol/spring-idol.xml");

Performer performer = (Performer) ctx.getBean("duke");
performer.perform();
```

Although this isn't the real competition, the previous code gives Duke a chance to practice. When run, this code prints the following:

```
JUGGLING 3 BEANBAGS
```

By default, Duke juggles only three beanbags at once. But juggling three beanbags isn't all that impressive—anybody can do that. If Duke is to have any hope of winning the talent competition, he's going to need to juggle many more beanbags at once. Let's see how to configure Duke to be a champion juggler.

2.1.3 Injecting through constructors

To really impress the judges, Duke has decided to break the world record by juggling as many as 15 beanbags at once.[2]

Recall from listing 2.1 that the Juggler class can be constructed in two different ways:

- Using the default constructor
- Using a constructor that takes an int argument which indicates the number of beanbags that the Juggler will attempt to keep in the air

Although the declaration of the duke bean in section 2.1.2 is valid, it uses the Juggler's default constructor, which limits Duke to juggling only three beanbags at once. To make Duke a world-record juggler, we'll need to use the other constructor. The following XML redeclares Duke as a 15-beanbag juggler:

---

1 Emphasis on "in essence." Actually, Spring creates its beans using reflection.

2 Juggling trivia: Who holds the actual world record for juggling beanbags depends on how many beanbags are juggled and for how long. Bruce Sarafian holds several records, including juggling 12 beanbags for 12 catches. Another record-holding juggler is Anthony Gatto, who juggled 7 balls for 10 minutes and 12 seconds in 2005. Another juggler, Peter Bone, claims to have juggled as many as 13 beanbags for 13 catches—but there's no video evidence of the feat.

```
<bean id="duke"
      class="com.springinaction.springidol.Juggler">
    <constructor-arg value="15" />
</bean>
```

The `<constructor-arg>` element is used to give Spring additional information to use when constructing a bean. If no `<constructor-arg>`s are given, as in section 2.1.2, the default constructor is used. But here you've given a `<constructor-arg>` with a value attribute set to 15, so the `Juggler`'s other constructor will be used instead.

Now when Duke performs, the following is printed:

```
JUGGLING 15 BEANBAGS
```

Juggling 15 beanbags at once is mighty impressive. But there's something we didn't tell you about Duke. Not only is Duke a good juggler, but he's also skilled at reciting poetry. Juggling while reciting poetry takes a lot of mental discipline. If Duke can juggle while reciting a Shakespearean sonnet then he should be able to establish himself as the clear winner of the competition. (I told you this wouldn't be like those other talent shows!)

INJECTING OBJECT REFERENCES WITH CONSTRUCTORS

Because Duke is more than just an average juggler—he's a poetic juggler—we need to define a new type of juggler for him to be. `PoeticJuggler` is a class more descriptive of Duke's talent.

Listing 2.2 A juggler who waxes poetic

```
package com.springinaction.springidol;

public class PoeticJuggler extends Juggler {
  private Poem poem;

  public PoeticJuggler(Poem poem) {                    <-- Inject poem
    super();
    this.poem = poem;
  }
                                                       Inject beanbag
  public PoeticJuggler(int beanBags, Poem poem) {      <-- count and poem
    super(beanBags);
    this.poem = poem;
  }

  public void perform() throws PerformanceException {
    super.perform();
    System.out.println("While reciting...");
    poem.recite();
  }
}
```

This new type of juggler does everything a regular juggler does, but it also has a reference to a poem to be recited. Speaking of the poem, here's an interface that generically defines what a poem looks like:

```
package com.springinaction.springidol;

public interface Poem {
  void recite();
}
```

One of Duke's favorite Shakespearean sonnets is "When in disgrace with fortune and men's eyes." `Sonnet29` is an implementation of the `Poem` interface that defines this sonnet.

Listing 2.3 A class that represents a great work of the Bard

```
package com.springinaction.springidol;

public class Sonnet29 implements Poem {
  private static String[] LINES = {
      "When, in disgrace with fortune and men's eyes,",
      "I all alone beweep my outcast state",
      "And trouble deaf heaven with my bootless cries",
      "And look upon myself and curse my fate,",
      "Wishing me like to one more rich in hope,",
      "Featured like him, like him with friends possess'd,",
      "Desiring this man's art and that man's scope,",
      "With what I most enjoy contented least;",
      "Yet in these thoughts myself almost despising,",
      "Haply I think on thee, and then my state,",
      "Like to the lark at break of day arising",
      "From sullen earth, sings hymns at heaven's gate;",
      "For thy sweet love remember'd such wealth brings",
      "That then I scorn to change my state with kings." };

  public Sonnet29() {
  }

  public void recite() {
    for (int i = 0; i < LINES.length; i++) {
      System.out.println(LINES[i]);
    }
  }
}
```

`Sonnet29` can be declared as a Spring <bean> with the following XML:

```
<bean id="sonnet29"
      class="com.springinaction.springidol.Sonnet29" />
```

With the poem chosen, all you need to do is give it to Duke. Now that Duke is a `PoeticJuggler`, his <bean> declaration will need to change slightly:

```
<bean id="poeticDuke"
      class="com.springinaction.springidol.PoeticJuggler">
    <constructor-arg value="15" />
    <constructor-arg ref="sonnet29" />
</bean>
```

As you can see from listing 2.2, there's no default constructor. The only way to construct a `PoeticJuggler` is to use a constructor that takes arguments. In this listing, you're using the constructor that takes an int and a Poem as arguments. The duke bean declaration configures the number of beanbags as 15 through the int argument using <constructor-arg>'s value attribute.

But you can't use value to set the second constructor argument because a Poem isn't a simple type. Instead, the ref attribute is used to indicate that the value passed to the constructor should be a reference to the bean whose ID is sonnet29. Although the Spring container does much more than just construct beans, you may imagine that when Spring encounters the sonnet29 and duke <bean>s, it performs some logic that's essentially the same as the following lines of Java:

```
Poem sonnet29 = new Sonnet29();
Performer duke = new PoeticJuggler(15, sonnet29);
```

Now when Duke performs, he not only juggles but will also recite Shakespeare, resulting in the following being printed to the standard output stream:

```
JUGGLING 15 BEANBAGS WHILE RECITING... When, in
disgrace with fortune and men's eyes, I all alone beweep my outcast
state And trouble deaf heaven with my bootless cries And look upon
myself and curse my fate, Wishing me like to one more rich in hope,
Featured like him, like him with friends possess'd, Desiring this
man's art and that man's scope, With what I most enjoy contented
least; Yet in these thoughts myself almost despising, Haply I think
on thee, and then my state, Like to the lark at break of day arising
From sullen earth, sings hymns at heaven's gate; For thy sweet love
remember'd such wealth brings That then I scorn to change my state
with kings.
```

Creating beans through constructor injection is great, but what if the bean you want to declare doesn't have a public constructor? Let's see how to wire in beans that are created through factory methods.

CREATING BEANS THROUGH FACTORY METHODS

Sometimes the only way to instantiate an object is through a static factory method. Spring is ready-made to wire factory-created beans through the <bean> element's factory-method attribute.

To illustrate, consider the case of configuring a singleton[3] class as a bean in Spring. Singleton classes generally ensure that only one instance is created by only allowing creation through a static factory method. The Stage class in the following listing is a basic example of a singleton class.

Listing 2.4 The Stage singleton class

```
package com.springinaction.springidol;

public class Stage {
  private Stage() {
  }
```

[3] I'm talking about the Gang of Four Singleton pattern here, not the Spring notion of singleton bean definitions.

```
  private static class StageSingletonHolder {
    static Stage instance = new Stage();            <-- Lazily loads instance
  }

  public static Stage getInstance() {
    return StageSingletonHolder.instance;          <-- Return instance
  }
}
```

In the *Spring Idol* competition, we want to ensure that there's only one stage for the performers to show their stuff. `Stage` has been implemented as a singleton to ensure that there's no way to create more than one instance of `Stage`.

But note that `Stage` doesn't have a public constructor. Instead, the static `getInstance()` method returns the same instance every time it's called. (For thread safety, `getInstance()` employs a technique known as "initialization on demand holder" to create the singleton instance.[4]) How can we configure `Stage` as a bean in Spring without a public constructor?

Fortunately, the <bean> element has a `factory-method` attribute that lets you specify a static method to be invoked instead of the constructor to create an instance of a class. To configure `Stage` as a bean in the Spring context, you simply use `factory-method` as follows:

```
<bean id="theStage"
      class="com.springinaction.springidol.Stage"
      factory-method="getInstance" />
```

Here I've shown you how to use `factory-method` to configure a singleton as a bean in Spring, but it's perfectly suitable for any occasion where you need to wire an object produced by a static method. You'll see more of `factory-method` in chapter 4 when we use it to get references to AspectJ aspects so that they can be injected with dependencies.

2.1.4 Bean scoping

By default, all Spring beans are singletons. When the container dispenses a bean (either through wiring or as the result of a call to the container's `getBean()` method) it'll always hand out the exact same instance of the bean. But there may be times when you need a unique instance of a bean each time it's asked for. How can you override Spring's default singleton nature?

When declaring a <bean> in Spring, you have the option of declaring a scope for that bean. To force Spring to produce a new bean instance each time one is needed, you should declare the bean's `scope` attribute to be `prototype`. For example, suppose that tickets for a performance are declared as a bean in Spring:

```
<bean id="ticket"
      class="com.springinaction.springidol.Ticket" scope="prototype" />
```

4 For information on the "initialization on demand holder" idiom, see http://mng.bz/IGYx.

It's important that everyone attending the performance be given a distinct ticket. If the `ticket` bean were a singleton, everyone would receive the same ticket. This would work out fine for the first person to arrive, but everyone else would be accused of ticket counterfeiting!

By setting the `scope` attribute to `prototype`, we can be assured that a distinct instance will be given out to everyone who the `ticket` bean is wired into.

In addition to `prototype`, Spring offers a handful of other scoping options out of the box, as listed in table 2.2.

Table 2.2 Spring's bean scopes let you declare the scope under which beans are created without hard-coding the scoping rules in the bean class itself.

Scope	What it does
`singleton`	Scopes the bean definition to a single instance per Spring container (default).
`prototype`	Allows a bean to be instantiated any number of times (once per use).
`request`	Scopes a bean definition to an HTTP request. Only valid when used with a web-capable Spring context (such as with Spring MVC).
`session`	Scopes a bean definition to an HTTP session. Only valid when used with a web-capable Spring context (such as with Spring MVC).
`global-session`	Scopes a bean definition to a global HTTP session. Only valid when used in a portlet context.

For the most part, you'll probably want to leave scoping to the default `singleton`, but `prototype` scope may be useful in situations where you want to use Spring as a factory for new instances of domain objects. If domain objects are configured as prototype beans, you can easily configure them in Spring, just like any other bean. But Spring is guaranteed to always dispense a unique instance each time a prototype bean is asked for.

The astute reader will recognize that Spring's notion of singletons is limited to the scope of the Spring context. Unlike true singletons, which guarantee only a single instance of a class per classloader, Spring's singleton beans only guarantee a single instance of the bean definition per the application context—nothing is stopping you from instantiating that same class in a more conventional way or even defining several <bean> declarations that instantiate the same class.

2.1.5 *Initializing and destroying beans*

When a bean is instantiated, it may be necessary to perform some initialization to get it into a usable state. Likewise, when the bean is no longer needed and is removed from the container, some cleanup may be in order. To accommodate setup and tear-down of beans, Spring provides hooks into the bean lifecycle.

To define setup and teardown for a bean, simply declare the `<bean>` with `init-method` and/or `destroy-method` parameters. The `init-method` attribute specifies a method that is to be called on the bean immediately upon instantiation. Similarly, `destroy-method` specifies a method that is called just before a bean is removed from the container.

To illustrate, imagine that we have a Java class called `Auditorium` which represents the performance hall where the talent competition will take place. `Auditorium` will likely do a lot of things, but for now let's focus on two things that are important at the beginning and the end of the show: turning on the lights and then turning them back off.

To support these essential activities, the `Auditorium` class might have `turnOnLights()` and `turnOffLights()` methods:

```
public class Auditorium {
    public void turnOnLights() {
        ...
    }

    public void turnOffLights() {
        ...
    }
}
```

The details of what takes place within the `turnOnLights()` and `turnOffLights()` methods isn't terribly important. What's important is that the `turnOnLights()` method be called at the start and `turnOffLights()` be called at the end. For that, let's use the `init-method` and `destroy-method` attributes when declaring the `auditorium` bean:

```
<bean id="auditorium"
      class="com.springinaction.springidol.Auditorium"
      init-method="turnOnLights"
     destroy-method="turnOffLights"/>
```

When declared this way, the `turnOnLights()` method will be called soon after the `auditorium` bean is instantiated, allowing it the opportunity to light up the performance venue. And, just before the bean is removed from the container and discarded, `turnOffLights()` will be called to turn the lights off.

> **`InitializingBean` and `DisposableBean`**
> An optional way to define init and destroy methods for a bean is to write the bean class to implement Spring's `InitializingBean` and `DisposableBean` interfaces. The Spring container treats beans that implement these interfaces in a special way by allowing them to hook into the bean lifecycle. `InitializingBean` declares an `afterPropertiesSet()` method that serves as the init method. As for `DisposableBean`, it declares a `destroy()` method that gets called when a bean is removed from the application context.

> **(continued)**
> The chief benefit of using these lifecycle interfaces is that the Spring container can automatically detect beans that implement them without any external configuration. The disadvantage of implementing these interfaces is that you couple your application's beans to Spring's API. For this reason alone, I recommend that you rely on the `init-method` and `destroy-method` attributes to initialize and destroy your beans. The only scenario where you might favor Spring's lifecycle interfaces is if you're developing a framework bean that's to be used specifically within Spring's container.

DEFAULTING INIT-METHOD AND DESTROY-METHOD

If many of the beans in a context definition file will have initialization or destroy methods with the same name, you don't have to declare `init-method` or `destroy-method` on each individual bean. Instead you can take advantage of the `default-init-method` and `default-destroy-method` attributes on the <beans> element:

```
<?xml version="1.0" encoding="UTF-8"?>
<beans xmlns="http://www.springframework.org/schema/beans"
   xmlns:xsi="http://www.w3.org/2001/XMLSchema-instance"
   xsi:schemaLocation="http://www.springframework.org/schema/beans
   http://www.springframework.org/schema/beans/spring-beans-3.0.xsd"
   default-init-method="turnOnLights"
   default-destroy-method="turnOffLights"> ...
</beans>
```

The `default-init-method` attribute sets an initialization method across all beans in a given context definition. Likewise, `default-destroy-method` sets a common destroy method for all beans in the context definition. In this case, we're asking Spring to initialize all beans in the context definition file by calling `turnOnLights()` and to tear them down with `turnOffLights()` (if those methods exist—otherwise nothing happens).

2.2 Injecting into bean properties

Typically, a JavaBean's properties are private and will have a pair of accessor methods in the form of `setXXX()` and `getXXX()`. Spring can take advantage of a property's setter method to configure the property's value through setter injection.

To demonstrate Spring's other form of DI, let's welcome our next performer to the stage. Kenny is a talented instrumentalist, as defined by the `Instrumentalist` class.

Listing 2.5 Defining a performer who is talented with musical instruments

```
package com.springinaction.springidol;

public class Instrumentalist implements Performer {
  public Instrumentalist() {
  }
```

```
  public void perform() throws PerformanceException {
    System.out.print("Playing " + song + " : ");
    instrument.play();
  }

  private String song;

  public void setSong(String song) {              <—— Inject song
    this.song = song;
  }

  public String getSong() {
    return song;
  }

  public String screamSong() {
    return song;
  }

  private Instrument instrument;

  public void setInstrument(Instrument instrument) {    <— Inject instrument
    this.instrument = instrument;
  }
}
```

From listing 2.5, we can see that an `Instrumentalist` has two properties: `song` and `instrument`. The `song` property holds the name of the song that the instrumentalist will play and is used in the `perform()` method. The `instrument` property holds a reference to an `Instrument` that the instrumentalist will play. An `Instrument` is defined by the following interface:

```
package com.springinaction.springidol;

public interface Instrument {
  public void play();
}
```

Because the `Instrumentalist` class has a default constructor, Kenny could be declared as a <bean> in Spring with the following XML:

```
<bean id="kenny"
      class="com.springinaction.springidol.Instrumentalist" />
```

Although Spring will have no problem instantiating `kenny` as an `Instrumentalist`, Kenny will have a hard time performing without a `song` or an `instrument`. Let's look at how to give Kenny his `song` and `instrument` by using setter injection.

2.2.1 *Injecting simple values*

Bean properties can be configured in Spring using the `<property>` element. `<property>` is similar to `<constructor-arg>` in many ways, except that instead of injecting values through a constructor argument, `<property>` injects by calling a property's setter method.

To illustrate, let's give Kenny a song to perform using setter injection. The following XML shows an updated declaration of the kenny bean:

```
<bean id="kenny"
      class="com.springinaction.springidol.Instrumentalist">
    <property name="song" value="Jingle Bells" />
</bean>
```

Once the Instrumentalist has been instantiated, Spring will use property setter methods to inject values into the properties specified by <property> elements. The <property> element in this XML instructs Spring to call setSong() to set a value of "Jingle Bells" for the song property.

In this case, the value attribute of the <property> element is used to inject a String value into a property. But <property> isn't limited to injecting String values. The value attribute can also specify numeric (int, float, java.lang.Double, and so on) values as well as boolean values.

For example, let's pretend that the Instrumentalist class has an age property of type int to indicate the age of the instrumentalist. You could set Kenny's age using the following XML:

```
<bean id="kenny"
      class="com.springinaction.springidol.Instrumentalist">
  <property name="song" value="Jingle Bells" />
  <property name="age" value="37" />
</bean>
```

Note that the value attribute is used exactly the same when setting a numeric value as it is when setting a String value. Spring will determine the correct type for the value based on the property's type. Since the age property is an int, Spring knows to convert 37 to an int value before calling setAge().

Using <property> to configure simple properties of a bean is great, but there's more to DI than just wiring hardcoded values. The real value of DI is found in wiring an application's collaborating objects together so that they don't have to wire themselves together. To that aim, let's see how to give Kenny an instrument that he can play.

2.2.2 Referencing other beans

Kenny's a talented instrumentalist and can play virtually any instrument given to him. As long as it implements the Instrument interface, he can make music with it. Naturally, Kenny does have a favorite instrument. His instrument of choice is the saxophone, which is defined by the Saxophone class.

Listing 2.6 A saxophone implementation of Instrument

```
package com.springinaction.springidol;

public class Saxophone implements Instrument {
  public Saxophone() {
  }
```

```
  public void play() {
    System.out.println("TOOT TOOT TOOT");
  }
}
```

Before you can give Kenny a saxophone to play, you must declare it as a bean in the Spring container. The following XML should do:

```
<bean id="saxophone"
      class="com.springinaction.springidol.Saxophone" />
```

Note that the Saxophone class has no properties that need to be set. Consequently, there's no need for <property> declarations in the saxophone bean.

With the saxophone declared, we're ready to give it to Kenny to play. The following modification to the kenny bean uses setter injection to set the instrument property:

```
<bean id="kenny2"
      class="com.springinaction.springidol.Instrumentalist">
    <property name="song" value="Jingle Bells" />
    <property name="instrument" ref="saxophone" />
</bean>
```

Now the kenny bean has been injected with all of its properties and Kenny is ready to perform. As with Duke, you can prompt Kenny to perform by executing the following Java code (perhaps in a main() method):

```
ApplicationContext ctx = new ClassPathXmlApplicationContext(
        "com/springinaction/springidol/spring-idol.xml");
Performer performer = (Performer) ctx.getBean("kenny");
performer.perform();
```

This isn't the exact code that will run the *Spring Idol* competition, but it does give Kenny a chance to practice. When it's run, the following will be printed:

```
Playing Jingle Bells : TOOT TOOT TOOT
```

At the same time, it illustrates an important concept. If you compare this code with the code that instructed Duke to perform, you'll find that it isn't much different. In fact, the only difference is the name of the bean retrieved from Spring. The code is the same, even though one causes a juggler to perform and the other causes an instrumentalist to perform.

This isn't a feature of Spring as much as it's a benefit of coding to interfaces. By referring to a performer through the Performer interface, we can blindly cause any type of performer to perform, whether it's a poetic juggler or a saxophonist. Spring encourages the use of interfaces for this reason. And, as you're about to see, interfaces work hand in hand with DI to provide loose coupling.

As mentioned, Kenny can play virtually any instrument that's given to him as long as it implements the Instrument interface. Although he favors the saxophone, we could also ask Kenny to play piano. For example, consider the Piano class.

Listing 2.7 A piano implementation of `Instrument`

```
package com.springinaction.springidol;

public class Piano implements Instrument {
  public Piano() {
  }

  public void play() {
    System.out.println("PLINK PLINK PLINK");
  }
}
```

The `Piano` class can be declared as a `<bean>` in Spring using the following XML:

```
<bean id="piano"
        class="com.springinaction.springidol.Piano" />
```

Now that a piano is available, changing Kenny's instrument is as simple as changing the `kenny` bean declaration as follows:

```
<bean id="kenny"
      class="com.springinaction.springidol.Instrumentalist">
  <property name="song" value="Jingle Bells" />
  <property name="instrument" ref="piano" />
</bean>
```

With this change, Kenny will play a piano instead of a saxophone. But because the `Instrumentalist` class only knows about its `instrument` property through the `Instrument` interface, nothing about the `Instrumentalist` class needed to change to support a new implementation of `Instrument`. Although an `Instrumentalist` can play either a `Saxophone` or `Piano`, it's decoupled from both. If Kenny decides to take up the hammered dulcimer, the only change required will be to create a `HammeredDulcimer` class and to change the `instrument` property on the `kenny` bean declaration.

INJECTING INNER BEANS

We've seen that Kenny can play saxophone, piano, or any instrument that implements the `Instrument` interface. But it's also true that the `saxophone` and `piano` beans could also be shared with any other bean by injecting them into an `instrument` property. So, not only can Kenny play any `Instrument`, any `Instrumentalist` can play the `saxophone` bean. In fact, it's common for beans to be shared among other beans in an application.

The problem is that Kenny's concerned with the hygienic implications of sharing his saxophone with others. He'd rather keep his saxophone to himself. To help Kenny avoid germs, we'll use a handy Spring technique known as *inner beans*.

As a Java developer, you're probably already familiar with the concept of inner classes—classes that are defined within the scope of other classes. Similarly, inner beans are beans that are defined within the scope of another bean. To illustrate, consider this new configuration of the `kenny` bean where his `saxophone` is declared as an inner bean:

```
<bean id="kenny"
      class="com.springinaction.springidol.Instrumentalist">
  <property name="song" value="Jingle Bells" />
  <property name="instrument">
    <bean class="org.springinaction.springidol.Saxophone" />
  </property>
</bean>
```

As you can see, an inner bean is defined by declaring a `<bean>` element directly as a child of the `<property>` element to which it'll be injected. In this case, a `Saxophone` will be created and wired into Kenny's `instrument` property.

Inner beans aren't limited to setter injection. You may also wire inner beans into constructor arguments, as shown in this new declaration of the `duke` bean:

```
<bean id="duke"
      class="com.springinaction.springidol.PoeticJuggler">
  <constructor-arg value="15" />
  <constructor-arg>
    <bean class="com.springinaction.springidol.Sonnet29" />
  </constructor-arg>
</bean>
```

Here, a `Sonnet29` instance will be created as an inner bean and sent as an argument to the `PoeticJuggler`'s constructor.

Note that the inner beans don't have an `id` attribute set. Though it's perfectly legal to declare an ID for an inner bean, it's not necessary because you'll never refer to the inner bean by name. This highlights the main drawback of using inner beans: they can't be reused. Inner beans are only useful for injection once and can't be referred to by other beans.

You may also find that using inner-bean definitions has a negative impact on the readability of the XML in the Spring context files.

2.2.3 Wiring properties with Spring's p namespace

Wiring values and references into bean properties using the `<property>` element isn't that daunting. Nevertheless, Spring's `p` namespace offers a way to wire bean properties that doesn't require so many angle brackets.

The `p` namespace has a schema URI of http://www.springframework.org/schema/p. To use it, simply add a declaration for it in the Spring XML configuration:

```
<?xml version="1.0" encoding="UTF-8"?>
<beans xmlns="http://www.springframework.org/schema/beans"
 xmlns:p="http://www.springframework.org/schema/p"
 xmlns:xsi="http://www.w3.org/2001/XMLSchema-instance"
 xsi:schemaLocation="http://www.springframework.org/schema/beans
        http://www.springframework.org/schema/beans/spring-beans-3.0.xsd">
```

With it declared, you can now use `p:`-prefixed attributes of the `<bean>` element to wire properties. An an example, look at the following declaration of the `kenny` bean:

```
<bean id="kenny" class="com.springinaction.springidol.Instrumentalist"
      p:song = "Jingle Bells"
      p:instrument-ref = "saxophone" />
```

The p:song attribute is set to "Jingle Bells", wiring the song property with that value. Meanwhile, the p:instrument-ref attribute is set to "saxophone", effectively wiring the instrument property with a reference to the bean whose ID is *saxophone*. The -ref suffix serves as a clue to Spring that a reference should be wired instead of a literal value.

The choice between <property> and the p namespace is up to you. They work equally well. The primary benefit of the p namespace is that it's more terse. That works well when trying to write examples for a book with fixed margins. Therefore, you're likely to see me use the p namespace from time to time throughout this book—especially when horizontal space is tight.

At this point, Kenny's talent extends to virtually any instrument. Nevertheless, he does have one limitation: he can play only one instrument at a time. Next to take the stage in the *Spring Idol* competition is Hank, a performer who can simultaneously play multiple instruments.

2.2.4 Wiring collections

Up to now, you've seen how to use Spring to configure both simple property values (using the value attribute) and properties with references to other beans (using the ref attribute). But value and ref are only useful when your bean's properties are singular. How can Spring help you when your bean has properties that are plural—what if a property is a collection of values?

Spring offers four types of collection configuration elements that come in handy when configuring collections of values. Table 2.3 lists these elements and what they're good for.

The <list> and <set> elements are useful when configuring properties that are either arrays or some implementation of java.util.Collection. As you'll soon see, the actual implementation of the collection used to define the property has little correlation to the choice of <list> or <set>. Both elements can be used almost interchangeably with properties of any type of java.util.Collection.

As for <map> and <props>, these two elements correspond to collections that are java.util.Map and java.util.Properties, respectively. These types of collections

Table 2.3 Just as Java has several kinds of collections, Spring allows for injecting several kinds of collections

Collection element	Useful for...
<list>	Wiring a list of values, allowing duplicates
<set>	Wiring a set of values, ensuring no duplicates
<map>	Wiring a collection of name-value pairs where name and value can be of any type
<props>	Wiring a collection of name-value pairs where the name and value are both Strings

are useful when you need a collection that's made up of a collection of key-value pairs. The key difference between the two is that when using `<props>`, both the keys and values are `String`s, whereas `<map>` allows keys and values of any type.

To illustrate collection wiring in Spring, please welcome Hank to the *Spring Idol* stage. Hank's special talent is that he's a one-man band. Like Kenny, Hank's talent is playing several instruments, but Hank can play several instruments at the same time. Hank is defined by the `OneManBand` class.

Listing 2.8 A performer that's a one-man-band

```
package com.springinaction.springidol;

import java.util.Collection;

public class OneManBand implements Performer {
  public OneManBand() {
  }

  public void perform() throws PerformanceException {
    for (Instrument instrument : instruments) {
      instrument.play();
    }
  }

  private Collection<Instrument> instruments;

  public void setInstruments(Collection<Instrument> instruments) {
    this.instruments = instruments;          <- Inject instrument collection
  }
}
```

As you can see, a `OneManBand` iterates over a collection of instruments when it performs. What's most important here is that the collection of instruments is injected through the `setInstruments()` method. Let's see how Spring can provide Hank with his collection of instruments.

WIRING LISTS, SETS, AND ARRAYS

To give Hank a collection of instruments to perform with, let's use the `<list>` configuration element:

```
<bean id="hank"
      class="com.springinaction.springidol.OneManBand">
  <property name="instruments">
    <list>
      <ref bean="guitar" />
      <ref bean="cymbal" />
      <ref bean="harmonica" />
    </list>
  </property>
</bean>
```

The `<list>` element contains one or more values. Here `<ref>` elements are used to define the values as references to other beans in the Spring context, configuring Hank to play a guitar, cymbal, and harmonica. But it's also possible to use other value-setting Spring elements as the members of a <list>, including <value>, <bean>, and <null/>. In fact, a <list> may contain another <list> as a member for multidimensional lists.

In listing 2.8, OneManBand's instruments property is a java.util.Collection using Java 5 generics to constrain the collection to Instrument values. But <list> may be used with properties that are of any implementation of java.util.Collection or an array. In other words, the <list> element we just used would still work, even if the instruments property were to be declared as

```
java.util.List<Instrument> instruments;
```

or even if it were to be declared as

```
Instrument[] instruments;
```

Likewise, you could also use <set> to wire a collection or array property:

```
<bean id="hank"
      class="com.springinaction.springidol.OneManBand">
  <property name="instruments">
    <set>
      <ref bean="guitar" />
      <ref bean="cymbal" />
      <ref bean="harmonica" />
      <ref bean="harmonica" />
    </set>
  </property>
</bean>
```

Again, either <list> or <set> can be used to wire any implementation of java.util.Collection or an array. Just because a property is a java.util.Set, that doesn't mean that you must use <set> to do the wiring. Even though it may seem odd to configure a java.util.List property using <set>, it's certainly possible. In doing so, you'll be guaranteed that all members of the List will be unique.

WIRING MAP COLLECTIONS

When a OneManBand performs, each instrument's sound is printed as the perform() method iterates over the collection of instruments. But suppose that you also want to see which instrument is producing each sound. To accommodate this, consider the following changes to the OneManBand class.

Listing 2.9 Changing OneManBand's instrument collection to a Map

```
package com.springinaction.springidol;

import java.util.Map;
import com.springinaction.springidol.Instrument;
import com.springinaction.springidol.PerformanceException;
import com.springinaction.springidol.Performer;

public class OneManBand implements Performer {
  public OneManBand() {
  }
```

```
  public void perform() throws PerformanceException {
    for (String key : instruments.keySet()) {
      System.out.print(key + " : ");
      Instrument instrument = instruments.get(key);
      instrument.play();
    }
  }

  private Map<String, Instrument> instruments;

  public void setInstruments(Map<String, Instrument> instruments) {
    this.instruments = instruments;                        <-- Inject
  }                                                            instrument as map
}
```

In the new version of OneManBand, the instruments property is a java.util.Map where each member has a String as its key and an Instrument as its value. Because a Map's members are made up of key-value pairs, a simple <list> or <set> configuration element won't suffice when wiring the property.

Instead, the following declaration of the hank bean uses the <map> element to configure the instruments property:

```
<bean id="hank" class="com.springinaction.springidol.OneManBand">
  <property name="instruments">
    <map>
      <entry key="GUITAR" value-ref="guitar" />
      <entry key="CYMBAL" value-ref="cymbal" />
      <entry key="HARMONICA" value-ref="harmonica" />
    </map>
  </property>
</bean>
```

The <map> element declares a value of type java.util.Map. Each <entry> element defines a member of the Map. In the previous example, the key attribute specifies the key of the entry whereas the value-ref attribute defines the value of the entry as a reference to another bean within the Spring context.

Although our example uses the key attribute to specify a String key and value-ref to specify a reference value, the <entry> element actually has two attributes each for specifying the key and value of the entry. Table 2.4 lists those attributes.

<map> is only one way to inject key-value pairs into bean properties when either of the objects isn't a String. Let's see how to use Spring's <props> element to configure String-to-String mappings.

Table 2.4 An <entry> in a <map> is made up of a key and a value, either of which can be a primitive value or a reference to another bean. These attributes help specify the keys and values of an <entry>.

Attribute	Purpose
key	Specifies the key of the map entry as a String
key-ref	Specifies the key of the map entry as a reference to a bean in the Spring context
value	Specifies the value of the map entry as a String
value-ref	Specifies the value of the map entry as a reference to a bean in the Spring context

WIRING PROPERTIES COLLECTIONS

When declaring a `Map` of values for `OneManBand`'s `instrument` property, it was necessary to specify the value of each entry using `value-ref`. That's because each entry is ultimately another bean in the Spring context.

But if you find yourself configuring a `Map` whose entries have both `String` keys and `String` values, you may want to consider using `java.util.Properties` instead of a `Map`. The `Properties` class serves roughly the same purpose as `Map`, but limits the keys and values to `Strings`.

To illustrate, imagine that instead of being wired with a map of `Strings` and bean references, `OneManBand` is wired with a `String`-to-`String` `java.util.Properties` collection. The new `instruments` property might be changed to look like this:

```
private Properties instruments;
public void setInstruments(Properties instruments) {
    this.instruments = instruments;
}
```

To wire the instrument sounds into the `instruments` property, we use the <props> element in the following declaration of the `hank` bean:

```
<bean id="hank" class="com.springinaction.springidol.OneManBand">
  <property name="instruments">
    <props>
      <prop key="GUITAR">STRUM STRUM STRUM</prop>
      <prop key="CYMBAL">CRASH CRASH CRASH</prop>
      <prop key="HARMONICA">HUM HUM HUM</prop>
    </props>
  </property>
</bean>
```

The <props> element constructs a `java.util.Properties` value where each member is defined by a <prop> element. Each <prop> element has a `key` attribute that defines the key of each `Properties` member, while the value is defined by the contents of the <prop> element. In our example, the element whose key is "GUITAR" has a value of "STRUM STRUM STRUM".

This may be the most difficult Spring configuration element to talk about. That's because the term *property* is highly overloaded. It's important to keep the following straight:

- <property> is the element used to inject a value or bean reference into a property of a bean class.
- <props> is the element used to define a collection value of type `java.util.Properties`.
- <prop> is the element used to define a member of a <props> collection.

Up to this point, we've seen how to wire several things into bean properties and constructor arguments. We've wired simple values, references to other beans, and collections. Now, let's see how to wire nothing.

2.2.5 *Wiring nothing (null)*

You read that right. In addition to all of the other things Spring can wire into a bean property or constructor argument, it can also wire nothing. Or more accurately, Spring can wire a `null`.

You're probably rolling your eyes and thinking, "What's this guy talking about? Why would I ever want to wire `null` into a property? Aren't all properties `null` until they're set? What's the point?"

Though it's often true that properties start out `null` and will remain that way until set, some beans may themselves set a property to a non-`null` default value. What if, for some twisted reason, you want to force that property to be `null`? If that's the case, it's not sufficient to just assume that the property will be `null`—you must explicitly wire `null` into the property.

To set a property to `null`, you simply use the `<null/>` element. For example:

```
<property name="someNonNullProperty"><null/></property>
```

Another reason for explicitly wiring `null` into a property is to override an autowired property value. What's autowiring, you ask? Keep reading—we're going to explore autowiring in the next chapter.

For now, you'll want to hold on to your seats. We'll wrap up this chapter by looking at one of the coolest new features in Spring: the Spring Expression Language.

2.3 *Wiring with expressions*

So far all of the stuff we've wired into bean properties and constructor arguments has been statically defined in the Spring configuration XML. When we wired the name of a song into the `Instrumentalist` bean, that value was determined at development time. And when we wired references to other beans, those references were also statically determined while we wrote the Spring configuration.

What if we want to wire properties with values that aren't known until runtime?

Spring 3 introduced the *Spring Expression Language (SpEL)*, a powerful yet succinct way of wiring values into a bean's properties or constructor arguments using expressions that are evaluated at runtime. Using SpEL, you can pull off amazing feats of bean wiring that would be much more difficult (or even impossible) using Spring's traditional wiring style.

SpEL has a lot of tricks up its sleeves, including

- The ability to reference beans by their ID
- Invoking methods and accessing properties on objects
- Mathematical, relational, and logical operations on values
- Regular expression matching
- Collection manipulation

Writing a SpEL expression involves piecing together the various elements of the SpEL syntax. Even the most interesting SpEL expressions are often composed of simpler expressions. So before we can start running with SpEL, let's take our first steps with some of the most basic ingredients of a SpEL expression.

2.3.1 Expressing SpEL fundamentals

The ultimate goal of a SpEL expression is to arrive at some value after evaluation. In the course of calculating that value, other values are considered and operated upon. The simplest kinds of values that SpEL can evaluate may be literal values, references to a bean's properties, or perhaps a constant on some class.

LITERAL VALUES

The simplest possible SpEL expression is one that contains only a literal value. For example, the following is a perfectly valid SpEL expression:

```
5
```

Not surprisingly, this expression evaluates to an integer value of 5. We could wire this value into a bean's property by using `#{}` markers in a `<property>` element's `value` attribute like this:

```
<property name="count" value="#{5}"/>
```

The `#{}` markers are a clue to Spring that the content that they contain is a SpEL expression. They could be mixed with non-SpEL values as well:

```
<property name="message" value="The value is #{5}"/>
```

Floating-point numbers can also be expressed in SpEL. For example:

```
<property name="frequency" value="#{89.7}"/>
```

Numbers can even be expressed in scientific notation. As an example, the following snippet of code sets a `capacity` property to 10000.0 using scientific notation:

```
<property name="capacity" value="#{1e4}"/>
```

Literal `String` values can also be expressed in SpEL with either single or double quote marks. For example, to wire a literal `String` value into a bean property, we could express it like this:

```
<property name="name" value="#{'Chuck'}"/>
```

Or if you were using single quote marks for XML attribute values, then you'd want to use double quotes in the SpEL expression:

```
<property name='name' value='#{"Chuck"}'/>
```

A couple of other literal values you may use are the Boolean `true` and `false` values. For example, you could express a `false` like this:

```
<property name="enabled" value="#{false}"/>
```

Working with literal values in SpEL expressions is mundane. After all, we don't need SpEL to set an integer property to 5 or a Boolean property to `false`. I admit that there's not much use to SpEL expressions that only contain literal values. But remember that more interesting SpEL expressions are composed of simpler expressions. So it's good to know how to work with literal values in SpEL. We'll eventually need them as our expressions get more complex.

REFERENCING BEANS, PROPERTIES, AND METHODS

Another basic thing that a SpEL expression can do is to reference another bean by its ID. For example, you could use SpEL to wire one bean into another bean's property by using the bean ID as the SpEL expression:

```
<property name="instrument" value="#{saxophone}"/>
```

As you can see, we're using SpEL to wire the bean whose ID is "saxophone" into an instrument property. But wait... can't we do that without SpEL by using the ref attribute as follows?

```
<property name="instrument" ref="saxophone"/>
```

Yes, the outcome is the same. And yes, we didn't need SpEL to do that. But it's interesting that we can do that, and in a moment I'll show you a few tricks that take advantage of being able to wire bean references with SpEL. Right now I want to show how you can use a bean reference to access the properties of the bean in a SpEL expression.

Let's say that you want to configure a new Instrumentalist bean whose ID is carl. The funny thing about Carl is that he's a copycat performer. Instead of performing his own song, he's going to be wired to perform whatever song Kenny plays. When you configure the carl bean, you can use SpEL to copy Kenny's song into the song property like this:

```
<bean id="carl"
      class="com.springinaction.springidol.Instrumentalist">
    <property name="song" value="#{kenny.song}" />
</bean>
```

As illustrated in figure 2.1, the expression passed into Carl's song property is made up of two parts.

The first part (the part before the period delimiter) refers to the kenny bean by its ID. The second part refers to the song attribute of the kenny bean. By wiring the carl bean's song property this way, it's effectively as if you programmatically performed the following Java code:

```
Instrumentalist carl = new Instrumentalist();
carl.setSong(kenny.getSong());
```

Ah! We're finally doing something slightly interesting with SpEL. It's a humble expression, but I can't imagine an easier way to pull off the same thing without SpEL.

Trust me... we're just getting started.

Referencing a bean's properties isn't the only thing you can do with a bean. You could also invoke a method. For example, imagine

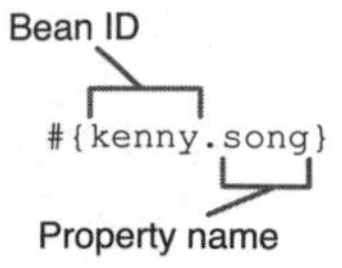

Bean ID
#{kenny.song}
Property name

Figure 2.1 Referring to another bean's property using the Spring Expression Language

that you have a `songSelector` bean which has a `selectSong()` method on it that returns a song to be sung. In that case, Carl could quit copycatting and start singing whatever song the `songSelector` bean suggests:

```
<property name="song" value="#{songSelector.selectSong()}"/>
```

Now suppose that (for whatever reason), Carl wants the song given to him in all uppercase. No problem... all you need to do is invoke the `toUpperCase()` method on the `String` value you're given:

```
<property name="song" value="#{songSelector.selectSong().toUpperCase()}"/>
```

That'll do the trick every time... as long as the `selectSong()` method doesn't return a `null`. If `selectSong()` were to return `null`, then you'd get a `NullPointerException` as the SpEL expression is being evaluated.

The way to avoid the dreaded `NullPointerException` in SpEL is to use the null-safe accessor:

```
<property name="song" value="#{songSelector.selectSong()?.toUpperCase()}"/>
```

Instead of a lonely dot (`.`) to access the `toUpperCase()` method, now you're using `?.` operator. This operator makes sure that the item to its left isn't null before accessing the thing to its right. So, if `selectSong()` were to return a null, then SpEL wouldn't even try to invoke `toUpperCase()` on it.

Writing expressions that work with other beans is a good start. But what if you need to invoke a static method or reference a constant? For that we'll need to see how to work with types in SpEL.

WORKING WITH TYPES

The key to working with class-scoped methods and constants in SpEL is to use the `T()` operator. For example, to express Java's `Math` class in SpEL, you'd need to use the `T()` operator like this:

```
T(java.lang.Math)
```

The result of the `T()` operator, as shown here, is a `Class` object that represents `java.lang.Math`. You could even wire it into a bean property of type `Class` if you want to. But the real value of the `T()` operator is that it gives us access to static methods and constants on a given class.

For example, suppose that you need to wire the value of pi into a bean property. In that case, simply reference the `Math` class's `PI` constant like this:

```
<property name="multiplier" value="#{T(java.lang.Math).PI}"/>
```

Similarly, static methods can also be invoked on the result of the `T()` operator. For instance, here's how to wire a random number (between 0 and 1) into a bean property:

```
<property name="randomNumber" value="#{T(java.lang.Math).random()}"/>
```

When the application is starting up and Spring is wiring the `randomNumber` property, it'll use the `Math.random()` method to determine a value for that property. This is another example of a SpEL expression that I can't think of a simpler way to do without SpEL.

Now that we've added a few of the most basic SpEL expressions to our bag of tricks, let's step things up a bit by looking at the types of operations we can perform on those simpler expressions.

2.3.2 Performing operations on SpEL values

SpEL offers several operations that you can apply on values in a SpEL expression. These operations are summarized in table 2.5.

Table 2.5 SpEL includes several operators that you can use to manipulate the values of an expression.

Operation type	Operators
Arithmetic	`+, -, *, /, %, ^`
Relational	`<, >, ==, <=, >=, lt, gt, eq, le, ge`
Logical	`and, or, not, |`
Conditional	`?:` (ternary), `?:` (Elvis)
Regular expression	`matches`

The first kind of operations we'll play with are the ones that let us perform basic math on values in a SpEL expression.

DOING MATH WITH SPEL

SpEL supports all of the basic arithmetic operators that Java supports, plus the carat (^) operator for performing a power of operation.

For example, to add two numbers together, the + operator can be used like this:

```
<property name="adjustedAmount" value="#{counter.total + 42}"/>
```

Here we're adding 42 to the value of the `counter` bean's `total` property. Note that although both sides of the + operator are numeric, they don't have to be literal values. In this case, the left side is a SpEL expression in its own right.

The other arithmetic operators work in SpEL just as you'd expect them to in Java. The - operator, for instance, performs subtraction:

```
<property name="adjustedAmount" value="#{counter.total - 20}"/>
```

The * operator performs multiplication:

```
<property name="circumference"
➥ value="#{2 * T(java.lang.Math).PI * circle.radius}"/>
```

The / operator performs division:

```
<property name="average" value="#{counter.total / counter.count}"/>
```

And the `%` operator performs a modulo operation:

```
<property name="remainder" value="#{counter.total % counter.count}"/>
```

Unlike Java, SpEL also offers a power-of operator in the form of the carat:

```
<property name="area" value="#{T(java.lang.Math).PI * circle.radius ^ 2}"/>
```

Even though we're talking about SpEL's arithmetic operators, it's worth mentioning that the + operator is overloaded to perform concatenation on `String` values. For example:

```
<property name="fullName"
    value="#{performer.firstName + ' ' + performer.lastName}"/>
```

Again, this is consistent Java in that the + operator can be used to concatenate `String` values there, too.

COMPARING VALUES

It's often useful to compare two values to decide whether they're equal or which is greater than the other. For that kind of comparison, SpEL offers all of the expected comparison operators that Java itself also offers.

As an example, to compare two numbers for equality, you can use the double-equal (==) operator:

```
<property name="equal" value="#{counter.total == 100}"/>
```

In this case, it's assumed that the `equal` property is a Boolean and it'll be wired with a `true` if the `total` property is equal to 100.

Similarly, the less-than (<) and greater-than (>) operators can be used to compare different values. Likewise, SpEL also supports the greater-than-or-equals (>=) and the less-than-or-equals (<=) operators. For example, the following is a perfectly valid SpEL expression:

```
counter.total <= 100000
```

Unfortunately, the less-than and greater-than symbols pose a problem when using these expressions in Spring's XML configuration, as they have special meaning in XML. So, when using SpEL in XML,[5] it's best to use SpEL's textual alternatives to these operators. For example:

```
<property name="hasCapacity" value="#{counter.total le 100000}"/>
```

Here, the `le` operator means less than or equals. The other textual comparison operators are cataloged in table 2.6.

You'll notice that even though the symbolic equals operator (==) doesn't present any issues in XML, SpEL offers a textual `eq` operator in the interest of consistency with the other operators, and because some developers may prefer the textual operators over the symbolic ones.

Operation	Symbolic	Textual
Equals	==	eq
Less than	<	lt
Less than or equals	<=	le
Greater than	>	gt
Greater than or equals	>=	ge

Table 2.6 SpEL includes several operators that you can use to manipulate the values of an expression.

[5] We'll see how to use SpEL outside of Spring XML configuration in the next chapter.

LOGICAL EXPRESSIONS

It's great that we can evaluate comparisons in SpEL, but what if you need to evaluate based on two comparisons? Or what if you want to negate some Boolean value? That's where the logical operators come into play. Table 2.7 lists all of SpEL's logical operators.

Table 2.7 SpEL includes several operators that you can use to manipulate the values of an expression.

Operator	Operation
`and`	A logical AND operation; both sides must evaluate true for the expression to be true
`or`	A logical OR operation; either side must evaluate true for the expression to be true
`not` or `!`	A logical NOT operation; negates the target of the operation

As an example, consider the following use of the `and` operator:

```
<property name="largeCircle"
          value="#{shape.kind == 'circle' and shape.perimeter gt 10000}"/>
```

In this case, the `largeCircle` property will be set to `true` if the `kind` property of `shape` is `"circle"` and the `perimeter` property is a number greater than 10000. Otherwise, it'll remain false.

To negate a Boolean expression, you have two operators to choose from: either the symbolic `!` operator or the textual `not` operator. For example, the following use of the `!` operator

```
<property name="outOfStock" value="#{!product.available}"/>
```

is equivalent to this use of the `not` operator:

```
<property name="outOfStock" value="#{not product.available}"/>
```

Strangely, SpEL doesn't offer symbolic equivalents for the `and` and `or` operators.

CONDITIONALLY EVALUATING

What if you want a SpEL expression to evaluate to one value if a condition is true and a different value otherwise? For example, let's say that Carl (the `Instrumentalist` from earlier) wants to play a piano if the song is "Jingle Bells," but he'll play a saxophone otherwise. In that case, you can use SpEL's ternary (`?:`) operator:

```
<property name="instrument"
   value="#{songSelector.selectSong()=='Jingle Bells'?piano:saxophone}"/>
```

As you can see, SpEL's ternary operator works the same as Java's ternary operator. In this case, the `instrument` property will be wired with a reference to the `piano` bean if the song selected is "Jingle Bells." Otherwise, it'll be wired with the bean whose ID is `saxophone`.

A common use of the ternary operator is to check for a `null` value and to wire a default value in the event of a `null`. For example, suppose we want to configure Carl to perform the same song as Kenny, unless Kenny doesn't have a song. In that case, Carl's song should default to "Greensleeves." The ternary operator could be used as follows to handle this case:

```
<property name="song"
          value="#{kenny.song != null ? kenny.song : 'Greensleeves'}"/>
```

Although that'll work, there's a bit of duplication in that we refer to `kenny.song` twice. SpEL offers a variant of the ternary operator that simplifies this expression:

```
<property name="song" value="#{kenny.song ?: 'Greensleeves'}"/>
```

As in the previous example, the expression will evaluate to the value of `kenny.song` or "Greensleeves" if `kenny.song` is `null`. When used this way, `?:` is referred to as the *Elvis operator*. This strange name comes from using the operator as a type of smiley where the question mark appears to form the shape of Elvis Presley's hair. [6]

REGULAR EXPRESSIONS IN SPEL

When working with text, it's sometimes useful to check whether that text matches a certain pattern. SpEL supports pattern matching in expressions with its `matches` operator.

The `matches` operator attempts to apply a regular expression (given as its right-side argument) against a `String` value (given as the left-side argument). The result of a `matches` evaluation is a Boolean value: `true` if the value matches the regular expression, `false` otherwise.

To demonstrate the `matches` operator, suppose that we want to check whether a `String` contains a valid email address. In that case, we could apply the `matches` operator like this:

```
<property name="validEmail" value=
  "#{admin.email matches '[a-zA-Z0-9._%+-]+@[a-zA-Z0-9.-]+\\.com'}"/>
```

Exploring the mysteries of the enigmatic regular expression syntax is outside the scope of this book. And I realize that the regular expression given here is not robust enough to cover all scenarios. But for the purposes of showing off the `matches` operator, it'll suffice.

Now that we've seen how to evaluate expressions concerning simple values, let's look at the kind of magic that SpEL can perform on collections.

2.3.3 *Sifting through collections in SpEL*

Some of SpEL's most amazing tricks involve working with collections. Sure, you can reference a single member of a collection in SpEL, just like in Java. But SpEL also has the power to select members of a collection based on the values of their properties. It can also extract properties out of the collection members into a new collection.

For demonstration purposes, suppose that you have a `City` class that's defined as follows (with getter/setter methods removed to conserve space):

---

[6] Don't blame me. I didn't come up with that name. But it kind of looks like Elvis's hair, doesn't it?

```
package com.habuma.spel.cities;
public class City {
  private String name;
  private String state;
  private int population;
}
```

And, let's suppose that you've configured a list of `City` objects in Spring by using the `<util:list>` element as shown next.

Listing 2.10 A list of cities, defined using Spring's `<util:list>` element

```
<util:list id="cities">
  <bean class="com.habuma.spel.cities.City"
     p:name="Chicago" p:state="IL" p:population="2853114"/>
  <bean class="com.habuma.spel.cities.City"
     p:name="Atlanta" p:state="GA" p:population="537958"/>
  <bean class="com.habuma.spel.cities.City"
     p:name="Dallas" p:state="TX" p:population="1279910"/>
  <bean class="com.habuma.spel.cities.City"
     p:name="Houston" p:state="TX" p:population="2242193"/>
  <bean class="com.habuma.spel.cities.City"
     p:name="Odessa" p:state="TX" p:population="90943"/>
  <bean class="com.habuma.spel.cities.City"
     p:name="El Paso" p:state="TX" p:population="613190"/>
  <bean class="com.habuma.spel.cities.City"
     p:name="Jal" p:state="NM" p:population="1996"/>
  <bean class="com.habuma.spel.cities.City"
     p:name="Las Cruces" p:state="NM" p:population="91865"/>
</util:list>
```

The `<util:list>` element comes from Spring's `util` namespace. It effectively creates a bean of type `java.util.List` that contains all of the values or beans that it contains. In this case, that's a list of eight `City` beans.

SpEL offers a few handy operators for working with collections such as this.

ACCESSING COLLECTION MEMBERS

The most basic thing we could do here is extract a single element out of the list and wire it into a property:

```
<property name="chosenCity" value="#{cities[2]}"/>
```

In this case, I've selected the third city out of the zero-based `cities` list and wired it into the `chosenCity` property. To spice up the example, I suppose you could randomly choose a city:

```
<property name="chosenCity"
          value="#{cities[T(java.lang.Math).random() * cities.size()]}"/>
```

In any event, the square-braces (`[]`) operator serves to access a member of the collection by its index.

The `[]` operator is also good for retrieving a member of a `java.util.Map` collection. For example, suppose the `City` objects were in a `Map` with their name as the key. In that case, we could retrieve the entry for Dallas like this:

```
<property name="chosenCity" value="#{cities['Dallas']}"/>
```

Another use of the `[]` operator is to retrieve a value from a `java.util.Properties` collection. For example, suppose that you were to load a properties configuration file into Spring using the `<util:properties>` element as follows:

```
<util:properties id="settings"
    location="classpath:settings.properties"/>
```

Here the `settings` bean will be a `java.util.Properties` that contains all of the entries in the file named `settings.properties`. With SpEL, you can access a property from that file in the same way you access a member of a `Map`. For example, the following use of SpEL reads a property whose name is `twitter.accessToken` from the `settings` bean:

```
<property name="accessToken" value="#{settings['twitter.accessToken']}"/>
```

In addition to reading properties from a `<util:properties>`-declared collection, Spring makes two special selections of properties available to SpEL: `systemEnvironment` and `systemProperties`.

`systemEnvironment` contains all of the environment variables on the machine running the application. It's just a `java.util.Properties` collection, so the square braces can be used to access its members by their key. For example, on my MacOS X machine, I can inject the user's home directory path into a bean property like this:

```
<property name="homePath" value="#{systemEnvironment['HOME']}"/>
```

Meanwhile, `systemProperties` contains all of the properties that were set in Java as the application started (typically using the `-D` argument). Therefore, if the JVM were started with `-Dapplication.home=/etc/myapp`, then you could wire that value into the `homePath` property with the following SpEL incantation:

```
<property name="homePath" value="#{systemProperties['application.home']}"/>
```

Although it doesn't have much to do with working with collections, it's worth noting that the `[]` operator can also be used on `String` values to retrieve a single character by its index within the `String`. For example, the following expression will evaluate to `"s"`:

```
'This is a test'[3]
```

Accessing individual members of a collection is handy. But with SpEL, we can also select members of a collection that meet certain criteria. Let's give collection selection a try.

SELECTING COLLECTION MEMBERS

Let's say that you want to narrow the list of cities down to only those whose population is greater than 100,000. One way to do this is to wire the entire `cities` bean into a property and place the burden of sifting out the smaller cities on the receiving bean. But with SpEL, it's a simple matter of using a selection operator (`.?[]`) when doing the wiring:

```
<property name="bigCities" value="#{cities.?[population gt 100000]}"/>
```

The selection operator will create a new collection whose members include only those members from the original collection that meet the criteria expressed between the square braces. In this case, the `bigCities` property will be wired with a list of `City` objects whose `population` property exceeds 100,000.

SpEL also offers two other selection operators, `.^[]` and `.$[]`, for selecting the first and last matching items (respectively) from a collection. For example, to select the first big city from `cities`:

```
<property name="aBigCity" value="#{cities.^[population gt 100000]}"/>
```

No ordering is done on the collection prior to selection, so the `City` representing Chicago would be wired into the `aBigCity` property. Likewise, the `City` object representing El Paso could be selected as follows:

```
<property name="aBigCity" value="#{cities.$[population gt 100000]}"/>
```

We'll revisit collection selection in a moment. But first, let's see how to project properties from a collection into a new collection.

PROJECTING COLLECTIONS

Collection projection involves collecting a particular property from each of the members of a collection into a new collection. SpEL's projection operator (`.![]`) can do exactly that.

For example, suppose that instead of a list of `City` objects, what you want is just a list of `String` objects containing the names of the cities. To get a list of just the city names, you could wire a `cityNames` property like this:

```
<property name="cityNames" value="#{cities.![name]}"/>
```

As a result of this expression, the `cityNames` property will be given a list of `Strings`, including values such as Chicago, Atlanta, Dallas, and so forth. The `name` property within the square braces decides what each member of the resulting list will contain.

But projection isn't limited to projecting a single property. With a slight change to the previous example, you can get a list of city and state names:

```
<property name="cityNames" value="#{cities.![name + ', ' + state]}"/>
```

Now the `cityNames` property will be given a list containing values such as "Chicago, IL", "Atlanta, GA", and "Dallas, TX".

For my final SpEL trick, let me bring collection selection and projection together. Here's how you might wire a list of only big city names into the `cityNames` property:

```
<property name="cityNames"
    value="#{cities.?[population gt 100000].![name + ', ' + state]}"/>
```

Since the outcome of the selection operation is a new list of `City` objects, there's no reason why I can't use projection on that new collection to get the names of all of the big cities.

This demonstrates that you can assemble simple SpEL expressions into more interesting (and more complex) expressions. It's easy to see how that's a powerful feature.

But it doesn't take much of a stretch to realize that it's also dangerous. SpEL expressions are ultimately just `Strings` that are tricky to test and have no IDE support for syntax checking.

I encourage you to use SpEL wherever it can simplify what would otherwise be difficult (or even impossible) wirings. But be careful to not get too carried away with SpEL. Fight the temptation to put too much logic into a SpEL expression.

We'll see some more SpEL later on and used in ways other than bean wiring. In the next chapter we'll break SpEL out of XML and use it in annotation-driven wiring. And, as we'll see in chapter 9, SpEL plays a significant role in the latest version of Spring Security.

2.4 Summary

At the core of the Spring Framework is the Spring container. Spring comes with several implementations of its container, but they all fall into one of two categories. A `BeanFactory` is the simplest form of container, providing basic DI and bean-wiring services. But when more advanced framework services are needed, Spring's `ApplicationContext` is the container to use.

In this chapter, you've seen how to wire beans together within the Spring container. Wiring is typically performed within a Spring container using an XML file. This XML file contains configuration information for all of the components of an application, along with information that helps the container perform DI to associate beans with other beans that they depend on.

Now that you know how to wire beans using XML, I'll show you how to use less XML. In the next chapter, we'll look at how to take advantage of automatic wiring and annotations to reduce the amount of XML configuration in a Spring application.

3 Minimizing XML configuration in Spring

This chapter covers

- Automatic bean wiring
- Automatic bean discovery
- Annotation-oriented bean wiring
- Java-based Spring configuration

So far, we've seen how to declare beans using the `<bean>` element and inject `<bean>` with values using either the `<constructor-arg>` or `<property>` element. That's all well and good for a small application where you only have a handful of beans. But as your application grows, so will the amount of XML configuration you'll write.

Fortunately, Spring offers a few tricks to help cut down on the amount of XML configuration required:

- Autowiring helps reduce or even eliminate the need for `<property>` and `<constructor-arg>` elements by letting Spring automatically figure out how to wire bean dependencies.
- Autodiscovery takes autowiring a step further by letting Spring figure out which classes should be configured as Spring beans, reducing the need for the `<bean>` element.

When used together, autowiring and autodiscovery can dramatically reduce the amount of XML Spring configuration. Often you'll need only a handful of lines of XML, regardless of how many beans are in your Spring application context.

We'll start this chapter by looking at how to take advantage of Spring autowiring and autodiscovery to cut down on the amount of XML needed to configure a Spring application. Then to wrap up the chapter, we'll look at Spring's Java-based configuration, which relies on good old Java code instead of XML to configure a Spring application.

3.1 Automatically wiring bean properties

If I were to say "The moon is bright tonight," it's not likely that you'd respond by asking "Which moon?" That's because we both reside on the Earth and in that context it's obvious that I'm talking about Luna, the Earth's moon. If I were to say the same thing while we were standing on Jupiter, you'd be justified in asking which of the planet's 63 natural satellites I had in mind. But on Earth, there's no ambiguity.[1] Similarly, when it comes to wiring bean properties, it's sometimes quite obvious which bean reference should be wired into a given property. If your application context only has one bean of type `javax.sql.DataSource`, then any bean that needs a `DataSource` will certainly need *that* `DataSource`. After all, it's the only `DataSource` to be had.

Taking advantage of such obvious wirings, Spring offers autowiring. Rather than explicitly wiring bean properties, why not let Spring sort out those cases when there's no question about which bean reference should be wired?

3.1.1 The four kinds of autowiring

When it comes to automatically wiring beans with their dependencies, Spring has a lot of clues to work from. As a result, Spring provides four flavors of autowiring:

- `byName`—Attempts to match all properties of the autowired bean with beans that have the same name (or ID) as the properties. Properties for which there's no matching bean will remain unwired.
- `byType`—Attempts to match all properties of the autowired bean with beans whose types are assignable to the properties. Properties for which there's no matching bean will remain unwired.
- `constructor`—Tries to match up a constructor of the autowired bean with beans whose types are assignable to the constructor arguments.
- `autodetect`—Attempts to apply `constructor` autowiring first. If that fails, `byType` will be tried.

Each of these options has its pros and cons. Let's first look at how to have Spring autowire a bean's properties using the names of those properties as a guide.

[1] Of course, if we were standing on Jupiter, the brightness of any of its moons would be of little concern given the intense atmospheric pressure and all of the unbreathable methane.

AUTOWIRING BY NAME

In Spring, everything is given a name. Thus bean properties are given names, as are the beans that are wired into those properties. Suppose that the name of a property happens to match the name of the bean that's to be wired into that property. That happy coincidence could serve as a hint to Spring that the bean should be automatically wired into the property.

For example, let's revisit the kenny bean from the previous chapter:

```
<bean id="kenny2"
      class="com.springinaction.springidol.Instrumentalist">
    <property name="song" value="Jingle Bells" />
    <property name="instrument" ref="saxophone" />
</bean>
```

Here you've explicitly configured Kenny's instrument property using <property>. For a moment, let's pretend that you declared the Saxophone as a <bean> with an id of instrument:

```
<bean id="instrument"
      class="com.springinaction.springidol.Saxophone" />
```

If this were the case, the id of the Saxophone bean would be the same as the name of the instrument property. Spring can take advantage of this to automatically configure Kenny's instrument by setting the autowire property:

```
<bean id="kenny"
    class="com.springinaction.springidol.Instrumentalist"
    autowire="byName">
  <property name="song" value="Jingle Bells" />
</bean>
```

byName autowiring establishes a convention where a property will automatically be wired with a bean of the same name. In setting the autowire property to byName, you're telling Spring to consider all properties of kenny and look for beans that are declared with the same names as the properties. In this case, Spring finds that the instrument property is eligible for autowiring through setter injection. As illustrated in figure 3.1, if there's a bean in the context whose id is instrument, it'll be autowired into the instrument property.

The downside of using byName autowiring is that it assumes that you'll have a bean whose name is the same as the name of the property of another bean. In our example, it would require creating a bean whose name is instrument. If multiple Instrumentalist beans are configured to be autowired by name, then all of them will be playing the same instrument. This may not be a problem in all circumstances, but it's something to keep in mind.

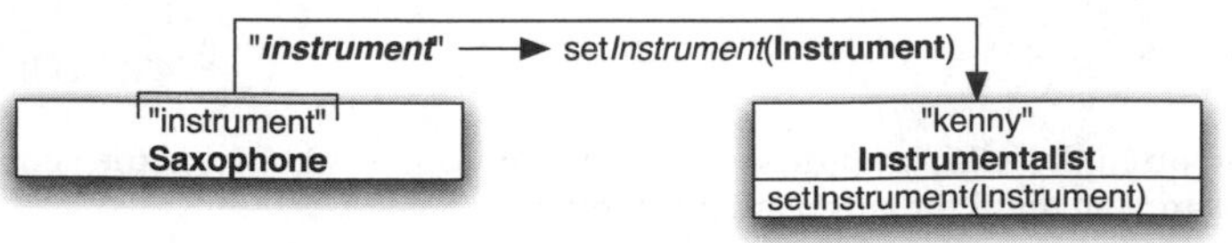

Figure 3.1 When autowiring by name, a bean's name is matched against properties that have the same name.

AUTOWIRING BY TYPE

Autowiring using `byType` works in a similar way to `byName`, except that instead of considering a property's name, the property's type is examined. When attempting to autowire a property by type, Spring will look for beans whose type is assignable to the property's type.

For example, suppose that the `kenny` bean's `autowire` property is set to `byType` instead of `byName`. The container will search itself for a bean whose type is `Instrument` and wire that bean into the `instrument` property. As shown in figure 3.2, the `saxophone` bean will be automatically wired into Kenny's `instrument` property because both the `instrument` property and the `saxophone` bean are of type `Instrument`.

But there's a limitation to autowiring by type. What happens if Spring finds more than one bean whose type is assignable to the `autowired` property? In such a case, Spring isn't going to guess which bean to `autowire` and will instead throw an exception. Consequently, you're allowed to have only one bean configured that matches the `autowired` property. In the *Spring Idol* competition, there are likely to be several beans whose types are subclasses of `Instrument`.

To overcome ambiguities with autowiring by type, Spring offers two options: you can either identify a primary candidate for autowiring or you can eliminate beans from autowiring candidacy.

To identify a primary autowire candidate, you'll work with the `<bean>` element's `primary` attribute. If only one autowire candidate has the `primary` attribute set to `true`, then that bean will be chosen in favor of the other candidates.

But here's the weird side of the `primary` attribute: it defaults to `true`. That means that all autowire candidates will be primary (and thus none will be preferred). So, to use `primary`, you'll need to set it to `false` for all of the beans that are *not* the primary choice. For example, to establish that the `saxophone` bean isn't the primary choice when autowiring `Instruments`:

```
<bean id="saxophone"
      class="com.springinaction.springidol.Saxophone"
      primary="false" />
```

The `primary` attribute is only useful for identifying a preferred autowire candidate. If you'd rather eliminate some beans from consideration when autowiring, then you can set their `autowire-candidate` attribute to `false`, as follows:

```
<bean id="saxophone"
      class="com.springinaction.springidol.Saxophone"
      autowire-candidate="false" />
```

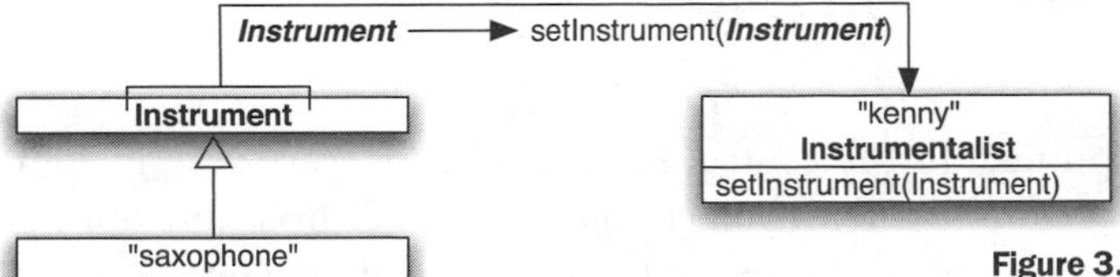

Figure 3.2 Autowiring by type matches beans to properties of the same type.

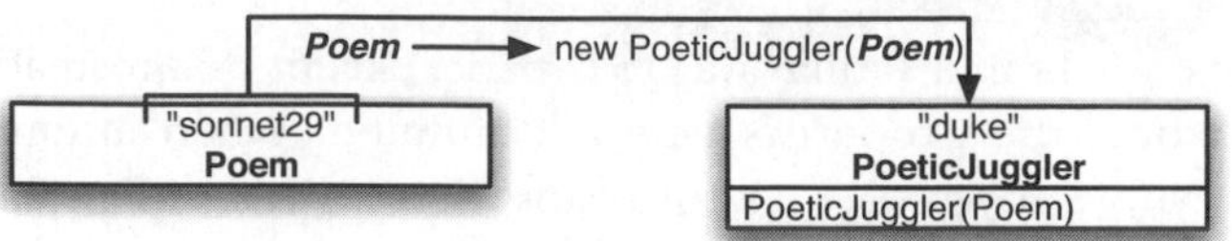

Figure 3.3 When autowired by constructor, the dukePoeticJuggler is instantiated with the constructor that takes a Poem argument.

Here, we've asked Spring to disregard the saxophone bean as a candidate when performing autowiring.

AUTOWIRING CONSTRUCTORS

If your bean is configured using constructor injection, you may choose to put away the <constructor-arg> elements and let Spring automatically choose constructor arguments from beans in the Spring context.

For example, consider the following redeclaration of the duke bean:

```
<bean id="duke"
      class="com.springinaction.springidol.PoeticJuggler"
      autowire="constructor" />
```

In this new declaration of duke, the <constructor-arg> elements are gone and the autowire attribute has been set to constructor. This tells Spring to look at PoeticJuggler's constructors and try to find beans in the Spring configuration to satisfy the arguments of one of the constructors. You've already declared the sonnet29 bean, which is a Poem and matches the constructor argument of one of PoeticJuggler's constructors. Therefore, Spring will use that constructor, passing in the sonnet29 bean, when constructing the duke bean, as expressed in figure 3.3.

Autowiring by constructor shares the same limitations as byType. Spring won't attempt to guess which bean to autowire when it finds multiple beans that match a constructor's arguments. Furthermore, if a class has multiple constructors, any of which can be satisfied by autowiring, Spring won't attempt to guess which constructor to use.

BEST-FIT AUTOWIRING

If you want to autowire your beans, but you can't decide which type of autowiring to use, have no fear. You can set the autowire attribute to autodetect to let Spring make the decision for you. For example:

```
<bean id="duke"
      class="com.springinaction.springidol.PoeticJuggler"
      autowire="autodetect" />
```

When a bean has been configured to autowire by autodetect, Spring will attempt to autowire by constructor first. If a suitable constructor-to-bean match can't be found, then Spring will attempt to autowire by type.

3.1.2 Default autowiring

If you find yourself putting the same autowire attribute on every bean in your application context (or even most of them), you can simplify things by asking Spring to apply the same autowiring style to all beans that it creates. All you need to do is add a default-autowire attribute to the root <beans> element:

```
<?xml version="1.0" encoding="UTF-8"?>
<beans xmlns="http://www.springframework.org/schema/beans"
    xmlns:xsi="http://www.w3.org/2001/XMLSchema-instance"
    xsi:schemaLocation="http://www.springframework.org/schema/beans
        http://www.springframework.org/schema/beans/spring-beans-3.0.xsd"
    default-autowire="byType">

</beans>
```

By default, `default-autowire` is set to `none`, indicating that no beans should be autowired unless they're individually configured for autowiring with the `autowire` attribute. Here we've set it to `byType` to indicate that we want the properties of every bean to be automatically wired using that style of autowiring. But you can set `default-autowire` to any of the valid autowiring types to be applied to all beans in a Spring configuration file.

Note that I said that `default-autowire` would be applied to all beans in a given Spring configuration file; I didn't say that it would be applied to all beans in a Spring application context. You could have multiple configuration files that define a single application context, each with their own default autowiring setting.

Also, just because you've defined a default autowiring scheme, that doesn't mean that you're stuck with it for all of your beans. You can still override the default on a bean-by-bean basis using the `autowire` attribute.

3.1.3 Mixing auto with explicit wiring

Just because you choose to autowire a bean, that doesn't mean you can't explicitly wire some properties. You can still use the `<property>` element on any property just as if you hadn't set `autowire`.

For example, to explicitly wire Kenny's `instrument` property even though he's set to autowire by type, use this code:

```
<bean id="kenny"
      class="com.springinaction.springidol.Instrumentalist"
      autowire="byType">
      <property name="song" value="Jingle Bells" />
      <property name="instrument" ref="saxophone" />
</bean>
```

As illustrated here, mixing automatic and explicit wiring is also a great way to deal with ambiguous autowiring that might occur when autowiring using `byType`. There may be several beans in the Spring context that implement `Instrument`. To keep Spring from throwing an exception due to the ambiguity of several `Instruments` to choose from, we can explicitly wire the `instrument` property, effectively overriding autowiring.

We mentioned earlier that you could use `<null/>` to force an autowired property to be `null`. This is a special case of mixing autowiring with explicit wiring. For example, if you wanted to force Kenny's `instrument` to be `null`, you'd use the following configuration:

```
<bean id="kenny"
      class="com.springinaction.springidol.Instrumentalist"
      autowire="byType">
      <property name="song" value="Jingle Bells" />
      <property name="instrument"><null/></property>
</bean>
```

This is just for illustration's sake, of course. Wiring `null` into `instrument` will result in a `NullPointerException` being thrown when the `perform()` method is invoked.

One final note on mixed wiring: when using constructor autowiring, you must let Spring wire all of the constructor arguments—you can't mix `<constructor-arg>` elements with constructor autowiring.

3.2 Wiring with annotations

Since Spring 2.5, one of the most interesting ways of wiring beans in Spring has been to use annotations to automatically wire bean properties. Autowiring with annotations isn't much different than using the `autowire` attribute in XML. But it does allow for more fine-grained autowiring, where you can selectively annotate certain properties for autowiring.

Annotation wiring isn't turned on in the Spring container by default. So, before we can use annotation-based autowiring, we'll need to enable it in our Spring configuration. The simplest way to do that is with the `<context:annotation-config>` element from Spring's `context` configuration namespace:

```
<?xml version="1.0" encoding="UTF-8"?>
<beans xmlns="http://www.springframework.org/schema/beans"
    xmlns:xsi="http://www.w3.org/2001/XMLSchema-instance"
    xmlns:context="http://www.springframework.org/schema/context"
    xsi:schemaLocation="http://www.springframework.org/schema/beans
        http://www.springframework.org/schema/beans/spring-beans-3.0.xsd
        http://www.springframework.org/schema/context
        http://www.springframework.org/schema/context/spring-context-3.0.xsd">

  <context:annotation-config />

  <!-- bean declarations go here -->

</beans>
```

`<context:annotation-config>` tells Spring that you intend to use annotation-based wiring in Spring. Once it's in place you can start annotating your code to indicate that Spring should automatically wire values into properties, methods, and constructors.

Spring 3 supports a few different annotations for autowiring:

- Spring's own `@Autowired` annotation
- The `@Inject` annotation from JSR-330
- The `@Resource` annotation from JSR-250

We'll look at how to use Spring's `@Autowired` first. Then we'll try out standards-based dependency injection with JSR-330's `@Inject` and JSR-250's `@Resource`.

3.2.1 Using @Autowired

Suppose that you want to use @Autowired to have Spring autowire the instrument property of the Instrumentalist bean. You could annotate the setInstrument() method like this:

```
@Autowired
public void setInstrument(Instrument instrument) {
  this.instrument = instrument;
}
```

Now you can get rid of the <property> element that wires the Instrumentalist with an instrument. When Spring sees that you've annotated setInstrument() with @Autowired it'll try to perform byType autowiring on the method.

What's especially interesting about @Autowired is that you don't have to use it with a setter method. You can use it on any method to automatically wire in bean references:

```
@Autowired
public void heresYourInstrument(Instrument instrument) {
  this.instrument = instrument;
}
```

The @Autowired annotation can even be used on constructors:

```
@Autowired
public Instrumentalist(Instrument instrument) {
  this.instrument = instrument;
}
```

When used with constructors, @Autowired indicates that the constructor should be autowired when creating the bean, even if no <constructor-arg> elements are used to configure the bean in XML.

What's more, you can directly annotate properties and do away with the setter methods altogether:

```
@Autowired
private Instrument instrument;
```

As you can see, @Autowired won't even be thwarted by the private keyword. Even though the instrument property is private, it'll still be autowired. Is there no limit to @Autowired's reach?

Actually, there are a couple of circumstances that could keep @Autowired from getting its job done. Specifically, there must be exactly one bean that's applicable for wiring into the @Autowired property or parameter. If there are no applicable beans or if multiple beans could be autowired, then @Autowired will run into some trouble.

Fortunately, there's a way that we can help @Autowired out in those circumstances. First, let's look at how to keep @Autowired from failing when there isn't a matching bean.

OPTIONAL AUTOWIRING

By default, @Autowired has a strong contract, requiring that the thing it annotates is wired. If no bean can be wired into the @Autowired-annotated property or argument, then autowiring fails (with a nasty NoSuchBeanDefinitionException). That may be what you want—to have Spring fail early when autowiring goes bad rather than later with a NullPointerException.

But it's also possible that the property being wired is truly optional and a null value is acceptable. In that case, you can configure optional autowiring by setting @Autowired's required attribute to false. For example:

```
@Autowired(required=false)
private Instrument instrument;
```

Here, Spring will try to wire the instrument property. But if no bean of type Instrument can be found, then no problem. The property will be left null.

Note that the required attribute can be used anywhere @Autowired can be used. But when used with constructors, only one constructor can be annotated with @Autowired and required set to true. All other @Autowired-annotated constructors must have required set to false. Moreover, when multiple constructors are annotated with @Autowired, Spring will choose the constructor which has the most arguments that can be satisfied.

QUALIFYING AMBIGUOUS DEPENDENCIES

On the other hand, maybe the problem's not a lack of beans for Spring autowiring to choose from. Maybe it's an abundance of (or at least two) beans, each of which is equally qualified to be wired into a property or parameter.

For example, suppose you have two beans that implement Instrument. In that event, there's no way for @Autowired to choose which one you really want. So, instead of guessing, a NoSuchBeanDefinitionException will be thrown and wiring will fail.

To help @Autowired figure out which bean you want, you can accompany it with Spring's @Qualifier annotation.

For example, to ensure that Spring selects a guitar for the eddie bean to play, even if there are other beans that could be wired into the instrument property, you can use @Qualifier to specify a bean named guitar:

```
@Autowired
@Qualifier("guitar")
private Instrument instrument;
```

As shown here, the @Qualifier annotation will try to wire in a bean whose ID matches guitar.

On the surface, it would seem that using @Qualifier is a means of switching @Autowired's by-type autowiring into explicit by-name wiring. And, as used here, that's effectively what's happening. But it's important to know that @Qualifier is really about narrowing the selection of autowire candidate beans. It just so happens that specifying a bean's ID is one way to narrow the selections down to a single bean.

In addition to narrowing by a bean's ID, it's also possible to narrow by a qualifier that's applied to a bean itself. For example, suppose that the guitar bean were declared in XML as follows:

```
<bean class="com.springinaction.springidol.Guitar">
  <qualifier value="stringed" />
</bean>
```

Here the `<qualifier>` element qualifies the `guitar` bean as a stringed instrument. But instead of specifying the qualifier in XML, you could have also annotated the `Guitar` class itself with the `@Qualifier` annotation:

```
@Qualifier("stringed")
public class Guitar implements Instrument {
  ...
}
```

Qualifying autowired beans with `String` identifiers, whether they're the bean's ID or some other qualifier, is simple enough. But you can take qualifiers so much further. In fact, you can even create your own custom qualifier annotations.

CREATING CUSTOM QUALIFIERS

To create a custom qualifier annotation, all you need to do is to define an annotation that's itself annotated with `@Qualifier`. For example, let's create our own `@StringedInstrument` annotation to serve as a qualifier. The following listing shows the custom qualifier annotation.

Listing 3.1 Use `@Qualifier` to create your own qualifier annotation.

```
package com.springinaction.springidol.qualifiers;
import java.lang.annotation.ElementType;
import java.lang.annotation.Retention;
import java.lang.annotation.RetentionPolicy;
import java.lang.annotation.Target;
import org.springframework.beans.factory.annotation.Qualifier;

@Target({ElementType.FIELD, ElementType.PARAMETER, ElementType.TYPE})
@Retention(RetentionPolicy.RUNTIME)
@Qualifier
public @interface StringedInstrument {
}
```

With the `@StringedInstrument` annotation defined, you can now use it instead of `@Qualifier` to annotate `Guitar`:

```
@StringedInstrument
public class Guitar implements Instrument {
  ...
}
```

Then, you can qualify the `@Autowiredinstrument` property with `@StringedInstrument`:

```
@Autowired
@StringedInstrument
private Instrument instrument;
```

When Spring tries to autowire the `instrument` property, it'll narrow the selection of all `Instrument` beans down to just those that are annotated with `@StringedInstrument`. As long as only one bean is annotated with `@StringedInstrument`, it'll be wired into the `instrument` property.

If there's more than one @StringedInstrument-annotated bean, then you'll need to provide further qualification to narrow it down. For example, suppose that in addition to the Guitar bean, you also have a HammeredDulcimer bean which is also annotated with @StringedInstrument. One key difference between a guitar and a hammered dulcimer is that guitars are strummed whereas hammered dulcimers are hit with small wooden sticks (called hammers).

So, to qualify the Guitar class further, you could define another qualifier annotation called @Strummed:

```
@Target({ElementType.FIELD, ElementType.PARAMETER, ElementType.TYPE})
@Retention(RetentionPolicy.RUNTIME)
@Qualifier
public @interface Strummed {
}
```

Now you can annotate the instrument property with @Strummed to narrow the selection down to strummed string instruments:

```
@Autowired
@StringedInstrument
@Strummed
private Instrument instrument;
```

If the Guitar class is the only class annotated with @Strummed and @StringedInstrument, then it'll be the one injected into instrument.

I suppose we could discuss the implications of adding a Ukelele or a Mandolin bean to the mix, but we have to end this somewhere. Suffice it to say that you'd need further qualification to deal with these additional strummed and stringed instruments.

Spring's @Autowired annotation is one way to cut down on the amount of Spring configuration XML. But it does create a Spring-specific dependency within the classes that use it (even if that dependency is just an annotation). Fortunately, Spring also supports a standard Java alternative to @Autowired. Let's look at how to use @Inject from the Dependency Injection for Java specification.

3.2.2 Applying standards-based autowiring with @Inject

In an effort to unify the programming model among the various dependency injection frameworks, the Java Community Process recently published the Dependency Injection for Java specification. Known in the Java Community Process as JSR-330 or more commonly as *at inject*, this specification brings a common dependency injection model to Java. As of Spring 3, Spring supports the at inject model.[2]

The centerpiece of JSR-330 is the @Inject annotation. This annotation is an almost complete drop-in replacement for Spring's @Autowired annotation. So, instead of using the Spring-specific @Autowired annotation, you might choose to use @Inject on the instrument property:

---

[2] Spring isn't alone in its support for JSR-330. Google Guice and Picocontainer also support the JSR-330 model.

```
@Inject
private Instrument instrument;
```

Just like @Autowired, @Inject can be used to autowire properties, methods, and constructors. Unlike @Autowired, @Inject doesn't have a required attribute. Therefore, @Inject-annotated dependencies are expected to be fulfilled, failing with an exception if they're not.

JSR-330 has another trick up its sleeve in addition to the @Inject annotation. Rather than inject a reference directly, you could ask @Inject to inject a Provider. The Provider interface enables, among other things, lazy injection of bean references and injection of multiple instances of a bean.

For example, let's say you have a KnifeJuggler class that needs to be injected with one or more instances of Knife. Assuming that the Knife bean is declared as having prototype scope, the following KnifeJuggler constructor will be able to retrieve five Knife beans:

```
private Set<Knife> knives;

@Inject
public KnifeJuggler(Provider<Knife> knifeProvider) {
  knives = new HashSet<Knife>();
  for (int i = 0; i < 5; i++) {
    knives.add(knifeProvider.get());
  }
}
```

Instead of receiving a Knife instance at construction, KnifeJuggler will receive a Provider<Knife>. At this point, only the provider is injected. No actual Knife object will be injected until the get() method is called on the provider. In this case, the get() method is called five times. And since the Knife bean is a prototype, we know that the Set of knives will be given five distinct Knife objects to work it.

QUALIFYING @INJECTED PROPERTIES

As you've seen, @Inject and @Autowired have a lot in common. And like @Autowired, the @Inject annotation is prone to ambiguous bean definitions. @Inject's answer to the @Qualifier annotation is the @Named annotation.

The @Named annotation works much like Spring's @Qualifier, as you can see here:

```
@Inject
@Named("guitar")
private Instrument instrument;
```

The key difference between Spring's @Qualifier and JSR-330's @Named is one of semantics. Whereas @Qualifier helps narrow the selection of matching beans (using the bean's ID by default), @Named specifically identifies a selected bean by its ID.

CREATING CUSTOM JSR-330 QUALIFIERS

As it turns out, JSR-330 has its own @Qualifier annotation in the javax.inject package. Unlike Spring's @Qualifier, the JSR-330 version isn't intended to be used on its own. Instead, you're expected to use it to create custom qualifier annotations, much as we did with Spring's @Qualifier.[3]

For example, the following listing shows a new @StringedInstrument annotation that's created using JSR-330's @Qualifier instead of Spring's @Qualifier.

Listing 3.2 Creating a custom qualifier using JSR-330's @Qualifier

```
package com.springinaction.springidol;
import java.lang.annotation.ElementType;
import java.lang.annotation.Retention;
import java.lang.annotation.RetentionPolicy;
import java.lang.annotation.Target;

import javax.inject.Qualifier;

@Target({ElementType.FIELD, ElementType.PARAMETER, ElementType.TYPE})
@Retention(RetentionPolicy.RUNTIME)
@Qualifier
public @interface StringedInstrument {
}
```

As you can see, the only real difference between listing 3.2 and 3.1 is the import statement for the @Qualifier annotation. In listing 3.1 we used the one from the org.springframework.beans.factory.annotation package. But this time, we're using the standards-friendly @Qualifier from the javax.inject package. Otherwise, they're virtually the same.

Annotation-based autowiring is great for wiring bean references and reducing <property> elements in our Spring XML configuration. But can annotations be used to wire values into String and other primitive values?

3.2.3 Using expressions with annotation injection

As long as you're using annotations to autowire bean references into your Spring beans, you may want to also use annotations to wire simpler values. Spring 3.0 introduced @Value, a new wiring annotation that lets you wire primitive values such as int, boolean, and String using annotations.

The @Value annotation is simple to use but, as you'll soon see, is also powerful. To use it, annotate a property, method, or method parameter with @Value and pass in a String expression to be wired into the property. For example:

```
@Value("Eruption")
private String song;
```

Here we're wiring a String value into a String property. But the String parameter passed into @Value is just an expression—it can evaluate down to any type and thus @Value can be applied to just about any kind of property.

Wiring hardcoded values using @Value is interesting, but not all that necessary. If you're hardcoding the values in Java code, then why not disregard @Value altogether

[3] In fact, the @Named annotation is just an annotation that's itself annotated with @Qualifier.

and just hardcode the value directly on the property? @Value seems like extra baggage in that case.

As it turns out, simple values aren't where @Value shines. Instead, @Value finds its power with SpEL expressions. Recall that SpEL lets you dynamically evaluate complex expressions, at runtime, into values to be wired into bean properties. That makes @Value a powerful wiring option.

For example, rather than hardcoding a static value into the song property, let's use SpEL to pull a value from a system property:

```
@Value("#{systemProperties.myFavoriteSong}")
private String song;
```

Now @Value shows its stuff. It's not just a courier of static values—it's an effective, annotation-driven method of wiring dynamically evaluated SpEL expressions.

As you can see, autowiring is a powerful technique. Letting Spring automatically figure out how to wire beans together can help you reduce the amount of XML configuration in your application. What's more, autowiring can take decoupling to a whole new level by decoupling bean declarations from each other.

Speaking of rising to new levels, let's now look at bean autodiscovery to see how we can rely on Spring to not only wire beans together, but also automatically figure out which beans should be registered in a Spring context in the first place.

3.3 Automatically discovering beans

When you added <context:annotation-config> to your Spring configuration, you told Spring that you wanted it to honor a certain set of annotations in the beans that you declared and to use those beans to guide bean wiring. Even though <context:annotation-config> can go a long way toward eliminating most uses of <property> and <constructor-arg> elements from your Spring configuration, you still must explicitly declare beans using <bean>.

But Spring has another trick up its sleeve. The <context:component-scan> element does everything that <context:annotation-config> does, plus it configures Spring to automatically discover beans and declare them for you. What this means is that most (or all) of the beans in your Spring application can be declared and wired without using <bean>.

To configure Spring for autodiscovery, use <context:component-scan> instead of <context:annotation-config>:

```
<beans xmlns="http://www.springframework.org/schema/beans"
 xmlns:xsi="http://www.w3.org/2001/XMLSchema-instance"
 xmlns:context="http://www.springframework.org/schema/context"
 xsi:schemaLocation="http://www.springframework.org/schema/beans
     http://www.springframework.org/schema/beans/spring-beans-3.0.xsd
     http://www.springframework.org/schema/context
     http://www.springframework.org/schema/context/spring-context-3.0.xsd">
```

```
  <context:component-scan
      base-package="com.springinaction.springidol">
  </context:component-scan>

</beans>
```

The <context:component-scan> element works by scanning a package and all of its subpackages, looking for classes that could be automatically registered as beans in the Spring container. The base-package attribute tells <context:component-scan> the package to start its scan from.

So, how does <context:component-scan> know which classes to register as Spring beans?

3.3.1 Annotating beans for autodiscovery

By default, <context:component-scan> looks for classes that are annotated with one of a handful of special stereotype annotations:

- @Component—A general-purpose stereotype annotation indicating that the class is a Spring component
- @Controller—Indicates that the class defines a Spring MVC controller
- @Repository—Indicates that the class defines a data repository
- @Service—Indicates that the class defines a service
- Any custom annotation that is itself annotated with @Component

For example, suppose that our application context only has the eddie and guitar beans in it. We can eliminate the explicit <bean> declarations from the XML configuration by using <context:component-scan> and annotating the Instrumentalist and Guitar classes with @Component.

First, let's annotate the Guitar class with @Component:

```
package com.springinaction.springidol;

import org.springframework.stereotype.Component;

@Component
public class Guitar implements Instrument {
  public void play() {
    System.out.println("Strum strum strum");
  }
}
```

When Spring scans the com.springinaction.springidol package, it'll find that Guitar is annotated with @Component and will automatically register it in Spring. By default, the bean's ID will be generated by camel-casing the class name. In the case of Guitar that means that the bean ID will be guitar.

Now let's annotate the Instrumentalist class:

```
package com.springinaction.springidol;

import org.springframework.beans.factory.annotation.Autowired;
import org.springframework.stereotype.Component;
```

```
@Component("eddie")
public class Instrumentalist implements Performer {
  // ...
}
```

In this case, we've specified a bean ID as a parameter to `@Component`. The bean ID would've been "instrumentalist," but to keep it consistent with the previous examples, we've explicitly named it `eddie`.

Annotation-based autodiscovery is just one option available when using `<context:component-scan>`. Let's see how to configure `<context:component-scan>` to look for bean candidates using other means.

3.3.2 Filtering component-scans

As it turns out, `<context:component-scan>` is flexible with regard to how it scans for bean candidates. By adding `<context:include-filter>` and/or `<context:exclude-filter>` subelements to `<context:component-scan>`, you can tweak component-scanning behavior to your heart's content.

To demonstrate component-scan filtering, consider what it would take to have `<context:component-scan>` automatically register all classes that are implementations of `Instrument` using the annotation-based strategy. We'd have to visit the source code for each of the `Instrument` implementations and annotate them with `@Component` (or one of the other stereotype annotations). At the least, that'd be inconvenient. And if we were working with a third-party implementation of `Instrument` we may not even have access to the source code to be able to add that annotation.

So, instead of relying on annotation-based component scanning, you can ask `<context:component-scan>` to automatically register all classes that are assignable to `Instrument` by adding an include filter, as follows:

```
<context:component-scan
    base-package="com.springinaction.springidol">
  <context:include-filter type="assignable"
      expression="com.springinaction.springidol.Instrument"/>
</context:component-scan>
```

The `type` and the `expression` attributes of `<context:include-filter>` work together to define a component-scanning strategy. In this case, we're asking for all classes that are assignable to `Instrument` to be automatically registered as Spring beans. But you can choose from other kinds of filtering, as cataloged in table 3.1.

Table 3.1 Component scanning can be customized using any of five kinds of filters.

Filter type	Description
`annotation`	Filters scan classes looking for those annotated with a given annotation at the type level. The annotation to scan for is specified in the `expression` attribute.
`assignable`	Filters scan classes looking for those that are assignable to the type specified in the `expression` attribute.

Table 3.1 Component scanning can be customized using any of five kinds of filters. *(continued)*

Filter type	Description
`aspectj`	Filters scan classes looking for those that match the AspectJ type expression specified in the `expression` attribute.
`custom`	Uses a custom implementation of `org.springframework.core.type.TypeFilter`, as specified in the `expression` attribute.
`regex`	Filters scan classes looking for those whose class names match the regular expression specified in the `expression` attribute.

Just as `<context:include-filter>` can be used to tell `<context:component-scan>` what it should register as beans, you can use `<context:exclude-filter>` to tell it what not to register. For example, to register all `Instrument` implementations except for those annotated with a custom `@SkipIt` annotation:

```
<context:component-scan
    base-package="com.springinaction.springidol">
  <context:include-filter type="assignable"
      expression="com.springinaction.springidol.Instrument"/>
  <context:exclude-filter type="annotation"
      expression="com.springinaction.springidol.SkipIt"/>
</context:component-scan>
```

When it comes to filtering `<context:component-scan>`, the possibilities are virtually endless. But you'll find that the default annotation-based strategy is the most commonly used. And it'll be the one you'll see most often throughout this book.

3.4 Using Spring's Java-based configuration

Believe it or not, not all developers are fans of XML. In fact, some are card-carrying members of the He-Man XML Haters Club. They'd love nothing more than to rid the world of the dreaded angle bracket. Spring's long history of using XML in its configuration has turned off a few of those who oppose XML.

If you're one who abhors XML, then Spring 3 has something special for you. Now you have the option of configuring a Spring application with almost no XML, using pure Java. And even if you don't hate XML, you may want to try out Spring's Java-based configuration because, as you'll soon see, the Java-based configuration knows a few tricks that its XML counterpart doesn't.

3.4.1 Setting up for Java-based configuration

Even though Spring's Java configuration option enables you to write most of your Spring configuration without XML, you'll still need a minimal amount of XML to bootstrap the Java configuration:

```
<?xml version="1.0" encoding="UTF-8"?>
<beans xmlns="http://www.springframework.org/schema/beans"
    xmlns:xsi="http://www.w3.org/2001/XMLSchema-instance"
    xmlns:context="http://www.springframework.org/schema/context"
```

```
    xsi:schemaLocation="http://www.springframework.org/schema/beans
        http://www.springframework.org/schema/beans/spring-beans-3.0.xsd
        http://www.springframework.org/schema/context
        http://www.springframework.org/schema/context/spring-context-3.0.xsd">

  <context:component-scan
     base-package="com.springinaction.springidol" />

</beans>
```

We've already seen how `<context:component-scan>` automatically registers beans that are annotated with certain stereotype annotations. But it also automatically loads in Java-based configuration classes that are annotated with `@Configuration`. In this case, the `base-package` attribute tells Spring to look in `com.springinaction.springidol` to find classes that are annotated with `@Configuration`.

3.4.2 *Defining a configuration class*

When we first started looking at Spring's XML-based configuration, I showed you a snippet of XML with the `<beans>` element from Spring's `beans` namespace at its root. The Java-based equivalent to that XML is a Java class annotated with `@Configuration`. For example:

```
package com.springinaction.springidol;
import org.springframework.context.annotation.Configuration;

@Configuration
public class SpringIdolConfig {

  // Bean declaration methods go here

}
```

The `@Configuration` annotation serves as a clue to Spring that this class will contain one or more Spring bean declarations. Those bean declarations are just methods that are annotated with `@Bean`. Let's see how to use `@Bean` to wire beans using Spring's Java-based configuration.

3.4.3 *Declaring a simple bean*

In the previous chapter, we used Spring's `<bean>` element to declare a `Juggler` bean whose ID was `duke`. Had we chosen Java-based configuration to wire up the *Spring Idol* beans, the `duke` bean would be defined in a method that's annotated with `@Bean`:

```
@Bean
public Performer duke() {
  return new Juggler();
}
```

This simple method is the Java configuration equivalent of the `<bean>` element we created earlier. The `@Bean` tells Spring that this method will return an object that should be registered as a bean in the Spring application context. The bean will get its ID from the method name. Everything that happens in the method ultimately leads to the creation of the bean.

In this case, the bean declaration is simple. The method creates and returns an instance of `Juggler`. That object will be registered in the Spring application context with an ID of `duke`.

Although this bean declaration method is largely equivalent to the XML version, it illustrates one strength that Spring's Java configuration has over its XML counterpart. In the XML version, both the bean's type and its ID were identified by `String` attributes. The downside of `String` identifiers is that they don't lend themselves to compile-time checking. If we were to rename the `Juggler` class, we may forget to change the XML configuration to match.

In Spring's Java-based configuration, there are no `String` attributes. Both the bean's ID and its type are expressed as part of a method signature. The actual creation of the bean is defined in the method body. Because it's all Java, you gain some benefit in terms of compile-time checking to ensure that your bean's type is a real type and that its ID is unique.

3.4.4 Injecting with Spring's Java-based configuration

If declaring beans with Spring's Java-based configuration is nothing more than writing a method that returns an instance of a class, then how does dependency injection work in Java-based configuration? It's actually simple, following common Java idioms.

For example, let's first look at how to inject values into a bean. Earlier, we saw how to create a `Juggler` bean that juggles 15 beanbags by using the `<constructor-arg>` element in XML configuration. In the Java-based configuration, we can just pass the number directly into the constructor:

```
@Bean
public Performer duke15() {
  return new Juggler(15);
}
```

As you can see, the Spring Java–based configuration feels natural, as it lets you define your beans using Java the way you always have. Setter injection is also natural Java:

```
@Bean
public Performer kenny() {
  Instrumentalist kenny = new Instrumentalist();
  kenny.setSong("Jingle Bells");
  return kenny;
}
```

Wiring simple values is straightforward enough. What about wiring in references to other beans? It's just as easy.

To illustrate, let's first set things up by declaring a `sonnet29` bean in Java:

```
@Bean
private Poem sonnet29() {
  return new Sonnet29();
}
```

This is another simple Java-based bean declaration, not much different than what we've already done with the duke bean. Now, let's create a PoeticJuggler bean, wiring the sonnet29 bean in through its constructor:

```
@Bean
public Performer poeticDuke() {
  return new PoeticJuggler(sonnet29());
}
```

Wiring in another bean is a simple matter of referring to that bean's method. But don't let the simplicity fool you. More is going on here than meets the eye.

In Spring Java Configuration, referring to a bean through its declaration method isn't the same as calling the method. If it were, then each time we call sonnet29(), we'd get a new instance of that bean. Spring is more clever than that.

By annotating the sonnet29() method with @Bean, we're telling Spring that we want that method to define a bean to be registered in the Spring application context. Then, whenever we refer to that method in another bean declaration method, Spring will intercept the call to the method and try to find the bean in its context instead of letting the method create a new instance.

3.5 Summary

Over the years, Spring has taken a lot of flak for XML verbosity. Despite the great strides in simplicity that Spring has brought to enterprise Java, a lot of developers haven't been able to look past all those angle brackets.

To answer the critics, Spring offers several ways of reducing and even eliminating Spring configuration XML. In this chapter we've seen how <property> and <constructor-arg> elements can be replaced with autowiring. Entire <bean> configuration elements can be handled automatically by Spring using component scanning. We've also seen how Spring configuration can be expressed in Java instead of XML, eliminating XML from Spring applications altogether.

At this point we've seen several ways to declare beans in Spring and wire their dependencies. In the next chapter, we'll take a look at how Spring supports aspect-oriented programming and see how AOP can be used to embellish beans with behavior that, although important to the functionality of an application, isn't a core concern of the beans that the aspects affect.

4 Aspect-oriented Spring

This chapter covers

- Basics of aspect-oriented programming
- Creating aspects from POJOs
- Using @AspectJ annotations
- Injecting dependencies into AspectJ aspects

As I'm writing this chapter, Texas (where I reside) is going through several days of record-high temperatures. It's hot. In weather like this, air conditioning is a must. But the downside of air conditioning is that it uses electricity, and electricity costs money. There's little we can do to avoid paying for a cool and comfortable home. That's because every home has a meter that measures every kilowatt, and once a month someone comes by to read that meter so that the electric company accurately knows how much to bill us.

Now imagine what would happen if the meter went away and nobody came by to measure our electricity usage. Suppose that it were up to each homeowner to contact the electric company and report their electricity usage. Although it's possible that some obsessive homeowners would keep careful record of their lights, televisions, and air conditioning, most wouldn't bother. Most would estimate their usage and others wouldn't bother reporting it at all. It's too much trouble to monitor electrical usage and the temptation to not pay is too great.

Electricity on the honor system might be great for consumers, but it would be less than ideal for the electric companies. That's why we all have electric meters on our homes and why a meter reader drops by once per month to report the consumption to the electric company.

Some functions of software systems are like the electric meters on our homes. The functions need to be applied at multiple points within the application, but it's undesirable to explicitly call them at every point.

Monitoring electricity consumption is an important function, but it isn't foremost in most homeowners' minds. Mowing the lawn, vacuuming the carpet, and cleaning the bathroom are the kinds of things that homeowners are actively involved in. Monitoring the amount of electricity used by their house is a passive event from the homeowner's point of view. (Although it'd be great if mowing the lawn were also a passive event—especially on these hot days.)

In software, several activities are common to most applications. Logging, security, and transaction management are important, but should they be activities that your application objects are actively participating in? Or would it be better for your application objects to focus on the business domain problems they're designed for and leave certain aspects to be handled by someone else?

In software development, functions that span multiple points of an application are called *cross-cutting concerns*. Typically, these cross-cutting concerns are conceptually separate from (but often embedded directly within) the application's business logic. Separating these cross-cutting concerns from the business logic is where aspect-oriented programming (AOP) goes to work.

In chapter 2, you learned how to use dependency injection (DI) to manage and configure your application objects. Whereas DI helps you decouple your application objects from each other, AOP helps you decouple cross-cutting concerns from the objects that they affect.

Logging is a common example of the application of aspects. But it's not the only thing aspects are good for. Throughout this book, you'll see several practical applications of aspects, including declarative transactions, security, and caching.

This chapter explores Spring's support for aspects, including how to declare regular classes to be aspects and how to use annotations to create aspects. In addition, you'll see how AspectJ—another popular AOP implementation—can complement Spring's AOP framework. But first, before we get carried away with transactions, security, and caching, let's see how aspects are implemented in Spring, starting with a primer on a few of AOP's fundamentals.

4.1 What's aspect-oriented programming?

As stated earlier, aspects help to modularize cross-cutting concerns. In short, a cross-cutting concern can be described as any functionality that affects multiple points of an application. Security, for example, is a cross-cutting concern, in that many methods in an application can have security rules applied to them. Figure 4.1 gives a visual depiction of cross-cutting concerns.

Figure 4.1 represents a typical application that's broken down into modules. Each module's main concern is to provide services for its particular domain. But each module also requires similar ancillary functionalities, such as security and transaction management.

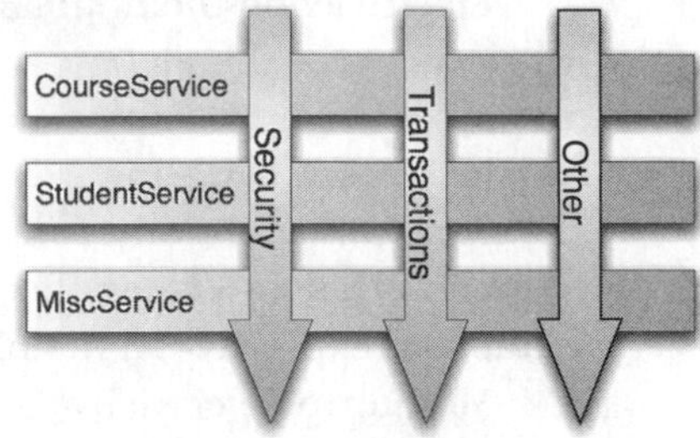

Figure 4.1 Aspects modularize cross-cutting concerns, applying logic that spans multiple application objects.

A common object-oriented technique for reusing common functionality is to apply inheritance or delegation. But inheritance can lead to a brittle object hierarchy if the same base class is used throughout an application, and delegation can be cumbersome because complicated calls to the delegate object may be required.

Aspects offer an alternative to inheritance and delegation that can be cleaner in many circumstances. With AOP, you still define the common functionality in one place, but you can declaratively define how and where this functionality is applied without having to modify the class to which you're applying the new feature. Cross-cutting concerns can now be modularized into special classes called *aspects*. This has two benefits. First, the logic for each concern is now in one place, as opposed to being scattered all over the code base. Second, our service modules are now cleaner since they only contain code for their primary concern (or core functionality) and secondary concerns have been moved to aspects.

4.1.1 Defining AOP terminology

Like most technologies, AOP has formed its own jargon. Aspects are often described in terms of advice, pointcuts, and join points. Figure 4.2 illustrates how these concepts are tied together.

Unfortunately, many of the terms used to describe AOP features aren't intuitive. Nevertheless, they're now part of the AOP idiom, and in order to understand AOP, you must know these terms. Before you walk the walk, you have to learn to talk the talk.

ADVICE

When a meter reader shows up at your house, his purpose is to report the number of kilowatt hours back to the electric company. Sure, he has a list of houses that he must visit and the information that he reports is important. But the actual act of recording electricity usage is the meter reader's main job.

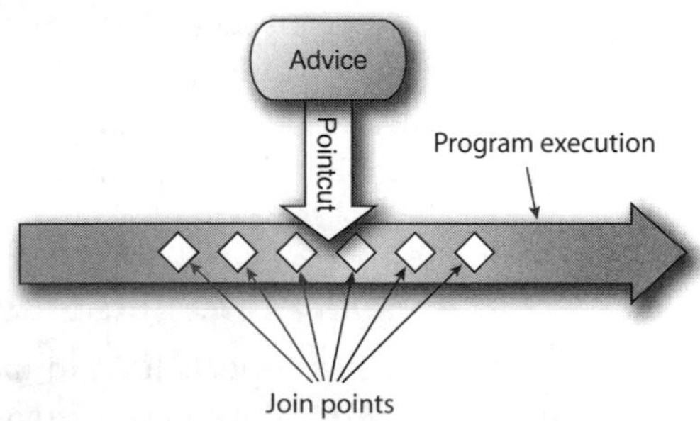

Figure 4.2 An aspect's functionality (advice) is woven into a program's execution at one or more join points.

Likewise, aspects have a purpose—a job they're meant to do. In AOP terms, the job of an aspect is called *advice*.

Advice defines both the *what* and the *when* of an aspect. In addition to describing the job that an aspect will perform, advice addresses the question of when to perform the job. Should it be applied before a method is invoked? After the method is invoked? Both before and after method invocation? Or should it only be applied if a method throws an exception?

Spring aspects can work with five kinds of advice:

- *Before*—The advice functionality takes place before the advised method is invoked.
- *After*—The advice functionality takes place after the advised method completes, regardless of the outcome.
- *After-returning*—The advice functionality takes place after the advised method successfully completes.
- *After-throwing*—The advice functionality takes place after the advised method throws an exception.
- *Around*—The advice wraps the advised method, providing some functionality before and after the advised method is invoked.

JOIN POINTS

An electric company services several houses, perhaps even an entire city. Each house will have an electric meter that needs to be read and thus each house is a potential target for the meter reader. The meter reader could potentially read all kinds of devices, but to do his job, he needs to target electric meters that are attached to houses.

In the same way, your application may have thousands of opportunities for advice to be applied. These opportunities are known as join points. A *join point* is a point in the execution of the application where an aspect can be plugged in. This point could be a method being called, an exception being thrown, or even a field being modified. These are the points where your aspect's code can be inserted into the normal flow of your application to add new behavior.

POINTCUTS

It's not possible for any one meter reader to visit all houses serviced by the electric company. Instead, each one is assigned a subset of all of the houses to visit. Likewise, an aspect doesn't necessarily advise all join points in an application. *Pointcuts* help narrow down the join points advised by an aspect.

If advice defines the *what* and *when* of aspects, then pointcuts define the *where*. A pointcut definition matches one or more join points at which advice should be woven. Often you specify these pointcuts using explicit class and method names or through regular expressions that define matching class and method name patterns. Some AOP frameworks allow you to create dynamic pointcuts that determine whether to apply advice based on runtime decisions, such as the value of method parameters.

ASPECTS

When a meter reader starts his day, he knows both what he's supposed to do (report electricity usage) and which houses to collect that information from. Thus he knows everything he needs to know to get his job done.

An *aspect* is the merger of advice and pointcuts. Taken together, advice and pointcuts define everything there is to know about an aspect—what it does and where and when it does it.

INTRODUCTIONS

An *introduction* allows you to add new methods or attributes to existing classes. For example, you could create an `Auditable` advice class that keeps the state of when an object was last modified. This could be as simple as having one method, `setLastModified(Date)`, and an instance variable to hold this state. The new method and instance variable can then be introduced to existing classes without having to change them, giving them new behavior and state.

WEAVING

Weaving is the process of applying aspects to a target object to create a new proxied object. The aspects are woven into the target object at the specified join points. The weaving can take place at several points in the target object's lifetime:

- *Compile time*—Aspects are woven in when the target class is compiled. This requires a special compiler. AspectJ's weaving compiler weaves aspects this way.
- *Classload time*—Aspects are woven in when the target class is loaded into the JVM. This requires a special `ClassLoader` that enhances that target class's bytecode before the class is introduced into the application. AspectJ 5's *load-time weaving (LTW)* support weaves aspects in this way.
- *Runtime*—Aspects are woven in sometime during the execution of the application. Typically, an AOP container will dynamically generate a proxy object that will delegate to the target object while weaving in the aspects. This is how Spring AOP aspects are woven.

That's a lot of new terms to get to know. Revisiting figure 4.2, you can now see how advice contains the cross-cutting behavior that needs to be applied to an application's objects. The join points are all the points within the execution flow of the application that are candidates to have advice applied. The pointcut defines where (at what join points) that advice is applied. The key concept you should take from this is that pointcuts define which join points get advised.

Now that you're familiar with some basic AOP terminology, let's see how these core AOP concepts are implemented in Spring.

4.1.2 Spring's AOP support

Not all AOP frameworks are created equal. They may differ in how rich their join point models are. Some allow you to apply advice at the field modification level, whereas others only expose the join points related to method invocations. They may also differ in how and when they weave the aspects. Whatever the case, the ability to create pointcuts that define the join points at which aspects should be woven is what makes it an AOP framework.

Much has changed in the AOP framework landscape in the past few years. There has been some housecleaning among the AOP frameworks, resulting in some frameworks merging and others going extinct. In 2005, the AspectWerkz project merged with AspectJ, marking the last significant activity in the AOP world and leaving us with three dominant AOP frameworks:

- AspectJ (http://eclipse.org/aspectj)
- JBoss AOP (http://www.jboss.org/jbossaop)
- Spring AOP (http://www.springframework.org)

Since this is a Spring book, we'll focus on Spring AOP. Even so, there's a lot of synergy between the Spring and AspectJ projects, and the AOP support in Spring borrows a lot from the AspectJ project.

Spring's support for AOP comes in four flavors:

- Classic Spring proxy-based AOP
- @AspectJ annotation-driven aspects
- Pure-POJO aspects
- Injected AspectJ aspects (available in all versions of Spring)

The first three items are all variations on Spring's proxy-based AOP. Consequently, Spring's AOP support is limited to method interception. If your AOP needs exceed simple method interception (constructor or property interception, for example), you'll want to consider implementing aspects in AspectJ, perhaps taking advantage of Spring DI to inject Spring beans into AspectJ aspects.

What? No classic Spring AOP?

The term *classic* usually carries a good connotation. Classic cars, classic golf tournaments, and classic Coca-Cola are all good things.

But Spring's classic AOP programming model isn't so great. Oh, it was good in its day. But now Spring supports much cleaner and easier ways to work with aspects. When held up against simple declarative AOP and annotation-based AOP, Spring's classic AOP seems bulky and overcomplicated. Working directly with `ProxyFactoryBean` can be wearying.

So I've chosen to not include any discussion of classic Spring AOP in this edition. If you're really curious about how it works, then you may look at the first two editions of this book. But I think you'll find that the new Spring AOP models are much easier to work with.

We'll explore more of these Spring AOP techniques in this chapter. But before we get started, it's important to understand a few key points of Spring's AOP framework.

SPRING ADVICE IS WRITTEN IN JAVA

All of the advice you create within Spring is written in a standard Java class. That way, you get the benefit of developing your aspects in the same integrated development environment (IDE) you'd use for your normal Java development. What's more, the pointcuts that define where advice should be applied are typically written in XML in your Spring configuration file. This means both the aspect's code and configuration syntax will be familiar to Java developers.

Contrast this with AspectJ. Although AspectJ now supports annotation-based aspects, AspectJ also comes as a language extension to Java. This approach has benefits and drawbacks. By having an AOP-specific language, you get more power and fine-grained control, as well as a richer AOP toolset. But you're required to learn a new tool and syntax to accomplish this.

SPRING ADVISES OBJECTS AT RUNTIME

In Spring, aspects are woven into Spring-managed beans at runtime by wrapping them with a proxy class. As illustrated in figure 4.3, the proxy class poses as the target bean, intercepting advised method calls and forwarding those calls to the target bean.

Between the time when the proxy intercepts the method call and the time when it invokes the target bean's method, the proxy performs the aspect logic.

Spring doesn't create a proxied object until that proxied bean is needed by the application. If you're using an `ApplicationContext`, the proxied objects will be created when it loads all of the beans from the `BeanFactory`. Because Spring creates proxies at runtime, you don't need a special compiler to weave aspects in Spring's AOP.

SPRING ONLY SUPPORTS METHOD JOIN POINTS

As mentioned earlier, multiple join point models are available through various AOP implementations. Because it's based on dynamic proxies, Spring only supports method join points. This is in contrast to some other AOP frameworks, such as AspectJ and JBoss, which provide field and constructor join points in addition to method pointcuts. Spring's lack of field pointcuts prevents you from creating very fine-grained advice, such as intercepting updates to an object's field. And without constructor pointcuts, there's no way to apply advice when a bean is instantiated.

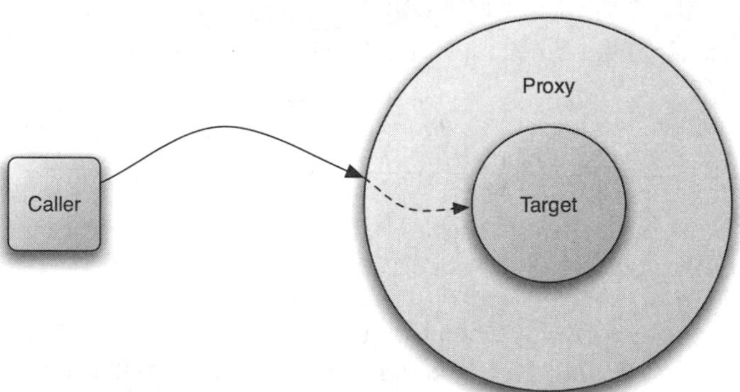

Figure 4.3 Spring aspects are implemented as proxies that wrap the target object. The proxy handles method calls, performs additional aspect logic, and then invokes the target method.

But method interception should suit most, if not all, of your needs. If you find yourself in need of more than method interception, you'll want to complement Spring AOP with AspectJ.

Now you have a general idea of what AOP does and how it's supported by Spring. It's time to get our hands dirty creating aspects in Spring. Let's start with Spring's declarative AOP model.

4.2 Selecting join points with pointcuts

As mentioned before, pointcuts are used to pinpoint where an aspect's advice should be applied. Along with an aspect's advice, pointcuts are among the most fundamental elements of an aspect. Therefore, it's important to know how to write pointcuts.

In Spring AOP, pointcuts are defined using AspectJ's pointcut expression language. If you're already familiar with AspectJ, then defining pointcuts in Spring should feel natural. But in case you're new to AspectJ, this section will serve as a quick lesson on writing AspectJ-style pointcuts. For a more detailed discussion on AspectJ and AspectJ's pointcut expression language, I strongly recommend Ramnivas Laddad's *AspectJ in Action, Second Edition*.

The most important thing to know about AspectJ pointcuts as they pertain to Spring AOP is that Spring only supports a subset of the pointcut designators available in AspectJ. Recall that Spring AOP is proxy-based and certain pointcut expressions aren't relevant to proxy-based AOP. Table 4.1 lists the AspectJ pointcut designators that are supported in Spring AOP.

Table 4.1 Spring leverages AspectJ's pointcut expression language for defining Spring aspects.

AspectJ designator	Description
`args()`	Limits join point matches to the execution of methods whose arguments are instances of the given types
`@args()`	Limits join point matches to the execution of methods whose arguments are annotated with the given annotation types
`execution()`	Matches join points that are method executions
`this()`	Limits join point matches to those where the bean reference of the AOP proxy is of a given type
`target()`	Limits join point matches to those where the target object is of a given type
`@target()`	Limits matching to join points where the class of the executing object has an annotation of the given type
`within()`	Limits matching to join points within certain types
`@within()`	Limits matching to join points within types that have the given annotation (the execution of methods declared in types with the given annotation when using Spring AOP)
`@annotation`	Limits join point matches to those where the subject of the join point has the given annotation

Attempting to use any of AspectJ's other designators will result in an `IllegalArgumentException` being thrown.

As you browse through the supported designators, note that the `execution` designator is the only one that actually performs matches. The other designators are used to limit those matches. This means that `execution` is the primary designator you'll use in every pointcut definition you write. You'll use the other designators to constrain the pointcut's reach.

4.2.1 Writing pointcuts

For example, the pointcut expression shown in figure 4.4 can be used to apply advice whenever an `Instrument`'s `play()` method is executed:

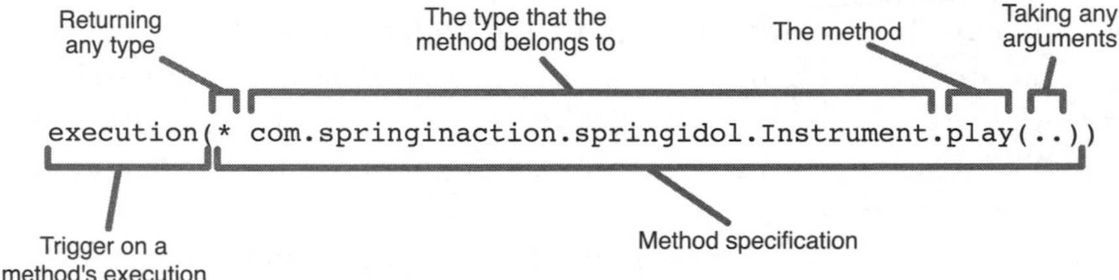

Figure 4.4 Selecting the `Instrument`'s `play()` method with an AspectJ pointcut expression

We used the `execution()` designator to select the `Instrument`'s `play()` method. The method specification starts with an asterisk, which indicates that we don't care what type the method returns. Then we specify the fully qualified class name and the name of the method we want to select. For the method's parameter list, we use the double-dot (`..`), indicating that the pointcut should select any `play()` method, no matter what the argument list is.

Now let's suppose that we want to confine the reach of that pointcut to only the `com.springinaction.springidol` package. In that case, we could limit the match by tacking on a `within()` designator, as shown in figure 4.5.

Note that we used the `&&` operator to combine the `execution()` and `within()` designators in an "and" relationship (where both designators must match for the pointcut to match). Similarly, we could've used the `||` operator to indicate an "or" relationship. And the `!` operator can be used to negate the effect of a designator.

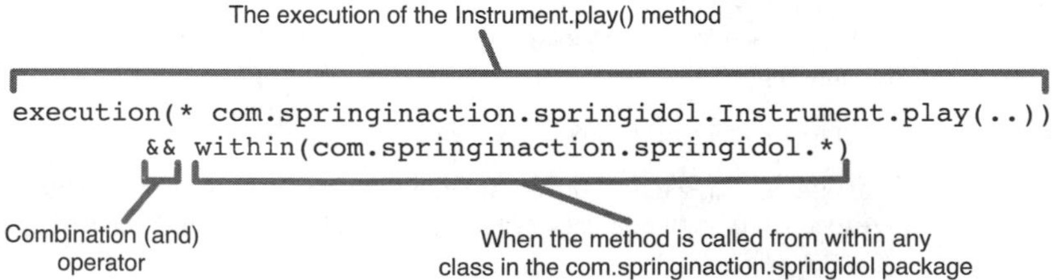

Figure 4.5 Limiting a pointcut's reach using the `within()` designator

Since ampersands have special meaning in XML, you're free to use and in place of && when specifying pointcuts in a Spring XML-based configuration. Likewise, or and not can be used in place of || and ! (respectively).

4.2.2 Using Spring's bean() designator

In addition to the designators listed in table 4.1, Spring 2.5 introduced a new bean() designator that lets you identify beans by their ID within a pointcut expression. bean() takes a bean ID or name as an argument and limits the pointcut's effect to that specific bean.

For example, consider the following pointcut:

```
execution(* com.springinaction.springidol.Instrument.play())
        and bean(eddie)
```

Here we're saying that we want to apply aspect advice to the execution of an Instruments play() method, but limited to the bean whose ID is eddie.

Narrowing a pointcut to a specific bean may be valuable in some cases, but we can also use negation to apply an aspect to all beans that don't have a specific ID:

```
execution(* com.springinaction.springidol.Instrument.play())
        and !bean(eddie)
```

In this case, the aspect's advice will be woven into all beans whose ID isn't eddie.

Now that we've covered the basics of writing pointcuts, let's see how to write the advice and declare the aspects that use those pointcuts.

4.3 Declaring aspects in XML

If you're familiar with Spring's classic AOP model, you'll know that working with ProxyFactoryBean is clumsy. The Spring development team recognized this and set out to provide a better way of declaring aspects in Spring. The outcome of this effort is found in Spring's aop configuration namespace. The AOP configuration elements are summarized in table 4.2.

Table 4.2 Spring's AOP configuration elements simplify declaration of POJO-based aspects.

AOP configuration element	Purpose
<aop:advisor>	Defines an AOP advisor.
<aop:after>	Defines an AOP after advice (regardless of whether the advised method returns successfully).
<aop:after-returning>	Defines an AOP after-returning advice.
<aop:after-throwing>	Defines an AOP after-throwing advice.
<aop:around>	Defines an AOP around advice.
<aop:aspect>	Defines an aspect.
<aop:aspectj-autoproxy>	Enables annotation-driven aspects using @AspectJ.

Table 4.2 Spring's AOP configuration elements simplify declaration of POJO-based aspects. *(continued)*

AOP configuration element	Purpose
`<aop:before>`	Defines an AOP before advice.
`<aop:config>`	The top-level AOP element. Most `<aop:*>` elements must be contained within `<aop:config>`.
`<aop:declare-parents>`	Introduces additional interfaces to advised objects that are transparently implemented.
`<aop:pointcut>`	Defines a pointcut.

In chapter 2, we demonstrated dependency injection by putting on a talent show called *Spring Idol.* In that example, we wired up several performers as Spring `<bean>`s to show their stuff. It was all greatly amusing. but a show like that needs an audience or else there's little point.

Therefore, to illustrate Spring AOP, let's create an `Audience` class for our talent show. The following class defines the functions of an audience.

Listing 4.1 The `Audience` class for our talent competition

```
package com.springinaction.springidol;

public class Audience {
  public void takeSeats() {                                    // Before performance
    System.out.println("The audience is taking their seats.");
  }

  public void turnOffCellPhones() {                            // Before performance
    System.out.println("The audience is turning off their cellphones");
  }

  public void applaud() {                                      // After performance
    System.out.println("CLAP CLAP CLAP CLAP CLAP");
  }

  public void demandRefund() {                                 // After bad performance
    System.out.println("Boo! We want our money back!");
  }
}
```

As you can see, there's nothing remarkable about the `Audience` class. It's a basic Java class with a handful of methods. And we can register it as a bean in the Spring application context like any other class:

```
<bean id="audience"
      class="com.springinaction.springidol.Audience" />
```

Despite its unassuming appearance, what's remarkable about `Audience` is that it has all the makings of an aspect. It just needs a little of Spring's special AOP magic.

4.3.1 Declaring before and after advice

Using Spring's AOP configuration elements, as shown in the following listing, you can turn the audience bean into an aspect.

Listing 4.2 Defining an audience aspect using Spring's AOP configuration elements

```
<aop:config>
  <aop:aspect ref="audience">                          Reference audience bean

    <aop:before pointcut=
        "execution(* com.springinaction.springidol.Performer.perform(..))"
      method="takeSeats" />                            Before performance

    <aop:before pointcut=
        "execution(* com.springinaction.springidol.Performer.perform(..))"
      method="turnOffCellPhones" />                    Before performance

    <aop:after-returning pointcut=
        "execution(* com.springinaction.springidol.Performer.perform(..))"
      method="applaud" />                              After performance

    <aop:after-throwing pointcut=
        "execution(* com.springinaction.springidol.Performer.perform(..))"
      method="demandRefund" />                         After bad performance

  </aop:aspect>
</aop:config>
```

The first thing to notice about the Spring AOP configuration elements is that most of them must be used within the context of the <aop:config> element. There are a few exceptions to this rule, but when it comes to declaring beans as aspects you'll always start with the <aop:config> element.

Within <aop:config> you may declare one or more advisors, aspects, or pointcuts. In listing 4.2, we declared a single aspect using the <aop:aspect> element. The ref attribute references the POJO bean that will be used to supply the functionality of the aspect—in this case, audience. The bean that's referenced by the ref attribute will supply the methods called by any advice in the aspect.

The aspect has four different bits of advice. The two <aop:before> elements define *method before advice* that will call the takeSeats() and turnOffCellPhones() methods (declared by the method attribute) of the Audience bean before any methods matching the pointcut are executed. The <aop:after-returning> element defines an *after-returning advice* to call the applaud() method after the pointcut. Meanwhile, the <aop:after-throwing> element defines an *after-throwing advice* to call the demand-Refund() method if any exceptions are thrown. Figure 4.6 shows how the advice logic is woven into the business logic.

In all advice elements, the pointcut attribute defines the pointcut where the advice will be applied. The value given to the pointcut attribute is a pointcut defined in AspectJ's pointcut expression syntax.

You'll notice that the value of the pointcut attribute is the same for all of the advice elements. That's because all of the advice is being applied to the same pointcut.

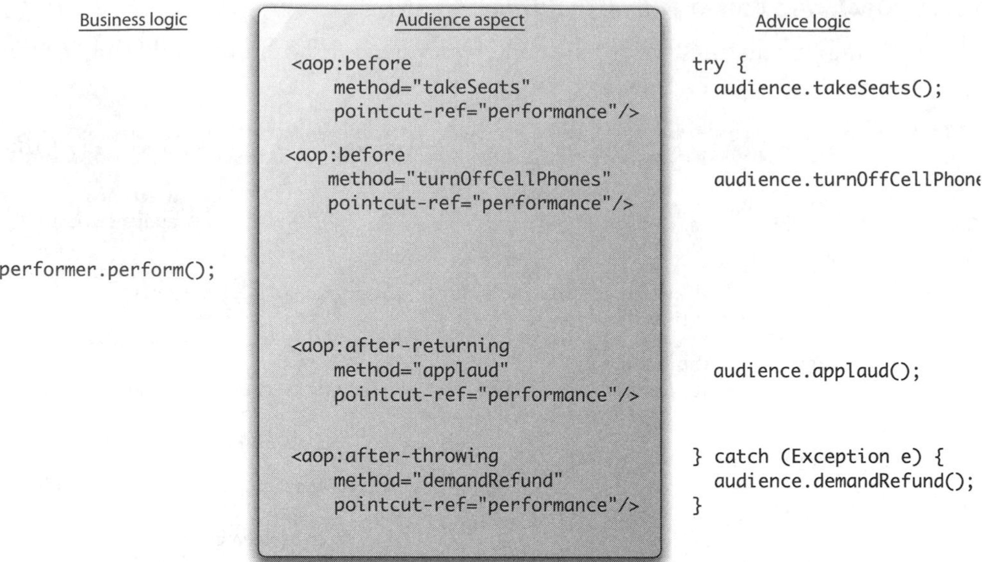

Figure 4.6 The `Audience` aspect includes four bits of advice which weave advice logic around methods that match the aspect's pointcut.

This presents a DRY (don't repeat yourself) principle violation. If you decide later to change the pointcut, you must change it in four different places.

To avoid duplication of the pointcut definition, you may choose to define a named pointcut using the `<aop:pointcut>` element. The following XML shows how the `<aop:pointcut>` element is used within the `<aop:aspect>` element to define a named pointcut that can be used by all of the advice elements.

Listing 4.3 Defining a named pointcut to eliminate redundant pointcut definitions

```
<aop:config>
  <aop:aspect ref="audience">
    <aop:pointcut id="performance" expression=
        "execution(* com.springinaction.springidol.Performer.perform(..))"
        />                                                  Define pointcut
    <aop:before
        pointcut-ref="performance"
        method="takeSeats" />
    <aop:before
        pointcut-ref="performance"
        method="turnOffCellPhones" />
    <aop:after-returning                                        Reference
        pointcut-ref="performance"                              pointcut
        method="applaud" />
    <aop:after-throwing
        pointcut-ref="performance"
        method="demandRefund" />
  </aop:aspect>
</aop:config>
```

Now the pointcut is defined in a single location and is referenced across multiple advice elements. The <aop:pointcut> element defines the pointcut to have an id of performance. Meanwhile, all of the advice elements have been changed to reference the named pointcut with the pointcut-ref attribute.

As used in listing 4.3, the <aop:pointcut> element defines a pointcut that can be referenced by all advices within the same <aop:aspect> element. But you can also define pointcuts that can be used across multiple aspects by placing the <aop:pointcut> elements within the scope of the <aop:config> element.

4.3.2 Declaring around advice

The current implementation of Audience works great. But basic before and after advice have some limitations. Specifically, it's tricky to share information between before advice and after advice without resorting to storing that information in member variables.

For example, suppose that in addition to putting away cell phones and applauding at the end, you also want the audience to keep their eyes on their watches and report how long the performance takes. The only way to accomplish this with before and after advice is to note the start time in before advice and report the length of time in some after advice. But you'd have to store the start time in a member variable. Since Audience is a singleton, it wouldn't be thread safe to retain state like that.

Around advice has an advantage over before and after advice in this regard. With around advice, you can accomplish the same thing as you can with distinct before and after advice, but do it in a single method. Since the entire set of advice takes place in a single method, there's no need to retain state in a member variable.

For example, consider the new watchPerformance() method.

Listing 4.4 The watchPerformance() method provides AOP around advice.

```
public void watchPerformance(ProceedingJoinPoint joinpoint) {
    try {
      System.out.println("The audience is taking their seats.");
      System.out.println("The audience is turning off their cellphones");
      long start = System.currentTimeMillis();          // Before performance

      joinpoint.proceed();                              // Proceed to advised method

      long end = System.currentTimeMillis();            // After performance
      System.out.println("CLAP CLAP CLAP CLAP CLAP");
      System.out.println("The performance took " + (end - start)
          + " milliseconds.");
    } catch (Throwable t) {
      System.out.println("Boo! We want our money back!");   // After bad performance
    }
  }
```

The first thing you'll notice about this new advice method is that it's given a ProceedingJoinPoint as a parameter. This object is necessary, as it's how we'll be able to invoke the advised method from within our advice. The advice method will do everything it needs to do and, when it's ready to pass control to the advised method, it'll call `ProceedingJoinPoint`'s `proceed()` method.

Note that it's crucial that you remember to include a call to the `proceed()` method. If you don't, then your advice will effectively block access to the advised method. Maybe that's what you want, but chances are good that you do want the advised method to be executed at some point.

What's also interesting is that just as you can omit a call to the `proceed()` method to block access to the advised method, you can also invoke it multiple times from within the advice. One reason for doing this may be to implement retry logic to perform repeated attempts on the advised method should it fail.

In the case of the audience aspect, the `watchPerformance()` method contains all of the functionality of the previous four advice methods, but all of it's contained in this single method, and this method is responsible for its own exception handling. You'll also note that just before the join point's `proceed()` method is called, the current time is recorded in a local variable. Just after the method returns, the elapsed time is reported.

Declaring around advice isn't dramatically different from declaring other types of advice. All you need to do is use the `<aop:around>` element.

Listing 4.5 Defining a named pointcut to eliminate redundant pointcut definitions

```
<aop:config>
  <aop:aspect ref="audience">
    <aop:pointcut id="performance2" expression=
        "execution(* com.springinaction.springidol.Performer.perform(..))"
        />

    <aop:around
        pointcut-ref="performance2"
        method="watchPerformance()" />
  </aop:aspect>
</aop:config>
```

Declare around advice

As with the other advice XML elements, `<aop:around>` is given a pointcut and the name of an advice method. Here we're using the same pointcut as before, but have set the `method` attribute to point to the new `watchPerformance()` method.

4.3.3 *Passing parameters to advice*

So far, our aspects have been simple, taking no parameters. The only exception is that the `watchPerformance()` method that we wrote for the around advice example took a `ProceedingJoinPoint` as a parameter. Other than that, the advice we've written hasn't bothered to look at any parameters passed to the advised methods. That's been okay, though, because the `perform()` method that we were advising didn't take any parameters.

Nevertheless, there are times when it may be useful for advice to not only wrap a method, but also inspect the values of the parameters passed to that method.

To see how this works, imagine a new type of contestant in the *Spring Idol* competition. This new contestant is a mind reader, as defined by the MindReader interface:

```
package com.springinaction.springidol;

public interface MindReader {
  void interceptThoughts(String thoughts);

  String getThoughts();
}
```

A MindReader does two basic things: it intercepts a volunteer's thoughts and reports those thoughts. A simple implementation of MindReader is the Magician class:

```
package com.springinaction.springidol;

public class Magician implements MindReader {
  private String thoughts;

  public void interceptThoughts(String thoughts) {
    System.out.println("Intercepting volunteer's thoughts");
    this.thoughts = thoughts;
  }

  public String getThoughts() {
    return thoughts;
  }
}
```

Now you need to give your mind reader someone whose mind he can read. For that, here's the Thinker interface:

```
package com.springinaction.springidol;

public interface Thinker {
  void thinkOfSomething(String thoughts);
}
```

The Volunteer class provides a basic implementation of Thinker:

```
package com.springinaction.springidol;

public class Volunteer implements Thinker {
  private String thoughts;

  public void thinkOfSomething(String thoughts) {
    this.thoughts = thoughts;
  }

  public String getThoughts() {
    return thoughts;
  }
}
```

The details of Volunteer aren't terribly interesting or important. What's interesting is how the Magician will intercept the Volunteer's thoughts using Spring AOP.

To pull off this feat of telepathy, you're going to use the same <aop:aspect> and <aop:before> elements as before. But this time you're going to configure them to pass the advised method's parameters to the advice.

```
<aop:config>
  <aop:aspect ref="magician">
    <aop:pointcut id="thinking"
      expression="execution(*
      com.springinaction.springidol.Thinker.thinkOfSomething(String))
            and args(thoughts)" />

    <aop:before
        pointcut-ref="thinking"
        method="interceptThoughts"
        arg-names="thoughts" />
  </aop:aspect>
</aop:config>
```

The key to the Magician's ESP is found in the pointcut definition and in the <aop:before>'s arg-names attribute. The pointcut identifies the Thinker's thinkOfSomething() method, specifying a String argument. And it follows up with an args parameter to identify the argument as thoughts.

Meanwhile, the <aop:before> advice declaration refers to the thoughts argument, indicating that it should be passed into the Magician's interceptThoughts() method.

Now, whenever the thinkOfSomething() method is invoked on the volunteer bean, the Magician will intercept those thoughts. To prove it, here's a simple test class with the following method:

```
@Test
public void magicianShouldReadVolunteersMind() {
  volunteer.thinkOfSomething("Queen of Hearts");

  assertEquals("Queen of Hearts", magician.getThoughts());
}
```

We'll talk more about writing unit tests and integration tests in Spring in the next chapter. For now, just note that the test will pass because the Magician will always know whatever the Volunteer is thinking.

Now let's see how to use Spring AOP to add new functionality to existing objects through the power of introduction.

4.3.4 *Introducing new functionality with aspects*

Some languages, such as Ruby and Groovy, have the notion of open classes. They make it possible to add new methods to an object or class without directly changing the definition of those objects/classes. Unfortunately, Java isn't quite that dynamic. Once a class has been compiled, there's little you can do to append new functionality to it.

But if you think about it, isn't that what we've been doing in this chapter with aspects? Sure, we haven't added any new methods to objects, but we're adding new functionality around the methods that the objects already have. If an aspect can wrap existing methods with additional functionality, why not add new methods to the object? In fact, using an AOP concept known as *introduction*, aspects can attach all new methods to Spring beans.

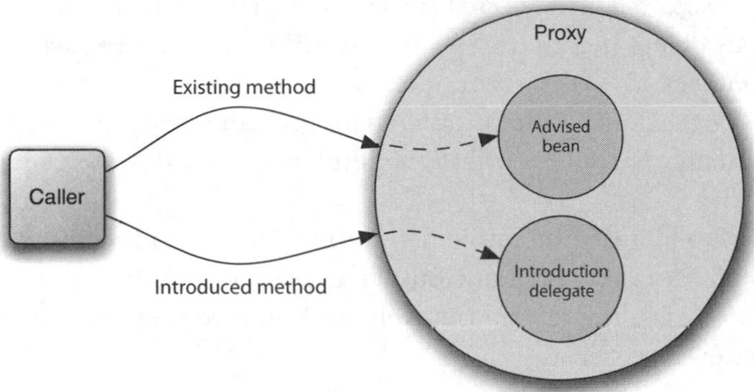

Figure 4.7 With Spring AOP, you can introduce new methods to a bean. A proxy intercepts the calls and delegates to a different object that implements the method.

Recall that in Spring, aspects are just proxies that implement the same interface(s) as the beans that they wrap. What if, in addition to implementing those interfaces, the proxy were to also be exposed through some new interface? Then any bean that's advised by the aspect will appear to implement the new interface, even if its underlying implementation class doesn't. Figure 4.7 illustrates how this works.

What you'll notice from figure 4.7 is that when a method on the introduced interface is called, the proxy delegates the call to some other object that provides the implementation of the new interface. Effectively this gives us one bean whose implementation is split across multiple classes.

Putting this idea to work, let's say that you want to introduce the following `Contestant` interface to all of the performers in our example:

```
package com.springinaction.springidol;

public interface Contestant {
  void receiveAward();
}
```

I suppose that we could visit all implementations of `Performer` and change them so that they also implement `Contestant`. But, from a design standpoint, that may not be the most prudent move (because `Contestants` and `Performers` aren't necessarily mutually inclusive concepts). Moreover, it may not even be possible to change all of the implementations of `Performer`, especially if we're working with third-party implementations and don't have the source code.

Thankfully, AOP introductions can help us out here without compromising design choices or requiring invasive changes to the existing implementations. To pull it off, you must use the `<aop:declare-parents>` element:

```
<aop:aspect>
  <aop:declare-parents
    types-matching="com.springinaction.springidol.Performer+"
    implement-interface="com.springinaction.springidol.Contestant"
    default-impl="com.springinaction.springidol.GraciousContestant"
    />
</aop:aspect>
```

As its name implies, `<aop:declare-parents>` declares that the beans it advises will have new parents in its object hierarchy. Specifically, in this case we're saying that the beans whose type matches the `Performer` interface (per the `types-matching` attribute) should have `Contestant` in their parentage (per the `implement-interface` attribute). The final matter to settle is where the implementation of the `Contestant`'s methods will come from.

There are two ways to identify the implementation of the introduced interface. In this case, we're using the `default-impl` attribute to explicitly identify the implementation by its fully-qualified class name. Alternatively, we could've identified it using the `delegate-ref` attribute:

```
<aop:declare-parents
  types-matching="com.springinaction.springidol.Performer+"
  implement-interface="com.springinaction.springidol.Contestant"
  delegate-ref="contestantDelegate"
  />
```

The `delegate-ref` attribute refers to a Spring bean as the introduction delegate. This assumes that a bean with an ID of `contestantDelegate` exists in the Spring context:

```
<bean id="contestantDelegate"
      class="com.springinaction.springidol.GraciousContestant" />
```

The difference between directly identifying the delegate using `default-impl` and indirectly using `delegate-ref` is that the latter will be a Spring bean that itself may be injected, advised, or otherwise configured through Spring.

4.4 Annotating aspects

A key feature introduced in AspectJ 5 is the ability to use annotations to create aspects. Prior to AspectJ 5, writing AspectJ aspects involved learning a Java language extension. But AspectJ's annotation-oriented model makes it simple to turn any class into an aspect by sprinkling a few annotations around. This new feature is commonly referred to as *@AspectJ*.

Looking back at our `Audience` class, we see that `Audience` contained all of the functionality needed for an audience, but none of the details to make it an aspect. That left us having to declare advice and pointcuts in XML.

But with @AspectJ annotations, we can revisit our `Audience` class and turn it into an aspect without the need for any additional classes or bean declarations. The following shows the new `Audience` class, now annotated to be an aspect.

Listing 4.6 Annotating `Audience` to be an aspect

```
package com.springinaction.springidol;

import org.aspectj.lang.annotation.AfterReturning;
import org.aspectj.lang.annotation.AfterThrowing;
import org.aspectj.lang.annotation.Aspect;
import org.aspectj.lang.annotation.Before;
import org.aspectj.lang.annotation.Pointcut;
```

```
@Aspect
public class Audience {
  @Pointcut(
        "execution(* com.springinaction.springidol.Performer.perform(..))")
  public void performance() {                            Define
  }                                                      pointcut

  @Before("performance()")                                           Before
  public void takeSeats() {                                          performance
    System.out.println("The audience is taking their seats.");
  }

  @Before("performance()")                                       Before
  public void turnOffCellPhones() {                              performance
    System.out.println("The audience is turning off their cellphones");
  }

  @AfterReturning("performance()")                                  After
  public void applaud() {                                           performance
    System.out.println("CLAP CLAP CLAP CLAP CLAP");
  }

  @AfterThrowing("performance()")                                After bad
  public void demandRefund() {                                   performance
    System.out.println("Boo! We want our money back!");
  }
}
```

The new `Audience` class is now annotated with `@Aspect`. This annotation indicates that `Audience` isn't just any POJO but is an aspect.

The `@Pointcut` annotation is used to define a reusable pointcut within an @AspectJ aspect. The value given to the `@Pointcut` annotation is an AspectJ pointcut expression—here indicating that the pointcut should match the `perform()` method of a `Performer`. The name of the pointcut is derived from the name of the method to which the annotation is applied. Therefore, the name of this pointcut is `performance()`. The actual body of the `performance()` method is irrelevant and in fact should be empty. The method itself is just a marker, giving the `@Pointcut` annotation something to attach itself to.

Each of the audience's methods has been annotated with advice annotations. The `@Before` annotation has been applied to both `takeSeats()` and `turnOffCellPhones()` to indicate that these two methods are before advice. The `@AfterReturning` annotation indicates that the `applaud()` method is an after-returning advice method. And the `@AfterThrowing` annotation is placed on `demandRefund()` so that it'll be called if any exceptions are thrown during the performance.

The name of the `performance()` pointcut is given as the value parameter to all of the advice annotations. This tells each advice method where it should be applied.

Note that aside from the annotations and the no-op `performance()` method, the `Audience` class is functionally unchanged. This means that it's still a simple Java object and can be used as such. It can also still be wired in Spring as follows:

```
<bean id="audience"
     class="com.springinaction.springidol.Audience" />
```

Because the `Audience` class contains everything that's needed to define its own pointcuts and advice, there's no more need for pointcut and advice declarations in the XML configuration. There's one last thing to do to make Spring apply `Audience` as an aspect. You must declare an autoproxy bean in the Spring context that knows how to turn @AspectJ-annotated beans into proxy advice.

For that purpose, Spring comes with an autoproxy creator class called `AnnotationAwareAspectJAutoProxyCreator`. You could register an `AnnotationAwareAspectJAutoProxyCreator` as a <bean> in the Spring context, but that would require a lot of typing (believe me… I've typed it a few times before). Instead, to simplify that rather long name, Spring also provides a custom configuration element in the `aop` namespace that's much easier to remember:

```
<aop:aspectj-autoproxy />
```

`<aop:aspectj-autoproxy/>` will create an `AnnotationAwareAspectJAutoProxyCreator` in the Spring context and will automatically proxy beans whose methods match the pointcuts defined with `@Pointcut` annotations in `@Aspect`-annotated beans.

To use the `<aop:aspectj-autoproxy>` configuration element, you'll need to remember to include the `aop` namespace in your Spring configuration file:

```
<beans xmlns="http://www.springframework.org/schema/beans"
 xmlns:xsi="http://www.w3.org/2001/XMLSchema-instance"
 xmlns:aop="http://www.springframework.org/schema/aop"
 xsi:schemaLocation="http://www.springframework.org/schema/beans
     http://www.springframework.org/schema/beans/spring-beans-3.0.xsd
     http://www.springframework.org/schema/aop
     http://www.springframework.org/schema/aop/spring-aop-3.0.xsd">
```

You should be aware that `<aop:aspectj-autoproxy>` only uses @AspectJ's annotations as a guide for creating proxy-based aspects. Under the covers, it's still Spring-style aspects. This is significant because it means that although you're using @AspectJ's annotations, you're still limited to proxying method invocations. If you want to be able to exploit the full power of AspectJ, you'll have to use the AspectJ runtime and not rely on Spring to create proxy-based aspects.

It's also worth mentioning at this point that both the `<aop:aspect>` element and the @AspectJ annotations are effective ways to turn a POJO into an aspect. But `<aop:aspect>` has one distinct advantage over @AspectJ in that you don't need the source code of the class that's to provide the aspect's functionality. With @AspectJ, you must annotate the class and methods, which requires having the source code. But `<aop:aspect>` can reference any bean.

Now let's see how to create around advice using @AspectJ annotations.

4.4.1 Annotating around advice

Just as with Spring's XML-based AOP, you're not limited to before and after advice types when using @AspectJ annotations. You may also choose to create around advice. For that, you must use the `@Around` annotation, as in the following example:

```
@Around("performance()")
  public void watchPerformance(ProceedingJoinPoint joinpoint) {
    try {
      System.out.println("The audience is taking their seats.");
      System.out.println("The audience is turning off their cellphones");

      long start = System.currentTimeMillis();
      joinpoint.proceed();
      long end = System.currentTimeMillis();

      System.out.println("CLAP CLAP CLAP CLAP CLAP");

      System.out.println("The performance took " + (end - start)
          + " milliseconds.");
    } catch (Throwable t) {
      System.out.println("Boo! We want our money back!");
    }
  }
```

Here the `@Around` annotation indicates that the `watchPerformance()` method is to be applied as around advice to the `performance()` pointcut. This should look oddly familiar, as it's the same `watchPerformance()` method that we saw before. The only difference is that it's now annotated with `@Around`.

As you may recall from before, around advice methods must remember to explicitly invoke `proceed()` so that the proxied method will be invoked. But simply annotating a method with `@Around` isn't enough to provide a `proceed()` method to call. Therefore, methods that are to be around advice must take a `ProceedingJoinPoint` object as an argument and then call the `proceed()` method on that object.

4.4.2 *Passing arguments to annotated advice*

Supplying parameters to advice using @AspectJ annotation isn't much different than how we did it with Spring's XML-based aspect declaration. In fact, for the most part, the XML elements we used earlier translate almost straight into equivalent @AspectJ annotations, as you can see in the new `Magician` class.

Listing 4.7 Using @AspectJ annotations to turn a `Magician` into an aspect

```
package com.springinaction.springidol;

import org.aspectj.lang.annotation.Aspect;
import org.aspectj.lang.annotation.Before;
import org.aspectj.lang.annotation.Pointcut;

@Aspect
public class Magician implements MindReader {
  private String thoughts;

  @Pointcut("execution(* com.springinaction.springidol."
      + "Thinker.thinkOfSomething(String)) && args(thoughts)")
  public void thinking(String thoughts) {
  }

  @Before("thinking(thoughts)")
  public void interceptThoughts(String thoughts) {
```

Declare parameterized pointcut

Pass parameters into advice

```
    System.out.println("Intercepting volunteer's thoughts : " + thoughts);
    this.thoughts = thoughts;
  }

  public String getThoughts() {
    return thoughts;
  }
}
/
```

The `<aop:pointcut>` element has become the `@Pointcut` annotation and the `<aop:before>` element has become the `@Before` annotation. The only significant change here is that @AspectJ can lean on Java syntax to determine the details of the parameters passed into the advice. Therefore, there's no need for an annotation-based equivalent to the `<aop:before>` element's `arg-names`.

4.4.3 Annotating introductions

Earlier, I showed you how to use `<aop:declare-parents>` to introduce an interface onto an existing bean without changing the bean's source code. Now let's have another look at that example, but this time using annotation-based AOP.

The annotation equivalent of `<aop:declare-parents>` is @AspectJ's `@DeclareParents`. `@DeclareParents` works almost exactly like its XML counterpart when used inside of an `@Aspect`-annotated class. The following shows how to use `@DeclareParents`.

Listing 4.8 Introducing the `Contestant` interface using @AspectJ annotations

```
package com.springinaction.springidol;

import org.aspectj.lang.annotation.Aspect;
import org.aspectj.lang.annotation.DeclareParents;

@Aspect
public class ContestantIntroducer {

  @DeclareParents(                                          // Mix in Contestant interface
      value = "com.springinaction.springidol.Performer+",
      defaultImpl = GraciousContestant.class)
  public static Contestant contestant;
}
```

As you can see, `ContestantIntroducer` is an aspect. But unlike the aspects we've created so far, it doesn't provide before, after, or around advice. Instead, it introduces the `Contestant` interface onto `Performer` beans. Like `<aop:declare-parents>`, `@DeclareParents` annotation is made up of three parts:

- The `value` attribute is equivalent to `<aop:declare-parents>`'s `types-matching` attribute. It identifies the kinds of beans that should be introduced with the interface.

- The `defaultImpl` attribute is equivalent to `<aop:declare-parents>`'s `default-impl` attribute. It identifies the class that will provide the implementation for the introduction.
- The static property that is annotated by `@DeclareParents` specifies the interface that is to be introduced.

As with any aspect, you'll need to declare `ContestantIntroducer` as a bean in the Spring application context:

```
<bean class="com.springinaction.springidol.ContestantIntroducer" />
```

`<aop:aspectj-autoproxy>` will take it from there. When it discovers a bean annotated with `@Aspect`, it'll automatically create a proxy that delegates calls to either the proxied bean or to the introduction implementation, depending on whether the method called belongs to the proxied bean or to the introduced interface.

One thing you'll notice is that `@DeclareParents` doesn't have an equivalent to `<aop:declare-parents>`'s `delegate-ref` attribute. That's because `@DeclareParents` is an @AspectJ annotation. @AspectJ is a project that's separate from Spring and thus its annotations aren't bean-aware. The implications here are that if you want to delegate to a bean that's configured with Spring, then `@DeclareParents` may not fit the bill and you'll have to resort to using `<aop:declare-parents>`.

Spring AOP enables separation of cross-cutting concerns from an application's business logic. But as we've seen, Spring aspects are still proxy-based and are limited to advising method invocations. If you need more than just method proxy support, you'll want to consider using AspectJ. In the next section, you'll see how traditional AspectJ aspects can be used within a Spring application.

4.5 Injecting AspectJ aspects

Although Spring AOP is sufficient for many applications of aspects, it's a weak AOP solution when contrasted with AspectJ. AspectJ offers many types of pointcuts that aren't possible with Spring AOP.

Constructor pointcuts, for example, are convenient when you need to apply advice upon the creation of an object. Unlike constructors in some other object-oriented languages, Java constructors are different from normal methods. This makes Spring's proxy-based AOP woefully inadequate for advising creation of an object.

For the most part, AspectJ aspects are independent of Spring. Although they can be woven into any Java-based application, including Spring applications, there's little involvement on Spring's part in applying AspectJ aspects.

But any well-designed and meaningful aspect will likely depend on other classes to assist in its work. If an aspect depends on one or more classes when executing its advice, you can instantiate those collaborating objects with the aspect itself. Or, better yet, you can use Spring's dependency injection to inject beans into AspectJ aspects.

To illustrate, let's create a new aspect for the *Spring Idol* competition. A talent competition needs a judge. So, let's create a judge aspect in AspectJ. `JudgeAspect` is such an aspect.

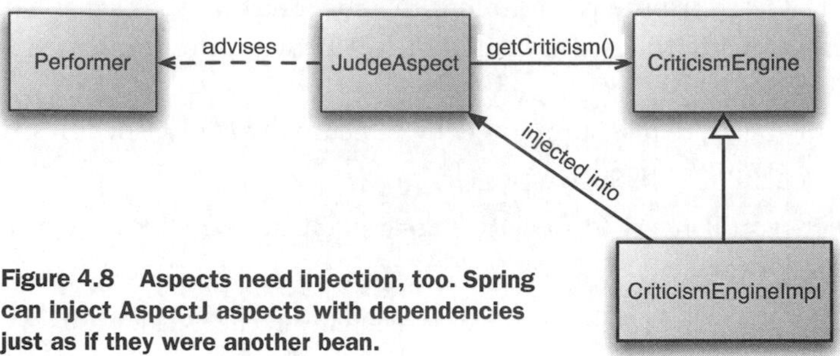

Figure 4.8 Aspects need injection, too. Spring can inject AspectJ aspects with dependencies just as if they were another bean.

Listing 4.9 An AspectJ implementation of a talent competition judge

```
package com.springinaction.springidol;

public aspect JudgeAspect {
  public JudgeAspect() {}

  pointcut performance() : execution(* perform(..));

  after() returning() : performance() {
    System.out.println(criticismEngine.getCriticism());
  }

  // injected
  private CriticismEngine criticismEngine;
  public void setCriticismEngine(CriticismEngine criticismEngine) {
    this.criticismEngine = criticismEngine;
  }
}
```

The chief responsibility for `JudgeAspect` is to make commentary on a performance after the performance has completed. The `performance()` pointcut in listing 4.9 matches the `perform()` method. When it's married with the `after()returning()` advice, you get an aspect that reacts to the completion of a performance.

What makes listing 4.9 interesting is that the judge doesn't make commentary on its own. Instead, `JudgeAspect` collaborates with a `CriticismEngine` object, calling its `getCriticism()` method, to produce critical commentary after a performance. To avoid unnecessary coupling between `JudgeAspect` and the `CriticismEngine`, the `JudgeAspect` is given a reference to a `CriticismEngine` through setter injection. This relationship is illustrated in figure 4.8.

`CriticismEngine` itself is an interface that declares a simple `getCriticism()` method. Here's the implementation of `CriticismEngine`.

Listing 4.10 An implementation of the `CriticismEngine` used by `JudgeAspect`

```
package com.springinaction.springidol;

public class CriticismEngineImpl implements CriticismEngine {
  public CriticismEngineImpl() {}
```

```
  public String getCriticism() {
    int i = (int) (Math.random() * criticismPool.length);

    return criticismPool[i];
  }

  // injected
  private String[] criticismPool;
  public void setCriticismPool(String[] criticismPool) {
    this.criticismPool = criticismPool;
  }
}
```

`CriticismEngineImpl` implements the `CriticismEngine` interface by randomly choosing a critical comment from a pool of injected criticisms. This class can be declared as a Spring <bean> using the following XML:

```
<bean id="criticismEngine"
    class="com.springinaction.springidol.CriticismEngineImpl">
  <property name="criticisms">
    <list>
      <value>I'm not being rude, but that was appalling.</value>
      <value>You may be the least talented
          person in this show.</value>
      <value>Do everyone a favor and keep your day job.</value>
    </list>
  </property>
</bean>
```

So far, so good. You now have a `CriticismEngine` implementation to give to `JudgeAspect`. All that's left is to wire `CriticismEngineImpl` into `JudgeAspect`.

Before I show you how to do the injection, you should know that AspectJ aspects can be woven into your application without involving Spring at all. But if you want to use Spring's dependency injection to inject collaborators into an AspectJ aspect, you'll need to declare the aspect as a <bean> in Spring's configuration. The following <bean> declaration injects the `criticismEngine` bean into `JudgeAspect`:

```
<bean class="com.springinaction.springidol.JudgeAspect"
    factory-method="aspectOf">
  <property name="criticismEngine" ref="criticismEngine" />
</bean>
```

For the most part, this <bean> declaration isn't much different from any other <bean> you may find in Spring. But the big difference is the use of the `factory-method` attribute. Normally Spring beans are instantiated by the Spring container, but AspectJ aspects are created by the AspectJ runtime. By the time Spring gets a chance to inject the `CriticismEngine` into `JudgeAspect`, `JudgeAspect` has already been instantiated.

Since Spring isn't responsible for the creation of `JudgeAspect`, it isn't possible to simply declare `JudgeAspect` as a bean in Spring. Instead, we need a way for Spring to get a handle to the `JudgeAspect` instance that has already been created by AspectJ so that we can inject it with a `CriticismEngine`. Conveniently, all AspectJ aspects provide a static `aspectOf()` method that returns the singleton instance of the aspect. So to get an instance of the aspect, you must use `factory-method` to invoke the `aspectOf()` method instead of trying to call `JudgeAspect`'s constructor.

In short, Spring doesn't use the `<bean>` declaration from earlier to create an instance of the `JudgeAspect`—it has already been created by the AspectJ runtime. Instead, Spring retrieves a reference to the aspect through the `aspectOf()` factory method and then performs dependency injection on it as prescribed by the `<bean>` element.

4.6 Summary

AOP is a powerful complement to object-oriented programming. With aspects, you can now group application behavior that was once spread throughout your applications into reusable modules. You can then declare exactly where and how this behavior is applied. This reduces code duplication and lets your classes focus on their main functionality.

Spring provides an AOP framework that lets you insert aspects around method executions. You've learned how you can weave advice before, after, and around a method invocation, as well as add custom behavior for handling exceptions.

You have several choices in how you can use aspects in your Spring applications. Wiring advice and pointcuts in Spring is much easier with the addition of @AspectJ annotation support and a simplified configuration schema.

Finally, there are times when Spring AOP isn't powerful enough and you must turn to AspectJ for more powerful aspects. For those situations, we looked at how to use Spring to inject dependencies into AspectJ aspects.

At this point, we've covered the basics of the Spring Framework. You've seen how to configure the Spring container and how to apply aspects to Spring-managed objects. As you've seen, these core techniques offer great opportunity to create applications composed of loosely coupled objects. In the next chapter, we'll look at how loose coupling through DI and AOP foster developer-driven testing and see how to keep your Spring code covered by tests.

Part 2

Spring application essentials

In part 1, you learned about Spring's core container and its support for dependency injection (DI) and aspect-oriented programming (AOP). With that foundation set, part 2 will explore the framework features that Spring provides for building enterprise applications.

Most applications ultimately persist business information in a relational database. Chapter 5, "Hitting the database," will guide you in using Spring's support for data persistence. You'll be introduced to Spring's JDBC support, which helps you remove much of the boilerplate code associated with JDBC. You'll also see how Spring integrates with the object-relational mapping persistence options, Hibernate and JPA.

Once you're persisting your data, you'll want to ensure that its integrity is preserved. In chapter 6, "Managing transactions," you'll learn how to declaratively apply transactional policies to your application objects using AOP.

In chapter 7, "Building web applications with Spring MVC," you'll learn the basics of using Spring MVC, a web framework built on the principles of the Spring Framework. You'll discover Spring MVC's vast selection of controllers for handling web requests and see how to transparently bind request parameters to your business objects while providing validation and error handling at the same time.

Chapter 8, "Working with Spring Web Flow," will show you how to build conversational, flow-based web applications using the Spring Web Flow framework.

As security is an important aspect of many applications, chapter 9, "Securing Spring," will show you how to use Spring Security to protect the information your application contains.

5 Hitting the database

This chapter covers

- Defining Spring's data access support
- Configuring database resources
- Working with Spring's JDBC templates
- Using Spring with Hibernate and JPA

With the core of the Spring container now under your belt, it's time to put it to work in real applications. A perfect place to start is with a requirement of nearly any enterprise application: persisting data. Every one of us has probably dealt with database access in an application in the past. In practice, we know that data access has many pitfalls. We have to initialize our data access framework, open connections, handle various exceptions, and close connections. If we get any of this wrong, we could potentially corrupt or delete valuable company data. In case you haven't experienced the consequences of mishandled data access, it's a *Bad Thing*.

Since we strive for *Good Things*, we turn to Spring. Spring comes with a family of data access frameworks that integrate with a variety of data access technologies. Whether you're persisting your data via direct JDBC, iBATIS, or an object relational mapping (ORM) framework such as Hibernate, Spring removes the tedium of data access from your persistence code. Instead, you can lean on Spring to handle the low-level data access work for you so that you can turn your attention to managing your application's data.

Starting in this chapter, we'll build a Twitter-like application based on Spring called Spitter. This application will be the primary example for the rest of this book. The first order of business is to develop Spitter's persistence layer.

As we develop the persistence layer, we're faced with some choices. We could use JDBC, Hibernate, the Java Persistence API (JPA), or any of a number of persistence frameworks. Fortunately, Spring supports all of those persistence mechanisms. We'll take each of them for a spin in this chapter.

But first, let's lay some groundwork by getting familiar with Spring's persistence philosophy.

5.1 Learning Spring's data access philosophy

From the previous chapters, you know that one of Spring's goals is to allow you to develop applications following the sound object-oriented (OO) principle of coding to interfaces. Spring's data access support is no exception.

DAO[1] stands for *data access object*, which perfectly describes a DAO's role in an application. DAOs exist to provide a means to read and write data to the database. They should expose this functionality through an interface by which the rest of the application will access them. Figure 5.1 shows the proper approach to designing your data access tier.

As you can see, the service objects are accessing the DAOs through interfaces. This has a couple of positive consequences. First, it makes your service objects easily testable, since they're not coupled to a specific data access implementation. In fact, you could create mock implementations of these data access interfaces. That would allow you to test your service object without ever having to connect to the database, which would significantly speed up your unit tests and rule out the chance of a test failure due to inconsistent data.

In addition, the data access tier is accessed in a persistence technology-agnostic manner. The chosen persistence approach is isolated to the DAO while only the

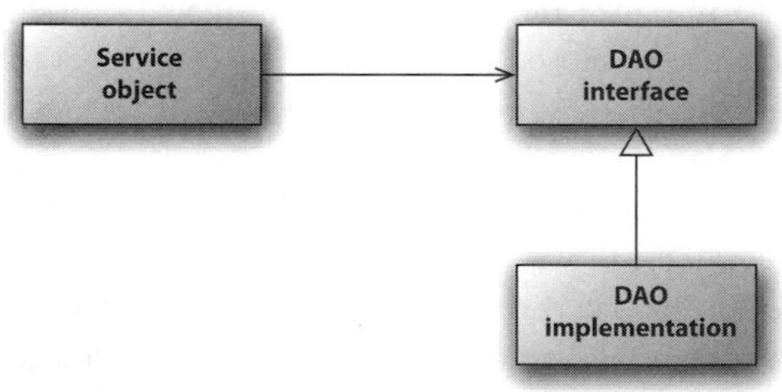

Figure 5.1 Service objects don't handle their own data access. Instead, they delegate data access to DAOs. The DAO's interface keeps it loosely coupled to the service object.

[1] Many developers, including Martin Fowler, refer to the persistence objects of an application as *repositories.* Though I appreciate the thinking that leads to the repository moniker, I believe that the word repository is already overloaded, even without adding this additional meaning. So forgive me, but I'm going to buck the popular trend—I'll continue referring to these objects as DAOs.

relevant data access methods are exposed through the interface. This makes for a flexible application design and allows the chosen persistence framework to be swapped out with minimal impact to the rest of the application. If the implementation details of the data access tier were to leak into other parts of the application, the entire application would become coupled with the data access tier, leading to a rigid application design.

> **NOTE** If after reading the last couple of paragraphs, you feel that I have a strong bias toward hiding the persistence layer behind interfaces, then I'm happy that I was able to get that point across. I believe that interfaces are key to writing loosely coupled code and that they should be used at all layers of an application, not just at the data access layer. That said, it's also important to note that though Spring encourages the use of interfaces, Spring doesn't require them—you're welcome to use Spring to wire a bean (DAO or otherwise) directly into a property of another bean without an interface between them.

One way Spring helps you insulate your data access tier from the rest of your application is by providing a consistent exception hierarchy that's used across all of its DAO frameworks.

5.1.1 Getting to know Spring's data access exception hierarchy

There's an old joke about a skydiver who's blown off course and ends up landing in a tree, dangling above the ground. After awhile someone walks by and the skydiver asks where he is.

> The passerby answers, "You're about 20 feet off the ground."
> The skydiver replies "You must be a software analyst."
> "You're right. How did you know?" asks the passerby.
> "Because what you told me was 100 percent accurate, but completely worthless."

That story has been told several times, with the profession or nationality of the passerby different each time. But the story reminds me of JDBC's `SQLException`. If you've ever written JDBC code (without Spring), you're probably keenly aware that you can't do anything with JDBC without being forced to catch `SQLException`. `SQLException` means that something went wrong while trying to access a database. But there's little about that exception that tells you what went wrong or how to deal with it.

Some common problems that might cause an `SQLException` to be thrown include

- The application is unable to connect to the database.
- The query being performed has errors in its syntax.
- The tables and/or columns referred to in the query don't exist.
- An attempt was made to insert or update values that violate a database constraint.

The big question surrounding `SQLException` is how it should be handled when it's caught. As it turns out, many of the problems that trigger an `SQLException` can't be remedied within a `catch` block. Most `SQLException`s that are thrown indicate a fatal condition. If the application can't connect to the database, that usually means that the application will be unable to continue. Likewise, if there are errors in the query, little can be done about it at runtime.

If there's nothing that can be done to recover from an `SQLException`, why are we forced to catch it?

Even if you have a plan for dealing with some `SQLException`s, you'll have to catch the `SQLException` and dig around in its properties for more information on the nature of the problem. That's because `SQLException` is treated as a one-size-fits-all exception for problems related to data access. Rather than have a different exception type for each possible problem, `SQLException` is the exception that's thrown for all data access problems.

Some persistence frameworks offer a richer hierarchy of exceptions. Hibernate, for example, offers almost two dozen different exceptions, each targeting a specific data access problem. This makes it possible to write `catch` blocks for the exceptions that you want to deal with.

Even so, Hibernate's exceptions are specific to Hibernate. As stated before, we'd like to isolate the specifics of the persistence mechanism to the data access layer. If Hibernate-specific exceptions are being thrown, then the fact that we're dealing with Hibernate will leak into the rest of the application. Either that, or you'll be forced to catch persistence platform exceptions and rethrow them as platform-agnostic exceptions.

On one hand, JDBC's exception hierarchy is too generic—it's not really much of a hierarchy at all. On the other hand, Hibernate's exception hierarchy is proprietary to Hibernate. What we need is a hierarchy of data access exceptions that are descriptive but not directly associated with a specific persistence framework.

SPRING'S PERSISTENCE PLATFORM-AGNOSTIC EXCEPTIONS

Spring JDBC provides a hierarchy of data access exceptions that solve both problems. In contrast to JDBC, Spring provides several data access exceptions, each descriptive of the problem that they're thrown for. Table 5.1 shows some of Spring's data access exceptions lined up against the exceptions offered by JDBC.

As you can see, Spring has an exception for virtually anything that could go wrong when reading or writing to a database. And the list of Spring's data access exceptions is more vast than what's shown in table 5.1. (I would've listed them all, but I didn't want JDBC to get an inferiority complex.)

Even though Spring's exception hierarchy is far richer than JDBC's simple `SQLException`, it isn't associated with any particular persistence solution. This means that you can count on Spring to throw a consistent set of exceptions, regardless of which persistence provider you choose. This helps to keep your persistence choice confined to the data access layer.

Table 5.1 JDBC's exception hierarchy versus Spring's data access exceptions

JDBC's exceptions	Spring's data access exceptions
BatchUpdateException DataTruncation SQLException SQLWarning	CannotAcquireLockException CannotSerializeTransactionException CleanupFailureDataAccessException ConcurrencyFailureException DataAccessException DataAccessResourceFailureException DataIntegrityViolationException DataRetrievalFailureException DeadlockLoserDataAccessException EmptyResultDataAccessException IncorrectResultSizeDataAccessException IncorrectUpdateSemanticsDataAccessException InvalidDataAccessApiUsageException InvalidDataAccessResourceUsageException OptimisticLockingFailureException PermissionDeniedDataAccessException PessimisticLockingFailureException TypeMismatchDataAccessException UncategorizedDataAccessException

LOOK, MA! NO CATCH BLOCKS!

What isn't evident from table 5.1 is that all of those exceptions are rooted with `DataAccessException`. What makes `DataAccessException` special is that it's an unchecked exception. In other words, you don't have to catch any of the data access exceptions thrown from Spring (although you're perfectly welcome to if you'd like).

`DataAccessException` is just one example of Spring's across-the-board philosophy of checked versus unchecked exceptions. Spring takes the stance that many exceptions are the result of problems that can't be addressed in a `catch` block. Instead of forcing developers to write `catch` blocks (which are often left empty), Spring promotes the use of unchecked exceptions. This leaves the decision of whether to catch an exception in the developer's hands.

To take advantage of Spring's data access exceptions, you must use one of Spring's supported data access templates. Let's look at how Spring templates can greatly simplify data access.

5.1.2 Templating data access

You've probably traveled by plane before. If so, you'll surely agree that one of the most important parts of traveling is getting your luggage from point A to point B. There are many steps to this process. When you arrive at the terminal, your first stop will be at the counter to check your luggage. Next, security will scan it to ensure the safety of the flight. Then it takes a ride on the "luggage train" on its way to being placed on the plane. If you need to catch a connecting flight, your luggage needs to be moved as well. When you arrive at your final destination, the luggage has to be removed from the plane and placed on the carousel. Finally, you go down to the baggage claim area and pick it up.

Even though there are many steps to this process, you're only actively involved in a couple of those steps. The carrier itself is responsible for driving the process. You're only involved when you need to be; the rest is taken care of. This mirrors a powerful design pattern: the Template Method pattern.

A template method defines the skeleton of a process. In our example, the process is moving luggage from departure city to arrival city. The process itself is fixed; it never changes. The overall sequence of events for handling luggage occurs the same way every time: luggage is checked in, luggage is loaded onto the plane, and so forth. Some steps of the process are fixed as well—some steps happen the same every time. When the plane arrives at its destination, every piece of luggage is unloaded one at a time and placed on a carousel to be taken to baggage claim.

At certain points, the process delegates its work to a subclass to fill in some implementation-specific details. This is the variable part of the process. For example, the handling of luggage starts with a passenger checking in the luggage at the counter. This part of the process always has to happen at the beginning, so its sequence in the process is fixed. Because each passenger's luggage check-in is different, the implementation of this part of the process is determined by the passenger. In software terms, a template method delegates the implementation-specific portions of the process to an interface. Different implementations of this interface define specific implementations of this portion of the process.

This is the same pattern that Spring applies to data access. No matter what technology we're using, certain data access steps are required. For example, we always need to obtain a connection to our data store and clean up resources when we're done. These are the fixed steps in a data access process. But each data access method we write is slightly different. We query for different objects and update the data in different ways. These are the variable steps in the data access process.

Spring separates the fixed and variable parts of the data access process into two distinct classes: *templates* and *callbacks*. Templates manage the fixed part of the process, whereas your custom data access code is handled in the callbacks. Figure 5.2 shows the responsibilities of both of these classes.

As you can see in figure 5.2, Spring's template classes handle the fixed parts of data access—controlling transactions, managing resources, and handling exceptions.

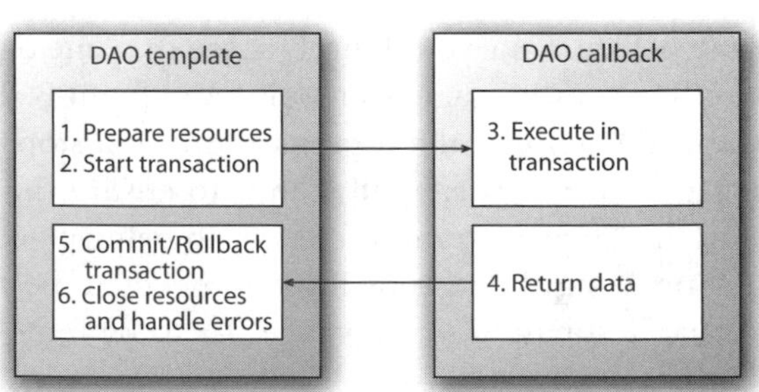

Figure 5.2 Spring's DAO template classes take responsibility for the common data access duties. For the application-specific tasks, it calls back into a custom DAO callback object.

Meanwhile, the specifics of data access as they pertain to your application—creating statements, binding parameters, and marshaling result sets—are handled in the callback implementation. In practice, this makes for an elegant framework because all you have to worry about is your data access logic.

Spring comes with several templates to choose from, depending on your persistence platform choice. If you're using straight JDBC, then you'll want to use `JdbcTemplate`. But if you favor one of the object-relational mapping frameworks, then perhaps `HibernateTemplate` or `JpaTemplate` is more suitable. Table 5.2 lists all of Spring's data access templates and their purposes.

Table 5.2 Spring comes with several data access templates, each suitable for a different persistence mechanism.

Template class (`org.springframework.*`)	Used to template. . .
`jca.cci.core.CciTemplate`	JCA CCI connections
`jdbc.core.JdbcTemplate`	JDBC connections
`jdbc.core.namedparam.NamedParameterJdbcTemplate`	JDBC connections with support for named parameters
`jdbc.core.simple.SimpleJdbcTemplate`	JDBC connections, simplified with Java 5 constructs
`orm.hibernate.HibernateTemplate`	Hibernate 2.*x* sessions
`orm.hibernate3.HibernateTemplate`	Hibernate 3.*x* sessions
`orm.ibatis.SqlMapClientTemplate`	iBATIS SqlMap clients
`orm.jdo.JdoTemplate`	Java Data Object implementations
`orm.jpa.JpaTemplate`	Java Persistence API entity managers

As you'll see, using a data access template simply involves configuring it as a bean in the Spring context and then wiring it into your application DAO. Or you can take advantage of Spring's DAO support classes to further simplify configuration of your application DAOs. Direct wiring of the templates is fine, but Spring also provides a set of convenient DAO base classes that can manage templates for you. Let's see how these template-based DAO classes work.

5.1.3 Using DAO support classes

The data access templates aren't all there is to Spring's data access framework. Each template also provides convenience methods that simplify data access without the need to create an explicit callback implementation. Furthermore, on top of the template-callback design, Spring provides DAO support classes that are meant to be subclassed by your own DAO classes. Figure 5.3 illustrates the relationship between a template class, a DAO support class, and your own custom DAO implementation.

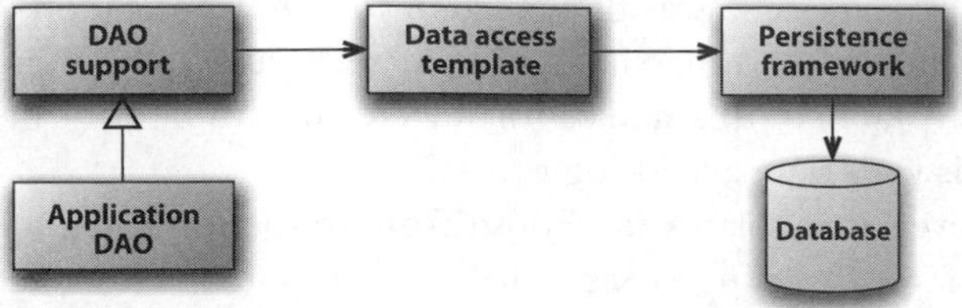

Figure 5.3 The relationship between an application DAO and Spring's DAO support and template classes

Later, as we examine Spring's individual data access support options, we'll see how the DAO support classes provide convenient access to the template class that they support. When writing your application DAO implementation, you can subclass a DAO support class and call a template retrieval method to have direct access to the underlying data access template. For example, if your application DAO subclasses `JdbcDaoSupport`, then you only need to call `getJdbcTemplate()` to get a `JdbcTemplate` to work with.

Plus, if you need access to the underlying persistence platform, each of the DAO support classes provides access to whatever class it uses to communicate with the database. For instance, the `JdbcDaoSupport` class contains a `getConnection()` method for dealing directly with the JDBC connection.

Just as Spring provides several data access template implementations, it also provides several DAO support classes—one for each template. Table 5.3 lists the DAO support classes that come with Spring.

Even though Spring provides support for several persistence frameworks, there isn't enough space to cover them all in this chapter. Therefore, we're going to focus on what I believe are the most beneficial persistence options and the ones that you'll most likely be using.

Table 5.3 Spring's DAO support classes provide convenient access to their corresponding data access template.

DAO support class (`org.springframework.*`)	Provides DAO support for. . .
`jca.cci.support.CciDaoSupport`	JCA CCI connections
`jdbc.core.support.JdbcDaoSupport`	JDBC connections
`jdbc.core.namedparam.NamedParameterJdbcDaoSupport`	JDBC connections with support for named parameters
`jdbc.core.simple.SimpleJdbcDaoSupport`	JDBC connections, simplified with Java 5 constructs
`orm.hibernate.support.HibernateDaoSupport`	Hibernate 2.*x* sessions
`orm.hibernate3.support.HibernateDaoSupport`	Hibernate 3.*x* sessions
`orm.ibatis.support.SqlMapClientDaoSupport`	iBATIS SqlMap clients
`orm.jdo.support.JdoDaoSupport`	Java Data Object implementations
`orm.jpa.support.JpaDaoSupport`	Java Persistence API entity managers

We'll start with basic JDBC access, as it's the most basic way to read and write data from a database. Then we'll look at Hibernate and JPA, two of the most popular POJO-based ORM solutions.

But first things first—most of Spring's persistence support options will depend on a data source. So, before we can get started with creating templates and DAOs, we need to configure Spring with a data source for the DAOs to access the database.

5.2 Configuring a data source

Regardless of which form of Spring DAO support you use, you'll likely need to configure a reference to a data source. Spring offers several options for configuring data source beans in your Spring application, including

- Data sources that are defined by a JDBC driver
- Data sources that are looked up by JNDI
- Data sources that pool connections

For production-ready applications, I recommend using a data source that draws its connections from a connection pool. When possible, I prefer to retrieve the pooled data source from an application server via JNDI. With that preference in mind, let's start by looking at how to configure Spring to retrieve a data source from JNDI.

5.2.1 Using JNDI data sources

Spring applications will often be deployed to run within a Java EE application server such as WebSphere, JBoss, or even a web container like Tomcat. These servers allow you to configure data sources to be retrieved via JNDI. The benefit of configuring data sources in this way is that they can be managed completely external to the application, allowing the application to ask for a data source when it's ready to access the database. Moreover, data sources managed in an application server are often pooled for greater performance and can be hot-swapped by system administrators.

With Spring, we can configure a reference to a data source that's kept in JNDI and wire it into the classes that need it as if it were just another Spring bean. The `<jee:jndi-lookup>` element from Spring's `jee` namespace makes it possible to retrieve any object, including data sources, from JNDI and make it available as a Spring bean. For example, if our application's data source were configured in JNDI, we might use `<jee:jndi-lookup>` like this to wire it into Spring:

```
<jee:jndi-lookup id="dataSource"
    jndi-name="/jdbc/SpitterDS"
    resource-ref="true" />
```

The `jndi-name` attribute is used to specify the name of the resource in JNDI. If only the `jndi-name` property is set, then the data source will be looked up using the name given as is. But if the application is running within a Java application server, then you'll want to set the `resource-ref` property to `true` so that the value given in `jndi-name` will be prepended with `java:comp/env/`.

5.2.2 Using a pooled data source

If you're unable to retrieve a data source from JNDI, the next best thing is to configure a pooled data source directly in Spring. Although Spring doesn't provide a pooled data source, there's a suitable one available in the Jakarta Commons Database Connection Pooling (DBCP) project (http://jakarta.apache.org/commons/dbcp).

DBCP includes several data sources that provide pooling, but the `BasicDataSource` is one that's often used because it's simple to configure in Spring and because it resembles Spring's own `DriverManagerDataSource` (which we'll talk about next).

For the Spitter application, we'll configure a `BasicDataSource` bean as follows:

```
<bean id="dataSource"
      class="org.apache.commons.dbcp.BasicDataSource">
  <property name="driverClassName" value="org.hsqldb.jdbcDriver" />
  <property name="url"
           value="jdbc:hsqldb:hsql://localhost/spitter/spitter" />
  <property name="username" value="sa" />
  <property name="password" value="" />
  <property name="initialSize" value="5" />
  <property name="maxActive" value="10" />
</bean>
```

The first four properties are elemental to configuring a `BasicDataSource`. The `driverClassName` property specifies the fully qualified name of the JDBC driver class. Here we've configured it with the JDBC driver for the Hypersonic database. The `url` property is where we set the complete JDBC URL for the database. Finally, the `username` and `password` properties are used to authenticate when we're connecting to the database.

Those four basic properties define connection information for `BasicDataSource`. In addition, several properties can be used to configure the data source pool itself. Table 5.4 lists a few of the most useful pool-configuration properties of `BasicDataSource`.

Table 5.4 `BasicDataSource`'s pool-configuration properties

Pool-configuration property	What it specifies
`initialSize`	The number of connections created when the pool is started.
`maxActive`	The maximum number of connections that can be allocated from the pool at the same time. If zero, there's no limit.
`maxIdle`	The maximum number of connections that can be idle in the pool without extras being released. If zero, there's no limit.
`maxOpenPreparedStatements`	The maximum number of prepared statements that can be allocated from the statement pool at the same time. If zero, there's no limit.
`maxWait`	How long the pool will wait for a connection to be returned to the pool (when there are no available connections) before an exception is thrown. If -1, wait indefinitely.

Table 5.4 `BasicDataSource`'s pool-configuration properties *(continued)*

Pool-configuration property	What it specifies
`minEvictableIdleTimeMillis`	How long a connection can remain idle in the pool before it's eligible for eviction.
`minIdle`	The minimum number of connections that can remain idle in the pool without new connections being created.
`poolPreparedStatements`	Whether or not to pool prepared statements (Boolean).

For our purposes, we've configured the pool to start with five connections. Should more connections be needed, `BasicDataSource` is allowed to create them, up to a maximum of ten active connections.

5.2.3 JDBC driver-based data source

The simplest data source you can configure in Spring is one that's defined through a JDBC driver. Spring offers two such data source classes to choose from (both in the `org.springframework.jdbc.datasource` package):

- `DriverManagerDataSource`—Returns a new connection every time that a connection is requested. Unlike DBCP's `BasicDataSource`, the connections provided by `DriverManagerDataSource` aren't pooled.
- `SingleConnectionDataSource`—Returns the same connection every time a connection is requested. Although `SingleConnectionDataSource` isn't exactly a pooled data source, you can think of it as a data source with a pool of exactly one connection.

Configuring either of these data sources is similar to how we configured DBCP's `BasicDataSource`:

```
<bean id="dataSource"
      class="org.springframework.jdbc.datasource.
          DriverManagerDataSource">
  <property name="driverClassName"
            value="org.hsqldb.jdbcDriver" />
  <property name="url"
            value="jdbc:hsqldb:hsql://localhost/spitter/spitter" />
  <property name="username" value="sa" />
  <property name="password" value="" />
</bean>
```

The only difference is that since neither `DriverManagerDataSource` nor `SingleConnectionDataSource` provides a connection pool, there are no pool configuration properties to set.

Although `SingleConnectionDataSource` and `DriverManagerDataSource` are great for small applications and running in development, you should seriously consider the implications of using either in a production application. Because `SingleConnectionDataSource` has one and only one database connection to work with, it doesn't work well in a multithreaded application. At the same time, even though DriverManagerDataSource is capable of supporting multiple threads, it incurs a performance cost for creating a new connection each time a connection is requested. Because of these limitations, I strongly recommend using pooled data sources.

Now that we've established a connection to the database through a data source, we're ready to actually access the database. As I've already mentioned, Spring affords us several options for working with databases, including JDBC, Hibernate, and the Java Persistence API (JPA). In the next section we'll see how to build the persistence layer of a Spring application using Spring's support for JDBC. But if Hibernate or JPA are more your style, then feel free to jump ahead to sections 5.4 and 5.5.

5.3 Using JDBC with Spring

There are many persistence technologies out there. Hibernate, iBATIS, and JPA are just a few. Despite this, a good number of applications are writing Java objects to a database the old-fashioned way: they earn it. No, wait—that's how people make money. The tried-and-true method for persisting data is with good old JDBC.

And why not? JDBC doesn't require mastering another framework's query language. It's built on top of SQL, which is the data access language. Plus, you can more finely tune the performance of your data access when you use JDBC than with practically any other technology. And JDBC allows you to take advantage of your database's proprietary features, where other frameworks may discourage or flat-out prohibit this.

What's more, JDBC lets you work with data at a much lower level than the persistence frameworks, allowing you to access and manipulate individual columns in a database. This fine-grained approach to data access comes in handy in applications, such as reporting applications, where it doesn't make sense to organize the data into objects, just to then unwind it back into raw data.

But all is not sunny in the world of JDBC. With its power, flexibility, and other niceties also come some not-so-niceties.

5.3.1 Tackling runaway JDBC code

Though JDBC gives you an API that works closely with your database, you're responsible for handling everything related to accessing the database. This includes managing database resources and handling exceptions.

If you've ever written JDBC that inserts data into the database, the following shouldn't be too alien to you.

Listing 5.1 Using JDBC to insert a row into a database

```
private static final String SQL_INSERT_SPITTER =
    "insert into spitter (username, password, fullname) values (?, ?, ?)";
private DataSource dataSource;
public void addSpitter(Spitter spitter) {
  Connection conn = null;
  PreparedStatement stmt = null;
```

```
  try {
    conn = dataSource.getConnection();                    Get connection
    stmt = conn.prepareStatement(SQL_INSERT_SPITTER);     Create statement
    stmt.setString(1, spitter.getUsername());             Bind parameters
    stmt.setString(2, spitter.getPassword());
    stmt.setString(3, spitter.getFullName());
    stmt.execute();                                       Execute statement
  } catch (SQLException e) {
    // do something...not sure what, though               Handle exceptions (somehow)
  } finally {
    try {
      if (stmt != null) {                                 Clean up
        stmt.close();
      }
      if (conn != null) {
        conn.close();
      }
    } catch (SQLException e) {
      // I'm even less sure about what to do here
    }
  }
}
```

Holy runaway code, Batman! That's more than 20 lines of code to insert a simple object into a database. As far as JDBC operations go, this is about as simple as it gets. So why does it take this many lines to do something so simple? Actually, it doesn't. Only a handful of lines actually do the insert. But JDBC requires that you properly manage connections and statements and somehow handle the `SQLException` that may be thrown.

Speaking of that `SQLException`: not only is it not clear how you should handle it (because it's not clear what went wrong), but you're forced to catch it twice! You must catch it if something goes wrong while inserting a record, and you have to catch it again if something goes wrong when closing the statement and connection. Seems like a lot of work to handle something that usually can't be handled programmatically.

Now look at the following listing, where we use traditional JDBC to update a row in the Spitter table in the database.

Listing 5.2 Using JDBC to update a row in a database

```
private static final String SQL_UPDATE_SPITTER =
      "update spitter set username = ?, password = ?, fullname = ?"
      + "where id = ?";
public void saveSpitter(Spitter spitter) {
  Connection conn = null;
  PreparedStatement stmt = null;
  try {
    conn = dataSource.getConnection();                    Get connection
```

```
    stmt = conn.prepareStatement(SQL_UPDATE_SPITTER);        Create statement

    stmt.setString(1, spitter.getUsername());                Bind parameters
    stmt.setString(2, spitter.getPassword());
    stmt.setString(3, spitter.getFullName());
    stmt.setLong(4, spitter.getId());

    stmt.execute();                  Execute statement
  } catch (SQLException e) {
    // Still not sure what I'm supposed to do here           Handle exceptions (somehow)
  } finally {
    try {
      if (stmt != null) {            Clean up
        stmt.close();
      }
      if (conn != null) {
        conn.close();
      }
    } catch (SQLException e) {
      // or here
    }
  }
}
```

At first glance, listing 5.2 may appear to be identical to listing 5.1. In fact, disregarding the SQL `String` and the line where the statement is created, they're identical. Again, that's a lot of code to do something as simple as update a single row in a database. What's more, that's a lot of repeated code. Ideally, we'd only have to write the lines that are specific to the task at hand. After all, those are the only lines that distinguish listing 5.2 from listing 5.1. The rest is just boilerplate code.

To round out our tour of conventional JDBC, let's see how you might retrieve data out of the database. As you can see in the following, that's not pretty, either.

Listing 5.3 Using JDBC to query a row from a database

```
private static final String SQL_SELECT_SPITTER =
      "select id, username, fullname from spitter where id = ?";
public Spitter getSpitterById(long id) {
  Connection conn = null;
  PreparedStatement stmt = null;
  ResultSet rs = null;
  try {
    conn = dataSource.getConnection();                  Get connection

    stmt = conn.prepareStatement(SQL_SELECT_SPITTER);   Create statement

    stmt.setLong(1, id);             Bind parameter

    rs = stmt.executeQuery();        Execute query

    Spitter spitter = null;
    if (rs.next()) {                 Process results
      spitter = new Spitter();
      spitter.setId(rs.getLong("id"));
      spitter.setUsername(rs.getString("username"));
```

```
      spitter.setPassword(rs.getString("password"));
      spitter.setFullName(rs.getString("fullname"));
    }
    return spitter;
  } catch (SQLException e) {                         Handle exceptions
                                                     (somehow)
  } finally {
    if(rs != null) {
      try {                           Clean up
        rs.close();
      } catch(SQLException e) {}
    }

    if(stmt != null) {
      try {
      stmt.close();
      } catch(SQLException e) {}
    }

    if(conn != null) {
      try {
        conn.close();
      } catch(SQLException e) {}
    }
  }

  return null;
}
```

That's about as verbose as the insert and update examples—maybe more. It's like the Pareto principle[2] flipped on its head: 20 percent of the code is needed to actually query a row whereas 80 percent is boilerplate code.

By now you should see that much of JDBC code is boilerplate code for creating connections and statements and exception handling. With my point made, I'll end the torture here and not make you look at any more of this nasty code.

But the fact is that this boilerplate code is important. Cleaning up resources and handling errors is what makes data access robust. Without it, errors would go undetected and resources would be left open, leading to unpredictable code and resource leaks. So not only do we need this code, we also need to make sure that it's correct. This is all the more reason to let a framework deal with the boilerplate code so that we know that it's written once and written right.

5.3.2 Working with JDBC templates

Spring's JDBC framework will clean up your JDBC code by shouldering the burden of resource management and exception handling. This leaves you free to write only the code necessary to move data to and from the database.

[2] http://en.wikipedia.org/wiki/Pareto%27s_principle

As I explained in section 5.3.1, Spring abstracts away the boilerplate data access code behind template classes. For JDBC, Spring comes with three template classes to choose from:

- `JdbcTemplate`—The most basic of Spring's JDBC templates, this class provides simple access to a database through JDBC and simple indexed-parameter queries.
- `NamedParameterJdbcTemplate`—This JDBC template class enables you to perform queries where values are bound to named parameters in SQL, rather than indexed parameters.
- `SimpleJdbcTemplate`—This version of the JDBC template takes advantage of Java 5 features such as autoboxing, generics, and variable parameter lists to simplify how a JDBC template is used.

At one time, you had to weigh your choice of JDBC template carefully. But as of the most recent versions of Spring, the decision is much easier. In Spring 2.5, the named parameter features of `NamedParameterJdbcTemplate` were merged into `SimpleJdbcTemplate`. And as of Spring 3.0, support for older versions of Java (prior to Java 5) has been dropped—so there's almost no reason to choose the plain `JdbcTemplate` over `SimpleJdbcTemplate`. In light of these changes, we'll focus solely on `SimpleJdbcTemplate` in this chapter.

ACCESSING DATA USING SIMPLEJDBCTEMPLATE

All that a `SimpleJdbcTemplate` needs to do its work is a `DataSource`. This makes it easy enough to configure a `SimpleJdbcTemplate` bean in Spring with the following XML:

```
<bean id="jdbcTemplate"
      class="org.springframework.jdbc.core.simple.SimpleJdbcTemplate">
   <constructor-arg ref="dataSource" />
</bean>
```

The actual `DataSource` being referred to by the `dataSource` property can be any implementation of `javax.sql.DataSource`, including those we created in section 5.2.

Now we can wire the `jdbcTemplate` bean into our DAO and use it to access the database. For example, suppose that the Spitter DAO is written to use `SimpleJdbcTemplate`:

```
public class JdbcSpitterDAO implements SpitterDAO {
...
  private SimpleJdbcTemplate jdbcTemplate;
  public void setJdbcTemplate(SimpleJdbcTemplate jdbcTemplate) {
    this.jdbcTemplate = jdbcTemplate;
  }
}
```

You'd then wire the `jdbcTemplate` property of `JdbcSpitterDAO` as follows:

```
<bean id="spitterDao"
      class="com.habuma.spitter.persistence.SimpleJdbcTemplateSpitterDao">
  <property name="jdbcTemplate" ref="jdbcTemplate" />
</bean>
```

With a SimpleJdbcTemplate at our DAO's disposal, we can greatly simplify the addSpitter() method from listing 5.1. The new SimpleJdbcTemplate-based addSpitter() method is shown next.

Listing 5.4 A SimpleJdbcTemplate-based addSpitter() method

```
public void addSpitter(Spitter spitter) {
  jdbcTemplate.update(SQL_INSERT_SPITTER,          <- Update Spitter
          spitter.getUsername(),
          spitter.getPassword(),
          spitter.getFullName(),
          spitter.getEmail(),
          spitter.isUpdateByEmail());
  spitter.setId(queryForIdentity());
}
```

I think you'll agree that this version of addSpitter() is significantly simpler. There's no more connection or statement creation code—and no more exception-handling code. There's nothing but pure data insertion code.

Just because you don't see a lot of boilerplate code, that doesn't mean it's not there. It's cleverly hidden inside of the JDBC template class. When the update() method is called, SimpleJdbcTemplate will get a connection, create a statement, and execute the insert SQL.

What you also don't see is how the SQLException is handled. Internally, SimpleJdbcTemplate will catch any SQLExceptions that are thrown. It'll then translate the generic SQLException into one of the more specific data access exceptions from table 5.1 and rethrow it. Because Spring's data access exceptions are all runtime exceptions, we didn't have to catch it in the addSpitter() method.

Reading data is also simplified with JdbcTemplate. The following shows a new version of getSpitterById() that uses SimpleJdbcTemplate callbacks to map a result set to domain objects.

Listing 5.5 Querying for a Spitter using SimpleJdbcTemplate

```
public Spitter getSpitterById(long id) {
  return jdbcTemplate.queryForObject(               <- Queries for Spitter
          SQL_SELECT_SPITTER_BY_ID,
      new ParameterizedRowMapper<Spitter>() {
        public Spitter mapRow(ResultSet rs, int rowNum)
            throws SQLException {
          Spitter spitter = new Spitter();            <- Maps results to object
          spitter.setId(rs.getLong(1));
          spitter.setUsername(rs.getString(2));
          spitter.setPassword(rs.getString(3));
          spitter.setFullName(rs.getString(4));
          return spitter;
        }
      },
      id                                 <- Binds parameters
      );
}
```

This getSpitterById() method uses SimpleJdbcTemplate's queryForObject() method to query for a Spitter from the database. The queryForObject() method takes three parameters:

- A String containing the SQL to be used to select the data from the database
- A ParameterizedRowMapper object that extracts values from a ResultSet and constructs a domain object (in this case a Spitter)
- A variable argument list of values to be bound to indexed parameters of the query

The real magic happens in the ParameterizedRowMapper object. For every row that results from the query, JdbcTemplate will call the mapRow() method of the RowMapper. Within ParameterizedRowMapper, we've written the code that creates a Spitter object and populates it with values from the ResultSet.

Just like addSpitter(), the getSpitterById() method is free from JDBC boilerplate code. Unlike traditional JDBC, there's no resource management or exception-handling code. Methods that use SimpleJdbcTemplate are laser-focused on retrieving a Spitter object from the database.

USING NAMED PARAMETERS

The addSpitter() method in listing 5.4 used indexed parameters. This meant that we had to take notice of the order of the parameters in the query and list the values in the correct order when passing them to the update() method. If we were to ever change the SQL in such a way that the order of the parameters would change, we'd also need to change the order of the values.

Optionally, we could use named parameters. Named parameters let us give each parameter in the SQL an explicit name and to refer to the parameter by that name when binding values to the statement. For example, suppose that the SQL_INSERT_SPITTER query were defined as follows:

```
private static final String SQL_INSERT_SPITTER =
      "insert into spitter (username, password, fullname) " +
      "values (:username, :password, :fullname)";
```

With named parameter queries, the order of the bound values isn't important. We can bind each value by name. If the query changes and the order of the parameters is no longer the same, we won't have to change the binding code.

In Spring 2.0 you'd have to rely on a special JDBC template class called NamedParameterJdbcTemplate to use named parameter queries. Prior to Spring 2.0, it wasn't even possible. But starting with Spring 2.5, the named parameter features of NamedParameterJdbcTemplate have been merged into SimpleJdbcTemplate, so you're already set to update your addSpitter() method to use named parameters. The following listing shows the new named-parameter version of addSpitter().

Listing 5.6 Using named parameters with Spring JDBC templates

```
public void addSpitter(Spitter spitter) {
  Map<String, Object> params = new HashMap<String, Object>();
  params.put("username", spitter.getUsername());          // Bind parameters
  params.put("password", spitter.getPassword());
  params.put("fullname", spitter.getFullName());

  jdbcTemplate.update(SQL_INSERT_SPITTER, params);          // Perform insert
  spitter.setId(queryForIdentity());
}
```

The first thing you'll notice is that this version of `addSpitter()` is a bit longer than the previous version. That's because named parameters are bound through a `java.util.Map`. Nevertheless, every line is focused on the goal of inserting a `Spitter` object into the database. There's still no resource management or exception-handling code cluttering up the chief purpose of the method.

USING SPRING'S DAO SUPPORT CLASSES FOR JDBC

For each of our application's JDBC-backed DAO classes, we'll need to be sure to add a `SimpleJdbcTemplate` property and setter method. And we'll need to be sure to wire the `SimpleJdbcTemplate` bean into the `SimpleJdbcTemplate` property of each DAO. That's not a big deal if the application only has one DAO, but if you have multiple DAOs, that's a lot of repeated code.

One solution would be for you to create a common parent class for all your DAO objects where the `SimpleJdbcTemplate` property resides. Then all of your DAO classes would extend that class and use the parent class's `SimpleJdbcTemplate` for its data access. Figure 5.4 shows the proposed relationship between an application DAO and the base DAO class.

The idea of creating a base DAO class that holds the JDBC template is such a good idea that Spring comes with just such a base class out of the box. Actually, it comes with three such classes—`JdbcDaoSupport`, `SimpleJdbcDaoSupport`, and `NamedParameterJdbcDaoSupport`—one to mirror each of Spring's JDBC templates. To use one of these DAO support classes, start by changing your DAO class to extend it. For example:

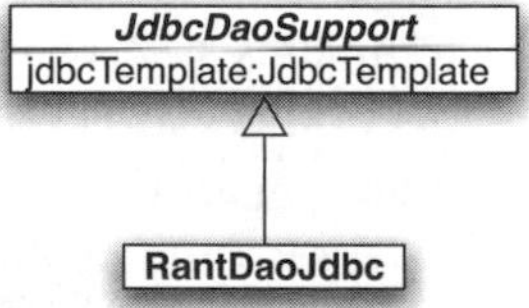

Figure 5.4 Spring's DAO support classes define a placeholder for the JDBC template objects so that subclasses won't have to manage their own JDBC templates.

```
public class JdbcSpitterDao extends SimpleJdbcDaoSupport
    implements SpitterDao {
...
}
```

The `SimpleJdbcDaoSupport` provides convenient access to the `SimpleJdbcTemplate` through the `getSimpleJdbcTemplate()` method. For example, the `addSpitter()` method may be written like this:

```
public void addSpitter(Spitter spitter) {
  getSimpleJdbcTemplate().update(SQL_INSERT_SPITTER,
          spitter.getUsername(),
          spitter.getPassword(),
          spitter.getFullName(),
          spitter.getEmail(),
          spitter.isUpdateByEmail());
  spitter.setId(queryForIdentity());
}
```

When configuring your DAO class in Spring, you could directly wire a `SimpleJdbcTemplate` bean into its `jdbcTemplate` property as follows:

```
<bean id="spitterDao"
      class="com.habuma.spitter.persistence.JdbcSpitterDao">
  <property name="jdbcTemplate" ref="jdbcTemplate" />
</bean>
```

This will work, but it isn't much different from how you configured the DAO that didn't extend `SimpleJdbcDaoSupport`. Alternatively, you can skip the middleman (or middle bean, as the case may be) and wire a data source directly into the `dataSource` property that `JdbcSpitterDao` inherits from `SimpleJdbcDaoSupport`:

```
<bean id="spitterDao"
      class="com.habuma.spitter.persistence.JdbcSpitterDao">
  <property name="dataSource" ref="dataSource" />
</bean>
```

When `JdbcSpitterDao` has its `dataSource` property configured, it'll internally create a `SimpleJdbcTemplate` instance for you. This eliminates the need to explicitly declare a `SimpleJdbcTemplate` bean in Spring.

JDBC is the most basic way to access data in a relational database. Spring's JDBC templates save you the hassle of dealing with the boilerplate code that handles connection resources and exception handling, leaving you to focus on the actual work of querying and updating data.

Even though Spring takes much of the pain out of working with JDBC, it can still become cumbersome as applications grow larger and more complex. To help manage the persistence challenges of large applications, you may want to graduate to a persistence framework such as Hibernate. Let's see how to plug Hibernate in the persistence layer of a Spring application.

5.4 Integrating Hibernate with Spring

When we were kids, riding a bike was fun, wasn't it? We'd ride to school in the mornings. When school let out, we'd cruise to our best friend's house. When it got late and our parents were yelling at us for staying out past dark, we'd peddle home for the night. Gee, those days were fun.

Then we grew up, and now we need more than a bike. Sometimes we have to travel a long distance to work. Groceries have to be hauled, and ours kids need to get to soccer practice. And if you live in Texas, air conditioning is a must! Our needs have simply outgrown our bikes.

JDBC is the bike of the persistence world. It's great for what it does, and for some jobs it works fine. But as our applications become more complex, so do our persistence requirements. We need to be able to map object properties to database columns and have our statements and queries created for us, freeing us from typing an endless string of question marks. We also need features that are more sophisticated:

- *Lazy loading*—As our object graphs become more complex, we sometimes don't want to fetch entire relationships immediately. To use a typical example, suppose we're selecting a collection of `PurchaseOrder` objects, and each of these objects contains a collection of `LineItem` objects. If we're only interested in `PurchaseOrder` attributes, it makes no sense to grab the `LineItem` data. This could be expensive. Lazy loading allows us to grab data only as it's needed.
- *Eager fetching*—This is the opposite of lazy loading. Eager fetching allows you to grab an entire object graph in one query. In the cases where we know that we need a `PurchaseOrder` object and its associated `LineItems`, eager fetching lets us get this from the database in one operation, saving us from costly round-trips.
- *Cascading*—Sometimes changes to a database table should result in changes to other tables as well. Going back to our purchase order example, when an `Order` object is deleted, we also want to delete the associated `LineItems` from the database.

Several frameworks are available that provide these services. The general name for these services is *object-relational mapping (ORM)*. Using an ORM tool for your persistence layer can save you literally thousands of lines of code and hours of development time. This lets you switch your focus from writing error-prone SQL code to addressing your application requirements.

Spring provides support for several persistence frameworks, including Hibernate, iBATIS, Java Data Objects (JDO), and the Java Persistence API (JPA).

As with Spring's JDBC support, Spring's support for ORM frameworks provides integration points to the frameworks as well as some additional services:

- Integrated support for Spring declarative transactions
- Transparent exception handling
- Thread-safe, lightweight template classes
- DAO support classes
- Resource management

I don't have enough space in this chapter to cover all of the ORM frameworks that are supported by Spring. That's okay, because Spring's support for one ORM solution is similar to the next. Once you get the hang of using one ORM framework with Spring, you'll find it easy to switch to another one.

Let's get started by looking at how Spring integrates with what's perhaps the most popular ORM framework in use—Hibernate. Later in this chapter, we'll also look at how Spring integrates with JPA (in section 5.5).

Hibernate is an open source persistence framework that has gained significant popularity in the developer community. It provides not only basic object-relational mapping but also all the other sophisticated features you'd expect from a full-featured ORM tool, such as caching, lazy loading, eager fetching, and distributed caching.

In this section, we'll focus on how Spring integrates with Hibernate, without dwelling too much on the intricate details of using Hibernate. If you need to learn more about working with Hibernate, I recommend either *Java Persistence with Hibernate* (Manning, 2006) or the Hibernate website at http://www.hibernate.org.

5.4.1 A Hibernate overview

In the previous section we looked at how to work with JDBC through Spring's JDBC templates. As it turns out, Spring's support for Hibernate offers a similar template class to abstract Hibernate persistence. Historically, `HibernateTemplate` was the way to work with Hibernate in a Spring application. Like its JDBC counterpart, `HibernateTemplate` took care of the intricacies of working with Hibernate by catching Hibernate-specific exceptions and rethrowing them as one of Spring's unchecked data access exceptions.

One of the responsibilities of `HibernateTemplate` is to manage Hibernate `Sessions`. This involves opening and closing sessions as well as ensuring one session per transaction. Without `HibernateTemplate`, you'd have no choice but to clutter your DAOs with boilerplate session management code.

The downside of `HibernateTemplate` is that it's somewhat intrusive. When we use Spring's `HibernateTemplate` in a DAO (whether directly or through `HibernateDaoSupport`), the DAO class is coupled to the Spring API. Although this may not be of much concern to some developers, others may find Spring's intrusion into their DAO code undesirable.

Even though `HibernateTemplate` is still around, it's no longer considered the best way of working with Hibernate. *Contextual sessions*, introduced in Hibernate 3, are a way in which Hibernate itself manages one `Session` per transaction. There's no need for `HibernateTemplate` to ensure this behavior. This keeps your DAO classes free of Spring-specific code.

Since contextual sessions are the accepted best practice for working with Hibernate, we'll focus on them and not spend any more time on `HibernateTemplate`. If you're still curious about `HibernateTemplate` and want to see how it works, I refer you to the second edition of this book or to the example code that can be downloaded from http://www.manning.com/walls4/, where I include a `HibernateTemplate` example.

Before we dive into working with Hibernate's contextual sessions, we need to set the stage for Hibernate by configuring a Hibernate session factory in Spring.

5.4.2 Declaring a Hibernate session factory

Natively, the main interface for working with Hibernate is `org.hibernate.Session`. The `Session` interface provides basic data access functionality such as the ability to save, update, delete, and load objects from the database. Through the Hibernate `Session`, an application's DAO will perform all of its persistence needs.

The standard way to get a reference to a Hibernate `Session` object is through an implementation of Hibernate's `SessionFactory` interface. Among other things, `SessionFactory` is responsible for opening, closing, and managing Hibernate `Session`s.

In Spring, the way to get a Hibernate `SessionFactory` is through one of Spring's Hibernate session factory beans. These session factory beans are implementations of Spring's `FactoryBean` interface that produce a Hibernate `SessionFactory` when wired into any property of type `SessionFactory`. This makes it possible to configure your Hibernate session factory alongside the other beans in your application's Spring context.

When it comes to configuring a Hibernate session factory bean, you have a choice to make. The decision hinges on whether you want to configure your persistent domain objects using Hibernate's XML mapping files or with annotations. If you choose to define your object-to-database mapping in XML, you'll need to configure `LocalSessionFactoryBean` in Spring :

```
<bean id="sessionFactory"
      class="org.springframework.orm.hibernate3.LocalSessionFactoryBean">
  <property name="dataSource" ref="dataSource" />
  <property name="mappingResources">
   <list>
    <value>Spitter.hbm.xml </value>
   </list>
  </property>
  <property name="hibernateProperties">
   <props>
    <prop key="dialect">org.hibernate.dialect.HSQLDialect</prop>
   </props>
  </property>
</bean>
```

`LocalSessionFactoryBean` is configured here with three properties. The `dataSource` property is wired with a reference to a `DataSource` bean. The `mappingResources` property lists one or more Hibernate mapping files that define the persistence strategy for the application. Finally, `hibernateProperties` is where we configure the minutia of how Hibernate should operate. In this case, we're saying that Hibernate will be working with a Hypersonic database and should use the `HSQLDialect` to construct SQL accordingly.

If annotation-oriented persistence is more your style, then you'll need to use `AnnotationSessionFactoryBean` instead of `LocalSessionFactoryBean`:

```
<bean id="sessionFactory"
      class="org.springframework.orm.hibernate3.annotation.
  ➥AnnotationSessionFactoryBean">
  <property name="dataSource" ref="dataSource" />
  <property name="packagesToScan"
```

```
      value="com.habuma.spitter.domain" />
  <property name="hibernateProperties">
    <props>
      <prop key="dialect">org.hibernate.dialect.HSQLDialect</prop>
    </props>
  </property>
</bean>
```

As with `LocalSessionFactoryBean`, the `dataSource` and `hibernateProperties` properties tell where to find a database connection and what kind of database we'll be dealing with.

But instead of listing Hibernate mapping files, we can use the `packagesToScan` property to tell Spring to scan one or more packages looking for domain classes that are annotated for persistence with Hibernate. This includes classes that are annotated with JPA's `@Entity` or `@MappedSuperclass` and Hibernate's own `@Entity` annotation.

A list of one

`AnnotationSessionFactoryBean`'s `packagesToScan` property takes an array of `String`s specifying the packages to look for persistent classes in. Normally, I might specify such a list as follows:

```
<property name="packagesToScan">
    <list>
        <value>com.habuma.spitter.domain</value>
    </list>
</property>
```

But since I'm only asking it to scan a single package, I'm taking advantage of a built-in property editor that automatically converts a single `String` value into a `String` array.

If you'd prefer, you may also explicitly list out all of your application's persistent classes by specifying a list of fully qualified class names in the `annotatedClasses` property:

```
<property name="annotatedClasses">
    <list>
        <value>com.habuma.spitter.domain.Spitter</value>
        <value>com.habuma.spitter.domain.Spittle</value>
   </list>
</property>
```

The `annotatedClasses` property is fine for hand-picking a few domain classes. But `packagesToScan` is more appropriate if you have a lot of domain classes and don't want to list them all or if you want the freedom to add or remove domain classes without revisiting the Spring configuration.

With a Hibernate session factory bean declared in the Spring application context, we're ready to start creating our DAO classes.

5.4.3 Building Spring-free Hibernate

As mentioned before, without contextual sessions, Spring's Hibernate templates would handle the task of ensuring one session per transaction. But now that Hibernate manages this, there's no need for a template class. That means that you can wire a Hibernate session directly into your DAO classes.

Listing 5.7 Hibernate's contextual sessions enable Spring-free Hibernate DAOs.

```
package com.habuma.spitter.persistence;
import java.util.List;
import org.hibernate.SessionFactory;
import org.hibernate.classic.Session;
import org.springframework.beans.factory.annotation.Autowired;
import org.springframework.stereotype.Repository;
import com.habuma.spitter.domain.Spitter;
import com.habuma.spitter.domain.Spittle;

@Repository
public class HibernateSpitterDao implements SpitterDao {
  private SessionFactory sessionFactory;

  @Autowired
  public HibernateSpitterDao(SessionFactory sessionFactory) {     // Construct DAO
    this.sessionFactory = sessionFactory;
  }

  private Session currentSession() {
    return sessionFactory.getCurrentSession();    // Retrieve current Session from SessionFactory
  }

  public void addSpitter(Spitter spitter) {
    currentSession().save(spitter);                // Use current Session
  }

  public Spitter getSpitterById(long id) {
    return (Spitter) currentSession().get(Spitter.class, id);
  }

  public void saveSpitter(Spitter spitter) {
    currentSession().update(spitter);
  }
...
}
```

There are several things to take note of in listing 5.7. First, note that we're using Spring's `@Autowired` annotation to have Spring automatically inject a `SessionFactory` into `HibernateSpitterDao`'s `sessionFactory` property. Then, in the `currentSession()` method, we use that `SessionFactory` to get the current transaction's session.

Also note that we've annotated the class with `@Repository`. This accomplishes two things for us. First, `@Repository` is another one of Spring's stereotype annotations that, among other things, are scanned by Spring's `<context:component-scan>`. This means that we won't have to explicitly declare a `HibernateSpitterDao` bean, as long as we configure `<context:component-scan>` like so:

```
<context:component-scan
     base-package="com.habuma.spitter.persistence" />
```

In addition to helping to reduce XML-based configuration, `@Repository` serves another purpose. Recall that one of the jobs of a template class is to catch platform-specific exceptions and rethrow them as one of Spring's unified unchecked exceptions. But if we're using Hibernate contextual sessions and not a Hibernate template, then how can the exception translation take place?

To add exception translation to a template-less Hibernate DAO, we just need to add a `PersistenceExceptionTranslationPostProcessor` bean to the Spring application context:

```
<bean class="org.springframework.dao.annotation.
  ➥PersistenceExceptionTranslationPostProcessor"/>
```

`PersistenceExceptionTranslationPostProcessor` is a bean post processor which adds an advisor to any bean that's annotated with `@Repository` so that any platform-specific exceptions are caught and then rethrown as one of Spring's unchecked data access exceptions.

And now the Hibernate version of our DAO is complete. And we were about to develop it without directly depending on any Spring-specific classes (aside from the `@Repository` annotation). That same template-less approach can also be applied when developing a pure JPA-based DAO. So, let's take one more stab at developing a `SpitterDao` implementation, this time using JPA.

5.5 Spring and the Java Persistence API

From its beginning, the EJB specification has included the concept of entity beans. In EJB, *entity beans* are a type of EJB that describes business objects that are persisted in a relational database. Entity beans have undergone several tweaks over the years, including *bean-managed persistence (BMP)* entity beans and *container-managed persistence (CMP)* entity beans.

Entity beans both enjoyed the rise and suffered the fall of EJB's popularity. In recent years, developers have traded in their heavyweight EJBs for simpler POJO-based development. This presented a challenge to the Java Community Process to shape the new EJB specification around POJOs. The result is JSR-220—also known as *EJB 3*.

The Java Persistence API (JPA) emerged out of the rubble of EJB 2's entity beans as the next-generation Java persistence standard. JPA is a POJO-based persistence mechanism that draws ideas from both Hibernate and *Java Data Objects (JDO)*, and mixes Java 5 annotations in for good measure.

With the Spring 2.0 release came the premiere of Spring integration with JPA. The irony is that many blame (or credit) Spring with the demise of EJB. But now that Spring provides support for JPA, many developers are recommending JPA for persistence in Spring-based applications. In fact, some say that Spring-JPA is the dream team for POJO development.

The first step toward using JPA with Spring is to configure an entity manager factory as a bean in the Spring application context.

5.5.1 Configuring an entity manager factory

In a nutshell, JPA-based applications use an implementation of `EntityManagerFactory` to get an instance of an `EntityManager`. The JPA specification defines two kinds of entity managers:

- *Application-managed*—Entity managers are created when an application directly requests one from an entity manager factory. With application-managed entity managers, the application is responsible for opening or closing entity managers and involving the entity manager in transactions. This type of entity manager is most appropriate for use in standalone applications that don't run within a Java EE container.
- *Container-managed*—Entity managers are created and managed by a Java EE container. The application doesn't interact with the entity manager factory at all. Instead, entity managers are obtained directly through injection or from JNDI. The container is responsible for configuring the entity manager factories. This type of entity manager is most appropriate for use by a Java EE container that wants to maintain some control over JPA configuration beyond what's specified in persistence.xml.

Both kinds of entity manager implement the same `EntityManager` interface. The key difference isn't in the `EntityManager` itself, but rather in how the `EntityManager` is created and managed. Application-managed `EntityManagers` are created by an `EntityManagerFactory` obtained by calling the `createEntityManagerFactory()` method of the `PersistenceProvider`. Meanwhile, container-managed `EntityManagerFactorys` are obtained through `PersistenceProvider`'s `createContainerEntityManagerFactory()` method.

So what does this all mean for Spring developers wanting to use JPA? Not much. Regardless of which variety of `EntityManagerFactory` you want to use, Spring will take responsibility for managing `EntityManagers` for you. If using an application-managed entity manager, Spring plays the role of an application and transparently deals with the `EntityManager` on your behalf. In the container-managed scenario, Spring plays the role of the container.

Each flavor of entity manager factory is produced by a corresponding Spring factory bean:

- `LocalEntityManagerFactoryBean` produces an application-managed `EntityManagerFactory`.
- `LocalContainerEntityManagerFactoryBean` produces a container-managed `EntityManagerFactory`.

It's important to point out that the choice made between an application-managed `EntityManagerFactory` and a container-managed `EntityManagerFactory` is completely transparent to a Spring-based application. Spring's `JpaTemplate` hides the intricate details of dealing with either form of `EntityManagerFactory`, leaving your data access code to focus on its true purpose: data access.

The only real difference between application-managed and container-managed entity manager factories, as far as Spring is concerned, is how each is configured within the Spring application context. Let's start by looking at how to configure the application-managed `LocalEntityManagerFactoryBean` in Spring. Then we'll see how to configure a container-managed `LocalContainerEntityManagerFactoryBean`.

CONFIGURING APPLICATION-MANAGED JPA

Application-managed entity manager factories derive most of their configuration information from a configuration file called persistence.xml. This file must appear in the META-INF directory within the classpath.

The purpose of the persistence.xml file is to define one or more persistence units. A persistence unit is a grouping of one or more persistent classes that correspond to a single data source. In simple terms, persistence.xml enumerates one or more persistent classes along with any additional configuration such as data sources and XML-based mapping files. Here's a typical example of a persistence.xml file as it pertains to the Spitter application:

```
<persistence xmlns="http://java.sun.com/xml/ns/persistence"
    version="1.0">
  <persistence-unit name="spitterPU">
    <class>com.habuma.spitter.domain.Spitter</class>
    <class>com.habuma.spitter.domain.Spittle</class>
    <properties>
      <property name="toplink.jdbc.driver"
          value="org.hsqldb.jdbcDriver" />
      <property name="toplink.jdbc.url" value=
          "jdbc:hsqldb:hsql://localhost/spitter/spitter" />
      <property name="toplink.jdbc.user"
          value="sa" />
      <property name="toplink.jdbc.password"
          value="" />
    </properties>
  </persistence-unit>
</persistence>
```

Because so much configuration goes into a persistence.xml file, little configuration is required (or even possible) in Spring. The following <bean> declares a `LocalEntityManagerFactoryBean` in Spring:

```
<bean id="emf"
      class="org.springframework.orm.jpa.LocalEntityManagerFactoryBean">
  <property name="persistenceUnitName" value="spitterPU" />
</bean>
```

The value given to the `persistenceUnitName` property refers to the persistence unit name as it appears in persistence.xml.

The reason why much of what goes into creating an application-managed `EntityManagerFactory` is contained in persistence.xml has everything to do with what it means to be application managed. In the application-managed scenario (not involving Spring), an application is entirely responsible for obtaining an `EntityManagerFactory` through the JPA implementation's `PersistenceProvider`. The application code would become incredibly bloated if it had to define the persistence unit every time it requested an `EntityManagerFactory`. By specifying it in persistence.xml, JPA can look in this well-known location for persistence unit definitions.

But with Spring's support for JPA, we'll never deal directly with the `PersistenceProvider`. Therefore, it seems silly to extract configuration information into persistence.xml. In fact, doing so prevents us from configuring the `EntityManagerFactory` in Spring (so that, for example, we can provide a Spring-configured data source).

For that reason, we should turn our attention to container-managed JPA.

CONFIGURING CONTAINER-MANAGED JPA

Container-managed JPA takes a different approach. When running within a container, an `EntityManagerFactory` can be produced using information provided by the container—Spring, in our case.

Instead of configuring data source details in persistence.xml, you can configure this information in the Spring application context. For example, the following `<bean>` declaration shows how to configure container-managed JPA in Spring using `LocalContainerEntityManagerFactoryBean`.

```
<bean id="emf" class=
      "org.springframework.orm.jpa.LocalContainerEntityManagerFactoryBean">
  <property name="dataSource" ref="dataSource" />
  <property name="jpaVendorAdapter" ref="jpaVendorAdapter" />
</bean>
```

Here we've configured the `dataSource` property with a Spring-configured data source. Any implementation of `javax.sql.DataSource` is appropriate, such as those that we configured in section 5.2. Although a data source may still be configured in persistence.xml, the data source specified through this property takes precedence.

The `jpaVendorAdapter` property can be used to provide specifics about the particular JPA implementation to use. Spring comes with a handful of JPA vendor adaptors to choose from:

- `EclipseLinkJpaVendorAdapter`
- `HibernateJpaVendorAdapter`
- `OpenJpaVendorAdapter`
- `TopLinkJpaVendorAdapter`

In this case, we're using Hibernate as a JPA implementation, so we've configured it with a `HibernateJpaVendorAdapter`:

```
<bean id="jpaVendorAdapter"
      class="org.springframework.orm.jpa.vendor.HibernateJpaVendorAdapter">
  <property name="database" value="HSQL" />
  <property name="showSql" value="true"/>
  <property name="generateDdl" value="false"/>
  <property name="databasePlatform"
          value="org.hibernate.dialect.HSQLDialect" />
</bean>
```

Database platform	Value for `database` property
IBM DB2	DB2
Apache Derby	DERBY
H2	H2
Hypersonic	HSQL
Informix	INFORMIX
MySQL	MYSQL
Oracle	ORACLE
PostgresQL	POSTGRESQL
Microsoft SQL Server	SQLSERVER
Sybase	SYBASE

Table 5.5 The Hibernate JPA vendor adapter supports several databases. You can specify which database to use by setting its `database` property.

Several properties are set on the vendor adapter, but the most important one is the `database` property, where we've specified the Hypersonic database as the database we'll be using. Other values supported for this property include those listed in table 5.5.

Certain dynamic persistence features require that the class of persistent objects be modified with instrumentation to support the feature. Objects whose properties are lazily loaded (they won't be retrieved from the database until they're accessed) must have their class instrumented with code that knows to retrieve unloaded data upon access. Some frameworks use dynamic proxies to implement lazy loading. Others, such as JDO, perform class instrumentation at compile time.

Which entity manager factory bean you choose will depend primarily on how you'll use it. For simple applications, `LocalEntityManagerFactoryBean` may be sufficient. But because `LocalContainerEntityManagerFactoryBean` enables us to configure more of JPA in Spring, it's an attractive choice and likely the one that you'll choose for production use.

PULLING AN ENTITYMANAGERFACTORY FROM JNDI

It's also worth noting that if you're deploying your Spring application in some application servers, an `EntityManagerFactory` may have already been created for you and may be waiting in JNDI to be retrieved. In that case, you can use the `<jee:jndi-lookup>` element from Spring's `jee` namespace to nab a reference to the `EntityManagerFactory`:

```
<jee:jndi-lookup id="emf" jndi-name="persistence/spitterPU" />
```

Regardless of how you get your hands on an `EntityManagerFactory`, once you have one, you're ready to start writing a DAO. Let's do that now.

5.5.2 *Writing a JPA-based DAO*

Just like all of Spring's other persistence integration options, Spring-JPA integration comes in template form with `JpaTemplate` and a corresponding `JpaDaoSupport` class. Nevertheless, template-based JPA has been set aside in favor of a pure JPA approach. This is analogous to the Hibernate contextual sessions that we used in section 5.4.3.

Since pure JPA is favored over template-based JPA, we'll focus on building Spring-free JPA DAOs in this section. Specifically, `JpaSpitterDao` in the following listing shows how to develop a JPA DAO without resorting to using Spring's `JpaTemplate`.

Listing 5.8 A pure JPA DAO doesn't use any Spring templates.

```
package com.habuma.spitter.persistence;
import java.util.List;

import javax.persistence.EntityManager;
import javax.persistence.PersistenceContext;

import org.springframework.dao.DataAccessException;
import org.springframework.stereotype.Repository;
import org.springframework.transaction.annotation.Transactional;

import com.habuma.spitter.domain.Spitter;
import com.habuma.spitter.domain.Spittle;

@Repository("spitterDao")
@Transactional
public class JpaSpitterDao implements SpitterDao {
  private static final String RECENT_SPITTLES =
      "SELECT s FROM Spittle s";
  private static final String ALL_SPITTERS =
      "SELECT s FROM Spitter s";
  private static final String SPITTER_FOR_USERNAME =
      "SELECT s FROM Spitter s WHERE s.username = :username";
  private static final String SPITTLES_BY_USERNAME =
      "SELECT s FROM Spittle s WHERE s.spitter.username = :username";

  @PersistenceContext
  private EntityManager em;                       <- Inject EntityManager

  public void addSpitter(Spitter spitter) {
    em.persist(spitter);                          <- Use EntityManager
  }

  public Spitter getSpitterById(long id) {
    return em.find(Spitter.class, id);
  }

  public void saveSpitter(Spitter spitter) {
    em.merge(spitter);
  }
...
}
```

JpaSpitterDao uses a EntityManager to handle persistence. By working with a EntityManager, the DAO remains pure and resembles how a similar DAO may appear in a non-Spring application. But where does it get the EntityManager?

Note that the em property is annotated with @PersistentContext. Put plainly, that annotation indicates that an instance of EntityManager should be injected into em. To enable EntityManager injection in Spring, we'll need to configure a PersistenceAnnotationBeanPostProcessor in Spring's application context:

```
<bean class="org.springframework.orm.jpa.support.
    ➥PersistenceAnnotationBeanPostProcessor"/>
```

You may have also noticed that JpaSpitterDao is annotated with @Repository and @Transactional. @Transactional indicates that the persistence methods in this DAO will be involved in a transactional context. We'll talk more about @Transactional in the next chapter when we cover Spring's support for declarative transactions.

As for @Repository, it serves the same purpose here as it did when we developed the Hibernate contextual session version of the DAO. Without a template to handle exception translation, we need to annotate our DAO with @Repository so that PersistenceExceptionTranslationPostProcessor will know that this is one of those beans for whom exceptions should be translated into one of Spring's unified data access exceptions.

Speaking of PersistenceExceptionTranslationPostProcessor, we'll need to remember to wire it up as a bean in Spring just as we did for the Hibernate example:

```
<bean class="org.springframework.dao.annotation.
   ➥PersistenceExceptionTranslationPostProcessor"/>
```

Note that exception translation, whether it be with JPA or Hibernate, isn't mandatory. If you'd prefer that your DAO throw JPA-specific or Hibernate-specific exceptions, then you're welcome to forgo PersistenceExceptionTranslationPostProcessor and let the native exceptions flow freely. But if you do use Spring's exception translation, you'll be unifying all of your data access exceptions under Spring's exception hierarchy, which will make it easier to swap out persistence mechanisms later.

5.6 Summary

Data is the life blood of an application. Some of the data-centric among us may even contend that data *is* the application. With such significance being placed on data, it's important that we develop the data access portion of our applications in a way that's robust, simple, and clear.

Spring's support for JDBC and ORM frameworks takes the drudgery out of data access by handling common boilerplate code that exists in all persistence mechanisms, leaving you to focus on the specifics of data access as they pertain to your application.

One way that Spring simplifies data access is by managing the lifecycle of database connections and ORM framework sessions, ensuring that they're opened and closed as necessary. In this way, management of persistence mechanisms is virtually transparent to your application code.

Also, Spring can catch framework-specific exceptions (some of which are checked exceptions) and convert them to one of a hierarchy of unchecked exceptions that are consistent among all persistence frameworks supported by Spring. This includes converting nebulous `SQLExceptions` thrown by JDBC into meaningful exceptions that describe the actual problem that led to the exception being thrown.

In this chapter, we saw how to build the persistence layer of a Spring application using JDBC, Hibernate, or JPA. Which you choose is largely a matter of taste, but because we developed our persistence layer behind a common Java interface, the rest of our application can remain unaware of how data is ferried to and from the database.

Transaction management is another aspect of data access that Spring can make simple and transparent. In the next chapter, we'll explore how to use Spring AOP for declarative transaction management.

6 Managing transactions

This chapter covers

- Integrating with transaction managers
- Managing transactions programmatically
- Using declarative transactions
- Describing transactions using annotations

Take a moment to recall your younger days. If you were like many children, you spent more than a few carefree moments on the playground swinging on the swings, traversing the monkey bars, getting dizzy while spinning on the merry-go-round, and going up and down on the teeter-totter.

The problem with the teeter-totter is that it's practically impossible to enjoy on your own. To truly enjoy a teeter-totter, you need another person: you and a friend both have to agree to play on the teeter-totter. This agreement is an all-or-nothing proposition. Either both of you will teeter-totter or you won't. If either of you fails to take your respective seat on each end of the teeter-totter, then there will be no teeter-tottering—just a sad kid sitting motionless on the end of a slanted board.[1]

[1] Since the first edition of this book, I've confirmed that this qualifies as the most uses of the word *teeter-totter* in a technical book. That's a bit of trivia to challenge your friends with.

In software, all-or-nothing operations are called *transactions*. Transactions allow you to group several operations into a single unit of work that either fully happens or fully doesn't happen. If everything goes well, then the transaction is a success. But if anything goes wrong, the slate is wiped clean and it's as if nothing ever happened.

Probably the most common example of a real-world transaction is a money transfer. Imagine that you were to transfer $100 from your savings account to your checking account. The transfer involves two operations: $100 is deducted from the savings account and $100 is added to the checking account. The money transfer must be performed completely or not at all. If the deduction from the savings account works but the deposit into the checking account fails, you'll be out $100 (good for the bank, bad for you). On the other hand, if the deduction fails but the deposit succeeds, you'll be ahead $100 (good for you, bad for the bank). It's best for both parties involved if the entire transfer is rolled back if either operation fails.

In the previous chapter, we examined Spring's data access support and saw several ways to read from and write data to the database. When writing to a database, we must ensure that the integrity of the data is maintained by performing the updates within a transaction. Spring has rich support for transaction management, both programmatic and declarative. In this chapter, we'll see how to apply transactions to your application code so that when things go right, they're made permanent. And when things go wrong... nobody needs to know. (Almost nobody. You may still want to log the problem for the sake of auditing.)

6.1 Understanding transactions

To illustrate transactions, consider the purchase of a movie ticket. Purchasing a ticket typically involves the following actions:

- The number of available seats will be examined to verify that enough seats are available for your purchase.
- The number of available seats is decremented by one for each ticket purchased.
- You provide payment for the ticket.
- The ticket is issued to you.

If everything goes well, you'll be enjoying a blockbuster movie and the theater will be a few dollars richer. But what if something goes wrong? For instance, what if you paid with a credit card that had reached its limit? Certainly, you wouldn't receive a ticket and the theater wouldn't receive payment. If the number of seats isn't reset to its value before the purchase, the movie may artificially run out of seats (and thus lose sales). Or consider what would happen if everything else works fine but the ticket issue fails. You'd be short a few dollars and be stuck at home watching reruns on cable TV.

To ensure that neither you nor the theater loses out, these actions should be wrapped in a transaction. As a transaction, they're all treated as a single action, guaranteeing that either they'll all fully succeed or all be rolled back as if these steps never happened. Figure 6.1 illustrates how this transaction plays out.

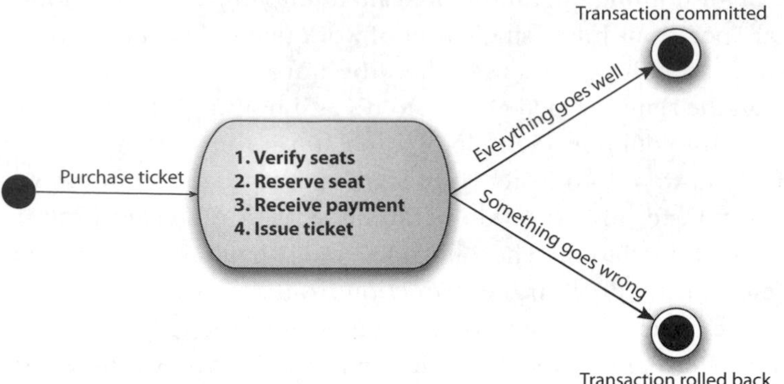

Figure 6.1 The steps involved when purchasing a movie ticket should be all or nothing. If every step is successful, then the entire transaction is successful. Otherwise, the steps should be rolled back—as if they never happened.

Transactions play an important role in software, ensuring that data and resources are never left in an inconsistent state. Without them, there's potential for data to be corrupted or inconsistent with the business rules of the application.

Before we get too carried away with Spring's transaction support, it's important to understand the key ingredients of a transaction. Let's take a quick look at the four factors that guide transactions and how they work.

6.1.1 Explaining transactions in only four words

In the grand tradition of software development, an acronym has been created to describe transactions: *ACID*. In short, ACID stands for

- *Atomic*—Transactions are made up of one or more activities bundled together as a single unit of work. Atomicity ensures that all the operations in the transaction happen or that none of them happen. If all the activities succeed, the transaction is a success. If any of the activities fails, the entire transaction fails and is rolled back.
- *Consistent*—Once a transaction ends (whether successful or not), the system is left in a state consistent with the business that it models. The data shouldn't be corrupted with respect to reality.
- *Isolated*—Transactions should allow multiple users to work with the same data, without each user's work getting tangled up with the others. Therefore, transactions should be isolated from each other, preventing concurrent reads and writes to the same data from occurring. (Note that isolation typically involves locking rows and/or tables in a database.)
- *Durable*—Once the transaction has completed, the results of the transaction should be made permanent so that they'll survive any sort of system crash. This typically involves storing the results in a database or some other form of persistent storage.

In the movie ticket example, a transaction could ensure atomicity by undoing the result of all the steps if any step fails. Atomicity supports consistency by ensuring that the system's data is never left in an inconsistent, partially done state. Isolation also supports consistency by preventing another concurrent transaction from stealing seats out from under you while you're still in the process of purchasing them.

Finally, the effects are durable because they'll have been committed to some persistent storage. In the event of a system crash or other catastrophic event, you shouldn't have to worry about results of the transaction being lost.

For a more detailed explanation of transactions, I suggest that you read Martin Fowler's *Patterns of Enterprise Application Architecture* (Addison-Wesley Professional, 2002). Specifically, chapter 5 discusses concurrency and transactions.

Now that you know the makings of a transaction, let's see the transaction capabilities available to a Spring application.

6.1.2 Understanding Spring's transaction management support

Spring, like EJB, provides support for both programmatic and declarative transaction management. But Spring's transaction management capabilities exceed those of EJB.

Spring's support for programmatic transaction management differs greatly from that of EJB. Unlike EJB, which is coupled with a Java Transaction API (JTA) implementation, Spring employs a callback mechanism that abstracts away the actual transaction implementation from the transactional code. In fact, Spring's transaction management support doesn't even require a JTA implementation. If your application uses only a single persistent resource, Spring can use the transactional support offered by the persistence mechanism. This includes JDBC, Hibernate, and the Java Persistence API (JPA). But if your application has transaction requirements that span multiple resources, Spring can support distributed (XA) transactions using a third-party JTA implementation. We'll discuss Spring's support for programmatic transactions in section 6.3.

Where programmatic transaction management affords you flexibility in precisely defining transaction boundaries in your code, declarative transactions (which are based on Spring AOP) help you decouple an operation from its transaction rules. Spring's support for declarative transactions is reminiscent of EJB's *container-managed transactions (CMTs)*. Both allow you to define transaction boundaries declaratively. But Spring's declarative transactions go beyond CMTs by allowing you to declare additional attributes such as isolation level and timeouts. We'll begin working with Spring's declarative transaction support in section 6.4.

Choosing between programmatic and declarative transaction management is largely a decision of fine-grained control versus convenience. When you program transactions into your code, you gain precise control over transaction boundaries, beginning and ending them precisely where you want. Typically, you won't require the fine-grained control offered by programmatic transactions and will choose to declare your transactions in the context definition file.

Regardless of whether you choose to program transactions into your beans or to declare them as aspects, you'll be using a Spring transaction manager to interface with a platform-specific transaction implementation. Let's see how Spring's transaction managers free you from dealing directly with platform-specific transaction implementations.

6.2 Choosing a transaction manager

Spring doesn't directly manage transactions. Instead, it comes with a selection of transaction managers that delegate responsibility for transaction management to a platform-specific transaction implementation provided by either JTA or the persistence mechanism. Spring's transaction managers are listed in table 6.1.

Each of these transaction managers acts as a facade to a platform-specific transaction implementation. (Figure 6.2 illustrates the relationship between transaction managers and the underlying platform implementations for a few of the transaction managers.) This makes it possible for you to work with a transaction in Spring with little regard to what the actual transaction implementation is.

Table 6.1 Spring has transaction managers for every occasion.

Transaction manager (`org.springframework.*`)	Use it when...
`jca.cci.connection.CciLocalTransactionManager`	Using Spring's support for Java EE Connector Architecture (JCA) and the Common Client Interface (CCI).
`jdbc.datasource.DataSourceTransactionManager`	Working with Spring's JDBC abstraction support. Also useful when using iBATIS for persistence.
`jms.connection.JmsTransactionManager`	Using JMS 1.1+.
`jms.connection.JmsTransactionManager102`	Using JMS 1.0.2.
`orm.hibernate3.HibernateTransactionManager`	Using Hibernate 3 for persistence.
`orm.jdo.JdoTransactionManager`	Using JDO for persistence.
`orm.jpa.JpaTransactionManager`	Using the Java Persistence API (JPA) for persistence.
`transaction.jta.JtaTransactionManager`	You need distributed transactions or when no other transaction manager fits the need.
`transaction.jta.OC4JJtaTransactionManager`	Using Oracle's OC4J JEE container.
`transaction.jta.WebLogicJtaTransactionManager`	You need distributed transactions and your application is running within WebLogic.
`transaction.jta.WebSphereUowTransactionManager`	You need transactions managed by a `UOWManager` in WebSphere.

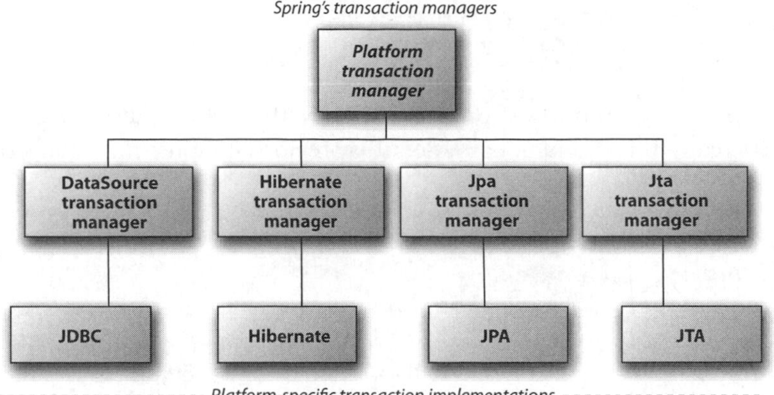

Figure 6.2 Spring's transaction managers delegate transaction-management responsibility to platform-specific transaction implementations.

To use a transaction manager, you'll need to declare it in your application context. In this section, you'll learn how to configure a few of Spring's most commonly used transaction managers, starting with `DataSourceTransactionManager`, which provides transaction support for plain JDBC and iBATIS.

6.2.1 JDBC transactions

If you're using straight JDBC for your application's persistence, `DataSourceTransactionManager` will handle transactional boundaries for you. To use `DataSourceTransactionManager`, wire it into your application's context definition using the following XML:

```
<bean id="transactionManager" class="org.springframework.jdbc.
    ➥datasource.DataSourceTransactionManager">
  <property name="dataSource" ref="dataSource"/>
</bean>
```

Note that the `dataSource` property is set with a reference to a bean named `dataSource`. Presumably, the `dataSource` bean is a `javax.sql.DataSource` bean defined elsewhere in your context definition file.

Behind the scenes, `DataSourceTransactionManager` manages transactions by making calls on the `java.sql.Connection` object retrieved from the `DataSource`. For instance, a successful transaction is committed by calling the `commit()` method on the connection. Likewise, a failed transaction is rolled back by calling the `rollback()` method.

6.2.2 Hibernate transactions

If your application's persistence is handled by Hibernate then you'll want to use `HibernateTransactionManager`. For Hibernate 3, you'll need to add the following <bean> declaration to the Spring context definition:

```
<bean id="transactionManager" class="org.springframework.
    ➥orm.hibernate3.HibernateTransactionManager">
  <property name="sessionFactory" ref="sessionFactory"/>
</bean>
```

The `sessionFactory` property should be wired with a Hibernate `SessionFactory`, here cleverly named `sessionFactory`. See the previous chapter for details on setting up a Hibernate session factory.

> **What if I'm using Hibernate 2?**
>
> If you're using the older Hibernate 2 for persistence, you won't be able to use the `HibernateTransactionManager` in Spring 3.0 or even Spring 2.5. Those versions of Spring don't include support for Hibernate 2. You'll have to go back to using Spring 2.0 if you insist on using an older version of Hibernate.
>
> But, if you roll back to using an older version of Spring with your older version of Hibernate, you should realize that you'll be giving up a lot of Spring features that we'll be talking about in this book. So, rather than roll back to an older version of Spring, I recommend upgrading to Hibernate 3.

`HibernateTransactionManager` delegates responsibility for transaction management to an `org.hibernate.Transaction` object that it retrieves from the Hibernate session. When a transaction successfully completes, `HibernateTransactionManager` will call the `commit()` method on the `Transaction` object. Similarly, when a transaction fails, the `rollback()` method will be called on the `Transaction` object.

6.2.3 Java Persistence API transactions

Hibernate has been Java's de facto persistence standard for a few years, but now the Java Persistence API (JPA) has entered the scene as the true standard for Java persistence. If you're ready to move up to JPA then you'll want to use Spring's `JpaTransactionManager` to coordinate transactions. Here's how you might configure `JpaTransactionManager` in Spring:

```
<bean id="transactionManager"
    class="org.springframework.orm.jpa.JpaTransactionManager">
  <property name="entityManagerFactory" ref="entityManagerFactory" />
</bean>
```

`JpaTransactionManager` only needs to be wired with a JPA entity manager factory (any implementation of `javax.persistence.EntityManagerFactory`). `JpaTransactionManager` will collaborate with the JPA `EntityManager` produced by the factory to conduct transactions.

In addition to applying transactions to JPA operations, `JpaTransactionManager` also supports transactions on simple JDBC operations on the same `DataSource` used by `EntityManagerFactory`. For this to work, `JpaTransactionManager` must also be wired with an implementation of `JpaDialect`. For example, suppose that you've configured `EclipseLinkJpaDialect` as follows:

```
<bean id="jpaDialect"
    class="org.springframework.orm.jpa.vendor.EclipseLinkJpaDialect" />
```

Then you must wire the jpaDialect bean into the JpaTransactionManager like this:

```
<bean id="transactionManager"
      class="org.springframework.orm.jpa.JpaTransactionManager">
  <property name="entityManagerFactory" ref="entityManagerFactory" />
  <property name="jpaDialect" ref="jpaDialect" />
</bean>
```

It's important to note that the JpaDialect implementation must support mixed JPA/JDBC access for this to work. All of Spring's vendor-specific implementations of JpaDialect (EclipseLinkJpaDialect, HibernateJpaDialect, OpenJpaDialect, and TopLinkJpaDialect) provide support for mixing JPA with JDBC. DefaultJpaDialect doesn't.

6.2.4 Java transaction API transactions

If none of the aforementioned transaction managers meet your needs or if your transactions span multiple transaction sources (for example, two or more different databases), you'll need to use JtaTransactionManager:

```
<bean id="transactionManager" class="org.springframework.
      ➥transaction.jta.JtaTransactionManager">
  <property name="transactionManagerName"
      value="java:/TransactionManager" />
</bean>
```

JtaTransactionManager delegates transaction management responsibility to a JTA implementation. JTA specifies a standard API to coordinate transactions between an application and one or more data sources. The transactionManagerName property specifies a JTA transaction manager to be looked up via JNDI.

JtaTransactionManager works with javax.transaction.UserTransaction and javax.transaction.TransactionManager objects, delegating responsibility for transaction management to those objects. A successful transaction will be committed with a call to the UserTransaction.commit() method. Likewise, if the transaction fails, the UserTransaction's rollback() method will be called.

By now, it should be clear which of Spring's transaction managers is a best fit for the Spitter application—insomuch as we've chosen a persistence mechanism. Now it's time to put that transaction manager to work. We'll start by using it to program transactions manually.

6.3 Programming transactions in Spring

There are two kinds of people: those who are control freaks and those who aren't. Control freaks like complete control over everything that happens and don't take anything for granted. If you're a developer and a control freak, you're probably the kind of person who prefers the command line and would rather write your own getter and setter methods than to delegate that work to an IDE.

Control freaks also like to know exactly what's going on in their code. When it comes to transactions, they want full control over where a transaction starts, where it commits, and where it ends. Declarative transactions aren't precise enough for them.

This isn't a bad thing, though. The control freaks are at least partially right. As you'll see later in this chapter, you're limited to declaring transaction boundaries at the method level. If you need more fine-grained control over transactional boundaries, programmatic transactions are the only way to go.

Consider the `saveSpittle()` method of `SpitterServiceImpl` as an example of a transactional method.

Listing 6.1 `saveSpittle()` saves a `Spittle`

```
public void saveSpittle(Spittle spittle) {
  spitterDao.saveSpittle(spittle);
}
```

Although this method appears rather simple, there may be more than meets the eye. As the `Spittle` is saved, the underlying persistence mechanism may have a lot to do. Even if it ends up being a simple matter of inserting a row into a database table, it's important to make sure that whatever happens takes place within the confines of a transaction. If it succeeds, the work should be committed. If it fails, then it should be rolled back.

One approach to adding transactions is to programmatically add transactional boundaries directly within the `saveSpittle()` method using Spring's `TransactionTemplate`. Like other template classes in Spring (such as `JdbcTemplate`, discussed in the previous chapter), `TransactionTemplate` utilizes a callback mechanism. Here's an updated `saveSpittle()` method to show how to add a transactional context using a `TransactionTemplate`.

Listing 6.2 Programmatically adding transactions to `saveSpittle()`

```
public void saveSpittle(final Spittle spittle) {
  txTemplate.execute(new TransactionCallback<Void>() {
    public Void doInTransaction(TransactionStatus txStatus) {
      try {
      spitterDao.saveSpittle(spittle);
      } catch (RuntimeException e) {
        txStatus.setRollbackOnly();
        throw e;
      }
      return null;
    }
  });
}
```

To use the `TransactionTemplate`, you start by implementing the `TransactionCallback` interface. Because `TransactionCallback` has only one method to implement, it's often easiest to implement it as an anonymous inner class, as shown in listing 6.2. As for the code that needs to be transactional, place it within the doIn-Transaction() method.

Calling the execute() method on the TransactionTemplate instance will execute the code contained within the TransactionCallback instance. If your code encounters a problem, calling setRollbackOnly() on the TransactionStatus object will roll back the transaction. Otherwise, if the doInTransaction() method returns successfully, the transaction will be committed.

Where does the TransactionTemplate instance come from? Good question. It should be injected into SpitterServiceImpl, as follows:

```
<bean id="spitterService"
      class="com.habuma.spitter.service.SpitterServiceImpl">
  ...
  <property name="transactionTemplate ">
    <bean class="org.springframework.transaction.support.
            TransactionTemplate">
      <property name="transactionManager"
          ref="transactionManager" />
    </bean>
  </property>
</bean>
```

Note that the TransactionTemplate is injected with a transactionManager. Under the hood, TransactionTemplate uses an implementation of PlatformTransaction-Manager to handle the platform-specific details of transaction management. Here we've wired in a reference to a bean named transactionManager, which could be any of the transaction managers listed in table 6.1.

Programmatic transactions are good when you want complete control over transactional boundaries. But, as you can see from the code in listing 6.1, they're intrusive. You had to alter the implementation of saveSpittle()—using Spring-specific classes—to employ Spring's programmatic transaction support.

Usually your transactional needs won't require such precise control over transactional boundaries. That's why you'll typically choose to declare your transactions outside your application code (in the Spring configuration file, for instance). The rest of this chapter will cover Spring's declarative transaction management.

6.4 Declaring transactions

Not long ago, declarative transaction management was only available in EJB containers. But now Spring offers support for declarative transactions to POJOs. This is a significant feature of Spring because you now have an alternative to EJB for declaring atomic operations.

Spring's support for declarative transaction management is implemented through Spring's AOP framework. This is a natural fit because transactions are a system-level service above an application's primary functionality. You can think of a Spring transaction as an aspect that "wraps" a method with transactional boundaries.

Spring provides three ways to declare transactional boundaries. Historically, Spring has always supported declarative transactions by proxying beans using Spring AOP and `TransactionProxyFactoryBean`. But since Spring 2.0, the preferred ways to declare transactions are to use Spring's `tx` configuration namespace and to use the `@Transactional` annotation.

Although the legacy `TransactionProxyFactoryBean` is still available in modern versions of Spring, it's effectively obsolete and so we won't look at it in any detail. Instead, we'll focus on the `tx` namespace and annotation-oriented declarative transactions later in this section. But first let's examine the attributes that define transactions.

6.4.1 Defining transaction attributes

In Spring, declarative transactions are defined with *transaction attributes*. A transaction attribute is a description of how transaction policies should be applied to a method. There are five facets of a transaction attribute, as illustrated in figure 6.3.

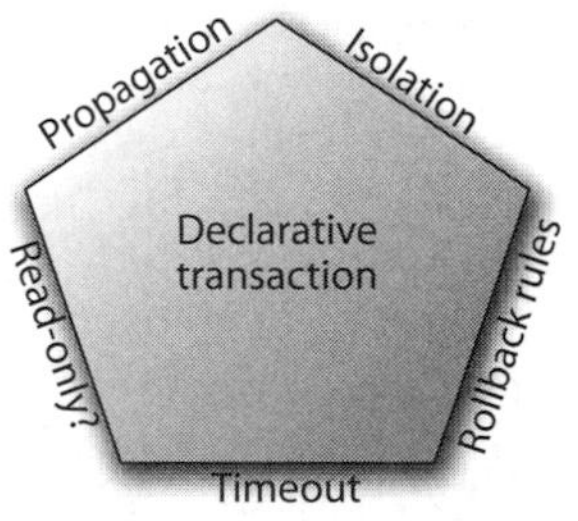

Figure 6.3 Declarative transactions are defined in terms of propagation behavior, isolation level, read-only hints, timeout, and rollback rules.

Although Spring provides several mechanisms for declaring transactions, all of them rely on these five parameters to govern how transaction policies are administered. Therefore, it's essential to understand these parameters in order to declare transaction policies in Spring.

Regardless of which declarative transaction mechanism you use, you'll have the opportunity to define these attributes. Let's examine each attribute to understand how it shapes a transaction.

PROPAGATION BEHAVIOR

The first facet of a transaction is *propagation behavior*. Propagation behavior defines the boundaries of the transaction with respect to the client and to the method being called. Spring defines seven distinct propagation behaviors, as described in table 6.2.

> **PROPAGATION CONSTANTS** The propagation behaviors described in table 6.2 are defined as constants in the `org.springframework.transaction.TransactionDefinition` interface.

The propagation behaviors in table 6.2 may look familiar. That's because they mirror the propagation rules available in EJB's container-managed transactions (CMTs). For instance, Spring's `PROPAGATION_REQUIRES_NEW` is equivalent to CMT's `RequiresNew`. Spring adds an additional propagation behavior not available in CMT, `PROPAGATION_NESTED`, to support nested transactions.

Propagation rules answer the question of whether a new transaction should be started or suspended, or if a method should even be executed within a transactional context at all.

Table 6.2 Propagation rules define when a transaction is created or when an existing transaction can be used. Spring provides several propagation rules to choose from.

Propagation behavior	What it means
PROPAGATION_MANDATORY	Indicates that the method must run within a transaction. If no existing transaction is in progress, an exception will be thrown.
PROPAGATION_NESTED	Indicates that the method should be run within a nested transaction if an existing transaction is in progress. The nested transaction can be committed and rolled back individually from the enclosing transaction. If no enclosing transaction exists, behaves like PROPAGATION_REQUIRED. Vendor support for this propagation behavior is spotty at best. Consult the documentation for your resource manager to determine if nested transactions are supported.
PROPAGATION_NEVER	Indicates that the current method shouldn't run within a transactional context. If an existing transaction is in progress, an exception will be thrown.
PROPAGATION_NOT_SUPPORTED	Indicates that the method shouldn't run within a transaction. If an existing transaction is in progress, it'll be suspended for the duration of the method. If using JTATransactionManager, access to TransactionManager is required.
PROPAGATION_REQUIRED	Indicates that the current method must run within a transaction. If an existing transaction is in progress, the method will run within that transaction. Otherwise, a new transaction will be started.
PROPAGATION_REQUIRES_NEW	Indicates that the current method must run within its own transaction. A new transaction is started and if an existing transaction is in progress, it'll be suspended for the duration of the method. If using JTATransactionManager, access to TransactionManager is required.
PROPAGATION_SUPPORTS	Indicates that the current method doesn't require a transactional context, but may run within a transaction if one is already in progress.

For example, if a method is declared to be transactional with PROPAGATION_REQUIRES_NEW behavior, it means that the transactional boundaries are the same as the method's own boundaries: a new transaction is started when the method begins and the transaction ends when the method returns or throws an exception. If the method has PROPAGATION_REQUIRED behavior, the transactional boundaries depend on whether a transaction is already under way.

ISOLATION LEVELS

The second dimension of a declared transaction is the *isolation level*. An isolation level defines how much a transaction may be impacted by the activities of other concurrent transactions. Another way to look at a transaction's isolation level is to think of it as how selfish the transaction is with the transactional data.

In a typical application, multiple transactions run concurrently, often working with the same data to get their jobs done. Concurrency, while necessary, can lead to the following problems:

- *Dirty reads* occur when one transaction reads data that has been written but not yet committed by another transaction. If the changes are later rolled back, the data obtained by the first transaction will be invalid.
- *Nonrepeatable reads* happen when a transaction performs the same query two or more times and each time the data is different. This is usually due to another concurrent transaction updating the data between the queries.
- *Phantom reads* are similar to nonrepeatable reads. These occur when a transaction (T1) reads several rows, and then a concurrent transaction (T2) inserts rows. Upon subsequent queries, the first transaction (T1) finds additional rows that weren't there before.

In an ideal situation, transactions would be completely isolated from each other, thus avoiding these problems. But perfect isolation can affect performance because it often involves locking rows (and sometimes complete tables) in the data store. Aggressive locking can hinder concurrency, requiring transactions to wait on each other to do their work.

Realizing that perfect isolation can impact performance and because not all applications will require perfect isolation, sometimes it's desirable to be flexible with regard to transaction isolation. Therefore, several levels of isolation are possible, as described in table 6.3.

Table 6.3 Isolation levels determine to what degree a transaction may be impacted by other transactions being performed in parallel.

Isolation level	What it means
`ISOLATION_DEFAULT`	Use the default isolation level of the underlying data store.
`ISOLATION_READ_UNCOMMITTED`	Allows you to read changes that haven't yet been committed. May result in dirty reads, phantom reads, and nonrepeatable reads.
`ISOLATION_READ_COMMITTED`	Allows reads from concurrent transactions that have been committed. Dirty reads are prevented, but phantom and nonrepeatable reads may still occur.
`ISOLATION_REPEATABLE_READ`	Multiple reads of the same field will yield the same results, unless changed by the transaction itself. Dirty reads and nonrepeatable reads are prevented, but phantom reads may still occur.
`ISOLATION_SERIALIZABLE`	This fully ACID-compliant isolation level ensures that dirty reads, nonrepeatable reads, and phantom reads are all prevented. This is the slowest of all isolation levels because it's typically accomplished by doing full table locks on the tables involved in the transaction.

ISOLATION LEVEL CONSTANTS The isolation levels described in table 6.3 are defined as constants in the `org.springframework.transaction.TransactionDefinition` interface.

`ISOLATION_READ_UNCOMMITTED` is the most efficient isolation level, but isolates the transaction the least, leaving the transaction open to dirty, nonrepeatable, and phantom reads. At the other extreme, `ISOLATION_SERIALIZABLE` prevents all forms of isolation problems but is the least efficient.

Be aware that not all data sources support all the isolation levels listed in table 6.3. Consult the documentation for your resource manager to determine what isolation levels are available.

READ-ONLY

The third characteristic of a declared transaction is whether it's a read-only transaction. If a transaction performs only read operations against the underlying data store, the data store may be able to apply certain optimizations that take advantage of the read-only nature of the transaction. By declaring a transaction as read-only, you give the underlying data store the opportunity to apply those optimizations as it sees fit.

Because read-only optimizations are applied by the underlying data store when a transaction begins, it only makes sense to declare a transaction as read-only on methods with propagation behaviors that may start a new transaction (`PROPAGATION_REQUIRED`, `PROPAGATION_REQUIRES_NEW`, and `PROPAGATION_NESTED`).

Furthermore, if you're using Hibernate as your persistence mechanism, declaring a transaction as read-only will result in Hibernate's flush mode being set to `FLUSH_NEVER`. This tells Hibernate to avoid unnecessary synchronization of objects with the database, thus delaying all updates until the end of the transaction.

TRANSACTION TIMEOUT

For an application to perform well, its transactions can't carry on for a long time. Therefore, the next trait of a declared transaction is its *timeout*.

Suppose that your transaction becomes unexpectedly long-running. Because transactions may involve locks on the underlying data store, long-running transactions can tie up database resources unnecessarily. Instead of waiting it out, you can declare a transaction to automatically roll back after a certain number of seconds.

Because the timeout clock begins ticking when a transaction starts, it only makes sense to declare a transaction timeout on methods with propagation behaviors that may start a new transaction (`PROPAGATION_REQUIRED`, `PROPAGATION_REQUIRES_NEW`, and `PROPAGATION_NESTED`).

ROLLBACK RULES

The final facet of the transaction pentagon is a set of rules that define which exceptions prompt a rollback and which ones don't. By default, transactions are rolled back only on runtime exceptions and not on checked exceptions. (This behavior is consistent with rollback behavior in EJBs.)

But you can declare that a transaction be rolled back on specific checked exceptions as well as runtime exceptions. Likewise, you can declare that a transaction not roll back on specified exceptions, even if those exceptions are runtime exceptions.

Now that you've had an overview of how transaction attributes shape the behavior of a transaction, let's see how to use these attributes when declaring transactions in Spring.

6.4.2 Declaring transactions in XML

In early version of Spring, declaring transactions involved wiring a special bean called `TransactionProxyFactoryBean`. The problem with `TransactionProxyFactoryBean` was that using it resulted in extremely verbose Spring configuration files. Fortunately, those days are gone and Spring now offers a `tx` configuration namespace that greatly simplifies declarative transactions in Spring.

Using the `tx` namespace involves adding it to your Spring configuration XML file:

```
<beans xmlns="http://www.springframework.org/schema/beans"
    xmlns:xsi="http://www.w3.org/2001/XMLSchema-instance"
    xmlns:aop="http://www.springframework.org/schema/aop"
    xmlns:tx="http://www.springframework.org/schema/tx"
    xsi:schemaLocation="http://www.springframework.org/schema/beans
        http://www.springframework.org/schema/beans/
            spring-beans-3.0.xsd
      http://www.springframework.org/schema/aop
      http://www.springframework.org/schema/aop/spring-aop-3.0.xsd
      http://www.springframework.org/schema/tx
      http://www.springframework.org/schema/tx/spring-tx-3.0.xsd">
```

Note that the `aop` namespace should also be included. This is important, because some of the declarative transaction configuration elements rely on a few of Spring's AOP configuration elements (as discussed in chapter 4).

The `tx` namespace provides a handful of new XML configuration elements, most notably the `<tx:advice>` element. The following XML snippet shows how `<tx:advice>` can be used to declare transactional policies similar to those we defined for the Spitter service in listing 6.2:

```
<tx:advice id="txAdvice">
  <tx:attributes>
    <tx:method name="add*" propagation="REQUIRED" />
    <tx:method name="*" propagation="SUPPORTS"
        read-only="true"/>
  </tx:attributes>
</tx:advice>
```

With `<tx:advice>`, the transaction attributes are defined in a `<tx:attributes>` element, which contains one or more `<tx:method>` elements. The `<tx:method>` element defines the transaction attributes for a given method (or methods) as defined by the `name` attribute (using wildcards).

`<tx:method>` has several attributes that help define the transaction policies for the method(s), as defined in table 6.4.

Table 6.4 The five facets of the transaction pentagon (see figure 6.3) are specified in the attributes of the `<tx:method>` element.

Attribute	Purpose
`isolation`	Specifies the transaction isolation level.
`propagation`	Defines the transaction's propagation rule.
`read-only`	Specifies that a transaction be read-only.

Rollback rules:
`rollback-for`
`no-rollback-for`
	`rollback-for` specifies checked exceptions for which a transaction should be rolled back and not committed.
	`no-rollback-for` specifies exceptions for which the transaction should continue and not be rolled back.

`timeout`	Defines a timeout for a long-running transaction.

As defined in the `txAdvice` transaction advice, the transactional methods configured are divided into two categories: those whose names begin with `add` and everything else. The `saveSpittle()` method falls into the first category and is declared to require a transaction. The other methods are declared with `propagation="supports"`—they'll run in a transaction if one already exists, but they don't need to run within a transaction.

When declaring a transaction using `<tx:advice>`, you'll still need a transaction manager just like you did when using `TransactionProxyFactoryBean`. Choosing convention over configuration, `<tx:advice>` assumes that the transaction manager will be declared as a bean whose `id` is `transactionManager`. If you happen to give your transaction manager a different `id` (`txManager`, for instance), you'll need to specify the `id` of the transaction manager in the `transactionmanager` attribute:

```
<tx:advice id="txAdvice"
      transaction-manager="txManager">
...
</tx:advice>
```

On its own, `<tx:advice>` only defines an AOP advice for advising methods with transaction boundaries. But this is only transaction advice, not a complete transactional aspect. Nowhere in `<tx:advice>` did we indicate which beans should be advised—we need a pointcut for that. To completely define the transaction aspect, we must define an advisor. This is where the `aop` namespace gets involved. The following XML defines an advisor that uses the `txAdvice` advice to advise any beans that implement the `SpitterService` interface:

```
<aop:config>
  <aop:advisor
      pointcut="execution(* *..SpitterService.*(..))"
      advice-ref="txAdvice"/>
</aop:config>
```

The pointcut attribute uses an AspectJ pointcut expression to indicate that this advisor should advise all methods of the SpitterService interface. The transaction advice, which is referenced with the advice-ref attribute to be the advice named txAdvice, defines which methods are actually run within a transaction as well as the transactional attributes for those methods.

Although the <tx:advice> element goes a long way toward making declarative transactions more palatable for Spring developers, Spring 2.0 has one more feature that makes it even nicer for those working in a Java 5 environment. Let's look at how Spring transactions can be annotation driven.

6.4.3 *Defining annotation-driven transactions*

The <tx:advice> configuration element greatly simplifies the XML required for declarative transactions in Spring. What if I told you that it could be simplified even further? What if I told you that you only need to add a single line of XML to your Spring context in order to declare transactions?

In addition to the <tx:advice> element, the tx namespace provides the <tx:annotation-driven> element. Using <tx:annotation-driven> is often as simple as the following line of XML:

```
<tx:annotation-driven />
```

That's it! If you were expecting more, I apologize. I could make it slightly more interesting by specifying a specific transaction manager bean with the transactionmanager attribute (which defaults to transactionManager):

```
<tx:annotation-driven transaction-manager="txManager" />
```

Otherwise, there's not much more to it. That single line of XML packs a powerful punch that lets you define transaction rules where they make the most sense: on the methods that are to be transactional.

Annotations are one of the biggest and most debated new features of Java 5. Annotations let you define metadata directly in your code rather than in external configuration files. I think they're a perfect fit for declaring transactions.

The <tx:annotation-driven> configuration element tells Spring to examine all beans in the application context and to look for beans that are annotated with @Transactional, either at the class level or at the method level. For every bean that is @Transactional, <tx:annotation-driven> will automatically advise it with transaction advice. The transaction attributes of the advice will be defined by parameters of the @Transactional annotation.

For example, the following shows SpitterServiceImpl, updated to include the @Transactional annotations.

Listing 6.3 Annotating the spitter service to be transactional

```
@Transactional(propagation=Propagation.SUPPORTS, readOnly=true)
public class SpitterServiceImpl implements SpitterService {
...
  @Transactional(propagation=Propagation.REQUIRED, readOnly=false)
  public void addSpitter(Spitter spitter) {
...
  }
...
}
```

At the class level, `SpitterServiceImpl` has been annotated with an `@Transactional` annotation that says that all methods will support transaction and be read-only. At the method level, the `saveSpittle()` method has been annotated to indicate that this method requires a transactional context.

6.5 Summary

Transactions are an important part of enterprise application development that leads to more robust software. They ensure an all-or-nothing behavior, preventing data from being inconsistent should the unexpected occur. They also support concurrency by preventing concurrent application threads from getting in each other's way as they work with the same data.

Spring supports both programmatic and declarative transaction management. In either case, Spring shields you from having to work directly with a specific transaction management implementation by abstracting the transaction management platform behind a common API.

Spring employs its own AOP framework to support declarative transaction management. Spring's declarative transaction support rivals that of EJB's CMT, enabling you to declare more than just propagation behavior on POJOs, including isolation levels, read-only optimizations, and rollback rules for specific exceptions.

This chapter showed you how to bring declarative transactions into the Java 5 programming model using annotations. With the introduction of Java 5 annotations, making a method transactional is simply a matter of tagging it with the appropriate transaction annotation.

As you've seen, Spring extends the power of declarative transactions to POJOs. This is an exciting development—declarative transactions were previously only available to EJBs. But declarative transactions are only the beginning of what Spring has to offer to POJOs. In the next chapter, you'll see how Spring extends declarative security to POJOs.

7 Building web applications with Spring MVC

This chapter covers

- Mapping requests to Spring controllers
- Transparently binding form parameters
- Validating form submissions
- Uploading files

As an enterprise Java developer, you've likely developed a web-based application or two. For many Java developers, web-based applications are their primary focus. If you do have this type of experience, you're well aware of the challenges that come with these systems. Specifically, state management, workflow, and validation are all important features that need to be addressed. None of these is made any easier given the HTTP protocol's stateless nature.

Spring's web framework is designed to help you address these concerns. Based on the Model-View-Controller (MVC) pattern, Spring MVC helps you build web-based applications that are as flexible and as loosely coupled as the Spring Framework itself.

In this chapter we'll explore the Spring MVC web framework. We'll build controllers using the new Spring MVC annotations to handle web requests. As we do, we'll strive to design our web layer in a RESTful way. Finally, we'll wrap up by looking at how to use Spring's JSP tags in views to send a response back to the user.

Before we go too deep with the specifics of Spring MVC controllers and handler mappings, let's start with a high-level view of Spring MVC and set up the basic plumbing needed to make Spring MVC work.

7.1 Getting started with Spring MVC

Have you ever seen the children's game Mousetrap? It's crazy. The goal is to send a small steel ball over a series of wacky contraptions in order to trigger a mousetrap. The ball goes over all kinds of intricate gadgets, from rolling down a curvy ramp to springing off a teeter-totter to spinning on a miniature Ferris wheel to being kicked out of a bucket by a rubber boot. It goes through all of this to spring a trap on a poor, unsuspecting plastic mouse.

At first glance, you may think that Spring's MVC framework is a lot like Mousetrap. Instead of moving a ball around through various ramps, teeter-totters, and wheels, Spring moves requests around between a dispatcher servlet, handler mappings, controllers, and view resolvers.

But don't draw too strong of a comparison between Spring MVC and the Rube Goldbergesque game of Mousetrap. Each of the components in Spring MVC performs a specific purpose. Let's start our exploration of Spring MVC by examining the lifecycle of a typical request.

7.1.1 Following a request through Spring MVC

Every time a user clicks a link or submits a form in their web browser, a request goes to work. A request's job description is that of a courier. Just like a postal carrier or a FedEx delivery person, a request lives to carry information from one place to another.

The request is a busy fellow. From the time it leaves the browser until it returns with a response, it'll make several stops, each time dropping off a bit of information and picking up some more. Figure 7.1 shows all the stops that the request makes.

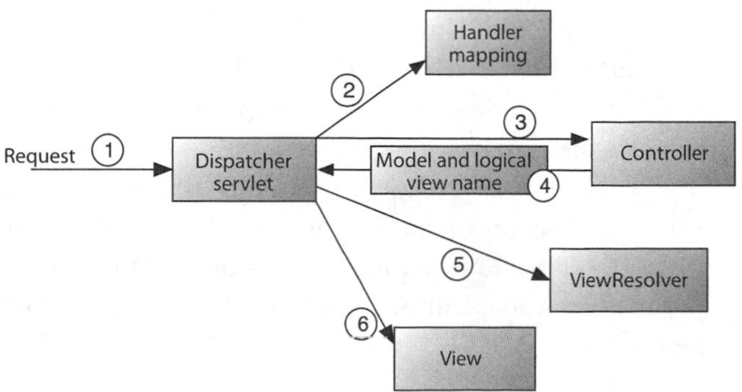

Figure 7.1 The web layer of the Spitter application includes two resource-oriented controllers along with a couple of utility controllers.

When the request leaves the browser, it carries information about what the user is asking for. At least, the request will be carrying the requested URL. But it may also carry additional data such as the information submitted in a form by the user.

The first stop in the request's travels is at Spring's `DispatcherServlet`. Like most Java-based web frameworks, Spring MVC funnels requests through a single front controller servlet. A front controller is a common web application pattern where a single servlet delegates responsibility for a request to other components of an application to perform actual processing. In the case of Spring MVC, `DispatcherServlet` is the front controller.

The `DispatcherServlet`'s job is to send the request on to a Spring MVC controller. A controller is a Spring component that processes the request. But a typical application may have several controllers and `DispatcherServlet` needs some help deciding which controller to send the request to. So the `DispatcherServlet` consults one or more handler mappings to figure out where the request's next stop will be. The handler mapping will pay particular attention to the URL carried by the request when making its decision.

Once an appropriate controller has been chosen, `DispatcherServlet` sends the request on its merry way to the chosen controller. At the controller, the request will drop off its payload (the information submitted by the user) and patiently wait while the controller processes that information. (Actually, a well-designed controller performs little or no processing itself and instead delegates responsibility for the business logic to one or more service objects.)

The logic performed by a controller often results in some information that needs to be carried back to the user and displayed in the browser. This information is referred to as the *model*. But sending raw information back to the user isn't sufficient—it needs to be formatted in a user-friendly format, typically HTML. For that the information needs to be given to a *view*, typically a JSP.

One of the last things that a controller does is package up the model data and identify the name of a view that should render the output. It then sends the request, along with the model and view name, back to the `DispatcherServlet`.

So that the controller doesn't get coupled to a particular view, the view name passed back to `DispatcherServlet` doesn't directly identify a specific JSP. In fact, it doesn't even necessarily suggest that the view is a JSP at all. Instead, it only carries a logical name which will be used to look up the actual view that will produce the result. The `DispatcherServlet` will consult a view resolver to map the logical view name to a specific view implementation, which may or may not be a JSP.

Now that `DispatcherServlet` knows which view will render the result, the request's job is almost over. Its final stop is at the view implementation (probably a JSP) where it delivers the model data. The request's job is finally done. The view will use the model data to render output that will be carried back to the client by the (not-so-hardworking) response object.

We'll dive into each of these steps in more detail throughout this chapter. But first things first—we need to set up Spring MVC and DispatcherServlet in the Spitter application.

7.1.2 Setting up Spring MVC

At the heart of Spring MVC is DispatcherServlet, a servlet that functions as Spring MVC's front controller. Like any servlet, DispatcherServlet must be configured in the web application's web.xml file. So the first thing we must do to use Spring MVC in our application is to place the following <servlet> declaration in the web.xml file:

```
<servlet>
    <servlet-name>spitter</servlet-name>
    <servlet-class>
       org.springframework.web.servlet.DispatcherServlet
     </servlet-class>
    <load-on-startup>1</load-on-startup>
</servlet>
```

The <servlet-name> given to the servlet is significant. By default, when DispatcherServlet is loaded, it'll load the Spring application context from an XML file whose name is based on the name of the servlet. In this case, because the servlet is named spitter, DispatcherServlet will try to load the application context from a file named spitter-servlet.xml (located in the application's WEB-INF directory).

Next we must indicate what URLs will be handled by the DispatcherServlet. It's common to find DispatcherServlet mapped to URL patterns such as *.htm, /*, or /app. But these URL patterns have a few problems:

- The *.htm pattern implies that the response will always be in HTML form (which, as we'll learn in chapter 11, isn't necessarily the case).
- Mapping it to /* doesn't imply any specify type of response, but indicates that DispatcherServlet will serve *all* requests. That makes serving static content such as images and stylesheets more difficult than necessary.
- The /app pattern (or something similar) helps us distinguish DispatcherServlet-served content from other types of content. But then we have an implementation detail (specifically, the /app path) exposed in our URLs. That leads to complicated URL rewriting tactics to hide the /app path.

Rather than use any of those flawed servlet-mapping schemes, I prefer mapping DispatcherServlet like this:

```
<servlet-mapping>
    <servlet-name>spitter</servlet-name>
    <url-pattern>/</url-pattern>
</servlet-mapping>
```

By mapping DispatcherServlet to /, I'm saying that it's the default servlet and that it'll be responsible for handling all requests, including requests for static content.

If it concerns you that DispatcherServlet will be handling those kinds of requests, then hold on for a bit. A handy configuration trick frees you, the developer, from having to worry about that detail much. Spring's mvc namespace includes a new <mvc:resources> element that handles requests for static content for you. All you must do is configure it in the Spring configuration.

That means that it's now time to create the spitter-servlet.xml file that DispatcherServlet will use to create an application context. The following listing shows the beginnings of the spitter-servlet.xml file.

Listing 7.1 <mvc:resources> sets up a handler for serving static resources.

```
<?xml version="1.0" encoding="UTF-8"?>
<beans xmlns="http://www.springframework.org/schema/beans"
       xmlns:xsi="http://www.w3.org/2001/XMLSchema-instance"
       xmlns:mvc="http://www.springframework.org/schema/mvc"
       xsi:schemaLocation="http://www.springframework.org/schema/mvc
         http://www.springframework.org/schema/mvc/spring-mvc-3.0.xsd
         http://www.springframework.org/schema/beans
         http://www.springframework.org/schema/beans/spring-beans-3.0.xsd">

  <mvc:resources mapping="/resources/**"
                 location="/resources/" />        <- Handle requests for static resources

</beans>
```

As I said earlier, all requests that go through DispatcherServlet must be handled in some way, commonly via controllers. Since requests for static content are also being handled by DispatcherServlet, we're going to need some way to tell DispatcherServlet how to serve those resources. But writing and maintaining a controller for that purpose seems too involved. Fortunately, the <mvc:resources> element is on the job.[1]

<mvc:resources> sets up a handler for serving static content. The mapping attribute is set to /resources/**, which includes an Ant-style wildcard to indicate that the path must begin with */resources*, but may include any subpath thereof. The location attribute indicates the location of the files to be served. As configured here, any requests whose paths begin with /resources will be automatically served from the /resources folder at the root of the application. Therefore, all of our images, stylesheets, JavaScript, and other static content needs to be kept in the application's /resources folder.

Now that we've settled the issue of how static content will be served, we can start thinking about how our application's functionality can be served. Since we're just getting started, we'll start simple by developing the Spitter application's home page.

---

1 The <mvc:resources> element was added in Spring 3.0.4. If you're using an older version of Spring, this facility won't be available.

7.2 Writing a basic controller

As we develop the web functionality for the Spitter application, we're going to develop resource-oriented controllers. Rather than write one controller for each use case in our application, we're going to write a single controller for each kind of resource that our application serves.

The Spitter application, being rather simple, has only two primary resource types: Spitters who are the users of the application and the spittles that they use to communicate their thoughts. Therefore, you'll need to write a spitter-oriented controller and a spittle-oriented controller. Figure 7.2 shows where these controllers fit into the overall application.

In addition to controllers for each of the application's core concepts, we also have two other utility controllers in 7.2. These controllers handle a few requests that are necessary, but don't directly map to a specific concept.

One of those controllers, `HomeController`, performs the necessary job of displaying the home page—a page that isn't directly associated with either `Spitters` or `Spittles`. That will be the first controller we write. But first, since we're developing annotation-driven controllers, there's a bit more setup to do.

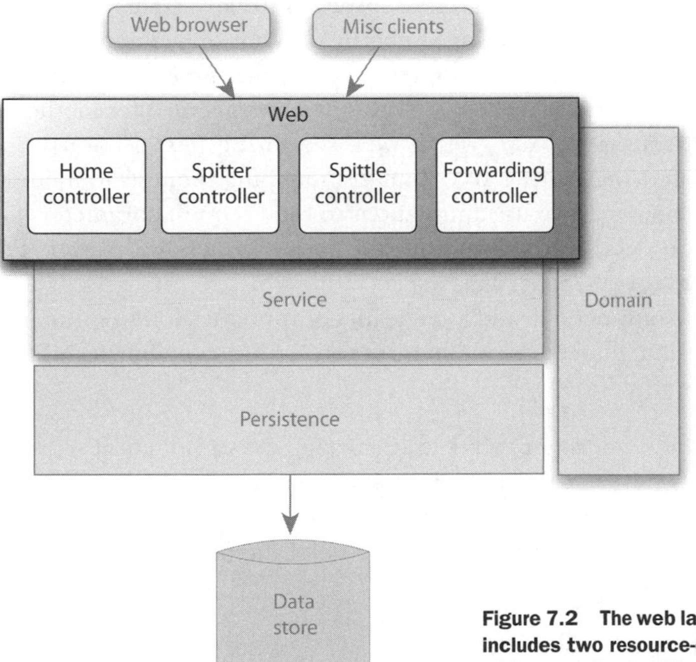

Figure 7.2 The web layer of the Spittle application includes two resource-oriented controllers along with a couple of utility controllers.

7.2.1 Configuring an annotation-driven Spring MVC

As I mentioned earlier, `DispatcherServlet` consults one or more handler mappings in order to know which controller to dispatch a request to. Spring comes with a handful of handler mapping implementations to choose from, including

- `BeanNameUrlHandlerMapping`—Maps controllers to URLs that are based on the controllers' bean names.
- `ControllerBeanNameHandlerMapping`—Similar to `BeanNameUrlHandlerMapping`, maps controllers to URLs that are based on the controllers' bean names. In this case, the bean names aren't required to follow URL conventions.
- `ControllerClassNameHandlerMapping`—Maps controllers to URLs by using the controllers' class names as the basis for their URLs.
- `DefaultAnnotationHandlerMapping`—Maps request to controller and controller methods that are annotated with `@RequestMapping`.
- `SimpleUrlHandlerMapping`—Maps controllers to URLs using a property collection defined in the Spring application context.

Using one of these handler mappings is usually just a matter of configuring it as a bean in Spring. But if no handler mapping beans are found, then `DispatcherServlet` creates and uses `BeanNameUrlHandlerMapping` and `DefaultAnnotationHandlerMapping`. Fortunately, we'll be working primarily with annotated controller classes, so the `DefaultAnnotationHandlerMapping` that `DispatcherServlet` gives us will do fine.

`DefaultAnnotationHandlerMapping` maps requests to controller methods that are annotated with `@RequestMapping` (which we'll see in the next section). But there's more to annotation-driven Spring MVC than just mapping requests to methods. As we build our controllers, we'll also use annotations to bind request parameters to handler method parameters, perform validation, and perform message conversion. Therefore, `DefaultAnnotationHandlerMapping` isn't enough.

Fortunately, you only need to add a single line of configuration to spitter-servlet.xml to flip on all of the annotation-driven features you'll need from Spring MVC:

```
<mvc:annotation-driven/>
```

Although small, the `<mvc:annotation-driven>` tag packs a punch. It registers several features, including JSR-303 validation support, message conversion, and support for field formatting.

We'll talk more about those features as we need them. For now, we have a home page controller to write.

7.2.2 Defining the home page controller

The home page is usually the first thing that visitors to a website will see. It's the front door to the rest of the site's functionality. In the case of the Spitter application, the home page's main job is to welcome visitors and to display a handful of recent spittles, hopefully enticing the visitors to join in on the conversation.

HomeController is a basic Spring MVC controller that handles requests for the home page.

Listing 7.2 HomeController welcomes the user to the Spitter application.

```
package com.habuma.spitter.mvc;
import javax.inject.Inject;
import java.util.Map;
import org.springframework.beans.factory.annotation.Autowired;
import org.springframework.stereotype.Controller;
import org.springframework.web.bind.annotation.RequestMapping;
import com.habuma.spitter.service.SpitterService;

@Controller                                                    <-- Declare as controller
public class HomeController {
  public static final int DEFAULT_SPITTLES_PER_PAGE = 25;

  private SpitterService spitterService;

  @Inject                                                      <-- Inject SpitterService
  public HomeController(SpitterService spitterService) {
    this.spitterService = spitterService;
  }

  @RequestMapping({"/","/home"})                               <-- Handle requests for home page

  public String showHomePage(Map<String, Object> model) {

    model.put("spittles", spitterService.getRecentSpittles(
              DEFAULT_SPITTLES_PER_PAGE));                     <-- Place spittles into model

    return "home";                                             <-- Return view name
  }
}
```

Although HomeController is simple, there's a lot to talk about here. First, the @Controller annotation indicates that this class is a controller class. This annotation is a specialization of the @Component annotation, which means that <context:component-scan> will pick up and register @Controller-annotated classes as beans, just as if they were annotated with @Component.

That means that we need to configure a <context:component-scan> in spitter-servlet.xml so that the HomeController class (and all of the other controllers we'll write) will be automatically discovered and registered as beans. Here's the relevant snippet of XML:

```
<context:component-scan base-package="com.habuma.spitter.mvc" />
```

Going back to the HomeController class, we know that it'll need to retrieve a list of the most recent spittles via a SpitterService. Therefore, we've written the constructor to take a SpitterService as an argument and have annotated it with @Inject annotation so that it'll automatically be injected when the controller is instantiated.

The real work takes place in the showHomePage() method. As you can see, it's annotated with @RequestMapping. This annotation serves two purposes. First, it identifies showHomePage() as a request-handling method. And, more specifically, it specifies that this method should handle requests whose path is either / or /home.

As a request-handling method, showHomePage() takes a Map of String-to-Object as a parameter. This Map represents the model—the data that's passed between the controller and a view. After retrieving a list of recent Spittles from the SpitterService's getRecentSpittles() method, that list is placed into the model Map so that it can be displayed when the view is rendered.

As we write more controllers we'll see that the signature of a request-handling method can include almost anything as an argument. Even though showHomePage() only needed the model Map, we could've added HttpServletRequest, HttpServletResponse, String, or numeric parameters that correspond to query parameters in the request, cookie values, HTTP request header values, or a number of other possibilities. For now, though, the model Map is all we need.

The last thing that showHomePage() does is return a String value that's the logical name of the view that should render the results. A controller class shouldn't play a direct part in rendering the results to the client, but should only identify a view implementation that'll render the data to the client. After the controller has finished its work, DispatcherServlet will use this name to look up the actual view implementation by consulting a view resolver.

We'll configure a view resolver soon. But first let's write a quick unit test to assert that HomeController is doing what we expect it to do.

TESTING THE CONTROLLER

What's most remarkable about HomeController (and most Spring MVC controllers) is that there's little that's Spring-specific about it. In fact, if you were to strip away the three annotations, this would be a POJO.

From a unit testing perspective, this is significant because it means that HomeController can be tested easily without having to mock anything or create any Spring-specific objects. HomeControllerTest demonstrates how you might test HomeController.

Listing 7.3 A test to assert that the HomeController does its job correctly

```
package com.habuma.spitter.mvc;

import static com.habuma.spitter.mvc.HomeController.*;
import static java.util.Arrays.*;
import static org.junit.Assert.*;
import static org.mockito.Mockito.*;

import java.util.HashMap;
import java.util.List;

import org.junit.Test;

import com.habuma.spitter.domain.Spittle;
import com.habuma.spitter.service.SpitterService;

public class HomeControllerTest {
  @Test
```

```
  public void shouldDisplayRecentSpittles() {
    List<Spittle> expectedSpittles =
      asList(new Spittle(), new Spittle(), new Spittle());

    SpitterService spitterService = mock(SpitterService.class);

    when(spitterService.getRecentSpittles(DEFAULT_SPITTLES_PER_PAGE)).
        thenReturn(expectedSpittles);

    HomeController controller =
                   new HomeController(spitterService);

    HashMap<String, Object> model = new HashMap<String, Object>();
    String viewName = controller.showHomePage(model);

    assertEquals("home", viewName);

    assertSame(expectedSpittles, model.get("spittles"));
    verify(spitterService).getRecentSpittles(DEFAULT_SPITTLES_PER_PAGE);
  }
}
```

Mock SpitterService

Create controller

Call handler method

Assert results

The only thing that HomeController needs to do its job is an instance of Spitter-Service, which Mockito[2] graciously provides as a mock implementation. Once the mock SpitterService is ready, you just need to create a new instance of Home-Controller and then call the showHomePage() method. Finally, you assert that the list of spittles returned from the mock SpitterService ends up in the model Map under the spittles key and that the method returns a logical view name of home.

As you can see, testing a Spring MVC controller is like testing any other POJO in your Spring application. Even though it'll ultimately be used to serve a web page, we didn't have to do anything special or web-specific to test it.

At this point we've developed a controller to handle requests for the home page. And we've written a test to ensure that the controller does what we think it should. One question is still unanswered, though. The showHomePage() method returned a logical view name. But how does that view name end up being used to render output to the user?

7.2.3 Resolving views

The last thing that must be done in the course of handling a request is rendering output to the user. This job falls to some view implementation—typically JavaServer Pages (JSP), but other view technologies such as Velocity or FreeMarker may be used. In order to figure out which view should handle a given request, DispatcherServlet consults a view resolver to exchange the logical view name returned by a controller for an actual view that should render the results.

In reality, a view resolver's job is to map a logical view name to some implementation of org.springframework.web.servlet.View. But it's sufficient for now to think of a view resolver as something that maps a view name to a JSP, as that's effectively what it does.

---

[2] http://mockito.org

Spring comes with several view resolver implementations to choose from, as described in table 7.1.

Table 7.1 When it's time to present information to a user, Spring MVC can select an appropriate view using one of several view resolvers.

View resolver	Description
BeanNameViewResolver	Finds an implementation of View that's registered as a <bean> whose ID is the same as the logical view name.
ContentNegotiatingViewResolver	Delegates to one or more other view resolvers, the choice of which is based on the content type being requested. (We'll talk more about this view resolver in chapter 11.)
FreeMarkerViewResolver	Finds a FreeMarker-based template whose path is determined by prefixing and suffixing the logical view name.
InternalResourceViewResolver	Finds a view template contained within the web application's WAR file. The path to the view template is derived by prefixing and suffixing the logical view name.
JasperReportsViewResolver	Finds a view defined as a Jasper Reports report file whose path is derived by prefixing and suffixing the logical view name.
ResourceBundleViewResolver	Looks up View implementations from a properties file.
TilesViewResolver	Looks up a view that is defined as a Tiles template. The name of the template is the same as the logical view name.
UrlBasedViewResolver	This is the base class for some of the other view resolvers, such as InternalResourceViewResolver. It can be used on its own, but it's not as powerful as its subclasses. For example, UrlBasedViewResolver is unable to resolve views based on the current locale.
VelocityLayoutViewResolver	This is a subclass of VelocityViewResolver that supports page composition via Spring's VelocityLayoutView (a view implementation that emulates Velocity's VelocityLayoutServlet).
VelocityViewResolver	Resolves a Velocity-based view where the path of a Velocity template is derived by prefixing and suffixing the logical view name.
XmlViewResolver	Finds an implementation of View that's declared as a <bean> in an XML file (/WEB-INF/views.xml). This view resolver is a lot like BeanNameViewResolver except that the view <bean>s are declared separately from those for the application's Spring context.
XsltViewResolver	Resolves an XSLT-based view where the path of the XSLT stylesheet is derived by prefixing and suffixing the logical view name.

There's neither time nor space enough for me to cover all of these view resolvers. But a few of them are quite useful and worth a closer look. We'll start by looking at `InternalResolverViewResolver`.

RESOLVING INTERNAL VIEWS

A lot of Spring MVC embraces a convention-over-configuration approach to development. `InternalResourceViewResolver` is one such convention-oriented element. It resolves a logical view name into a `View` object that delegates rendering responsibility to a template (usually a JSP) located in the web application's context. As illustrated in figure 7.3, it does this by taking the logical view name and surrounding it with a prefix and a suffix to arrive at the path of a template that's a resource within the web application.

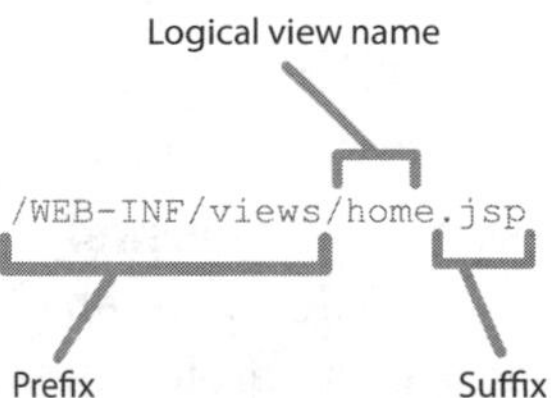

Figure 7.3 **`InternalResourceViewResolver` resolves a view template's path by attaching a specified prefix and suffix to the logical view name.**

Let's say that we've placed all of the JSPs for the Spitter application in the /WEB-INF/views/ directory. Given that arrangement, we'll need to configure an `InternalResourceViewResolver` bean in spitter-servlet.xml as follows:

```
<bean class=
      "org.springframework.web.servlet.view.InternalResourceViewResolver">
  <property name="prefix" value="/WEB-INF/views/"/>
  <property name="suffix" value=".jsp"/>
</bean>
```

When `DispatcherServlet` asks `InternalResourceViewResolver` to resolve a view, it takes the logical view name, prefixes it with /WEB-INF/views/ and suffixes it with .jsp. The result is the path of a JSP that will render the output. Internally, `InternalResourceViewResolver` then hands that path over to a `View` object that dispatches the request to the JSP. So, when `HomeController` returns *home* as the logical view name, it'll end up being resolved to the path /WEB-INF/views/home.jsp.

By default the `View` object that `InternalResourceViewResolver` creates is an instance of `InternalResourceView`, which simply dispatches the request to the JSP for rendering. But since home.jsp uses some JSTL tags, we may choose to replace `InternalResourceView` with `JstlView` by setting the `viewClass` property as follows:

```
<bean class=
      "org.springframework.web.servlet.view.InternalResourceViewResolver">
  <property name="viewClass"
     value="org.springframework.web.servlet.view.JstlView" />
  <property name="prefix" value="/WEB-INF/views/"/>
  <property name="suffix" value=".jsp"/>
</bean>
```

`JstlView` dispatches the request to JSP, just like `InternalResourceView`. But it also exposes JSTL-specific request attributes so that you can take advantage of JSTL's internationalization support.

Although we won't delve into the details of FreeMarkerViewResolver, JasperReportsViewResolver, VelocityViewResolver, VelocityLayoutViewResolver, or XsltViewResolver, they're all similar to InternalResourceViewResolver in that they resolve views by adding a prefix and a suffix to the logical view name to find a view template. Once you know how to use InternalResourceViewResolver, working with those other view resolvers should feel natural.

Using InternalResourceViewResolver to resolve to JSP views is fine for a simple web application with an uncomplicated look and feel. But websites often have interesting user interfaces with some common elements shared between pages. For those kinds of sites, a layout manager such as Apache Tiles is in order. Let's see how to configure Spring MVC to resolve Tiles layout views.

RESOLVING TILES VIEWS

Apache Tiles[3] is a templating framework for laying out pieces of a page as fragments that are assembled into a full page at runtime. Although it was originally created as part of the Struts framework, Tiles proved to be useful with other web frameworks. In fact, we'll use it with Spring MVC to lay out the look and feel of the Spitter application.

To use Tiles views in Spring MVC, the first thing to do is to register Spring's TilesViewResolver as a <bean> in spitter-servlet.xml:

```
<bean class=
    "org.springframework.web.servlet.view.tiles2.TilesViewResolver"/>
```

This modest <bean> declaration sets up a view resolver that attempts to find views that are Tiles template definitions where the logical view name is the same as the Tiles definition name.

What's missing here is how Spring knows about Tiles definitions. By itself, TilesViewResolver doesn't know anything about any Tiles definitions, but instead relies on a TilesConfigurer to keep track of that information. So we'll need to add a TilesConfigurer bean to spitter-servlet.xml:

```
<bean class=
    "org.springframework.web.servlet.view.tiles2.TilesConfigurer">
  <property name="definitions">
    <list>
      <value>/WEB-INF/viewsviews.xml</value>
    </list>
  </property>
</bean>
```

TilesConfigurer loads one or more Tiles definition files and make them available for TilesViewResolver to resolve views from. For the Spitter application we're going to have a few Tiles definition files, all named views.xml, spread around under the /WEB-INF/views folder. So we wire /WEB-INF/views/**/views.xml into the definitions property. The Ant-style ** pattern indicates that the entire directory hierarchy under /WEB-INF/views should be searched for files named views.xml.

3 http://tiles.apache.org

As for the contents of views.xml files, we'll build them up throughout this chapter, starting with just enough to render the home page. The following views.xml file defines the `home` tile definition as well as a common `template` definition to be used by other tile definitions.

Listing 7.4 Tiles defined

```
<!DOCTYPE tiles-definitions PUBLIC
      "-//Apache Software Foundation//DTD Tiles Configuration 2.1//EN"
      "http://tiles.apache.org/dtds/tiles-config_2_1.dtd">

<tiles-definitions>
   <definition name="template"
              template="/WEB-INF/views/main_template.jsp">        Define common layout
     <put-attribute name="top"
                    value="/WEB-INF/views/tiles/spittleForm.jsp" />
     <put-attribute name="side"
                    value="/WEB-INF/views/tiles/signinsignup.jsp" />
   </definition>

   <definition name="home" extends="template">        Define home tile

     <put-attribute name="content" value="/WEB-INF/views/home.jsp" />
   </definition>
</tiles-definitions>
```

The `home` definition extends the `template` definition, using home.jsp as the JSP that renders the main content of the page, but relying on `template` for all of the common features of the page.

It's the `home` template that `TilesViewResolver` will find when it tries to resolve the logical view name returned by `HomeController`'s `showHomePage()` methods. `DispatcherServlet` will send the request to Tiles to render the results using the `home` definition.

7.2.4 Defining the home page view

As you can see from listing 7.4, the home page is made up of several distinct pieces. The main_template.jsp file describes the common layout for all pages in the Spitter application, while home.jsp displays the main content for the home page. Plus, spittleForm.jsp and signinsignup.jsp provide some additional common elements.

For now we'll focus on home.jsp, as it's most pertinent to our discussion of displaying the home page. This JSP is where the home page request finishes its journey. It picks up the list of `Spittles` that `HomeController` placed into the model and renders them to be displayed in the user's browser. The following shows what home.jsp is made of.

Listing 7.5 The home page `<div>` element will be inserted into the template.

```
<%@ taglib prefix="c" uri="http://java.sun.com/jsp/jstl/core" %>
<%@ taglib prefix="s" uri="http://www.springframework.org/tags"%>
<%@ taglib prefix="t" uri="http://tiles.apache.org/tags-tiles"%>
```

```
<%@ taglib prefix="fmt" uri="http://java.sun.com/jsp/jstl/fmt"%>

<div>
  <h2>A global community of friends and strangers spitting out their
  inner-most and personal thoughts on the web for everyone else to
  see.</h2>
  <h3>Look at what these people are spitting right now...</h3>

  <ol class="spittle-list">
    <c:forEach var="spittle" items="${spittles}">          <!-- Iterate over list of Spittles -->

      <s:url value="/spitters/{spitterName}"
                 var="spitter_url" >                  <!-- Construct context-relative Spitter URL -->
        <s:param name="spitterName"
                     value="${spittle.spitter.username}" />
      </s:url>

      <li>
        <span class="spittleListImage">
          <img src=
            "http://s3.amazonaws.com/spitterImages/${spittle.spitter.id}.jpg"
             width="48"
             border="0"
             align="middle"
             onError=
      "this.src='<s:url value="/resources/images"/>/spitter_avatar.png';"/>
      </span>
      <span class="spittleListText">                 <!-- Display Spitter properties -->
        <a href="${spitter_url}">
          <c:out value="${spittle.spitter.username}" /></a>
          - <c:out value="${spittle.text}" /><br/>
         <small><fmt:formatDate value="${spittle.when}"
                                pattern="hh:mma MMM d, yyyy" /></small>
      </span>
      </li>
    </c:forEach>
  </ol>
</div>
```

Aside from a few friendly messages at the beginning, the crux of home.jsp is contained in the `<c:forEach>` tag, which cycles through the list of `Spittles`, rendering the details of each one as it goes. Since the `Spittles` were placed into the model with the key `spittles`, the list is referenced in the JSP using `${spittles}`.

> **THE MODEL AND REQUEST ATTRIBUTES: THE INSIDE STORY** It's not obvious, but `${spittles}` in home.jsp refers to a servlet request attribute named `spittles`. After `HomeController` finished its work and before home.jsp was called into action, `DispatcherServlet` copied all of the members of the model into request attributes with the same name.

Take notice of the `<s:url>` tag near the middle. We use this tag to create a servlet context–relative URL to the `Spitter` that authored each `Spittle`. The `<s:url>` tag is new to Spring 3.0 and works much like JSTL's `<c:url>` tag.

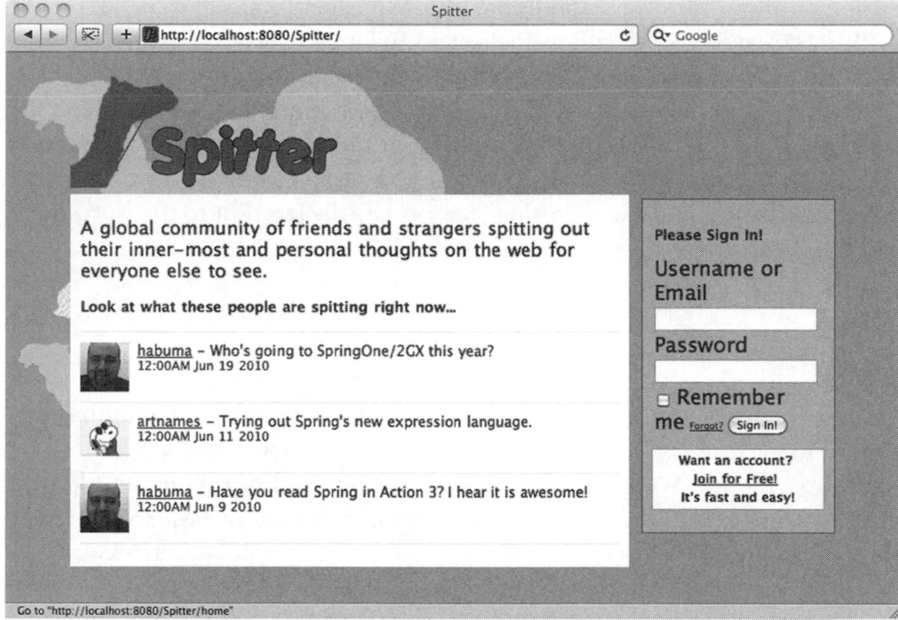

Figure 7.4 The Spitter application's home page displays a welcome message along with a list of recent spittles.

The main difference between Spring's `<s:url>` and JSTL's `<c:url>` is that `<s:url>` supports parameterized URL paths. In this case, the path is parameterized with the `Spitter`'s username. For example, if the `Spitter`'s username is *habuma* and the servlet context name is *Spitter*, then the resulting path will be /Spitter/spitters/habuma.

When rendered, this JSP along with the other JSPs in the same Tiles definition will display the Spitter application's home page, as shown in figure 7.4.

At this point, we've written our first Spring MVC controller, configured a view resolver, and defined a basic JSP view to display the results of invoking the controller. There's one tiny problem, though. An exception is waiting to happen in `HomeController` because `DispatcherServlet`'s Spring application context won't know where to find a `SpitterService` bean. Fortunately, it's an easy fix.

7.2.5 Rounding out the Spring application context

As I mentioned earlier, `DispatcherServlet` loads its Spring application context from a single XML file whose name is based on its `<servlet-name>`. But what about the other beans we've declared in previous chapters, such as the `SpitterService` bean? If `DispatcherServlet` is going to load its beans from a file named spitter-servlet.xml, then won't we need to declare those other beans in spitter-servlet.xml?

In the earlier chapters we've split our Spring configuration across multiple XML files: one for the service layer, one for the persistence layer, and another for the data source configuration. Although not strictly required, it's a good idea to organize our

Spring configuration across multiple files. With that in mind, it makes sense to put all of the web layer configuration in spitter-servlet.xml, the file loaded by `DispatcherServlet`. But we still need a way to load the other configuration files.

That's where `ContextLoaderListener` comes into play. `ContextLoaderListener` is a servlet listener that loads additional configuration into a Spring application context alongside the application context created by `DispatcherServlet`. To use `ContextLoaderListener`, add the following `<listener>` declaration to the web.xml file:

```
<listener>
    <listener-class>
        org.springframework.web.context.ContextLoaderListener
    </listener-class>
</listener>
```

We also need to tell `ContextLoaderListener` which Spring configuration file(s) it should load. If not specified otherwise, the context loader will look for a Spring configuration file at /WEB-INF/applicationContext.xml. But this single file doesn't lend itself to breaking up the application context into several pieces. So we'll need to override this default.

To specify one or more Spring configuration files for `ContextLoaderListener` to load, set the `contextConfigLocation` parameter in the servlet context:

```
<context-param>
    <param-name>contextConfigLocation</param-name>
    <param-value>
        /WEB-INF/spitter-security.xml
        classpath:service-context.xml
        classpath:persistence-context.xml
        classpath:dataSource-context.xml
    </param-value>
</context-param>
```

The `contextConfigLocation` parameter is specified as a list of paths. Unless specified otherwise, the paths are relative to the application root. But since our Spring configuration is split across multiple XML files that are scattered across several JAR files in the web application, we've prefixed some of them with `classpath:` to load them as resources from the application classpath and others with a path local to the web application.

You'll recognize that we've included the Spring configuration files that we created in previous chapters. You may also notice a few extra configuration files that we've not covered yet. Don't worry...we'll get to those in later chapters.

Now we have our first controller written and ready to serve requests for the Spitter application's home page. If all we needed is a home page, we'd be done. But there's more to Spitter than just the home page, so let's continue building out the application. The next thing we'll try is to write a controller that can handle input.

7.3 Handling controller input

HomeController had it easy. It didn't have to deal with user input or any parameters. It just handled a basic request and populated the model for the view to render. It couldn't have been much simpler.

But not all controllers live such simple lives. Controllers are often asked to perform some logic against one or more pieces of information that are passed in as URL parameters or as form data. Such is the case for both SpitterController and SpittleController. These two controllers will handle several kinds of requests, many of which take input of some kind.

One example of how SpitterController will handle input is in how it supports displaying a list of Spittles for a given Spitter. Let's drive out that functionality now to see how to write controllers that process input.

7.3.1 Writing a controller that processes input

One way that we could implement SpitterController is to have it respond to a URL with the Spitter's username as a request query parameter. For example, http://localhost:8080/spitter/spitters/spittles?spitter=habuma could be the URL for displaying all of the Spittles for a Spitter whose username is habuma.

The following shows an implementation of SpitterController that can respond to this kind of request.

Listing 7.6 A conventional approach to handling requests for a Spitter's spittles

```
package com.habuma.spitter.mvc;
import org.springframework.beans.factory.annotation.Autowired;
import org.springframework.stereotype.Controller;
import org.springframework.ui.Model;
import org.springframework.web.bind.annotation.RequestParam;
import org.springframework.web.bind.annotation.RequestMapping;
import com.habuma.spitter.domain.Spitter;
import com.habuma.spitter.service.SpitterService;
import static org.springframework.web.bind.annotation.RequestMethod.*;

@Controller
@RequestMapping("/spitter")                        <-- Root URL path
public class SpitterController {

  private final SpitterService spitterService;

  @Inject
  public SpitterController(SpitterService spitterService) {
    this.spitterService = spitterService;
  }
                                                        Handle GET requests
  @RequestMapping(value="/spittles", method=GET)    <-- for /spitter/spittles
  public String listSpittlesForSpitter(
        @RequestParam("spitter") String username, Model model) {
    Spitter spitter = spitterService.getSpitter(username);
    model.addAttribute(spitter);                         <-- Fill model
    model.addAttribute(spitterService.getSpittlesForSpitter(username));
```

```
    return "spittles/list";
  }
}
```

As you can see, we've annotated SpitterController with @Controller and @RequestMapping at the class level. As we've already discussed, @Controller is a clue to <context:component-scan> that this class should be automatically discovered and registered as a bean in the Spring application context.

You'll also notice that SpitterController is annotated with @RequestMapping at the class level. In HomeController we used @RequestMapping on the showHomePage() handler method, but this class-level use of @RequestMapping is different.

As used here, the class-level @RequestMapping defines the root URL path that this controller will handle. We'll ultimately have several handler methods in SpitterController, each handling different types of requests. But here @RequestMapping is saying that all of those requests will have paths that start with /spitters.

Within SpitterController we currently have a single method: listSpittlesForSpitter(). Like any good handler method, this method is annotated with @RequestMapping. It's not dramatically different from the one we used in HomeController. But there's more to this @RequestMapping than meets the eye.

Method-level @RequestMappings narrow the mapping defined by any class-level @RequestMapping. Here, SpitterController is mapped to /spitters at the class level and to /spittles at the method level. Taken together, that means that listSpittlesForSpitter() handles requests for /spitters/spittles. Moreover, the method attribute is set to GET indicating that this method will only handle HTTP GET requests for /spitters/spittles.

The listSpittlesForSpitter() method takes a Stringusername and a Model object as parameters.

The username parameter is annotated with @RequestParam("spitter") to indicate that it should be given the value of the spitter query parameter in the request. listSpittlesForSpitter() will use that parameter to look up the Spitter object and its list of Spittles.

You're probably scratching your head over the second parameter to

> **Do I really need @RequestParam?**
>
> The @RequestParam annotation isn't strictly required. @RequestParam is useful for binding query parameters to method parameters where the names don't match. As a matter of convention, any parameters of a handler method that aren't annotated otherwise will be bound to the query parameter of the same name. In the case of listSpittlesForSpitter(), if the parameter were named *spitter* or if the query parameter were called *username*, then we could leave the @RequestParam annotation off.
>
> @RequestParam also comes in handy when you compile your Java code without debugging information compiled in. In that circumstance, the name of the method parameter is lost and so there's no way to bind the query parameter to the method parameter by convention. For that reason, it's probably best to always use @RequestParam and not rely too heavily on the convention.

the listSpittlesForSpitter() method. When we wrote HomeController, we passed in a Map<String, Object> to represent the model. But here we're using a new Model parameter.

The truth be known, the object passed in as a Model likely is a Map<String, Object> under the covers. But Model provides a few convenient methods for populating the model, such as addAttribute(). The addAttribute() method does pretty much the same thing as Map's put() method, except that it figures out the key portion of the map on its own.

When adding a Spitter object to the model, addAttribute() gives it the name spitter, a name it arrives at by applying JavaBeans property naming rules to the object's class name. When adding a List of Spittles, it tacks *List* to the end the member type of the List, naming the attribute spittleList.

We're almost ready to call listSpittlesForSpitter() done. We've written the SpitterController and a handler method. All that's left is to write the view that will display that list of Spittles.

7.3.2 Rendering the view

When the list of Spittles is displayed to the user, we don't need much different than what we did for the home page. We just need to show the name of the Spitter (so that it's clear whom the list of Spittles belongs to) and then list each Spittle

To enable that, we first need to create a new Tiles definition. listSpittlesForSpitter() returns spittles/list as its logical view name, so the following Tile definition should do the trick:

```
<definition name="spittles/list" extends="template">
 <put-attribute name="content"
                value="/WEB-INF/views/spittles/list.jsp" />
</definition>
```

Just like the home Tile, this one adds another JSP page to the content attribute to be rendered within main_template.jsp. The list.jsp file used to display the list of Spittles is shown next.

Listing 7.7 The list.jsp file is a JSP that's used to display a list of Spittle objects.

```
<%@ taglib prefix="s" uri="http://www.springframework.org/tags"%>
<%@ taglib prefix="c" uri="http://java.sun.com/jsp/jstl/core"%>

<div>
  <h2>Spittles for ${spitter.username}</h2>             <—— Display username

  <table cellspacing="15">
    <c:forEach items="${spittleList}" var="spittle">         <—— List Spittles

    <tr>
      <td>
          <img src="<s:url value="/resources/images/spitter_avatar.png"/>"
               width="48" height="48" /></td>
```

```
        <td>
            <a href="<s:url value="/spitters/${spittle.spitter.username}"/>">
                        ${spittle.spitter.username}</a>
            <c:out value="${spittle.text}" /><br/>
            <c:out value="${spittle.when}" />
        </td>
      </tr>
      </c:forEach>
  </table>
</div>
```

Aesthetics aside, this JSP does what we need. Near the top, it displays a header indicating who the list of `Spittles` belongs to. This header references the `username` property of the `Spitter` object that `listSpittlesForSpitter()` placed into the model with `${spitter.username}`.

The better part of this JSP iterates through the list of `Spittles`, displaying their details. The JSTL `<c:forEach>` tag's `items` attribute references the list with `${spittleList}`—the name that `Model`'s `addAttribute()` gave it.

One minor thing to take note of is that we're using a hardcoded reference to spitter_avatar.png as the user's profile image. In section 7.5 we'll see how to let the user upload an image to their profile.

The result of list.jsp, as rendered in the context of the spittles/list view, is shown in figure 7.5.

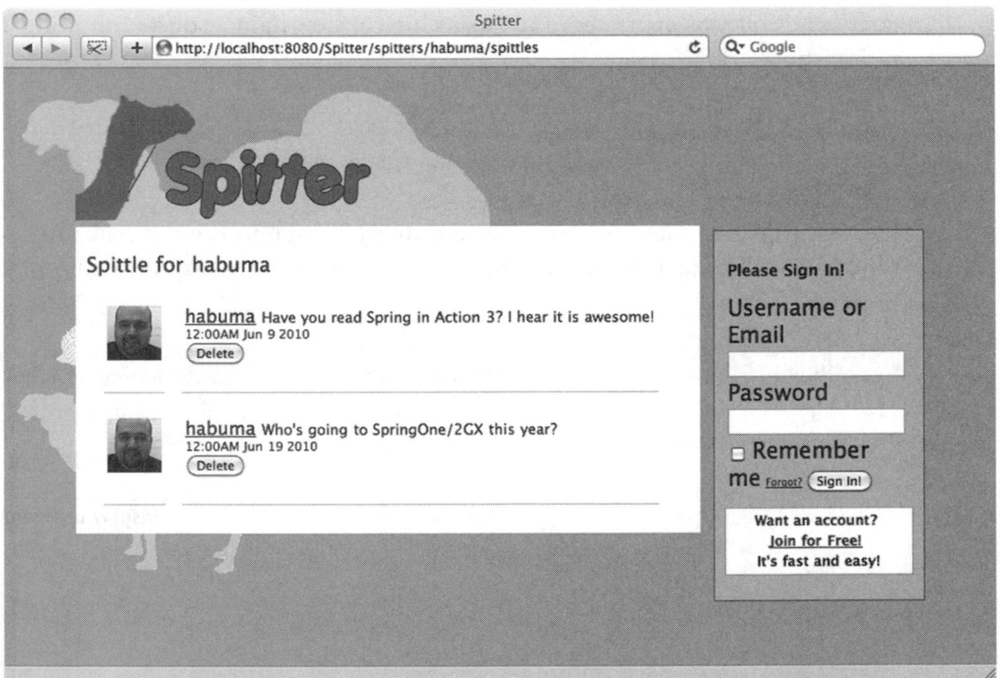

Figure 7.5 When taken together with other Tiles elements, list.jsp shows a list of spittles for a given user.

But first, we need to create a way for users to register to the application. In doing so, we'll get a chance to write a controller that handles form submissions.

7.4 Processing forms

Working with forms in a web application involves two operations: displaying the form and processing the form submission. Therefore, in order to register a new `Spitter` in our application, we're going to need to add two handler methods to `SpitterController` to handle each of the operations. Since we're going to need the form in the browser before we can submit it, we'll start by writing the handler method that displays the registration form.

7.4.1 Displaying the registration form

When the form is displayed, it'll need a `Spitter` object to bind to the form fields. Since this is a new `Spitter` that we're creating, a newly constructed, uninitialized `Spitter` object will be perfect. The following `createSpitterProfile()` handler method will create a `Spitter` object and place it in the model.

Listing 7.8 Displaying the form for registering a spitter

```
@RequestMapping(method=RequestMethod.GET, params="new")
public String createSpitterProfile(Model model) {
  model.addAttribute(new Spitter());
  return "spitters/edit";
}
```

As with other handler methods, `createSpitterProfile()` is annotated with `@RequestMapping`. But, unlike previous handler methods, this one doesn't specify a path. Therefore, this method handles requests for the path specified in the class-level `@RequestMapping`—`/spitters` in the case of `SpitterController`.

What the method's `@RequestMapping` does specify is that this method will handle HTTP GET requests only. What's more, note the `params` attribute, which is set to `new`. This means that this method will only handle HTTP GET requests for /spitters if the request includes a `new` query parameter. Figure 7.6 illustrates the kind of URL that `createSpitterProfile` will handle.

As for the inner workings of `createSpitterProfile()`, it simply creates a new instance of a `Spitter` and adds it to the model. It then wraps up by returning spitters/edit as the logical name of the view that will render the form.

Speaking of the view, let's create it next.

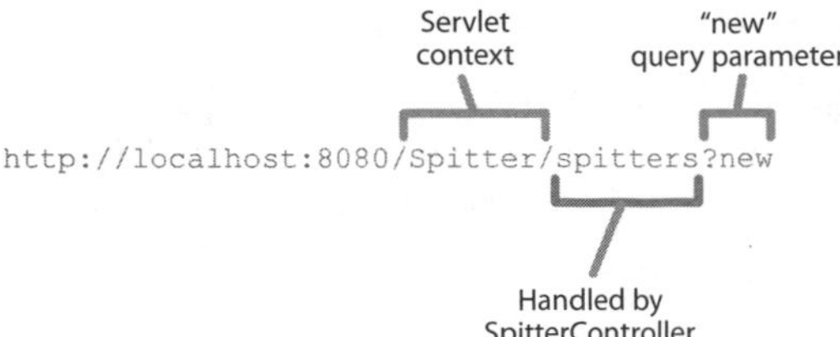

Figure 7.6 `@RequestMapping`'s `params` attribute can limit a handler method to only handling requests with certain parameters.

DEFINING THE FORM VIEW

As before, the logical view name returned from `createSpitterProfile()` will ultimately be mapped to a Tiles definition for rendering the form to the user. So we need to add a tile definition named `spitters/edit` to the Tiles configuration file. The following `<definition>` entry should do the trick.

```
<definition name="spitters/edit" extends="template">
 <put-attribute name="content"
               value="/WEB-INF/views/spitters/edit.jsp" />
</definition>
```

As before, the `content` attribute is where the main content of the page will go. In this case, it's the JSP file at /WEB-INF/views/spitters/edit.jsp, as shown next.

Listing 7.9 Rendering a form to capture user registration information

```
<%@ taglib prefix="sf" uri="http://www.springframework.org/tags/form"%>

<div>
<h2>Create a free Spitter account</h2>

<sf:form method="POST" modelAttribute="spitter">          <-- Bind form to model attribute
   <fieldset>
   <table cellspacing="0">
      <tr>
         <th><label for="user_full_name">Full name:</label></th>
         <td><sf:input path="fullName" size="15" id="user_full_name"/></td>
      </tr>
      <tr>
         <th><label for="user_screen_name">Username:</label></th>
         <td><sf:input path="username" size="15" maxlength="15"
             id="user_screen_name"/>                      <-- Username field
              <small id="username_msg">No spaces, please.</small>

            </td>
      </tr>
      <tr>
         <th><label for="user_password">Password:</label></th>
         <td><sf:password path="password" size="30"
                         showPassword="true"
                         id="user_password"/>             <-- Password field
             <small>6 characters or more (be tricky!)</small>
            </td>
      </tr>

      <tr>
         <th><label for="user_email">Email Address:</label></th>

         <td><sf:input path="email" size="30"
                 id="user_email"/>                        <-- Email field
             <small>In case you forget something</small>
            </td>
      </tr>
      <tr>
```

```
        <th></th>
        <td>
          <sf:checkbox path="updateByEmail"
                       id="user_send_email_newsletter"/>    Update-by-email
          <label for="user_send_email_newsletter"           checkbox
          >Send me email updates!</label>

        </td>
      </tr>
    </table>
</fieldset>
</sf:form>
</div>
```

What makes this JSP file different than the others we've created so far is that it uses Spring's form binding library. The `<sf:form>` tag binds the `Spitter` object (identified by the `modelAttribute` attribute) that `createSpitterProfile()` placed into the model to the various fields in the form.

The `<sf:input>`, `<sf:password>`, and `<sf:checkbox>` tags each have a `path` attribute that references the property of the `Spitter` object that the form is bound to. When the form is submitted, whatever values these fields contain will be placed into a `Spitter` object and submitted to the server for processing.

Note that the `<sf:form>` specifies that it'll be submitted as an HTTP POST request. What it doesn't specify is the URL. With no URL specified, it'll be submitted back to /spitters, the same URL path that displayed the form. That means that the next thing to do is to write another handler method that accepts POST requests for /spitters.

7.4.2 Processing form input

After the form is submitted, we'll need a handler method that takes a `Spitter` object (populated with data from the form) and saves it. Then, the last thing it should do is redirect to the user's profile page. The following listing shows `addSpitterFromForm()`, a method that processes the form submission.

Listing 7.10 The `addSpitter` method processes input from the spitter form.

```
@RequestMapping(method=RequestMethod.POST)
public String addSpitterFromForm(@Valid Spitter spitter,
                                 BindingResult bindingResult) {
  if(bindingResult.hasErrors()) {                       Check for errors
    return "spitters/edit";
  }

  spitterService.saveSpitter(spitter);        Save Spitter        Redirect
                                                                  after
  return "redirect:/spitters/" + spitter.getUsername();           POST
}
```

Note that the `addSpitterFromForm()` method is annotated with an `@RequestMapping` annotation that isn't much different than the `@RequestMapping` that adorns the `createSpitterProfile()` method. Neither specify a URL path, meaning that both handle requests for /spitters. The difference is that where `createSpitterProfile()` handles GET requests, `addSpitterFromForm()` handles POST requests. That's perfect, since that's how the form will be submitted.

And when that form is submitted, the fields in the request will be bound to the `Spitter` object that's passed in as an argument to `addSpitterFromForm()`. From there, it's sent to the `SpitterService`'s `saveSpitter()` method to be stored away in the database.

You may have also noticed that the `Spitter` parameter is annotated with `@Valid`. This indicates that the `Spitter` should pass validation before being passed in. We'll talk about validation in the next section.

Like the handler methods we've written before, this one ends by returning a `String` to indicate where the request should be sent next. This time, instead of specifying a logical view name, we're returning a special redirect view. The `redirect:` prefix signals that the request should be redirected to the path that it precedes. By redirecting to another page, we can avoid duplicate submission of the form if the user clicks the Refresh button in their browser.

As for the path that it's redirecting to, it'll take the form of `/spitters/{username}` where *{username}* represents the username of the `Spitter` that was just submitted. For example, if the user registered under the name habuma, then they'd be redirected to /spitters/habuma after the form submission.

HANDLING REQUESTS WITH PATH VARIABLES

The big question is what will respond to requests for /spitters/{username}? Actually, that's another handler method that we'll add to `SpitterController`:

```
@RequestMapping(value="/{username}", method=RequestMethod.GET)
public String showSpitterProfile(@PathVariable String username,
        Model model) {
  model.addAttribute(spitterService.getSpitter(username));
  return "spitters/view";
}
```

The `showSpitterProfile()` method isn't too dissimilar from the other handler methods we've seen. It's given a `String` parameter containing a username and uses it to retrieve a `Spitter` object. It then places that `Spitter` into the model and wraps up by returning the logical name of the view that will render the output.

But by now you've probably noticed a few things that make `showSpitterProfile()` different. First, the `value` attribute in the `@RequestMapping` contains some strange-looking curly braces. And the `username` parameter is annotated with `@PathVariable`.

Those two things work together to enable the `showSpitterProfile()` method to handle requests whose URLs have parameters embedded in their path. The `{username}` portion of the path is actually a placeholder that corresponds to the `username` method parameter that's annotated with `@PathVariable`. Whatever value is in that location in a request's path will be passed in as the value of `username`.

For example, if the request path is `/username/habuma`, then `habuma` will be passed in to `showSpitterProfile()` for the username.

We'll talk more about `@PathVariable` and how it helps us write handler methods that respond to RESTful URLs when we get to chapter 11.

But we still have some unfinished business with regard to `addSpitterFromForm()`. You've probably noticed that `addSpitterFromForm()`'s `Spitter` parameter is annotated with `@Valid`. Let's see how this annotation can be used to keep bad data from being submitted in a form.

7.4.3 Validating input

When a user registers with the Spitter application, there are certain requirements that we'd like to place on that registration. Specifically, a new user must give us their full name, email address, a username, and a password. Not only that, but the email address can't be just freeform text—it must look like an email address. Moreover, the password should be at least six characters long.

The `@Valid` annotation is the first line of defense against faulty form input. `@Valid` is actually a part of the JavaBean validation specification.[4] Spring 3 includes support for JSR-303, and we're using `@Valid` here to tell Spring that the `Spitter` object should be validated as it's bound to the form input.

Should anything go wrong while validating the `Spitter` object, the validation error will be carried to the `addSpitterFromForm()` method via the `BindingResult` that's passed in on the second parameter. If the `BindingResult`'s `hasErrors()` method returns `true`, then that means that validation failed. In that case, the method will return `spitters/edit` as the view name to display the form again so that the user can correct any validation errors.

But how will Spring know the difference between a valid `Spitter` and an invalid `Spitter`?

DECLARING VALIDATION RULES

Among other things, JSR-303 defines a handful of annotations that can be placed on properties to specify validation rules. We can use these annotations to define what "valid" means with regard to a `Spitter` object. The following shows the properties of the `Spitter` class that are annotated with validation annotations.

Listing 7.11 Annotating a `Spitter` for validation

```
@Size(min=3, max=20, message=
    "Username must be between 3 and 20 characters long.")        <- Enforce size
@Pattern(regexp="^[a-zA-Z0-9]+$",
        message="Username must be alphanumeric with no spaces")   <- Ensure no spaces
private String username;

@Size(min=6, max=20,
        message="The password must be at least 6 characters long.")
private String password;
```

4 Also known as JSR-303 (http://jcp.org/en/jsr/summary?id=303)

```
@Size(min=3, max=50, message=
    "Your full name must be between 3 and 50 characters long.")   <-- Enforce size
private String fullName;

@Pattern(regexp="[A-Za-z0-9._%+-]+@[A-Za-z0-9.-]+\.[A-Za-z]{2,4}",
        message="Invalid email address.")    <-- Match email pattern
private String email;
```

The first three properties in listing 7.11 are annotated with JSR-303's `@Size` annotation to validate that those fields meet certain expectations on their length. The `username` property must be at least 3 and at most 20 characters long, whereas the `fullName` property must be between 3 and 50 characters in length. As for the `password` property, it must be at least 6 characters long and not exceed 20 characters.

To make sure that the value given to the email property fits the format of an email address, we've annotated it with `@Pattern` and specified a regular expression to match it against in the `regexp` attribute.[5] Similarly, we've used `@Pattern` on the `username` property to ensure that the username is only made up of alphanumeric characters with no spaces.

In all of the validation annotations, we've set the `message` attribute with the message to be displayed in the form when validation fails so that the user knows what needs to be corrected.

With these annotations in place, when a user submits a registration form to `SpitterController`'s `addSpitterFromForm()` method, the values in the `Spitter` object's fields will be weighed against the validation annotations. If any of those rules are broken, then the handler method will send the user back to the form to fix the problem.

When they arrive back at the form, we'll need a way to tell them what the problem was. So we're going to have to go back to the form JSP and add some code to display the validation messages.

DISPLAYING VALIDATION ERRORS

Recall that the `BindingResult` passed in as a parameter to `addSpitterFromForm()` knew whether the form had any validation errors. And we were able to ask if there were any errors by calling its `hasErrors()` method. But what we didn't see was that the actual error messages are also in there, associated with the fields that failed validation.

One way of displaying those errors to the users is to access those field errors through `BindingResult`'s `getFieldError()` method. But a much better way is to use Spring's form binding JSP tag library to display the errors. More specifically, the `<sf:errors>` tag can render field validation errors. All we need to do is sprinkle a few `<sf:errors>` tags around our form JSP.

---

[5] Trust me...that gobbledygook will validate an email address.

Listing 7.12 The <sf:errors> JSP tag can be used to display form validation errors.

```
<%@ taglib prefix="sf" uri="http://www.springframework.org/tags/form"%>

<div>
<h2>Create a free Spitter account</h2>

<sf:form method="POST" modelAttribute="spitter"
         enctype="multipart/form-data">
   <fieldset>
   <table cellspacing="0">
      <tr>
         <th><sf:label path="fullName">Full name:</sf:label></th>
         <td><sf:input path="fullName" size="15" /><br/>
             <sf:errors path="fullName" cssClass="error" />        Display fullName errors
         </td>
      </tr>
      <tr>
         <th><sf:label path="username">Username:</sf:label></th>
         <td><sf:input path="username" size="15" maxlength="15" />
              <small id="username_msg">No spaces, please.</small><br/>
             <sf:errors path="username" cssClass="error" />        Display username errors
            </td>
      </tr>
      <tr>
         <th><sf:label path="password">Password:</sf:label></th>
         <td><sf:password path="password" size="30"
                              showPassword="true"/>
             <small>6 characters or more (be tricky!)</small><br/>
             <sf:errors path="password" cssClass="error" />        Display password errors

            </td>
      </tr>
      <tr>
         <th><sf:label path="email">Email Address:</sf:label></th>
         <td><sf:input path="email" size="30"/>
             <small>In case you forget something</small><br/>
             <sf:errors path="email" cssClass="error" />           Display email errors
            </td>
      </tr>
      <tr>
         <th></th>
         <td>
            <sf:checkbox path="updateByEmail"/>
            <sf:label path="updateByEmail"
            >Send me email updates!</sf:label>

         </td>
      </tr>
      <tr>
        <th><label for="image">Profile image:</label></th>
        <td><input name="image" type="file"/>
      </tr>
      <tr>
         <th></th>
         <td><input name="commit" type="submit"
```

```
                    value="I accept. Create my account." /></td>
      </tr>
    </table>
</fieldset>
</sf:form>
</div>
```

The <sf:errors> tag's path attribute specifies the form field for which errors should be displayed. For example, the following <sf:errors> displays errors (if there are any) for the field whose name is fullName:

```
<sf:errors path="fullName" cssClass="error" />
```

If there are multiple errors for a single field, they'll all be displayed, separated by an HTML <br/> tag. If you'd rather have them separated some other way, then you can use the delimiter attribute. The following <sf:errors> snippet uses delimiter to separate errors with a comma and a space:

```
<sf:errors path="fullName" delimiter=", "
    cssClass="error" />
```

Note that there are four <sf:errors> tags in this JSP, one on each of the fields for which we declared validation rules. The cssClass attribute refers to a class that's declared in CSS to display in red so that it catches the user's attention.

With these in place, errors will be displayed on the page if any validation errors occur. For example, figure 7.7 shows what the form would look like if the user were to submit the form without filling in any of the fields.

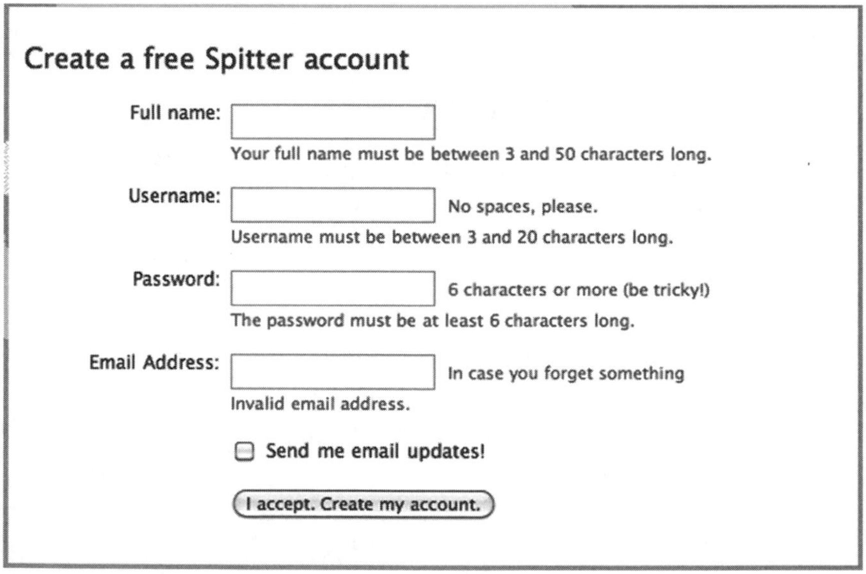

Figure 7.7 With the <sf:errors> JSP tag on the registration page, validation problems will be shown to the user for them to fix and try again.

As you can see, validation errors are displayed on a per-field basis. But if you'd prefer to display all of the errors in one place (perhaps at the top of the form), you'll only need a single `<sf:errors>` tag, with its `path` attribute set to `*`:

```
<sf:errors path="*" cssClass="error" />
```

Now you know how to write controller handler methods that process form data. The one thing that's common about all of the form fields we've seen thus far is that they're textual data and were probably entered into the form by the user typing on a keyboard. But what if the thing that the user needs to submit in a form can't be banged out on a keyboard? What if the user needs to submit an image or some other kind of file?

7.5 Handling file uploads

Earlier, in section 7.2.4, I punted on how the user's profile picture would be displayed, simply displaying a default spitter_avatar.png for all users. But real Spitter users will want more identity than some generic icon. To grant them more individuality, we'll let them upload their profile photos as part of registration.

To enable file uploads in the Spitter application, we'll need to do three things:

- Add a file upload field to the registration form
- Tweak `SpitterController`'s `addSpitterFromForm()` to receive the uploaded file
- Configure a multipart file resolver in Spring

Let's start at the top of the list and prepare the registration form JSP to take a file upload.

7.5.1 Adding a file upload field to the form

Most form fields are textual and can easily be submitted to the server as a set of name-value pairs. In fact, a typical form submission has a content type of `application/x-www-form-urlencoded` and takes the form of name-value pairs separated by ampersands.

But I think you'll agree that files are a different kind of thing than most other field values that will be submitted in a form. Uploaded files are typically binary files and don't fit well into the name-value pair paradigm. Therefore, if we're going to let users upload images to be associated with their profile, we'll need to encode the form submission in some other way.

When it comes to submitting forms with files in tow, `multipart/form-data` is the content type of choice. We'll need to configure the form to submit as `multipart/form-data` content type by setting the `<sf:form>`'s `enctype` attribute as follows:

```
<sf:form method="POST"
        modelAttribute="spitter"
        enctype="multipart/form-data">
```

With enctype set to multipart/form-data, each field will be submitted as a distinct part of the POST request and not as just another name-value pair. This makes it possible for one of those parts to contain uploaded image file data.

Now we can add a new field to the form. A standard HTML <input> field with type set to file will do the trick:

```
<tr>
  <th><label for="image">Profile image:</label></th>
  <td><input name="image" type="file"/>
</tr>
```

This bit of HTML will render a basic file selection field on the form. Most browsers display this as a text field with a button to the side. Figure 7.8 shows what it looks like when rendered in the Safari browser on Mac OS X.

All of the parts of the form are in place for our users to submit a profile photo. When the form is submitted, it'll be posted as a multipart form where one of the parts contains the image file's binary data. Now we need to ready the server side of our application to be able to receive that data.

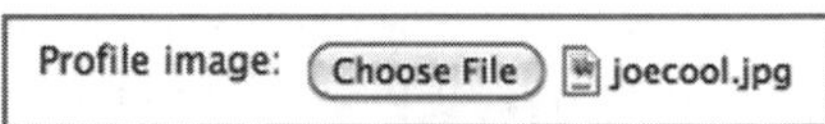

Figure 7.8 A file selection field in the Spitter registration form will enable users to put a face on their profile.

7.5.2 Receiving uploaded files

As before, the addSpitterFromForm() method will handle the registration form submissions. But we'll need to tweak that method to be able to accept an image upload. The following shows the new upload-ready addSpitterFromForm() method.

Listing 7.13 addSpitterFromForm() takes a MultipartFile as a parameter.

```
@RequestMapping(method=RequestMethod.POST)
public String addSpitterFromForm(@Valid Spitter spitter,
    BindingResult bindingResult,
    @RequestParam(value="image", required=false)        <- Accept file upload
        MultipartFile image) {
  if(bindingResult.hasErrors()) {
    return "spitters/edit";
  }

  spitterService.saveSpitter(spitter);

  try {
    if(!image.isEmpty()) {
      validateImage(image);                   <- Validate image

      saveImage(spitter.getId() + ".jpg", image); //       <- Save image file
    }
  } catch (ImageUploadException e) {
    bindingResult.reject(e.getMessage());
    return "spitters/edit";
  }

  return "redirect:/spitters/" + spitter.getUsername();
}
```

The first change made to addSpitterFromForm() is the addition of a new parameter. The image parameter is given as a MultipartFile and is annotated with @RequestParam to indicate that it's not required (so that a user can still register, even without a profile picture).

A little further down in the method, we check to make sure that the image isn't empty and, if it's not, then it's passed in to a validateImage() method and a saveImage() method. The validateImage(), as shown here, makes sure that the uploaded file meets our needs:

```
private void validateImage(MultipartFile image) {
  if(!image.getContentType().equals("image/jpeg")) {
    throw new ImageUploadException("Only JPG images accepted");
  }
}
```

We don't want to let users try to pass off zip or exe files as images. So validateImage() ensures that the uploaded file is a JPEG image. If this validation fails, an ImageUploadException (a simple extension of RuntimeException) will be thrown.

Once we're assured that the uploaded file is an image, we're ready to save it by calling the saveImage() method. The actual implementation of saveImage() could save the file almost anywhere, so long as it's available to the user's browser so that it can be rendered in the browser. Keeping it simple, let's start by writing an implementation of saveImage() that saves the image to the local file system.

SAVING FILES TO THE FILE SYSTEM

Even though our application will be accessible over the web, its resources ultimately reside in a file system on the host server. So it would seem natural to write the user profile pictures to a path on the local file system that the web server can serve the images from. The following implementation of saveImage does just that:

```
private void saveImage(String filename, MultipartFile image)
      throws ImageUploadException {
  try {
    File file = new File(webRootPath + "/resources/" + filename);
    FileUtils.writeByteArrayToFile(file, image.getBytes());
  } catch (IOException e) {
    throw new ImageUploadException("Unable to save image", e);
  }
}
```

Here, the first thing that saveImage() does is construct a java.io.File object whose path is based at the value of the webRootPath. We've purposefully left the value of that variable a mystery, as it depends on the server where the application is hosted. Suffice it to say that it could be configured by value injection, either through a setWebRootPath() method or perhaps using SpEL and an @Value annotation to read the value from a configuration file.

Once the `File` object is ready, we use `FileUtils` from Apache Commons IO[6] to write the image data to a file. If anything goes wrong, an `ImageUploadException` will be thrown.

Saving a file to the local file system like this works great, but leaves the management of the file system up to you. You'll be responsible for ensuring that there's plenty of space. It'll be up to you to make sure that it's backed up in case of a hardware failure. And it's your job to deal with synchronizing the image files across multiple servers in a cluster.

Another option is to let someone else take that hassle away from you. With a bit more code, we can save our images out on the cloud. Let's free ourselves from the burden of managing our own files by rewriting the `saveFile()` method to write to an Amazon S3 bucket.

SAVING FILES TO AMAZON S3

Amazon's *Simple Storage Service*, or *S3* as it's commonly referred to, is an inexpensive way to offload storage of files to Amazon's infrastructure. With S3, we can just write the files and let Amazon's system administrators do all of the grunt work.

The easiest way to use S3 in Java is with the JetS3t library.[7] JetS3t is an open source library for saving and reading files in the S3 cloud. We can use JetS3t to save user profile pictures. The following listing shows the new `saveImage()` method.

Listing 7.14 This `saveImage()` method posts a user's image to the Amazon S3 cloud

```
private void saveImage(String filename, MultipartFile image)
      throws ImageUploadException {

  try {
    AWSCredentials awsCredentials =
      new AWSCredentials(s3AccessKey, s3SecretKey);
    S3Service s3 = new RestS3Service(awsCredentials);     <-- Set up S3 service

    S3Bucket imageBucket = s3.getBucket("spitterImages");
    S3Object imageObject = new S3Object(filename);        <-- Create S3 bucket and object

    imageObject.setDataInputStream(
            new ByteArrayInputStream(image.getBytes()));
    imageObject.setContentLength(image.getBytes().length);
    imageObject.setContentType("image/jpeg");             <-- Set image data

    AccessControlList acl = new AccessControlList();      <-- Set permissions
    acl.setOwner(imageBucket.getOwner());
    acl.grantPermission(GroupGrantee.ALL_USERS,
            Permission.PERMISSION_READ);
    imageObject.setAcl(acl);

    s3.putObject(imageBucket, imageObject);               <-- Save image
  } catch (Exception e) {
    throw new ImageUploadException("Unable to save image", e);
  }
}
```

---

6 http://commons.apache.org/io/

7 http://bitbucket.org/jmurty/jets3t/wiki/Home

The first thing that `saveImage()` does is set up Amazon Web Service credentials. For this, you'll need an S3 access key and an S3 secret access key. These will be given to you by Amazon when you sign up for S3 service. They'll be given to `SpitterController` via value injection.

With the AWS credentials in hand, `saveImage()` creates an instance of JetS3t's `RestS3Service` through which it'll operate on the S3 file system. It gets a reference to the `spitterImages` bucket, creates an `S3Object` to contain the image, then fills that `S3Object` with image data.

Just before calling the `putObject()` method to write the image data to S3, `saveImage()` sets the permissions on the `S3Object` to allow all users to view it. This is important—without it, the images wouldn't be visible to our application's users.

As with the previous version of `saveImage()`, if anything goes wrong, a `ImageUploadException` will be thrown.

We're almost set for uploading profile pictures into the Spitter application. But there's one final bit of Spring configuration to tie it all together.

7.5.3 Configuring Spring for file uploads

On its own, `DispatcherServlet` doesn't know how to deal with multipart form data. We need a multipart resolver to extract the multipart data out of the POST request so that `DispatcherServlet` can give it to our controller.

To register a multipart resolver in Spring, we need to declare a bean that implements the `MultipartResolver` interface. Our choice of multipart resolvers is made easy by the fact that Spring only comes with one: `CommonsMultipartResolver`. It's configured in Spring as follows:

```
<bean id="multipartResolver" class=
    "org.springframework.web.multipart.commons.CommonsMultipartResolver"
    p:maxUploadSize="500000" />
```

Note that the multipart resolver's bean ID is significant. When `DispatcherServlet` looks for a multipart resolver, it'll look for it as a bean whose ID is `multipartResolver`. If the bean has any other ID, `DispatcherServlet` will overlook it.

7.6 Summary

In this chapter, we've built much of the web layer of the Spitter application. As we've seen, Spring comes with a powerful and flexible web framework. Employing annotations, Spring MVC offers a near-POJO development model, making simple work of developing controllers that handle requests and are simple to test. These controllers typically don't directly process requests, but instead delegate to other beans in the Spring application context that are injected into the controllers using Spring's dependency injection.

By employing handler mappings that choose controllers to handle requests and view resolvers to choose how results are rendered, Spring MVC maintains a loose coupling between how a controller is chosen to handle a request and how its view is chosen to display output. This sets Spring apart from many other MVC web frameworks, where choices are limited to one or two options.

Although the views developed in this chapter were written in JSP to produce HTML output, there's no reason why the model data produced by the controllers couldn't be rendered in some other form, including machine-readable XML or JSON. We'll see how to turn the Spitter application's web layer into a powerful web-based API in chapter 11 when we explore Spring's REST support further.

But for now, we'll continue looking at how to build user-facing web applications with Spring by exploring Spring Web Flow, an extension to Spring MVC that enables conversation-oriented web development in Spring.

8 Working with Spring Web Flow

This chapter covers

- Creating conversational web applications
- Defining flow states and actions
- Securing web flows

One of the strangely wonderful things about the internet is that it's so easy to get lost. There are so many things to see and read. The hyperlink is at the core of the internet's power. But at the same time it's no wonder they call it *the web*. Just like webs built by spiders, it traps anyone who happens to crawl across it.

I'll confess: one reason why it took me so long to write this book is because I once got lost in an endless path of Wikipedia links.

There are times when a web application must take control of a web surfer's voyage, leading the user step by step through the application. The quintessential example of such an application is the checkout process on an e-commerce site. Starting with the shopping cart, the application leads you through a process of entering shipping details, billing information, and ultimately an order confirmation.

Spring Web Flow is a web framework that enables development of elements following a prescribed flow. In this chapter, we're going to explore Spring Web Flow and see how it fits into the Spring web framework landscape.

It's possible to write a flowed application with any web framework. I've even seen a Struts application that had a certain flow built into it. But without a way to separate the flow from the implementation, you'll find that the definition of the flow is scattered across the various elements that make up the flow. There's no one place to go to fully understand the flow.

Spring Web Flow is an extension to Spring MVC that enables development of flow-based web applications. It does this by separating the definition of an application's flow from the classes and views that implement the flow's behavior.

As we get to know Spring Web Flow, we're going to take a break from the Spitter example and work on a new web application for taking pizza orders. We'll use Spring Web Flow to define the order process.

The first step to working with Spring Web Flow is to install it within your project. Let's start there.

8.1 Installing Spring Web Flow

Although Spring Web Flow is a subproject of the Spring Framework, it isn't part of the Spring Framework proper. Therefore, before we can get started building flow-based applications, we'll need to add Spring Web Flow to our project's classpath.

You can download Spring Web Flow from the project's website (http://www.springframework.org/webflow). Be sure to get the latest version (as I write this, that's version 2.2.1). Once you've downloaded and unzipped the distribution zip file, you'll find the following Spring Web Flow JAR files in the dist directory:

- org.springframework.binding-2.2.1.RELEASE.jar
- org.springframework.faces-2.2.1.RELEASE.jar
- org.springframework.js-2.2.1.RELEASE.jar
- org.springframework.js.resources-2.2.1.RELEASE.jar
- org.springframework.webflow-2.2.1.RELEASE.jar

For our example, we'll only need the *binding* and *webflow* JAR files. The others are for using Spring Web Flow with JSF and JavaScript.

8.1.1 Configuring Web Flow in Spring

Spring Web Flow is built upon a foundation of Spring MVC. That means that all requests to a flow first go through Spring MVC's `DispatcherServlet`. From there, a handful of special beans in the Spring application context must be configured to handle the flow request and execute the flow.

Several of the web flow beans are declared using elements from Spring Web Flow's Spring configuration XML namespace. Therefore, we'll need to add the namespace declaration to the context definition XML file:

```
<?xml version="1.0" encoding="UTF-8"?>
<beans xmlns="http://www.springframework.org/schema/beans"
 xmlns:xsi="http://www.w3.org/2001/XMLSchema-instance"
 xmlns:flow="http://www.springframework.org/schema/webflow-config"
```

```
xsi:schemaLocation="http://www.springframework.org/schema/webflow-config
  http://www.springframework.org/schema/webflow-config/
➥spring-webflow-config-2.0.xsd
  http://www.springframework.org/schema/beans
  http://www.springframework.org/schema/beans/spring-beans-3.0.xsd">
```

With the namespace declaration in place, we're now ready to start wiring up web flow beans, starting with the flow executor.

WIRING A FLOW EXECUTOR

As its name implies, the *flow executor* drives the execution of a flow. When a user enters a flow, the flow executor creates and launches an instance of the flow execution for that user. When the flow pauses (such as when a view is presented to the user), the flow executor also resumes the flow once the user has taken some action.

The `<flow:flow-executor>` element creates a flow executor in Spring:

```
<flow:flow-executor id="flowExecutor"
                    flow-registry="flowRegistry" />
```

Although the flow executor is responsible for creating and executing flows, it's not responsible for loading flow definitions. That responsibility falls to a flow registry, which we'll create next. Here, the flow registry is referred to by its ID: `flowRegistry`.[1]

CONFIGURING A FLOW REGISTRY

A *flow registry*'s job is to load flow definitions and make them available to the flow executor. We can configure a flow registry in the Spring configuration with the `<flow:flow-registry>` element like this:

```
<flow:flow-registry id="flowRegistry"
         base-path="/WEB-INF/flows">
   <flow:flow-location-pattern value="*-flow.xml" />
</flow:flow-registry>
```

As declared here, the flow registry will look for flow definitions under the /WEB-INF/flows directory, as specified in the `base-path` attribute. Per the `<flow:flow-location-pattern>` element, any XML file whose name ends with *-flow.xml* will be considered a flow definition.

All flows are referred to by their IDs. Using the `<flow:flow-location-pattern>` as we have, the flow ID will be the directory path relative to the `base-path`—or the part of the path represented with the double asterisk. Figure 8.1 shows how the flow ID is calculated in this scenario.

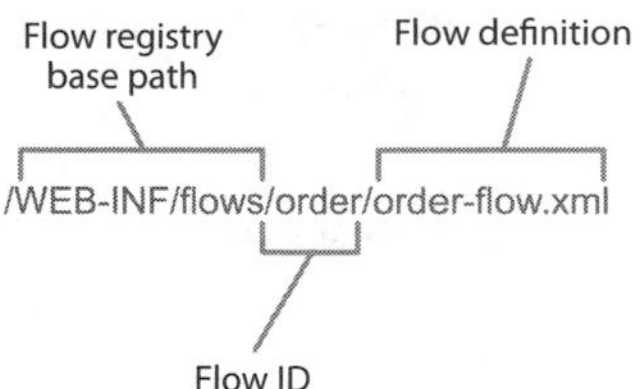

Figure 8.1 When using a flow location pattern, the path to the flow definition file relative to the base path will be used as the flow's ID.

[1] The `flow-registry` attribute is explicitly set here, but it wasn't necessary to do so. If it's not set, then it defaults to `flowRegistry`.

Alternatively, you could leave the base-path attribute off and explicitly identify the flow definition file's location:

```
<flow:flow-registry id="flowRegistry">
   <flow:flow-location path="/WEB-INF/flows/springpizza.xml" />
</flow:flow-registry>
```

Here, the <flow:flow-location> element is used instead of <flow:flow-location-pattern>. The path attribute directly points at the /WEB-INF/flows/springpizza.xml file as the flow definition. When configured this way, the flow's ID is derived from the base name of the flow definition file; *springpizza* in this case.

If you'd like to be even more explicit about the flow's ID, then you can set it with the id attribute of the <flow:flow-location> element. For example, to specify pizza as the flow's ID, configure the <flow:flow-location> like this:

```
<flow:flow-registry id="flowRegistry">
   <flow:flow-location id="pizza"
         path="/WEB-INF/flows/springpizza.xml" />
</flow:flow-registry>
```

HANDLING FLOW REQUESTS

As we saw in the previous chapter, DispatcherServlet typically dispatches requests to controllers. But for flows, we'll need a FlowHandlerMapping to help DispatcherServlet know that it should send flow requests to Spring Web Flow. The FlowHandlerMapping is configured in the Spring application context like this:

```
<bean class="org.springframework.webflow.mvc.servlet.FlowHandlerMapping">
  <property name="flowRegistry" ref="flowRegistry" />
</bean>
```

As you can see, the FlowHandlerMapping is wired with a reference to the flow registry so it knows when a request's URL maps to a flow. For example, if we have a flow whose ID is pizza, then FlowHandlerMapping will know to map a request to that flow if the request's URL pattern (relative to the application context path) is /pizza.

Whereas the FlowHandlerMapping's job is to direct flow requests to Spring Web Flow, it's the job of a FlowHandlerAdapter to answer that call. A FlowHandlerAdapter is equivalent to a Spring MVC controller in that it handles requests coming in for a flow and processes those requests. The FlowHandlerAdapter is wired as a Spring bean like this:

```
<bean class="org.springframework.webflow.mvc.servlet.FlowHandlerAdapter">
  <property name="flowExecutor" ref="flowExecutor" />
</bean>
```

This handler adapter is the bridge between DispatcherServlet and Spring Web Flow. It handles flow requests and manipulates the flow based on those requests. Here, it's wired with a reference to the flow executor to execute the flows that it handles requests for.

We've configured all of the beans and components that are needed for Spring Web Flow to work. What's left is to actually define a flow. We'll do that soon enough. But first, let's get to know the elements that are put together to make up a flow.

8.2 The components of a flow

In Spring Web Flow, a flow is defined by three primary elements: states, transitions, and flow data.

States are points in a flow where something happens. If you imagine a flow as being like a road trip, then states are the towns, truck stops, and scenic stops along the way. Instead of picking up a bag of Doritos and a Diet Coke, a state in a flow is where some logic is performed, some decision is made, or some page is presented to the user.

If flow states are like the points on a map where you might stop during a road trip, then *transitions* are the roads that connect those points. In a flow, you get from one state to another by way of a transition.

As you travel from town to town, you may pick up some souvenirs, memories, and empty snack bags along the way. Similarly, as a flow progresses, it collects some data: the current condition of the flow. I'm tempted to refer to it as the state of the flow, but the word *state* already has another meaning when talking about flows.

Let's take a closer look at how these three elements are defined in Spring Web Flow.

8.2.1 States

Spring Web Flow defines five different kinds of state, as shown in table 8.1.

The selection of states provided by Spring Web Flow makes it possible to construct virtually any arrangement of functionality into a conversational web application. Though not all flows will require all of the states described in table 8.1, you'll probably end up using most of them at one time or another.

Table 8.1 Spring Web Flow's selections of states

State type	What it's for
Action	Action states are where the logic of a flow takes place.
Decision	Decision states branch the flow in two directions, routing the flow based on the outcome of evaluation flow data.
End	The end state is the last stop for a flow. Once a flow has reached its end state, the flow is terminated.
Subflow	A subflow state starts a new flow within the context of a flow that is already underway.
View	A view state pauses the flow and invites the user to participate in the flow.

In a moment we'll see how to piece these different kinds of states together to form a complete flow. But first, let's get to know how each of these flow elements are manifested in a Spring Web Flow definition.

VIEW STATES

View states are used to display information to the user and to offer the user an opportunity to play an active role in the flow. The actual view implementation could be any of the views supported by Spring MVC, but is often implemented in JSP.

Within the flow definition XML file, the `<view-state>` element is used to define a view state:

```
<view-state id="welcome" />
```

In this simple example, the `id` attribute serves a dual purpose. It identifies the state within the flow. Also, because no view has been specified otherwise, it specifies `welcome` as the logical name of the view to be rendered when the flow reaches this state.

If you'd rather explicitly identify another view name, then you can do so with the `view` attribute:

```
<view-state id="welcome" view="greeting" />
```

If a flow presents a form to the user, you may want to specify the object to which the form will be bound. To do that, set the `model` attribute:

```
<view-state id="takePayment" model="flowScope.paymentDetails"/>
```

Here we've specified that the form in the `takePayment` view will be bound to the flow-scoped `paymentDetails` object. (We'll talk more about flow scopes and data in a moment.)

ACTION STATES

Whereas view states involve the users of the application in the flow, action states are where the application itself goes to work. Action states typically invoke some method on a Spring-managed bean and then transition to another state depending on the outcome of the method call.

In the flow definition XML, action states are expressed with the `<action-state>` element. Here's an example:

```
<action-state id="saveOrder">
  <evaluate expression="pizzaFlowActions.saveOrder(order)" />
  <transition to="thankYou" />
</action-state>
```

Although it's not strictly required, `<action-state>` elements usually have an `<evaluate>` element as a child. The `<evaluate>` element gives an action state something to do. The `expression` attribute is given an expression that's evaluated when the state is entered. In this case, `expression` is given a SpEL[2] expression which

---

[2] Starting with version 2.1.0, Spring Web Flow uses the Spring Expression Language, but can optionally use OGNL or the Unified EL if you'd prefer.

indicates that the saveOrder() method should be called on a bean whose ID is pizzaFlowActions.

DECISION STATES

It's possible for a flow to be purely linear, stepping from one state to another without taking any alternate routes. But more often a flow branches at one point or another, depending on the flow's current circumstances.

Decision states enable a binary branch in a flow execution. A decision state will evaluate a Boolean expression and will take one of two transitions, depending on whether the expression evaluates to true or false. Within the XML flow definition, decision states are defined by the <decision-state> element. A typical example of a decision state might look like this:

```
<decision-state id="checkDeliveryArea">
  <if test="pizzaFlowActions.checkDeliveryArea(customer.zipCode)"
      then="addCustomer"
      else="deliveryWarning" />
</decision-state>
```

As you can see, the <decision-state> element doesn't work alone. The <if> element is the heart of a decision state. It's where the expression is evaluated. If the expression evaluates to true, then the flow will transition to the state identified by the then attribute. But if it's false, then the flow will transition to the state named in the else attribute.

SUBFLOW STATES

You probably wouldn't write all of your application's logic in a single method. Instead, you'd probably break it up into multiple classes, methods, and other structures.

In the same way, it's a good idea to break flows down into discrete parts. The <subflow-state> element lets you call another flow from within an executing flow. It's analogous to calling a method from within another method.

A <subflow-state> might be declared as follows:

```
<subflow-state id="order" subflow="pizza/order">
  <input name="order" value="order"/>
  <transition on="orderCreated" to="payment" />
</subflow-state>
```

Here, the <input> element is used to pass the order object as input to the subflow. And, if the subflow ends with an <end-state> whose ID is orderCreated, then the flow will transition to the state whose ID is payment.

But I'm getting ahead of myself. We haven't talked about the <end-state> element or transitions yet. But we'll look at transitions soon in section 8.2.2. As for end states, that's what we'll look at next.

END STATES

Eventually all flows must come to an end. And that's what they'll do when they transition to an end state. The <end-state> element designates the end of a flow and typically appears like this:

```
<end-state id="customerReady" />
```

When the flow reaches an `<end-state>`, the flow ends. What happens next depends on a few factors:

- If the flow that's ending is a subflow, then the calling flow will proceed from the `<subflow-state>`. The `<end-state>`'s ID will be used as an event to trigger the transition away from the `<subflow-state>`.
- If the `<end-state>` has its `view` attribute set, the specified view will be rendered. The view may be a flow-relative path to a view template, prefixed with `externalRedirect:` to redirect to some page external to the flow, or prefixed with `flowRedirect:` to redirect to another flow.
- If the ending flow isn't a subflow and no `view` is specified, then the flow simply ends. The browser ends up landing on the flow's base URL, and with no current flow active, a new instance of the flow begins.

It's important to realize that a flow may have more than one end state. Since the end state's ID determines the event fired from a subflow, you may want to end the flow through multiple end states to trigger different events in the calling flow. Even in flows that aren't subflows, there may be several landing pages that follow the completion of a flow, depending on the course that the flow took.

Now that we've looked at the various kinds of states in a flow, we should take a moment to look at how the flow travels between states. Let's see how to pave some roads in a flow by defining transitions.

8.2.2 Transitions

As I've already mentioned, transitions connect the states within a flow. Every state in a flow, with the exception of end states, should have at least one transition so that the flow will know where to go once that state has completed. A state may have multiple transitions, each one representing a different path that could be taken upon completion of the state.

A transition is defined by the `<transition>` element, a child of the various state elements (`<action-state>`, `<view-state>`, and `<subflow-state>`). In its simplest form, the `<transition>` element identifies the next state in the flow:

```
<transition to="customerReady" />
```

The `to` attribute is used to specify the next state in the flow. When `<transition>` is declared with only a `to` attribute, the transition is the default transition for that state and will be taken if no other transitions are applicable.

More commonly transitions are defined to take place upon some event being fired. In a view state, the event is usually some action taken by the user. In an action state, the event is the result of evaluating an expression. In the case of a subflow state, the event is determined by the ID of the subflow's end state. In any event (no pun intended), you can specify the event to trigger the transition by specifying it in the `on` attribute:

```
<transition on="phoneEntered" to="lookupCustomer"/>
```

In this example, the flow will transition to the state whose ID is `lookupCustomer` if a `phoneEntered` event is fired.

The flow can also transition to another state in response to some exception being thrown. For example, if a customer record can't be found, you may want the flow to transition to a view state that presents a registration form. The following snippet shows that kind of transition:

```
<transition
    on-exception=
           "com.springinaction.pizza.service.CustomerNotFoundException"
    to="registrationForm" />
```

The `on-exception` attribute is much like the `on` attribute, except that it specifies an exception to transition on instead of an event. In this case, a `CustomerNotFoundException` will cause the flow to transition to the `registrationForm` state.

GLOBAL TRANSITIONS

After you've created a flow, you may find that there are several states that share some common transitions. For example, I wouldn't be surprised to find the following `<transition>` sprinkled all over a flow:

```
<transition on="cancel" to="endState" />
```

Rather than repeat common transitions in multiple states, you can define them as global transitions by placing the `<transition>` element as a child of a `<global-transitions>` element. For example:

```
<global-transitions>
  <transition on="cancel" to="endState" />
</global-transitions>
```

With this global transition in place, all states within the flow will have an implicit `cancel` transition.

We've talked about states and transitions. Before we get busy writing flows, let's look at flow data, the remaining member of the web flow triad.

8.2.3 *Flow data*

If you've ever played one of those old text-based adventure games, you know that as you move from location to location, you occasionally find objects laying around that you can pick up and carry with you. Sometimes you need an object right away. Other times, you may carry an object around through the entire game not knowing what it's for—until you get to that final puzzle and find that it's useful after all.

In many ways, flows are like those adventure games. As the flow progresses from one state to another, it picks up some data. Sometimes that data is only needed for a little while (maybe just long enough to display a page to the user). Other times, that data is carried around through the entire flow and is ultimately used as the flow completes.

DECLARING VARIABLES

Flow data is stored away in variables that can be referenced at various points in the flow. It can be created and accumulated in several ways. The simplest way to create a variable in a flow is by using the `<var>` element:

```
<var name="customer" class="com.springinaction.pizza.domain.Customer"/>
```

Here, a new instance of a `Customer` object is created and placed into the variable whose name is `customer`. This variable will be available to all states in a flow.

As part of an action state or upon entry to a view state, you may also create variables using the `<evaluate>` element. For example:

```
<evaluate result="viewScope.toppingsList"
   expression="T(com.springinaction.pizza.domain.Topping).asList()" />
```

In this case, the `<evaluate>` element evaluates an expression (a SpEL expression) and places the result in a variable named `toppingsList` that's view-scoped. (We'll talk more about scopes in a moment.)

Similarly, the `<set>` element can set a variable's value:

```
<set name="flowScope.pizza"
   value="new com.springinaction.pizza.domain.Pizza()" />
```

The `<set>` element works much the same as the `<evaluate>` element, setting a variable to the resulting value from an evaluated expression. Here, we're setting a flow-scoped `pizza` variable to a new instance of a `Pizza` object.

You'll see more specifics on how these elements are used in an actual flow when we get to section 8.3 and start building a real working web flow. But first, let's see what it means for a variable to be flow-scoped, view-scoped, or use some other scope.

SCOPING FLOW DATA

The data carried about in a flow will have varying lifespans and visibility, depending on the scope of the variable it's kept in. Spring Web Flow defines five scopes, as described in table 8.2.

Table 8.2 Spring Web Flow's selections of states

Scope	Lifespan and visibility
Conversation	Created when a top-level flow starts and destroyed when the top-level flow ends. Shared by a top-level flow and all of its subflows.
Flow	Created when a flow starts and destroyed when the flow ends. Only visible within the flow it was created by.
Request	Created when a request is made into a flow and destroyed when the flow returns.
Flash	Created when a flow starts and destroyed when the flow ends. It's also cleared out after a view state renders.
View	Created when a view state is entered and destroyed when the state exits. Visible only within the view state.

When declaring a variable using the `<var>` element, the variable is always flow-scoped within the flow defining the variable. When using `<set>` or `<evaluate>`, the scope is specified as a prefix for the `name` or `result` attribute. For example, to assign a value to a flow-scoped variable named `theAnswer`:

```
<set name="flowScope.theAnswer" value="42"/>
```

Now that we've seen all of the raw materials of a web flow, it's time to piece them together into a full-blown, fully functional web flow. As we do, keep your eyes peeled for examples of how to store data away in scoped variables.

8.3 Putting it all together: the pizza flow

As I mentioned earlier in this chapter, we're taking a break from the Spitter application. Instead, we've been asked to build out an online pizza ordering application where hungry web visitors can order their favorite Italian pie.[3]

As it turns out, the process of ordering a pizza can be defined nicely in a flow. We'll start by building a high-level flow that defines the overall process of ordering a pizza. Then we'll break that flow down into subflows that define the details at a lower level.

8.3.1 Defining the base flow

A new pizza chain, Spizza,[4] has decided to relieve the load on their stores' telephones by allowing customers to place orders online. When the customer visits the Spizza website, they'll identify themselves, select one or more pizzas to add to their order, provide payment information, and then submit the order and wait for the pizza to arrive, hot and fresh. Figure 8.2 illustrates this flow.

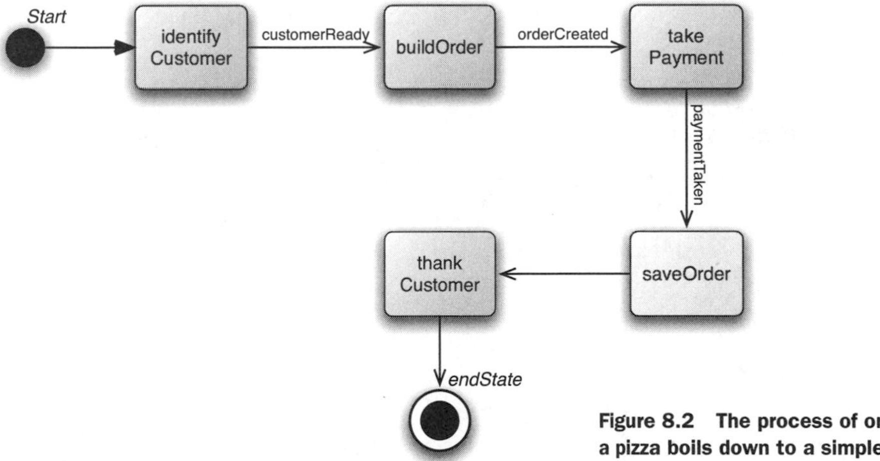

Figure 8.2 The process of ordering a pizza boils down to a simple flow.

[3] In truth, I couldn't think of any good way of working a flow into the Spitter application. So rather than shoehorn a Spring Web Flow example into Spitter, we're going to go with the pizza example.

[4] Yes, I know...there's a real Spizza pizza place in Singapore. This isn't that one.

The boxes in the diagram represent states and the arrows represent transitions. As you can see, the overall pizza flow is simple and linear. It should be easy to express this flow in Spring Web Flow. The only thing that makes it interesting is that the first three states can be more involved than suggested by a simple box.

The following shows the high-level pizza order flow as defined using Spring Web Flow's XML-based flow definition.

Listing 8.1 The pizza order flow, defined as a Spring Web Flow

```
<?xml version="1.0" encoding="UTF-8"?>
<flow xmlns="http://www.springframework.org/schema/webflow"
  xmlns:xsi="http://www.w3.org/2001/XMLSchema-instance"
  xsi:schemaLocation="http://www.springframework.org/schema/webflow
  http://www.springframework.org/schema/webflow/spring-webflow-2.0.xsd">

  <var name="order"
       class="com.springinaction.pizza.domain.Order"/>

  <subflow-
     state id="identifyCustomer" subflow="pizza/customer">     <-- Call customer subflow
    <output name="customer" value="order.customer"/>
    <transition on="customerReady" to="buildOrder" />
  </subflow-state>

  <subflow-state id="buildOrder" subflow="pizza/order">        <-- Call order subflow
    <input name="order" value="order"/>
    <transition on="orderCreated" to="takePayment" />
  </subflow-state>

  <subflow-state id="takePayment" subflow="pizza/payment">     <-- Call payment subflow
    <input name="order" value="order"/>
    <transition on="paymentTaken" to="saveOrder"/>
  </subflow-state>

  <action-state id="saveOrder">                                <-- Save order
    <evaluate expression="pizzaFlowActions.saveOrder(order)" />
    <transition to="thankCustomer" />
  </action-state>

  <view-state id="thankCustomer">                              <-- Thank customer
    <transition to="endState" />
  </view-state>

  <end-state id="endState" />

  <global-transitions>
    <transition on="cancel" to="endState" />                   <-- Global cancel transition
  </global-transitions>
</flow>
```

The first thing you see in the flow definition is the declaration of the `order` variable. Each time the flow starts, a new instance of `Order` is created. The `Order` class, as shown next, has properties for carrying all of the information about an order, including the customer information, the list of pizzas ordered, and the payment details.

Listing 8.2 An `Order` carries all of the details pertaining to a pizza order

```
package com.springinaction.pizza.domain;

import java.io.Serializable;
import java.util.ArrayList;
import java.util.List;

public class Order implements Serializable {
   private static final long serialVersionUID = 1L;

   private Customer customer;
   private List<Pizza> pizzas;
   private Payment payment;

   public Order() {
      pizzas = new ArrayList<Pizza>();
      customer = new Customer();
   }

   public Customer getCustomer() {
      return customer;
   }

   public void setCustomer(Customer customer) {
      this.customer = customer;
   }

   public List<Pizza> getPizzas() {
      return pizzas;
   }

   public void setPizzas(List<Pizza> pizzas) {
      this.pizzas = pizzas;
   }

   public void addPizza(Pizza pizza) {
      pizzas.add(pizza);
   }

   public float getTotal() {
      return 0.0f;
   }

   public Payment getPayment() {
      return payment;
   }

   public void setPayment(Payment payment) {
      this.payment = payment;
   }
}
```

The main portion of the flow definition is made up of the flow states. By default, the first state in the flow definition file is also the first state that will be visited in the flow. In this case, that's the `identifyCustomer` state (a subflow state). But if you'd like, you can explicitly identify any state as the starting state by setting the `start-state` attribute in the `<flow>` element:

```
<?xml version="1.0" encoding="UTF-8"?>
<flow xmlns="http://www.springframework.org/schema/webflow"
  xmlns:xsi="http://www.w3.org/2001/XMLSchema-instance"
  xsi:schemaLocation="http://www.springframework.org/schema/webflow
  http://www.springframework.org/schema/webflow/spring-webflow-2.0.xsd"
  start-state="identifyCustomer">
...
</flow>
```

Identifying a customer, building a pizza order, and taking payment are activities that are too complex to be crammed into a single state. That's why we'll define them later in more detail as flows in their own right. But for the purposes of the high-level pizza flow, these activities are expressed with the `<subflow-state>` element.

The `order` flow variable will be populated by the first three states and then saved in the fourth state. The `identifyCustomer` subflow state uses the `<output>` element to populate the `order`'s `customer` property, setting it to the output received from calling the customer subflow. The `buildOrder` and `takePayment` states take a different approach, using `<input>` to pass the `order` flow variable as input so that those subflows can populate the `order` internally.

After the order has been given a customer, some pizzas, and payment details, it's time to save it. The `saveOrder` state is an action state that handles that task. It uses `<evaluate>` to make a call to the `saveOrder()` method on the bean whose ID is `pizzaFlowActions`, passing in the order to be saved. When it's finished saving the order, it transitions to `thankCustomer`.

The `thankCustomer` state is a simple view state, backed by the JSP file at /WEB-INF/flows/pizza/thankCustomer.jsp, as shown next.

Listing 8.3 A JSP view that thanks the customer for their order

```
<html xmlns:jsp="http://java.sun.com/JSP/Page">
  <jsp:output omit-xml-declaration="yes"/>
  <jsp:directive.page contentType="text/html;charset=UTF-8" />

  <head><title>Spizza</title></head>

  <body>
    <h2>Thank you for your order!</h2>

    <![CDATA[
    <a href='${flowExecutionUrl}&_eventId=finished'>Finish</a>      <-- Fire finished event
   ]]>
    </body>
</html>
```

The "thank you" page thanks the customer for their order and gives a link for the customer to finish the flow. This link is the most interesting thing on the page because it shows one way that a user can interact with the flow.

Spring Web Flow provides a `flowExecutionUrl` variable, which contains the URL for the flow, for use in the view. The Finish link attaches an `_eventId` parameter to the URL to fire a `finished` event back to the web flow. That event sends the flow to the end state.

At the end state, the flow ends. Since there are no further details on where to go after the flow ends, the flow will start over again at the `identifyCustomer` state, ready to take another pizza order.

That covers the general flow for ordering a pizza. But there's more to the flow than what we see in listing 8.1. We still need to define the subflows for the `identifyCustomer`, `buildOrder`, and `takePayment` states. Let's build those flows next, starting with the one that identifies the customer.

8.3.2 Collecting customer information

If you've ordered a pizza before, you probably know the drill. The first thing they ask for is your phone number. Aside from giving them a way to call you if the delivery driver can't find your house, the phone number also serves as your identification to the pizza shop. If you're a repeat customer, they can use that phone number to look up your address so that they'll know where to deliver your order.

For a new customer, the phone number won't turn up any results. So the next information that they'll ask for is your address. At this point the pizzeria knows who you are and where to deliver your pizzas. But before they ask you what kind of pizza you want, they need to check to make sure that your address falls within their delivery area. If not, then you'll have to come in and pick up the pizza yourself.

The initial question and answer period that begins every pizza order can be illustrated with the flow diagram in figure 8.3.

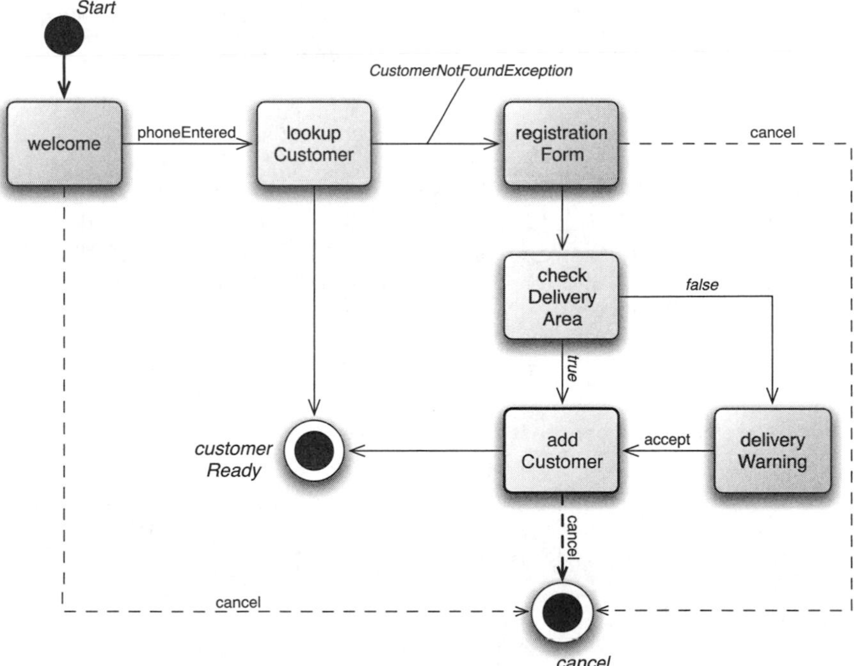

Figure 8.3 The flow for identifying a customer has a few more twists than the pizza flow.

This flow is more interesting than the top-level pizza flow. This flow isn't linear and branches in a couple of places depending on different conditions. For example, after looking up the customer, the flow could either end (if the customer was found) or transition to a registration form (if the customer was not found). Also, at the `checkDeliveryArea` state, the customer may or may not be warned that their address isn't in the delivery area.

The following shows the flow definition for identifying the customer.

Listing 8.4 Identifying the hungry pizza customer with a web flow

```
<?xml version="1.0" encoding="UTF-8"?>
<flow xmlns="http://www.springframework.org/schema/webflow"
  xmlns:xsi="http://www.w3.org/2001/XMLSchema-instance"
  xsi:schemaLocation="http://www.springframework.org/schema/webflow
  http://www.springframework.org/schema/webflow/spring-webflow-2.0.xsd">

  <var name="customer" class="com.springinaction.pizza.domain.Customer"/>

  <view-state id="welcome">                              <- Welcome customer
    <transition on="phoneEntered" to="lookupCustomer"/>
  </view-state>

  <action-state id="lookupCustomer">                   <- Look up customer
    <evaluate result="customer" expression=
        "pizzaFlowActions.lookupCustomer(requestParameters.phoneNumber)" />
    <transition to="registrationForm" on-exception=
        "com.springinaction.pizza.service.CustomerNotFoundException" />
    <transition to="customerReady" />
  </action-state>
                                                              Register new
  <view-state id="registrationForm" model="customer">    <- customer
    <on-entry>
      <evaluate expression=
          "customer.phoneNumber = requestParameters.phoneNumber" />
    </on-entry>
    <transition on="submit" to="checkDeliveryArea" />
  </view-state>
                                                       Check
  <decision-state id="checkDeliveryArea">          <- delivery area
    <if test="pizzaFlowActions.checkDeliveryArea(customer.zipCode)"
        then="addCustomer"
        else="deliveryWarning"/>
  </decision-state>
                                                  Show delivery
  <view-state id="deliveryWarning">            <- warning
    <transition on="accept" to="addCustomer" />
  </view-state>

  <action-state id="addCustomer">                          <- Add customer
    <evaluate expression="pizzaFlowActions.addCustomer(customer)" />
    <transition to="customerReady" />
  </action-state>

  <end-state id="cancel" />
  <end-state id="customerReady">
    <output name="customer" />
  </end-state>
```

```
  <global-transitions>
    <transition on="cancel" to="cancel" />
  </global-transitions>
</flow>
```

This flow introduces a few new tricks, including our first use of the `<decision-state>` element. Also, since it's a subflow of the `pizza` flow, it expects to receive an `Order` object as input.

As before, let's break down this flow definition state by state, starting with the `welcome` state.

ASKING FOR A PHONE NUMBER

The `welcome` state is a fairly straightforward view state that welcomes the customer to the Spizza website and asks them to enter their phone number. The state itself isn't particularly interesting. It has two transitions: one that directs the flow to the `lookupCustomer` state if a `phoneEntered` event is fired from the view, and another `cancel` transition, defined as a global transition, that reacts to a `cancel` event.

Where the `welcome` state gets interesting is in the view itself. The welcome view is defined in /WEB-INF/flows/pizza/customer/welcome.jspx, as shown next.

Listing 8.5 Welcoming the customer and asking for their phone number

```
<html xmlns:jsp="http://java.sun.com/JSP/Page"
     xmlns:form="http://www.springframework.org/tags/form">
  <jsp:output omit-xml-declaration="yes"/>
  <jsp:directive.page contentType="text/html;charset=UTF-8" />

  <head><title>Spizza</title></head>

  <body>
    <h2>Welcome to Spizza!!!</h2>

    <form:form>
      <input type="hidden" name="_flowExecutionKey"
             value="${flowExecutionKey}"/>          Flow execution key

      <input type="text" name="phoneNumber"/><br/>

      <input type="submit" name="_eventId_phoneEntered"
             value="Lookup Customer" />             Fire phoneEntered event
    </form:form>
  </body>
</html>
```

This simple form prompts the user to enter their phone number. But the form has two special ingredients that enable it to drive the flow.

First note the hidden `_flowExecutionKey` field. When a view state is entered, the flow pauses and waits for the user to take some action. The flow execution key is given to the view as a sort of "claim ticket" for the flow. When the user submits the form, the flow execution key is sent along with it in the `_flowExecutionKey` field and the flow resumes where it left off.

Also pay special attention to the submit button's name. The *_eventId_* portion of the button's name is a clue to Spring Web Flow that what follows is an event that should be fired. When the form is submitted by clicking that button, a phoneEntered event will be fired, triggering a transition to lookupCustomer.

LOOKING UP THE CUSTOMER

After the welcome form has been submitted, the customer's phone number is among the request parameters and is ready to be used to look up a customer. The lookupCustomer state's <evaluate> element is where that happens. It pulls the phone number off of the request parameters and passes it to the lookupCustomer() method on the pizzaFlowActions bean.

The implementation of lookupCustomer() is not important right now. It's sufficient to know that it will either return a Customer object or throw a CustomerNotFoundException.

In the former case, the Customer object is assigned to the customer variable (per the result attribute) and the default transition takes the flow to the customerReady state. But if the customer can't be found, then a CustomerNotFoundException will be thrown and the flow will transition to the registrationForm state.

REGISTERING A NEW CUSTOMER

The registrationForm state is where the user is asked for their delivery address. Like other view states we've seen, it'll render a JSP view. The JSP file is shown next.

Listing 8.6 Registering a new customer

```
<html xmlns:c="http://java.sun.com/jsp/jstl/core"
      xmlns:jsp="http://java.sun.com/JSP/Page"
      xmlns:spring="http://www.springframework.org/tags"
      xmlns:form="http://www.springframework.org/tags/form">

  <jsp:output omit-xml-declaration="yes"/>
  <jsp:directive.page contentType="text/html;charset=UTF-8" />

  <head><title>Spizza</title></head>

  <body>
    <h2>Customer Registration</h2>

    <form:form commandName="customer">
      <input type="hidden" name="_flowExecutionKey"
             value="${flowExecutionKey}"/>
      <b>Phone number: </b><form:input path="phoneNumber"/><br/>
      <b>Name: </b><form:input path="name"/><br/>
      <b>Address: </b><form:input path="address"/><br/>
      <b>City: </b><form:input path="city"/><br/>
      <b>State: </b><form:input path="state"/><br/>
      <b>Zip Code: </b><form:input path="zipCode"/><br/>
      <input type="submit" name="_eventId_submit"
             value="Submit" />
      <input type="submit" name="_eventId_cancel"
             value="Cancel" />
    </form:form>
    </body>
</html>
```

This isn't the first form we've seen in our flow. The `welcome` view state also displayed a form to the customer. That form was simple and had only a single field. It was easy enough to pull that field's value from the request parameters. The registration form, on the other hand, is more involved.

Instead of dealing with the fields one at a time through the request parameters, it makes more sense to bind the form to a `Customer` object—let the framework do all of the hard work.

CHECKING THE DELIVERY AREA

After the customer has given their address, we need to be sure that they live within the delivery area. If Spizza can't deliver to them, then we should let them know and advise them that they'll need to come in and pick up the pizzas themselves.

To make that decision, we use a decision state. The `checkDeliveryArea` decision state has an `<if>` element that passes the customer's Zip code into the `checkDelivery-Area()` method on the `pizzaFlowActions` bean. That method will return a Boolean value: `true` if the customer is in the delivery area, `false` otherwise.

If the customer is in the delivery area, then the flow transitions to the `addCustomer` state. If not, then the customer is taken to the `deliveryWarning` view state. The view behind the `deliveryWarning` is /WEB-INF/flows/pizza/customer/deliveryWarning.jspx and is shown next.

Listing 8.7 Warning a customer that pizza can't be delivered to their address

```
<html xmlns:jsp="http://java.sun.com/JSP/Page">
  <jsp:output omit-xml-declaration="yes"/>
  <jsp:directive.page contentType="text/html;charset=UTF-8" />

  <head><title>Spizza</title></head>

  <body>
        <h2>Delivery Unavailable</h2>

        <p>The address is outside of our delivery area. You may
        still place the order, but you will need to pick it up
        yourself.</p>

        <![CDATA[
        <a href="${flowExecutionUrl}&_eventId=accept">
                                Continue, I'll pick up the order</a> |
        <a href="${flowExecutionUrl}&_eventId=cancel">Never mind</a>
        ]]>
  </body>
</html>
```

The key flow-related items in deliveryWarning.jspx are the two links that offer the customer a chance to continue with the order or to cancel. Using the same `flow-ExecurtionUrl` variable that we used in the `welcome` state, these links will trigger either an `accept` event or a `cancel` event in the flow. If an accept event is sent, then the flow will transition to the `addCustomer` state. Otherwise, the global cancel transition will be followed and the subflow will transition to the `cancel` end state.

We'll talk about the end states in a moment. First, let's take a quick look at the `addCustomer` state.

STORING THE CUSTOMER DATA

By the time the flow arrives at the `addCustomer` state, the customer has entered their address. For future reference, that address needs to be stored away (probably in a database). The `addCustomer` state has an `<evaluate>` element that calls the `addCustomer()` method on the `pizzaFlowActions` bean, passing in the `customer` flow variable.

Once the evaluation is complete, the default transition will be taken and the flow will transition to the end state whose ID is `customerReady`.

ENDING THE FLOW

Normally a flow's end state isn't that interesting. But in this flow, there's not just one end state, but two. When a subflow ends, it fires a flow event that's equivalent to its end state's ID. If the flow only has one end state, then it'll always fire the same event. But with two or more end states, a flow can influence the direction of the calling flow.

When the customer flow goes down any of the normal paths, it'll ultimately land on the end state whose ID is `customerReady`. When the calling pizza flow resumes, it'll receive a `customerReady` event, which will result in a transition to the `buildOrder` state.

Note that the `customerReady` end state includes an `<output>` element. This element is a flow's equivalent of Java's `return` statement. It passes back some data from a subflow to the calling flow. In this case, the `<output>` is returning the `customer` flow variable so that the `identifyCustomer` subflow state in the pizza flow can assign it to the order.

On the other hand, if a `cancel` event is triggered at any time during the customer flow, it'll exit the flow through the end state whose ID is `cancel`. That will trigger a `cancel` event in the pizza flow and result in a transition (via the global transition) to the pizza flow's end state.

8.3.3 *Building an order*

After the customer has been identified, the next step in the main flow is to figure out what kind of pizzas they want. The order subflow, as illustrated in figure 8.4, is where the user is prompted to create pizzas and add them to the order.

As you can see, the `showOrder` state is the centerpiece of the order subflow. It's the first state that the user sees upon entering the flow and it's the state that the user is sent to after adding a new pizza to the order. It displays the current state of the order and offers the user a chance to add another pizza to the order.

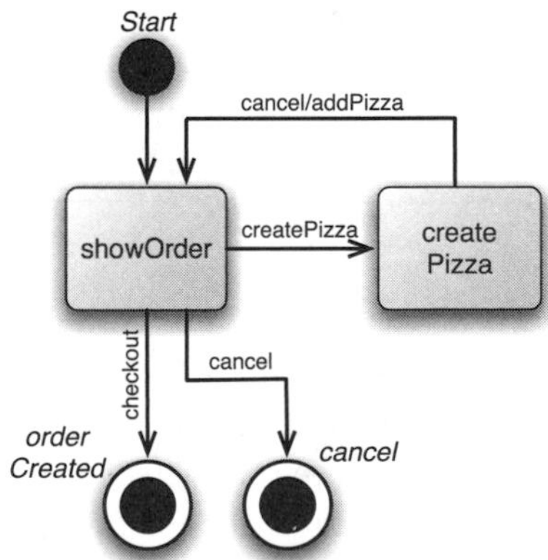

Figure 8.4 Pizzas are added via the order subflow.

Upon choosing to add a pizza to the order, the flow transitions to the `createPizza` state. This is another view state that gives the user a selection of pizza sizes and toppings to build a pizza with. From here the user may add a pizza or cancel. In either event the flow transitions back to the `showOrder` state.

From the `showOrder` state, the user may choose to either submit the order or cancel the order. Either choice will end the order subflow, but the main flow will go down different paths depending on which choice is made.

The following shows how the diagram translates into a Spring Web Flow definition.

Listing 8.8 The order subflow view states to display the order and to create a pizza

```
<?xml version="1.0" encoding="UTF-8"?>
<flow xmlns="http://www.springframework.org/schema/webflow"
  xmlns:xsi="http://www.w3.org/2001/XMLSchema-instance"
  xsi:schemaLocation="http://www.springframework.org/schema/webflow
  http://www.springframework.org/schema/webflow/spring-webflow-2.0.xsd">

  <input name="order" required="true" />

  <view-state id="showOrder">
    <transition on="createPizza" to="createPizza" />
    <transition on="checkout" to="orderCreated" />
    <transition on="cancel" to="cancel" />
  </view-state>

  <view-state id="createPizza" model="flowScope.pizza">
    <on-entry>
      <set name="flowScope.pizza"
          value="new com.springinaction.pizza.domain.Pizza()" />

      <evaluate result="viewScope.toppingsList" expression=
              "T(com.springinaction.pizza.domain.Topping).asList()" />
    </on-entry>
    <transition on="addPizza" to="showOrder">
      <evaluate expression="order.addPizza(flowScope.pizza)" />
    </transition>
    <transition on="cancel" to="showOrder" />
  </view-state>

  <end-state id="cancel" />
  <end-state id="orderCreated" />
</flow>
```

This subflow will actually operate on the `Order` object created in the main flow. Therefore, we need a way of passing the `Order` from the main flow to the subflow. As you'll recall from listing 8.1, we used the `<input>` element there to pass the `Order` into the flow. Here we're using it to accept that `Order` object. If you think of this subflow as being analogous to a method in Java, the `<input>` element used here is effectively defining the subflow's signature. This flow requires a single parameter called `order`.

Next we find the `showOrder` state, a basic view state with three different transitions: one for creating a pizza, one for submitting the order, and another to cancel the order.

The createPizza state is more interesting. Its view is a form that submits a new Pizza object to be added to the order. The <on-entry> element adds a new Pizza object to flow scope to be populated when the form is submitted. Note that the model of this view state references the same flow-scoped Pizza object. That Pizza object will be bound to the create pizza form, shown next.

Listing 8.9 Adding pizzas to an order with an HTML form bound to a flow-scoped object

```
<div xmlns:form="http://www.springframework.org/tags/form"
     xmlns:jsp="http://java.sun.com/JSP/Page">

  <jsp:output omit-xml-declaration="yes"/>
  <jsp:directive.page contentType="text/html;charset=UTF-8" />

    <h2>Create Pizza</h2>
    <form:form commandName="pizza">
      <input type="hidden" name="_flowExecutionKey"
          value="${flowExecutionKey}"/>

      <b>Size: </b><br/>
  <form:radiobutton path="size"
                    label="Small (12-inch)" value="SMALL"/><br/>
  <form:radiobutton path="size"
                    label="Medium (14-inch)" value="MEDIUM"/><br/>
  <form:radiobutton path="size"
                    label="Large (16-inch)" value="LARGE"/><br/>
  <form:radiobutton path="size"
                    label="Ginormous (20-inch)" value="GINORMOUS"/>
      <br/>
      <br/>

      <b>Toppings: </b><br/>
      <form:checkboxes path="toppings" items="${toppingsList}"
                       delimiter="&lt;br/&gt;"/><br/><br/>

      <input type="submit" class="button"
          name="_eventId_addPizza" value="Continue"/>
      <input type="submit" class="button"
          name="_eventId_cancel" value="Cancel"/>
    </form:form>
</div>
```

When the form is submitted via the Continue button, the size and topping selections will be bound to the Pizza object and the addPizza transition will be taken. The <evaluate> element associated with that transition indicates that the flow-scoped Pizza object should be passed in a call to the order's addPizza() method before transitioning to the showOrder state.

There are two ways to end the flow. The user can either click the Cancel button on the showOrder view or they can click the Checkout button. Either way, the flow transitions to an <end-state>. But the id of the end state chosen determines the event triggered on the way out of this flow, and ultimately determines the next step in the main flow. The main flow will either transition on cancel or will transition on orderCreated.

In the former case, the outer flow ends; in the latter case, it transitions to the `takePayment` subflow, which we'll look at next.

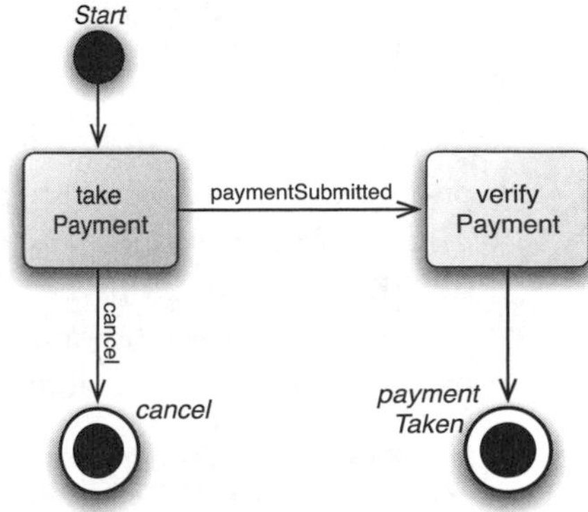

Figure 8.5 The final step in placing a pizza order is to take payment from the customer through the payment subflow.

8.3.4 *Taking payment*

It's not common to get a free pizza, and the Spizza pizzeria wouldn't stay in business long if they let their customers order pizzas without providing some form of payment. As the pizza flow nears an end, the final subflow prompts the user to enter payment details. This simple flow is illustrated in figure 8.5.

Like the order subflow, the payment subflow also accepts an `Order` object as input using the `<input>` element.

As you can see, upon entering the payment subflow, the user arrives at the `takePayment` state. This is a view state where the user can indicate that they'll pay by credit card, check, or cash. Upon submitting their payment information, they're taken to the `verifyPayment` state, an action state that verifies that their payment information is acceptable.

The payment subflow is defined in XML as shown.

Listing 8.10 The payment subflow has one view state and one action state.

```
<?xml version="1.0" encoding="UTF-8"?>
<flow xmlns="http://www.springframework.org/schema/webflow"
  xmlns:xsi="http://www.w3.org/2001/XMLSchema-instance"
  xsi:schemaLocation="http://www.springframework.org/schema/webflow
  http://www.springframework.org/schema/webflow/spring-webflow-2.0.xsd">

  <input name="order" required="true"/>

  <view-state id="takePayment" model="flowScope.paymentDetails">
    <on-entry>
      <set name="flowScope.paymentDetails"
          value="new com.springinaction.pizza.domain.PaymentDetails()" />

      <evaluate result="viewScope.paymentTypeList" expression=
               "T(com.springinaction.pizza.domain.PaymentType).asList()" />
    </on-entry>
    <transition on="paymentSubmitted" to="verifyPayment" />
    <transition on="cancel" to="cancel" />
  </view-state>

  <action-state id="verifyPayment">
    <evaluate result="order.payment" expression=
        "pizzaFlowActions.verifyPayment(flowScope.paymentDetails)" />
    <transition to="paymentTaken" />
  </action-state>
```

```
  <end-state id="cancel" />
  <end-state id="paymentTaken" />
</flow>
```

As the flow enters the takePayment view state, the <on-entry> element sets up the payment form by first using a SpEL expression to create a new PaymentDetails instance in flow scope. This will effectively be the backing object for the form. It also sets the view-scoped paymentTypeList variable to a list containing the values of the PaymentTypeenum (shown in listing 8.11). Here, SpEL's T() operator is used to get the PaymentType class so that the static toList() method can be invoked.

Listing 8.11 The PaymentType enumeration defines customer's choices for payment.

```
package com.springinaction.pizza.domain;

import static org.apache.commons.lang.WordUtils.*;

import java.util.Arrays;
import java.util.List;

public enum PaymentType {
  CASH, CHECK, CREDIT_CARD;

  public static List<PaymentType> asList() {
    PaymentType[] all = PaymentType.values();
    return Arrays.asList(all);
  }

  @Override
  public String toString() {
    return capitalizeFully(name().replace('_', ' '));
  }
}
```

Upon being presented with the payment form, the user may either submit a payment or cancel. Depending on the choice made, the payment subflow either ends through the paymentTaken<end-state> or the cancel<end-state>. As with other subflows, either <end-state> will end the subflow and return control to the main flow. But the id of the <end-state> taken will determine the transition taken next in the main flow.

Now we've stepped all of the way through the pizza flow and its subflows. We've seen a lot of what Spring Web Flow is capable of. Before we move past the Web Flow topic, let's take a quick look at what's involved with securing access to a flow or any of its states.

8.4 Securing web flows

In the next chapter, we'll see how to secure Spring applications using Spring Security. But while we're on the subject of Spring Web Flow, let's quickly look at how Spring Web Flow supports flow-level security when used along with Spring Security.

States, transitions, and even entire flows can be secured in Spring Web Flow by using the <secured> element as a child of those elements. For example, to secure access to a view state, you might use <secured> like this:

```
<view-state id="restricted">
  <secured attributes="ROLE_ADMIN" match="all"/>
</view-state>
```

As configured here, access to the view state will be restricted to only users who are granted ROLE_ADMIN access (per the `attributes` attribute). The `attributes` attribute takes a comma-separated list of authorities that the user must have to gain access to the state, transition, or flow. The `match` attribute can be set to either `any` or `all`. If it's set to `any`, then the user must be granted at least one of the authorities listed in `attributes`. If it's set to `all`, then the user must have been granted all of the authorities.

You may be wondering how a user is granted the authorities checked for by the `<secured>` element. For that matter, how does the user even log in to the application in the first place? The answers to those questions will be addressed in the next chapter.

8.5 Summary

Not all web applications are freely navigable. Sometimes, a user must be guided along, asked appropriate questions, and led to specific pages based on their responses. In these situations, an application feels less like a menu of options and more like a conversation between the application and the user.

In this chapter, we've explored Spring Web Flow, a web framework that enables development of conversational applications. Along the way, we built a flow-based application to take pizza orders. We started by defining the overall path that the application should take, starting with gathering customer information and concluding with the order being saved in the system.

A flow is made up of several states and transitions that define how the conversation will traverse from state to state. As for the states themselves, they come in one of several varieties: action states that perform some business logic, view states that involve the user in the flow, decision states that dynamically direct the flow, and end states that signify the end of a flow. In addition, there are subflow states, which are themselves defined by a flow.

Finally, we saw hints of how access to a flow, state, or transition can be restricted to users who are granted specific authorities. But we deferred conversation of how the user authenticates to the application and how the user is granted those authorities. That's where Spring Security comes in, and Spring Security is what we'll explore in the next chapter.

9 Securing Spring

This chapter covers

- Introducing Spring Security
- Securing web applications using servlet filters
- Authentication against databases and LDAP
- Transparently securing method invocations

Have you ever noticed that most people in television sitcoms don't lock their doors? It happens all the time. On *Seinfeld,* Kramer frequently let himself into Jerry's apartment to help himself to the goodies in Jerry's refrigerator. On *Friends,* the various characters often entered one another's apartments without warning or hesitation. Once, while in London, Ross even burst into Chandler's hotel room, narrowly missing Chandler in a compromising situation with Ross's sister.

In the days of *Leave it to Beaver,* it wasn't so unusual for people to leave their doors unlocked. But it seems crazy that in a day when we're concerned with privacy and security we see television characters enabling unhindered access to their apartments and homes.

It's a sad reality that there are villainous individuals roaming around seeking to steal our money, riches, cars, and other valuables. And it should be no surprise that as information is probably the most valuable item we have, crooks are looking for ways to steal our data and identity by sneaking into unsecured applications.

As software developers, we must take steps to protect the information that resides in our applications. Whether it's an email account protected with a username/password pair or a brokerage account protected with a trading PIN, security is a crucial *aspect* of most applications.

It's no accident that I chose to describe application security with the word "aspect." Security is a concern that transcends an application's functionality. For the most part, an application should play no part in securing itself. Although you could write security functionality directly into your application's code (and that's not uncommon), it's better to keep security concerns separate from application concerns.

If you're thinking that it's starting to sound as if security is accomplished using aspect-oriented techniques, you're right. In this chapter we're going to explore ways to secure your applications with aspects. But we won't have to develop those aspects ourselves—we're going to look at Spring Security, a security framework implemented with Spring AOP and servlet filters.[1]

9.1 Introducing Spring Security

Spring Security is a security framework that provides declarative security for your Spring-based applications. Spring Security provides a comprehensive security solution, handling authentication and authorization at both the web request level and at the method invocation level. Based on the Spring Framework, Spring Security takes full advantage of dependency injection (DI) and aspect-oriented techniques.

Spring Security got its start as Acegi Security. Acegi was a powerful security framework, but it had one big turn-off: it required a *lot* of XML configuration. I'll spare you the intricate details of what such a configuration may have looked like. Suffice it to say that it was common for a typical Acegi configuration to grow to several hundred lines of XML.

With version 2.0, Acegi Security became Spring Security. But the 2.0 release brought more than just a superficial name change. Spring Security 2.0 introduced a new security-specific XML namespace for configuring security in Spring. The new namespace, along with annotations and reasonable defaults, slimmed typical security configuration from hundreds of lines to only a dozen or so lines of XML. Spring Security 3.0, the most recent release, added SpEL to the mix, simplifying security configuration even more.

Spring Security tackles security from two angles. To secure web requests and restrict access at the URL level, Spring Security uses servlet filters. Spring Security can also secure method invocations using Spring AOP—proxying objects and applying advice that ensures that the user has proper authority to invoke secured methods.

---

[1] I'm probably going to get a lot of emails about this, but I have to say it anyway: servlet filters are a primitive form of AOP, with URL patterns as a kind of pointcut expression language. There... I've said it... I feel better now.

9.1.1 Getting started with Spring Security

No matter what kind of application you want to secure using Spring Security, the first thing to do is to add the Spring Security modules to the application's classpath. Spring Security 3.0 is divided into eight modules, as listed in table 9.1.

Table 9.1 Spring Security is partitioned into eight modules.

Module	Description
ACL	Provides support for domain object security through access control lists (ACLs)
CAS Client	Provides integration with JA-SIG's Central Authentication Service (CAS)
Configuration	Contains support for Spring Security's XML namespace
Core	Provides the essential Spring Security library
LDAP	Provides support for authentication using the Lightweight Directory Access Protocol (LDAP)
OpenID	Provides integration with the decentralized OpenID standard
Tag Library	Includes a set of JSP tags for view-level security
Web	Provides Spring Security's filter-based web security support

At the least, you'll want to include the Core and Configuration modules in your application's classpath. Spring Security is often used to secure web applications. That's certainly the case with the Spitter application, so we'll also need to add the web module. We'll also be taking advantage of Spring Security's JSP tag library, so we'll need to add that module to the mix.

Now we're ready to start declaring security configuration in Spring Security. Let's see how to get started with Spring Security's XML configuration namespace.

9.1.2 Using the Spring Security configuration namespace

When Spring Security was known as Acegi Security, all of the security elements were configured as <bean>s in the Spring application context. A common Acegi configuration scenario would contain dozens of <bean> declarations and span multiple pages. The long and short of it was that Acegi configuration was often longer than it was short.

Spring Security comes with a security-specific namespace that greatly simplifies security configuration in Spring. This new namespace, along with some sensible default behavior, reduces a typical security configuration from over 100 lines of XML to a dozen or so.

The only thing to do in preparation for using the security namespace is to include it in the XML file by adding the namespace declaration:

Listing 9.1 Adding the Spring Security namespace to a Spring configuration XML file

```
<beans xmlns="http://www.springframework.org/schema/beans"
    xmlns:security="http://www.springframework.org/schema/security"
    xmlns:xsi="http://www.w3.org/2001/XMLSchema-instance"
    xsi:schemaLocation="http://www.springframework.org/schema/beans
     http://www.springframework.org/schema/beans/spring-beans-3.0.xsd
     http://www.springframework.org/schema/security
     http://www.springframework.org/schema/security/spring-security-3.0.xsd">

</beans>
```

security:-prefixed elements go here

For the Spitter application, we've separated all of the security-specific configuration into a separate Spring configuration file called spitter-security.xml. Since all of the configuration in this file will be from the security namespace, we've changed the security namespace to be the primary namespace for that file.

Listing 9.2 Using the security namespace as the default namespace

```
<beans:beans xmlns:beans="http://www.springframework.org/schema/beans"
    xmlns="http://www.springframework.org/schema/security"
    xmlns:xsi="http://www.w3.org/2001/XMLSchema-instance"
    xsi:schemaLocation="http://www.springframework.org/schema/beans
     http://www.springframework.org/schema/beans/spring-beans-3.0.xsd
     http://www.springframework.org/schema/security
     http://www.springframework.org/schema/security/spring-security-3.0.xsd">

</beans:beans>
```

Non-prefixed security elements go here

With the security namespace as the primary namespace, we can avoid adding those pesky `security:` prefixes on all of the elements.

All of the Spring Security pieces are falling into place nicely. Now we're ready to add web-level security to the Spitter application.

9.2 Securing web requests

Everything you do with a Java web application starts with an `HttpServletRequest`. And if the request is the access point to a web application, then that's where security for a web application should begin.

The most basic form of request-level security involves declaring one or more URL patterns as requiring some level of granted authority and preventing users without that authority from accessing the content behind those URLs. Taking it a step further, you may want to require that certain URLs can only be accessed over HTTPS.

Before you can restrict access to users with certain privileges, there must be a way to know who's using the application. Therefore, the application will need to authenticate the user, prompting them to log in and identify themselves.

Spring Security supports these and many other forms of request-level security. To get started with web security in Spring, we must set up the servlet filters that provide the various security features.

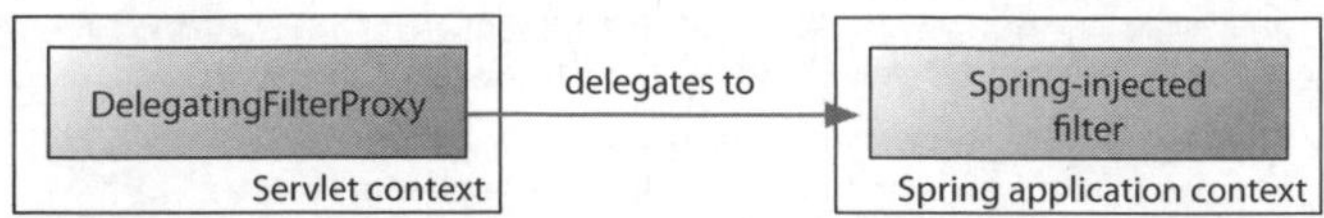

Figure 9.1 `DelegatingFilterProxy` proxies filter handling to a delegate filter bean in the Spring application context.

9.2.1 Proxying servlet filters

Spring Security employs several servlet filters to provide various aspects of security. As you might imagine, this could mean several `<filter>` declarations in your application's web.xml file. But rest easy—thanks to a little Spring magic, we'll only need to configure one filter in the application's web.xml file. Specifically, we'll need to add the following `<filter>`:

```
<filter>
    <filter-name>springSecurityFilterChain</filter-name>
    <filter-class>
        org.springframework.web.filter.DelegatingFilterProxy
    </filter-class>
</filter>
```

`DelegatingFilterProxy` is a special servlet filter that, by itself, doesn't do much. Instead, it delegates to an implementation of `javax.servlet.Filter` that's registered as a `<bean>` in the Spring application context, as illustrated in figure 9.1.

In order to do their job, Spring Security's filters must be injected with some other beans. It's not possible to inject beans into servlet filters registered in web.xml. But by using `DelegatingFilterProxy`, we can configure the actual filter in Spring, taking full advantage of Spring's support for dependency injection.

The value given as `DelegatingFilterProxy`'s `<filter-name>` is significant. This is the name used to look up the filter bean from the Spring application context. Spring Security will automatically create a filter bean whose ID is `springSecurityFilterChain`, so that's the name we've given to `DelegatingFilterProxy` in web.xml.

As for the `springSecurityFilterChain` bean itself, it's another special filter known as `FilterChainProxy`. It's a single filter that chains together one or more additional filters. Spring Security relies on several servlet filters to provide different security features. But you should almost never need to know these details, as you likely won't need to explicitly declare the `springSecurityFilterChain` bean or any of the filters it chains together. Spring Security will automatically create those beans for us when we configure the `<http>` element, which we'll do next.

9.2.2 Configuring minimal web security

Early versions of Spring Security required a seemingly endless amount of XML configuration to set up basic security features. In contrast, using recent versions of Spring Security, the following snippet of XML packs a lot of punch:

```
<http auto-config="true">
  <intercept-url pattern="/**" access="ROLE_SPITTER" />
</http>
```

These humble three lines of XML configure Spring security to intercept requests for all URLs (as specified by the Ant-style path in the pattern attribute of <intercept-url>) and restrict access to only authenticated users who have the ROLE_SPITTER role. The <http> element automatically sets up a FilterChainProxy (which is delegated to by the DelegatingFilterProxy we configured in web.xml) and all of the filter beans in the chain.

In addition to those filter beans, we also get a few more freebies by setting the auto-config attribute to true. Autoconfiguration gives our application a free login page, support for HTTP Basic authentication, and support for logging out. In fact, setting auto-config to true is equivalent to explicitly asking for those features like this:

```
<http>
    <form-login />
    <http-basic />
    <logout />
  <intercept-url pattern="/**" access="ROLE_SPITTER" />
</http>
```

Let's dig deeper into what these features give us and see how to use them.

LOGGING IN VIA A FORM

One of the benefits of setting auto-config to true is that Spring Security will automatically generate a login page for you. Here's the HTML for that form.

Listing 9.3 Spring Security can automatically generate a simple login form for you.

```
<html>
  <head><title>Login Page</title></head>
  <body onload='document.f.j_username.focus();'>
    <h3>Login with Username and Password</h3>
    <form name='f' method='POST'
          action='/Spitter/j_spring_security_check'>      <- Authentication filter path
      <table>
        <tr><td>User:</td><td>
            <input type='text' name='j_username' value=''>      <- Username field
          </td></tr>
        <tr><td>Password:</td><td>
            <input type='password' name='j_password'/>      <- Password field
          </td></tr>
        <tr><td colspan='2'><input name="submit" type="submit"/></td></tr>
        <tr><td colspan='2'><input name="reset" type="reset"/></td></tr>
      </table>
    </form>
  </body>
</html>
```

You can get to the automatically generated login form via the path /spring_security_login relative to the application's context URL. For example, when accessing the Spitter application on localhost, that URL is http://localhost:8080/Spitter/spring_security_login.

At first it may seem like a great deal that Spring Security gives you a login form for free. But as you can see, the form is simple and not a lot should be said about its aesthetics. It's plain and we'll probably want to replace it with a login page of our own design.

To put our own login page in place, we'll need to configure a `<form-login>` element to override the default behavior:

```
<http auto-config="true" use-expressions="false">
  <form-login login-processing-url="/static/j_spring_security_check"
              login-page="/login"
              authentication-failure-url="/login?login_error=t"/>
</http>
```

The `login` attribute specifies a new context-relative URL for the login page. In this case we state that the login page will reside at `/login` which is ultimately handled by a Spring MVC controller. Likewise, if authentication fails, the `authentication-failure-url` attribute is set to send the user back to the same login page.

Note that we've set the `login-processing-url` to `/static/j_spring_security_check`. This is the URL that the login form will submit back to to authenticate the user.

Even though we may not want to keep the user-generated login form, we can learn a lot from it. For starters, we know that Spring Security will process the login request at the path `/Spitter/j_spring_security_check`. And it's clear that the username and password should be submitted in the request as fields named `j_username` and `j_password`. Armed with that information, we can create our own custom login page.

For the Spitter application the new login page is a JSP that's served up by a Spring MVC controller. The JSP itself is shown next.

Listing 9.4 The Spitter application uses a custom login page defined as JSP.

```
<%@ taglib prefix="s" uri="http://www.springframework.org/tags"%>
<div>
   <h2>Sign in to Spitter</h2>

   <p>
    If you've been using Spitter from your phone,
    then that's amazing...we don't support IM yet.
   </p>

   <spring:url var="authUrl"
          value="/static/j_spring_security_check" />     <- Authentication filter path
   <form method="post" class="signin" action="${authUrl}">

    <fieldset>
    <table cellspacing="0">
    <tr>
    <th><label for="username_or_email">Username or Email</label></th>
    <td><input id="username_or_email"
```

```
                name="j_username"
                type="text" />              <-- Username field
        </td>
      </tr>
      <tr>
      <th><label for="password">Password</label></th>
        <td><input id="password"
                  name="j_password"                  Password
                  type="password" />             <-- field
            <small><a href="/account/resend_password">Forgot?</a></small>
        </td>
      </tr>
      <tr>
      <th></th>
      <td><input id="remember_me"
          name="_spring_security_remember_me"
          type="checkbox"/>                  <-- Remember-me box
          <label for="remember_me"
                class="inline">Remember me</label></td>
      </tr>
      <tr>
      <th></th>
      <td><input name="commit" type="submit" value="Sign In" /></td>
      </tr>
      </table>
      </fieldset>
    </form>

    <script type="text/javascript">
     document.getElementById('username_or_email').focus();
    </script>
</div>
```

Although our login page is different than the one that Spring Security gives us out of the box, the key thing is that the form submits j_username and j_password parameters with the user's credentials. Everything else is decoration.

Also note that listing 9.4 includes a "remember me" checkbox. We'll discuss the details of how that works later in section 9.4.4. But for now, let's see Spring Security's support for HTTP Basic authentication.

HANDLING BASIC AUTHENTICATION

Form-based authentication is ideal for human users of an application. But in chapter 11, we'll see how to turn some of our web application's pages into a RESTful API. When the user of the application is another application, prompting for login with a form just won't do.

HTTP Basic authentication is a way to authenticate a user to an application directly in the HTTP request itself. You may have seen HTTP Basic authentication before. When encountered by a web browser, it prompts the user with a plain modal dialog box.

But that's just how it's manifested in a web browser. In reality, it's an HTTP 401 response, indicating that a username and password must be presented with the request. This makes it suitable as a means for REST clients to authenticate against the services that they're consuming.

Not much customization is available with `<http-basic>`. HTTP Basic authentication is either turned on or it's not. So rather than dwell on the topic any further, let's move on to see what the `<logout>` element gives us.

LOGGING OUT

The `<logout>` element sets up a Spring Security filter that will invalidate a user session. When used as is, the filter set up by `<logout>` is mapped to /j_spring_security_logout. But so that this doesn't collide with how we've set up `DispatcherServlet`, we need to override the filter's URL much as we did for the login form. To do that, we need to set the `logout-url` attribute:

```
<logout logout-url="/static/j_spring_security_logout"/>
```

That wraps up our discussion of what autoconfiguration gives us. But there's more to explore in Spring Security. Let's take a closer look at the `<intercept-url>` element and see how it controls access at the request level.

9.2.3 Intercepting requests

In the previous section, we saw a simple example of the `<intercept-url>` element. But we didn't dig into it much… until now.

The `<intercept-url>` element is the first line of defense in the request-level security game. Its `pattern` attribute is given a URL pattern that will be matched against incoming requests. If any requests match the pattern, then that `<intercept-url>`'s security rules will be applied.

Let's revisit the `<intercept-url>` element from before:

```
<intercept-url pattern="/**" access="ROLE_SPITTER" />
```

The `pattern` attribute takes an Ant-style path by default. But if you'd prefer, setting the `<http>` element's `path-type` attribute to `regex` will change the `pattern` to taking regular expressions.

In this case, we've set the `pattern` attribute to `/**`, indicating that we want all requests, regardless of the URL, to require ROLE_SPITTER access. The `/**` has a broad reach, but you can be more specific.

Suppose that some special areas of the Spitter application are restricted to administrative users. For that, we can insert the following `<intercept-url>` just before the one we already have:

```
<intercept-url pattern="/admin/**" access="ROLE_ADMIN" />
```

Where our first `<intercept-url>` entry makes sure that the user has ROLE_SPITTER authority for most of the application, this `<intercept-url>` restricts access to the /admin branch of the site's hierarchy to users with ROLE_ADMIN authority.

You can use as many `<intercept-url>` entries as you like to secure various paths in your web application. But it's important to know that the `<intercept-url>` rules are applied top to bottom. Therefore, this new `<intercept-url>` should be placed before the original one or else it'll be eclipsed by the broad scope of the `/**` path.

SECURING WITH SPRING EXPRESSIONS

Listing required authorities is simple enough, but it's somewhat one-dimensional. What if you wanted to express security constraints that are based on more than just granted privileges?

In chapter 2, we saw how to use the Spring Expression Language (SpEL) as an advanced technique for wiring bean properties. As of version 3.0, Spring Security also supports SpEL as a means for declaring access requirements. To enable it, we must set the `use-expressions` attribute of `<http>` to `true`:

```
<http auto-config="true" use-expressions="true">
...
</http>
```

Now we can start using SpEL expressions in the `access` attribute. Here's how to use a SpEL expression to require ROLE_ADMIN access for the `/admin/**` URL pattern:

```
<intercept-url pattern="/admin/**" access="hasRole('ROLE_ADMIN')"/>
```

This `<intercept-url>` is effectively the same as the one we started with, except that it uses SpEL. The `hasRole()` expression evaluates to `true` if the current user has been granted the given authority. But `hasRole()` is only one of several security-specific expressions supported. Table 9.2 lists all of the SpEL expressions added by Spring Security 3.0.

Table 9.2 Spring Security extends the Spring Expression Language with a several security-specific expressions.

Security expression	What it evaluates to
`authentication`	The user's authentication object
`denyAll`	Always evaluates to `false`
`hasAnyRole(list of roles)`	`true` if the user has been granted any of the roles specified
`hasRole(role)`	`true` if the user has been granted the specified role
`hasIpAddress(IP Address)`	The user's IP address (only available in web security)
`isAnonymous()`	`true` if the current user is an anonymous user
`isAuthenticated()`	`true` if the current user is not anonymous
`isFullyAuthenticated()`	`true` if the current user is neither an anonymous nor a remember-me user
`isRememberMe()`	`true` if the current user was automatically authenticated via remember-me
`permitAll`	Always evaluates to `true`
`principal`	The user's principal object

With Spring Security's SpEL expressions at our disposal, we can do more than just limit access based on a user's granted authorities. For example, if you wanted to lock down the /admin/** URLs to not only require ROLE_ADMIN, but to also only be allowed from a given IP address, you might declare an <intercept-url> like this:

```
<intercept-url pattern="/admin/**"
    access="hasRole('ROLE_ADMIN') and hasIpAddress('192.168.1.2')"/>
```

With SpEL-based security constraints, the possibilities are virtually endless. I'll bet that you're already dreaming up interesting security constraints based on SpEL.

But for now, let's look at another one of <intercept-url>'s tricks: enforcing channel security.

FORCING REQUESTS TO HTTPS

Submitting data across HTTP can be a risky proposition. It may not be a big deal to send a spittle message in the clear over HTTP. But if you're passing sensitive information such as passwords and credit card numbers across HTTP, then you're asking for trouble. That's why sensitive information should be sent encrypted over HTTPS.

Working with HTTPS seems simple enough. All you have to do is add an s after the http in a URL and you're set. Right?

That's true, but it places responsibility for using the HTTPS channel in the wrong place. If you have dozens or hundreds of links and form actions that should be going to an HTTPS URL, it's too easy to forget to add that S. Chances are good that you'll miss one or two of them. Or you may overcorrect and use HTTPS in places where it's unnecessary.

The <intercept-url> element's requires-channel attribute shifts the responsibility for channel enforcement into the Spring Security configuration.

As an example, consider the Spitter application's registration form. Although Spitter doesn't ask for credit card numbers or social security numbers or anything terribly sensitive, the users may want that information to be kept private. In that case, we should configure an <intercept-url> element for the /spitter/form like this:

```
<intercept-url pattern="/spitter/form" requires-channel="https"/>
```

Anytime a request comes in for /spitter/form, Spring Security will see that it requires the https channel and automatically redirect the request to go over HTTPS. Likewise, the home page doesn't require HTTPS, so we can declare that it always should be sent over HTTP:

```
<intercept-url pattern="/home" requires-channel="http"/>
```

So far we've seen how to secure web applications as requests are made. The assumption has been that security would involve stopping a user from accessing a URL that they're not authorized to use. But it's also a good idea to never show links that a user won't be able to follow. Let's see how Spring Security offers security in the view.

9.3 Securing view-level elements

To support security in the view layer, Spring Security comes with a JSP tag library.[2] This tag library is small and includes only three tags, as listed in table 9.3.

Table 9.3 Spring Security supports security in the view layer with a JSP tag library.

JSP tag	What it does
`<security:accesscontrollist>`	Allows the body of the tag to be rendered if the currently authenticated user has one of the stipulated permissions in the specified domain object
`<security:authentication>`	Accesses properties of the current user's authentication object
`<security:authorize>`	Allows the body of the tag to be rendered if a specified security constraint has been met

To use the JSP tag library, we'll need to declare it in the JSP files where it's used:

```
<%@ taglib prefix="security"
         uri="http://www.springframework.org/security/tags" %>
```

Once the tag library has been declared in the JSP file, we're ready to use it. Let's look at each of the three JSP tags that come with Spring Security and see how they work.

9.3.1 Accessing authentication details

One of the simplest things that the Spring Security JSP tag library can do for us is provide convenient access to the user's authentication information. For example, it's common for websites to display a "welcome" or "hello" message in the page header, identifying the user by their username. That's precisely the kind of thing that the `<security:authentication>` can do for us. For example:

```
Hello <security:authentication property="principal.username" />!
```

The `property` attribute identifies a property of the user's authentication object. The properties available will vary depending on how the user was authenticated. But you can count on a few common properties to be available, including those listed in table 9.4.

In our example, the property being rendered is actually the nested `username` property of the `principal` property.

When used as shown in the previous example, `<security:authentication>` will render the property's value in the view. But if you'd rather assign it to a variable, then simply specify the name of the variable in the `var` attribute:

```
<security:authentication property="principal.username"
        var="loginId"/>
```

---

[2] If you prefer Velocity over JSP for rendering views, Spring Security also comes with a set of Velocity macros that are similar to its JSP tags.

Table 9.4 You can access several of the user's authentication details using the `<security:authentication>` JSP tag.

Authentication property	Description
`authorities`	A collection of `GrantedAuthority` objects that represent the privileges granted to the user
`credentials`	The credentials that were used to verify the principal (commonly, this is the user's password)
`details`	Additional information about the authentication (IP address, certificate serial number, session ID, and so on)
`principal`	The user's principal

The variable is created in page scope by default. But if you'd rather create it in some other scope such as request or session (or any of the scopes available from `javax.servlet.jsp.PageContext`), you can specify it via the `scope` attribute. For example, to create the variable in request scope, use the `<security:authentication>` tag like this:

```
<security:authentication property="principal.username"
        var="loginId" scope="request" />
```

The `<security:authentication>` tag is useful, but it's just the start of what Spring Security's JSP tag library can do. Let's see how to conditionally render content depending on the user's privileges.

9.3.2 Rendering with authorities

Sometimes portions of the view should or shouldn't be rendered, depending on what the user is privileged to do. There's no point in showing a login form to a user who's already logged in or in showing a personalized greeting to a user who's not logged in.

Spring Security's `<security:authorize>` JSP tag conditionally renders a portion of the view depending on the user's granted authorities. For example, in the Spitter application we don't want to show the form for adding a new spittle unless the user has the ROLE_SPITTER role. The following listing shows how to use the `<security:authorize>` tag to display the spittle form if the user has ROLE_SPITTER authority.

Listing 9.5 Conditional rendering with the `<security:authorize>` tag

```
<sec:authorize access="hasRole('ROLE_SPITTER')">        <- Only with ROLE_SPITTER authority

    <s:url value="/spittles" var="spittle_url" />
      <sf:form modelAttribute="spittle"

                action="${spittle_url}">
        <sf:label path="text"><s:message code="label.spittle"
                        text="Enter spittle:"/></sf:label>
        <sf:textarea path="text" rows="2" cols="40" />
            <sf:errors path="text" />
```

```
    <br/>
    <div class="spitItSubmitIt">
      <input type="submit" value="Spit it!"
           class="status-btn round-btn disabled" />
    </div>
  </sf:form>
</sec:authorize>
```

The access attribute is given a SpEL expression whose result determines whether <security:authorize>'s body is rendered. Here we're using the hasRole ('ROLE_SPITTER') expression to ensure that the user has the ROLE_SPITTER role. But you have the full power of SpEL at your disposal when setting the access attribute, including the Spring Security-provided expressions listed in table 9.2.

With these expressions available, you can cook up some interesting security constraints. For example, imagine that the application has some administrative functions that are only available to the user whose username is habuma. Maybe you'd use the isAuthenticated() and principal expressions like this:

```
<security:authorize
   access="isAuthenticated() and principal.username=='habuma'">
  <a href="/admin">Administration</a>
</security:authorize>
```

I'm sure you can dream up even more interesting expressions than that. I'll leave it up to your imagination to concoct more security constraints. The options are virtually limitless with SpEL.

But one thing about the example that I dreamt up still bugs me. Though I might want to restrict the administrative functions to habuma, perhaps doing it with a SpEL expression isn't ideal. Sure, it'll keep the link from being rendered in the view. But nothing's stopping anyone from manually entering the /admin URL in the browser's address line.

Drawing on what we learned earlier in this chapter, that should be an easy thing to fix. Adding a new <intercept-url> in the security configuration will tighten security around the /admin URL:

```
<intercept-url pattern="/admin/**"
    access="hasRole('ROLE_ADMIN') and hasIpAddress('192.168.1.2')"/>
```

Now the admin functionality is locked down. The URL is secured and the link to the URL won't appear unless the user is authorized to use it. But to do that we had to declare the SpEL expression in two places—in <intercept-url> and in the <security:authorize> tag's access attribute. Wouldn't it make more sense to only show the URL if the URL's security constraint was met?

That's what the <security:authorize> tag's url attribute is for. Unlike the access attribute where the security constraint is explicitly declared, the url attribute indirectly refers to the security constraints for a given URL pattern. Since we've already declared security constraints for /admin in the Spring Security configuration, we can use the url attribute like this:

```
<security:authorize url="/admin/**">
  <spring:url value="/admin" var="admin_url" />
  <br/><a href="${admin_url}">Admin</a>
</security:authorize>
```

Since the /admin URL is restricted to only authenticated users who have ROLE_ADMIN authority and to requests coming from a specific IP address, the body of the `<security:authorize>` tag will only be rendered if those conditions are met.

> **What about `<security:authorize>`'s other attributes?**
>
> In addition to the `access` and `url` attributes, `<security:authorize>` has three other attributes: `ifAllGranted`, `ifAnyGranted`, and `ifNotGranted`. These attributes make `<security:authorize>` conditionally render depending on what authorities have or haven't been granted to the user.
>
> Prior to Spring Security 3.0, these were the only attributes available for `<security:authorize>`. But with the introduction of SpEL and the `access` attribute, they become obsolete. They're still available, but the `access` attribute can do the same things and much more.

We've now seen how to declare various forms of security at the web layer. One question remains: where is user information kept? In other words, when someone tries to log in to the application, what repository of user information does Spring Security use to authenticate against?

Put simply, Spring Security is flexible enough to authenticate against virtually any kind of user repository. Let's look at a few of the authentication options Spring Security offers.

9.4 Authenticating users

Every application's a little different. That truth is evident in how every application stores user information. Sometimes it's kept in a relational database. Other times it might be in an LDAP-enabled directory. Some applications rely on a decentralized user identity system. And some may employ more than one strategy.

Fortunately, Spring Security is flexible and can handle almost any authentication strategy you need. Spring Security is prepared to cover many common authentication scenarios, including authenticating users against

- In-memory (Spring-configured) user repositories
- JDBC-based user repositories
- LDAP-based user repositories
- OpenID decentralized user identity systems
- Central Authentication System (CAS)
- X.509 certificates
- JAAS-based providers

If none of the out-of-the-box options suit you, then you can easily implement your own authentication strategy and wire it in.

Let's have a deeper look at a few of the most commonly used authentication options that Spring Security offers.

9.4.1 Configuring an in-memory user repository

One of the easiest authentication options available is to declare the user details directly in the Spring configuration. This is done by creating a user service using the `<user-service>` element from Spring Security's XML namespace:

```
<user-service id="userService">
  <user name="habuma" password="letmein"
               authorities="ROLE_SPITTER,ROLE_ADMIN"/>
  <user name="twoqubed" password="longhorns"
               authorities="ROLE_SPITTER"/>
  <user name="admin" password="admin"
               authorities="ROLE_ADMIN"/>
</user-service>
```

A user service is effectively a data access object that looks up user details when given a user's login ID. In the case of `<user-service>`, those user details are declared within `<user-service>`. There's one `<user>` element for each user that can log in to the application. The `name` and `password` attributes respectively specify the login name and password. Meanwhile, the `authorities` attribute is set to a comma-separated list of authorities—the things that the user is allowed to do.

Recall that earlier (in section 9.2.3) we configured Spring Security to restrict access to all URLs to only users with ROLE_SPITTER authority. In this case, the habuma and twoqubed users would be granted access, but the admin user would be denied.

The user service is now ready and waiting to look up user details for authentication. All that's left is to wire it into Spring Security's authentication manager:

```
<authentication-manager>
  <authentication-provider user-service-ref="userService" />
</authentication-manager>
```

The `<authentication-manager>` element registers an authentication manager. More specifically, it registers an instance of `ProviderManager`, an authentication manager that delegates authentication responsibility to one or more authentication providers. In this case, it's an authentication provider that relies on a user service to provide user details. We happen to have a user service handy. So all we have to do is wire it in through the `user-service-ref` attribute of `<authentication-provider>`.

Here we've declared the authentication provider and the user service independently and wired them together. Optionally, if it suits you better, you could also embed the user service within the authentication provider:

```
<authentication-provider>
  <user-service id="userService">
    <user name="habuma" password="letmein"
```

```
        authorities="ROLE_SPITTER,ROLE_ADMIN"/>
    ...
  </user-service>
</authentication-provider>
```

There's no significant benefit in embedding the <user-service> within <authentication-provider>, but if it helps you organize your Spring XML configuration, then that option is available.

Defining user details in the Spring application context is convenient for testing or when you're first starting to add security to your application. But it's not a very realistic way of managing users in a production application. More often user details are kept in a database or a directory server. Let's see how to register a user service that looks for user details in a relational database.

9.4.2 Authenticating against a database

Many applications store user information, including the username and password, in a relational database. If that's how your application keeps user information, Spring Security's <jdbc-user-service> is a good choice for your application.

The <jdbc-user-service> is used the same way that <user-service> is used. This includes wiring it into <authentication-provider>'s user-service-ref attribute or embedding it within <authentication-provider>. Here we're configuring a basic <jdbc-user-service> with an id so that it can be declared independently and wired into the <authentication-provider>:

```
<jdbc-user-service id="userService"
    data-source-ref="dataSource" />
```

The <jdbc-user-service> element uses a JDBC data source—wired in through its data-source-ref attribute—to query a database for user details. Without any further configuration, the user service queries for user information using the following SQL:

```
select username,password,enabled
  from users
 where username = ?
```

And, although we're talking about user authentication right now, part of the authentication involves looking up the user's granted authorities. By default, the basic <jdbc-user-service> configuration will use the following SQL to look up authorities given a username:

```
select username,authority
  from authorities
 where username = ?
```

This is great if your application's database happens to store user details and authorities in tables that match those queries. But I'll bet that's not the case for most applications. In fact, in the case of the Spitter application, user details are kept in the spitter table. Clearly the default behavior isn't going to work.

Table 9.5 The attributes of `<jdbc-user-service>` that can change the SQL used to query for user details

Attribute	What it does
`users-by-username-query`	Queries for a user's username, password, and enabled status given the username
`authorities-by-username-query`	Queries for a user's granted authorities given the username
`group-authorities-by-username-query`	Queries for a user's group authorities given the username

Fortunately, `<jdbc-user-service>` can easily be configured to use whatever queries best fit your application. Table 9.5 describes the attributes that can be used to tweak `<jdbc-user-service>`'s behavior.

For the Spitter application, we'll set the `users-by-username-query` and `authorities-by-username-query` attributes as follows:

```
<jdbc-user-service id="userService"
       data-source-ref="dataSource"
       users-by-username-query=
          "select username, password, true from spitter where username=?"
       authorities-by-username-query=
          "select username,'ROLE_SPITTER' from spitter where username=?" />
```

In the Spitter application, the username and password are stored in the `spitter` table in the `username` and `password` properties, respectively. But we haven't really considered the idea of a user being enabled or disabled and have been assuming that all users are enabled. So we've written the SQL to always return `true` for all users.

We also haven't given much thought to giving Spitter users different levels of authority. All Spitter users have the same authorities. In fact, the Spitter database schema doesn't have a table for storing user authorities. Therefore, we've set `authorities-by-username-query` with a concocted query that gives all users ROLE_SPITTER authority.

While relational databases are commonly where an application's user details are kept, just as often (or perhaps more often) you'll find applications that need to authenticate against a directory server using LDAP. Let's see how to configure Spring Security to use LDAP as a user repository.

9.4.3 *Authenticating against LDAP*

We've all seen an organizational chart or two before. Most organizations are structured hierarchically. Employees report to supervisors, supervisors to directors, directors to vice presidents, and so forth. Within that hierarchy you'll often find a similarly hierarchical set of security rules. Human resources personnel are probably granted different privileges than accounting personnel. Supervisors probably have more open access than those that report to them.

As useful as relational databases can be, they don't do well representing hierarchical data. LDAP directories, on the other hand, excel at storing information hierarchically. For that reason, it's common to find a company's organizational structure represented in an LDAP directory. Alongside, you'll often find the company's security constraints mapped to the entries in the directory.

To use LDAP-based authentication, we'll first need to use Spring Security's LDAP module and configure LDAP authentication within the Spring application context. When it comes to configuring LDAP authentication, we have two choices:

- With an LDAP-oriented authentication provider
- With an LDAP-oriented user service

For the most part, it's an even choice on which you should use. But there are some small considerations to make when choosing one over the other.

DECLARING AN LDAP AUTHENTICATION PROVIDER

For the in-memory and JDBC-based user services, we declared an `<authentication-provider>` and wired in the user service. We can do the same thing for an LDAP-oriented user service (and I'll show you how in a moment). But a more direct way is to use a special LDAP-oriented authentication provider by declaring an `<ldap-authentication-provider>` within the `<authentication-manager>`:

```
<authentication-manager alias="authenticationManager">
      <ldap-authentication-provider
          user-search-filter="(uid={0})"
          group-search-filter="member={0}"/>
    </authentication-manager>
```

The `user-search-filter` and `group-search-filter` attributes are used to provide a filter for the base LDAP queries, which are used to search for users and groups. By default, the base queries for both users and groups are empty, indicating that the search will be done from the root of the LDAP hierarchy. But we can change that by specifying a query base:

```
<ldap-user-service id="userService"
             user-search-base="ou=people"
             user-search-filter="(uid={0})"
             group-search-base="ou=groups"
             group-search-filter="member={0}" />
```

The `user-search-base` attribute provides a base query for finding users. Likewise, the `group-search-base` specifies the base query for finding groups. Rather than search from the root, we've specified that users be searched for where the organization unit is `people`. And groups should be searched for where the organizational unit is `groups`.

CONFIGURING PASSWORD COMPARISON

The default strategy to authenticate against LDAP is to perform a bind operation, authenticating the user directly to the LDAP server. Another option is to perform a comparison operation. This involves sending the entered password to the LDAP directory and asking the server to compare the password against a user's password attribute. Because the comparison is done within the LDAP server, the actual password remains secret.

If you'd rather authenticate by doing a password comparison, you can do so by declaring so with the `<password-compare>` element:

```
<ldap-authentication-provider
    user-search-filter="(uid={0})"
    group-search-filter="member={0}">
  <password-compare />
</ldap-authentication-provider>
```

As declared here, the password given in the login form will be compared with the value of the `userPassword` attribute in the user's LDAP entry. If the password is kept in a different attribute, then specify the password attribute's name with `password-attribute`:

```
<password-compare hash="md5"
    password-attribute="passcode" />
```

It's nice that the actual password is kept secret on the server when doing server-side password comparison. But the attempted password is still passed across the wire to the LDAP server and could be intercepted by a hacker. To prevent that, you can specify an encryption strategy by setting the `hash` attribute to one of the following values:

- `{sha}`
- `{ssha}`
- `md4`
- `md5`
- `plaintext`
- `sha`
- `sha-256`

In the example, we've encrypted passwords using MD5 by setting `hash` to `md5`.

REFERRING TO A REMOTE LDAP SERVER

The one thing I've left out up until now is where the LDAP server and data actually reside. We've happily been configuring Spring to authenticate against an LDAP server, but where's that server?

By default, Spring Security's LDAP authentication assumes that the LDAP server is listening on port 33389 on localhost. But if your LDAP server is on another machine, then you can use the `<ldap-server>` element to configure the location:

```
<ldap-server url="ldap://habuma.com:389/dc=habuma,dc=com" />
```

Here we use the `url` attribute to specify the location of the LDAP server.[3]

---

[3] Don't even try to use this LDAP URL. It's just an example. No LDAP server is actually listening there.

CONFIGURING AN EMBEDDED LDAP SERVER

If you don't happen to have an LDAP server laying around waiting to be authenticated against, then the `<ldap-server>` can also be used to configure an embedded LDAP server. Just leave off the `url` parameter. For example:

```
<ldap-server root="dc=habuma,dc=com" />
```

The `root` attribute is optional. But it defaults to `dc=springframework,dc=org`, which I suspect isn't what you'll want to use as the root for your LDAP server.

When the LDAP server starts, it will attempt to load data from any LDIF files that it can find in the classpath. LDIF (LDAP Data Interchange Format) is a standard way of representing LDAP data in a plain text file. Each record is comprised of one or more lines, each containing a name:value pair. Records are separated from each other by blank lines.[4]

If you'd rather be more explicit about which LDIF file gets loaded, you can use the `ldif` attribute:

```
<ldap-server root="dc=habuma,dc=com"
             ldif="classpath:users.ldif" />
```

Here we specifically ask the LDAP server to load its content from the users.ldif file at the root of the classpath. In case you're curious, the following listing shows the LDIF file that we've been using.

Listing 9.6 A sample LDIF file used to load user details into LDAP

```
dn: ou=groups,dc=habuma,dc=com
objectclass: top
objectclass: organizationalUnit
ou: groups

dn: ou=people,dc=habuma,dc=com
objectclass: top
objectclass: organizationalUnit
ou: people

dn: uid=habuma,ou=people,dc=habuma,dc=com
objectclass: top
objectclass: person
objectclass: organizationalPerson
objectclass: inetOrgPerson
cn: Craig Walls
sn: Walls
uid: habuma
userPassword: password

dn: uid=jsmith,ou=people,dc=habuma,dc=com
objectclass: top
objectclass: person
objectclass: organizationalPerson
objectclass: inetOrgPerson
```

[4] See http://tools.ietf.org/html/rfc2849 for more details on the LDIF specification.

```
cn: John Smith
sn: Smith
uid: jsmith
userPassword: password

dn: cn=spitter,ou=groups,dc=habuma,dc=com
objectclass: top
objectclass: groupOfNames
cn: spitter
member: uid=habuma,ou=people,dc=habuma,dc=com
```

Whether your user authenticates against a database or an LDAP directory, it's always more convenient for them not to have to directly authenticate at all. Let's see how to configure Spring Security to remember a user so that they don't have to log in every time they visit an application.

9.4.4 Enabling remember-me functionality

It's important for an application to be able to authenticate users. But from the user's perspective, it'd be nice if the application didn't always prompt them with a login every time they use it. That's why many websites offer remember-me functionality so that you can log in once and then be remembered by the application when you come back to it later.

Spring Security makes it easy to add remember-me functionality to an application. To turn on remember-me support, all we need to do is add a `<remember-me>` element within the `<http>` element:

```
<http auto-config="true" use-expressions="true">
  ...
  <remember-me
      key="spitterKey"
      token-validity-seconds="2419200" />
</http>
```

Here, we've turned on remember-me functionality along with a bit of special configuration. If you use the `<remember-me>` element with no attributes, this feature is accomplished by storing a token in a cookie that's valid for up to two weeks. But here we've specified that the token should stay valid for up to four weeks (2,419,200 seconds).

The token that's stored in the cookie is made up of the username, password, an expiration date, and a private key—all encoded in an MD5 hash before being written to the cookie. By default, the private key is `SpringSecured`, but we've set it to `spitterKey` to make it specific to the Spitter application.

Simple enough. Now that remember-me functionality is enabled, we'll need to make a way for users to indicate that they'd like the application to remember them. For that, the login request will need to include a `_spring_security_remember_me` parameter. A simple checkbox in the login form ought to do the job:

```
<input id="remember_me" name="_spring_security_remember_me"
       type="checkbox"/>
<label for="remember_me" class="inline">Remember me</label>
```

Up until now we've been mostly focused on securing web requests. Since Spring Security is often used to secure web applications, it tends to be forgotten that it can also be used to secure method invocations. Let's look at Spring Security's support for method-level security.

9.5 Securing methods

As I've hinted at before, security is an aspect-oriented concept. And Spring AOP is the basis for method-level security in Spring Security. But for the most part you'll never need to deal with Spring Security's aspects directly. All of the AOP involved in securing methods is packed into a single element: `<global-method-security>`. Here's a common way of using `<global-method-security>`.

```
<global-method-security secured-annotations="enabled" />
```

This sets up Spring Security for securing methods that are annotated with Spring Security's own `@Secured` annotation. This is just one of four ways that Spring Security supports method-level security:

- Methods annotated with `@Secured`
- Methods annotated with JSR-250's `@RolesAllowed`
- Methods annotated with Spring's pre- and post-invocation annotations
- Methods matching one or more explicitly declared pointcuts

Let's look at each style of method security.

9.5.1 Securing methods with @Secured

When `<global-method-security>` is configured with its `secured-annotations` attribute set to `enabled`, a pointcut is created such that the Spring Security aspects will wrap bean methods that are annotated with `@Secured`. For example:

```
@Secured("ROLE_SPITTER")
public void addSpittle(Spittle spittle) {
  // ...
}
```

The `@Secured` annotation takes an array of `String` as an argument. Each `String` value is a authorization, one of which is required to invoke the method. By passing in `ROLE_SPITTER`, we tell Spring Security to not allow the `saveSpittle()` method to be invoked unless the authenticated user has ROLE_SPITTER as one of their granted authorities.

If more than one value is passed into `@Secured`, then the authenticated user must be granted at least one of those authorities to gain access to the method. For example, the following use of `@Secured` indicates that the user must have ROLE_SPITTER *or* ROLE_ADMIN privilege to invoke the method:

```
@Secured({"ROLE_SPITTER", "ROLE_ADMIN"})
public void addSpittle(Spittle spittle) {
  // ...
}
```

When the method is invoked by an unauthenticated user or by a user not possessing the required privileges, the aspect wrapping the method will throw one of Spring Security's exceptions (probably a subclass of `AuthenticationException` or `AccessDeniedException`). Ultimately the exception will need to be caught. If the secured method is invoked in the course of a web request, the exception will be automatically handled by Spring Security's filters. Otherwise, you'll need to write the code to handle the exception.

The one drawback of the `@Secured` annotation is that it's a Spring-specific annotation. If you're more comfortable using standard annotations, then perhaps you should consider using `@RolesAllowed` instead.

9.5.2 Using JSR-250's @RolesAllowed

The `@RolesAllowed` annotation is equivalent to `@Secured` in almost every way. The only substantial difference is that `@RolesAllowed` is one of Java's standard annotations as defined in JSR-250.[5]

This difference carries more political consequence than technical. But using the standard `@RolesAllowed` annotation may have implications when used in the context of other frameworks or APIs that process that annotation.

Regardless, if you choose to use `@RolesAllowed`, you'll need to turn it on by setting `<global-method-security>`'s `jsr250-annotations` attribute to `enabled`:

```
<global-method-security jsr250-annotations="enabled" />
```

Although here we've only enabled `jsr250-annotations`, it's good to note that it's not mutually exclusive with `secured-annotations`. These two annotation styles can both be enabled at the same time. And they may even be used side by side with Spring's pre-/post-invocation security annotations, which is what we'll look at next.

9.5.3 Pre-/Post-invocation security with SpEL

Although `@Secured` and `@RolesAllowed` seem to do the trick when it comes to keeping unauthorized users out, that's about all that they can do. Sometimes security constraints are more interesting than just whether a user has privileges or not.

Spring Security 3.0 introduced a handful of new annotations that use SpEL to enable even more interesting security constraints on methods. These new annotations are described in table 9.6.

We'll look at specific examples of each of these in a moment. But first, it's important to know that if you want to use any of these annotations, you'll need to enable them by setting `<global-method-security>`'s `pre-post-annotations` to `enabled`:

```
<global-method-security pre-post-annotations="enabled" />
```

With the annotations enabled, you can start annotating methods to be secured. Let's start by looking at `@PreAuthorize`.

---

[5] http://jcp.org/en/jsr/summary?id=250

Table 9.6 Spring Security 3.0 offers four new annotations that can be used to secure methods with SpEL expressions.

Annotations	Description
`@PreAuthorize`	Restricts access to a method before invocation based on the result of evaluating an expression
`@PostAuthorize`	Allows a method to be invoked, but throws a security exception if the expression evaluates to false
`@PostFilter`	Allows a method to be invoked, but filters the results of that method per an expression
`@PreFilter`	Allows a method to be invoked, but filters input prior to entering the method

PRE-AUTHORIZING METHODS

At first glance, `@PreAuthorize` may appear to be nothing more than a SpEL-enabled equivalent to `@Secured` and `@RolesAllowed`. In fact, you could use `@PreAuthorize` to limit access based on the roles given to the authenticated user:

```
@PreAuthorize("hasRole('ROLE_SPITTER')")
public void addSpittle(Spittle spittle) {
  // ...
}
```

The `String` argument to `@PreAuthorize` is a SpEL expression. Here it uses the Spring Security-provided `hasRole()` function to authorize access to the method if the user has the ROLE_SPITTER role.

With SpEL expressions guiding access decisions, far more advanced security constraints can be written. For example, suppose that the average Spitter user can only write spittles of 140 characters or less, but premium users are allowed unlimited spittle lengths. Though `@Secured` and `@RolesAllowed` would be of no help here, `@PreAuthorize` is on the case:

```
@PreAuthorize("(hasRole('ROLE_SPITTER') and #spittle.text.length() <= 140)
                or hasRole('ROLE_PREMIUM')")
public void addSpittle(Spittle spittle) {
  // ...
}
```

The `#spittle` portion of the expression refers directly to the method parameter of the same name. This enables Spring Security to examine the parameters passed to the method and use those parameters in its authorization decision making. Here, we dig into the `Spitter`'s text to make sure it doesn't exceed the length allowed for standard Spitter users. Or if the user is a premium user, then the length doesn't matter.

POST-AUTHORIZING METHODS

A slightly less obvious way to authorize a method is to post-authorize the method. Post-authorization typically involves making security decisions based on the object returned from the secured method. This of course means that the method must be invoked and given a chance to produce a return value.

Aside from the timing of the authorization, @PostAuthorize works much the same as @PreAuthorize. For example, suppose that we want to secure the getSpittleById() method to only authorize access if the Spittle object returned belongs to the authenticated user. For that we could annotate getSpittleById() with @PostAuthorize like this:

```
@PostAuthorize("returnObject.spitter.username == principal.username")
public Spittle getSpittleById(long id) {
  // ...
}
```

For easy access to the object returned from the secured method, Spring Security provides the returnObject name in SpEL. Here we know that the returned object is a Spittle, so the expression digs into its spitter property and pulls the username property from that.

On the other side of the double-equal comparison, the expression digs into the built-in principal object to get its username property. principal is another one of Spring Security's special built-in names that represents the principal of the currently authenticated user.

If the Spittle object has a Spitter whose username property is the same as the principal's username, the Spittle will be returned to the caller. Otherwise, an AccessDeniedException will be thrown and the caller won't get to see the Spittle.

It's important to keep in mind that, unlike methods annotated with @PreAuthorize, @PostAuthorize-annotated methods will be executed first and intercepted afterward. That means that care should be taken to make sure that the method doesn't have any side effects that would be undesired if authorization fails.

POST-FILTERING METHODS

Sometimes it's not the method that's being secured, but rather the data being returned from that method. For example, suppose that you wanted to present a list of Spittles to the user, but limit that list to only those Spittles that the user is allowed to delete. In that case, you might annotate the method like this:

```
@PreAuthorize("hasRole('ROLE_SPITTER)")
@PostFilter("filterObject.spitter.username == principal.name")
public List<Spittle> getABunchOfSpittles() {
  ...
}
```

Here, the @PreAuthorize annotation only allows users with ROLE_SPITTER authority to execute the method. If the user makes it through that checkpoint, the method will execute and a List of Spittles will be returned. But the @PostFilter annotation will filter that list, ensuring that the user only sees those Spittle objects that belong to the user.

The filterObject referenced in the expression refers to an individual element (which we know to be a Spittle) in the List returned from the method. If that Spittle's Spitter has a username that's the same as the authenticated user (the principal.name in the expression), then the element will end up in the filtered list. Otherwise, it'll be left out.

I know what you're thinking. You could write your query such that it only returns Spittle objects belonging to our user. That'd be fine if the security rules were such that a user may only delete Spittles that belong to them.

To make things more interesting, let's suppose that in addition to being able to delete a Spittle that they own, a user is empowered to delete any Spittle that contains profanity. For that, you'll rewrite the @PostFilter expression as follows:

```
@PreAuthorize("hasRole('ROLE_SPITTER)")
@PostFilter("hasPermission(filterObject, 'delete')")
public List<Spittle> getSpittlesToDelete() {
  ...
}
```

As used here, the hasPermission() operation *should* evaluate to true if the user has delete permission for the Spittle identified by filterObject. I say that it *should* evaluate to true in that case, but the reality is that by default hasPermission() will always return false.

If hasPermission() always returns false by default, then what use is it? Well, the nice thing about a default behavior is that it can be overridden. Overriding the behavior of hasPermission() involves creating and registering a permission evaluator. That's what SpittlePermissionEvaluator in the following listing is for.

Listing 9.7 A permission evaluator provides the logic behind hasPermission()

```
package com.habuma.spitter.security;
import java.io.Serializable;
import org.springframework.security.access.PermissionEvaluator;
import org.springframework.security.core.Authentication;
import com.habuma.spitter.domain.Spittle;

public class SpittlePermissionEvaluator implements PermissionEvaluator {
    public boolean hasPermission(Authentication authentication,
            Object target, Object permission) {
        if (target instanceof Spittle) {
            Spittle spittle = (Spittle) target;
            if ("delete".equals(permission)) {
                return spittle.getSpitter().getUsername().equals(
                    authentication.getName()) || hasProfanity(spittle);
            }
        }
        throw new UnsupportedOperationException(
                "hasPermission not supported for object <" + target
                        + "> and permission <" + permission + ">");
    }

    public boolean hasPermission(Authentication authentication,
            Serializable targetId, String targetType, Object permission) {
        throw new UnsupportedOperationException();
    }
```

```
    private boolean hasProfanity(Spittle spittle) {
        ...
        return false;
    }
}
```

SpittlePermissionEvaluator implements Spring Security's PermissionEvaluator interface, which demands that two different hasPermission() methods be implemented. One of the hasPermission() methods takes an Object as the object to evaluate against in the second parameter. The other hasPermission() is useful when only the ID of the target object is available, and takes that ID as a Serializable in its second parameter.

For our purposes, we assume that we'll always have the Spittle object to evaluate permissions against, so the other method simply throws UnsupportedOperationException.

As for the other hasPermission() method, it checks to see that the object being evaluated is a Spittle and that we're checking for delete permission. If so, then it compares the Spitter's username against the authenticated user's name. It also checks whether the Spittle contains profanity by passing it into the hasProfanity() method.[6]

With the permission evaluator ready, you need to register it with Spring Security for it to back the hasPermission() operation in the expression given to @PostFilter. To do that, you'll need to create an expression handler bean and register it with <global-method-security>.

For the expression evaluator, you'll create a bean of type DefaultMethodSecurityExpressionHandler and inject its permissionEvaluator property with an instance of our SpittlePermissionEvaluator:

```
<beans:bean id="expressionHandler" class=
    "org.springframework.security.access.expression.method.
                                    ➥DefaultMethodSecurityExpressionHandler">
  <beans:property name="permissionEvaluator">
    <beans:bean class=
            "com.habuma.spitter.security.SpittlePermissionEvaluator" />
  </beans:property>
</beans:bean>
```

Then we can configure that expressionHandler bean with <global-method-security> like this:

```
<global-method-security pre-post-annotations="enabled">
    <expression-handler ref="expressionHandler"/>
</global-method-security>
```

Before, we configured a <global-method-security> without specifying an expression handler. But here we have replaced the default expression handler with one that knows about our permission evaluator.

---

[6] I've conveniently left the implementation of hasProfanity() as an exercise for the reader.

9.5.4 Declaring method-level security pointcuts

Method-level security constraints often vary from method to method. Annotating each method with the constraints that best serve that method makes a lot of sense. But sometimes it may make sense to apply the same authorization checks to several methods—cross-cutting authorization, so to speak.

To restrict access to multiple methods, we can use the `<protect-pointcut>` element as a child of the `<global-method-security>` element. For example:

```
<global-method-security>
  <protect-pointcut access="ROLE_SPITTER"
      expression=
          "execution(@com.habuma.spitter.Sensitive * *.*(String))"/>
</global-method-security>
```

The `expression` attribute is given an AspectJ pointcut expression. In this case, it identifies any methods that are annotated with a custom `@Sensitive` annotation. Meanwhile, the `access` attribute indicates which authorities the authenticated user must have to access the methods that are identified by the `expression` attribute.

9.6 Summary

Security is a crucial aspect of many applications. Spring Security provides a mechanism for securing your application that's simple, flexible, and powerful.

Using a series of servlet filters, Spring Security can control access to web resources, including Spring MVC controllers. And by employing aspects, you can also secure method invocations with Spring Security. But thanks to Spring Security's configuration namespace, you don't need to deal with the filters or aspects directly. Security can be declared concisely.

When it comes to authenticating users, Spring Security offers several options. We saw how to configure authentication against an in-memory user repository, a relational-database, and LDAP directory servers.

Next, we'll look at ways to integrate Spring applications with other applications. Starting in the next chapter, we'll look at how Spring supports several remoting options including RMI and web services.

Part 3

Integrating Spring

In parts 1 and 2, you learned the basics of working with Spring and the essentials of application development using Spring's persistence and transaction support and web framework. In part 3, you'll learn how to take your application further by integrating it with other applications and enterprise services.

In chapter 10, "Working with remote services," you'll learn how to expose your application objects as remote services. You'll also learn how to transparently access remote services as though they're any other object in your application. We'll explore remoting technologies including RMI, Hessian/Burlap, Spring's own HTTP invoker, and web services with JAX-RPC and JAX-WS.

In contrast to RPC-style remote services presented in chapter 10, chapter 11 explores building resource-oriented REST integration with Spring MVC.

Chapter 12, "Messaging in Spring," explores a different approach to application integration by showing how Spring can be used with JMS to asynchronously send and receive messages between applications.

Management and monitoring of Spring beans is the subject of chapter 13, "Managing Spring beans with JMX." In this chapter, you'll learn how Spring can automatically expose beans configured in Spring as JMX MBeans.

Wrapping up the book, chapter 14, "Odds and ends," covers a few topics that were important enough to discuss, but too small to warrant their own chapter. In this chapter you'll learn how to externalize configuration, wire JNDI resources as Spring beans, send email, schedules tasks, and declare methods to run asynchronously as background jobs.

10 Working with remote services

This chapter covers

- Accessing and exposing RMI services
- Using Hessian and Burlap services
- Working with Spring's HTTP invoker
- Using Spring with web services

Imagine for a moment that you're stranded on a deserted island. This may sound like a dream come true. After all, who wouldn't want to get some solitude on a beach, blissfully ignorant of the goings-on of the outside world?

But on a deserted island, it's not pina coladas and sunbathing all the time. Even if you enjoy the peaceful seclusion, it won't be long before you'll get hungry, bored, and lonely. You can only live on coconuts and spear-caught fish for so long. You'll eventually need food, fresh clothing, and other supplies. And if you don't get in contact with another human soon, you may end up talking to a volleyball!

Many applications that you'll develop are like island castaways. On the surface they might seem self-sufficient, but in reality, they probably collaborate with other systems, both within your organization and externally.

For example, consider a procurement system that needs to communicate with a vendor's supply chain system. Maybe your company's human resources system needs to integrate with the payroll system. Or the payroll system may need to communicate with an external system that prints and mails paychecks. No matter the circumstance, your application will need to communicate with other systems to access services remotely.

Several remoting technologies are available to you, as a Java developer, including

- Remote Method Invocation (RMI)
- Caucho's Hessian and Burlap
- Spring's own HTTP-based remoting
- Web services with JAX-RPC and JAX-WS

Regardless of which remoting technology you choose, Spring provides broad support for accessing and creating remote services with several different technologies. In this chapter, you'll learn how Spring both simplifies and complements these remoting services. But first, let's set the stage for this chapter with an overview of how remoting works in Spring.

10.1 An overview of Spring remoting

Remoting is a conversation between a client application and a service. On the client side, some functionality is required that isn't within the scope of the application. So the application reaches out to another system that can provide the functionality. The remote application exposes the functionality through a remote service.

Suppose that we'd like to make some of the Spitter application's functionality available as remote services for other applications to use. Perhaps in addition to the existing browser-based user interface, we'd like to make a desktop or mobile front end for Spitter, as illustrated in figure 10.1. To support that, we'll need to expose the basic functions of the `SpitterService` interface as a remote service.

The conversation between the other applications and Spitter begins with a *remote procedure call (RPC)* from the client applications. On the surface, an RPC is similar to a call to a method on a local object. Both are synchronous operations, blocking execution in the calling code until the called procedure is complete.

The difference is a matter of proximity, with an analogy to human communication. If you're at the proverbial watercooler at work discussing the outcome of the weekend's football game, you're conducting a local conversation—the conversation takes place between two people in the same room. Likewise, a local method call is one where execution flow is exchanged between two blocks of code within the same application.

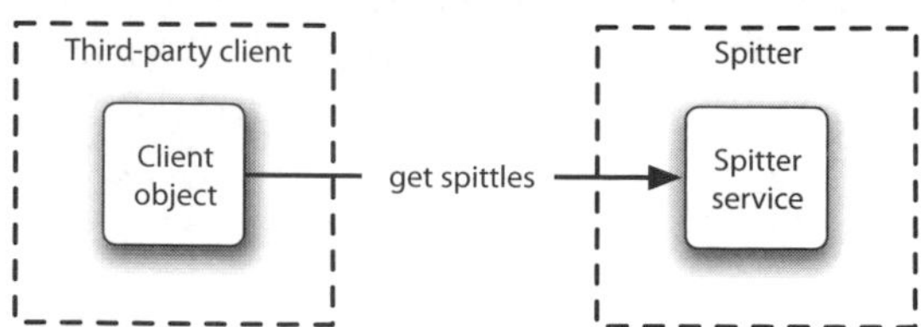

Figure 10.1 A third-party client can interact with the Spitter application by making remote calls to a service exposed by Spitter.

On the other hand, if you were to pick up the phone to call a client in another city, your conversation would be conducted remotely over the telephone network. Similarly, RPC is when execution flow is handed off from one application to another application, theoretically on a different machine in a remote location over the network.

Spring supports remoting for several different RPC models, including Remote Method Invocation (RMI), Caucho's Hessian and Burlap, and Spring's own HTTP invoker. Table 10.1 outlines each of these models and briefly discusses their usefulness in various situations.

Table 10.1 Spring supports RPC via several remoting technologies.

RPC model	Useful when...
Remote Method Invocation (RMI)	Accessing/exposing Java-based services when network constraints such as firewalls aren't a factor
Hessian or Burlap	Accessing/exposing Java-based services over HTTP when network constraints are a factor
HTTP invoker	Accessing/exposing Spring-based services when network constraints are a factor and you desire Java serialization over XML or proprietary serialization
JAX-RPC and JAX-WS	Accessing/exposing platform-neutral, SOAP-based web services

Regardless of which remoting model you choose, you'll find that a common theme runs through Spring's support for each model. This means that once you understand how to configure Spring to work with one of the models, you'll have a modest learning curve if you decide to use a different model.

In all models, services can be configured into your application as Spring-managed beans. This is accomplished using a proxy factory bean that enables you to wire remote services into properties of your other beans as if they were local objects. Figure 10.2 illustrates how this works.

The client makes calls to the proxy as if the proxy were providing the service functionality. The proxy communicates with the remote service on behalf of the client. It handles the details of connecting and making remote calls to the remote service.

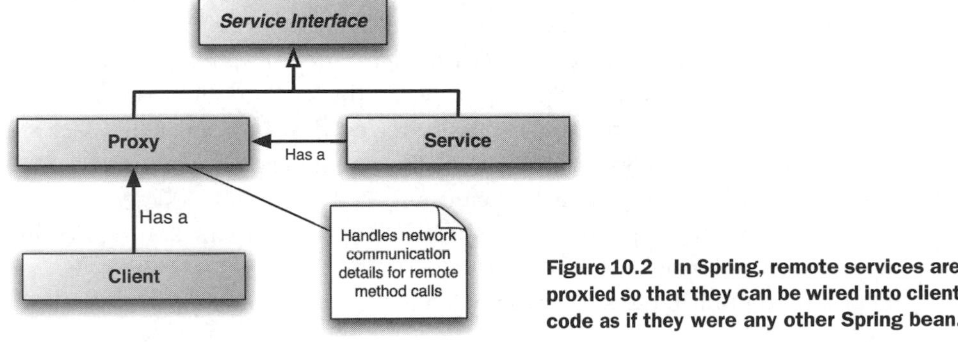

Figure 10.2 In Spring, remote services are proxied so that they can be wired into client code as if they were any other Spring bean.

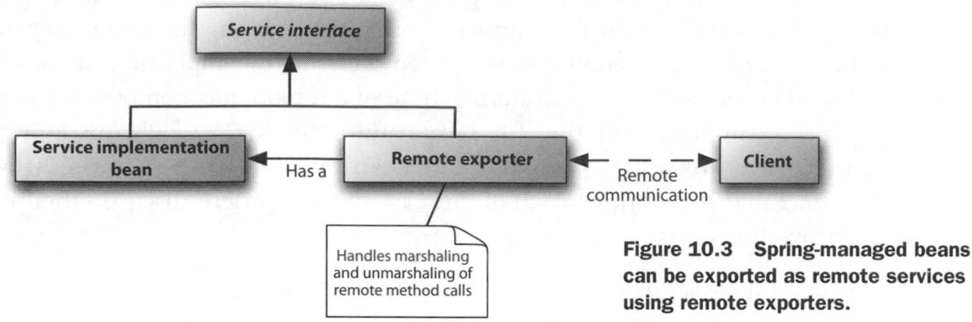

Figure 10.3 Spring-managed beans can be exported as remote services using remote exporters.

What's more, if the call to the remote service results in a `java.rmi.RemoteException`, the proxy handles that exception and rethrows it as an unchecked `RemoteAccessException`. Remote exceptions usually signal problems such as network or configuration issues that can't be gracefully recovered from. Since a client can usually do little to gracefully recover from a remote exception, rethrowing a `RemoteAccessException` makes it optional for the client to handle the exception.

On the service side, you're able to expose the functionality of any Spring-managed bean as a remote service using any of the models listed in table 10.1. Figure 10.3 illustrates how remote exporters expose bean methods as remote services.

Whether you'll be developing code that consumes remote services, implementing those services, or both, working with remote services in Spring is purely a matter of configuration. You won't have to write any Java code to support remoting. Your service beans don't have to be aware that they're involved in an RPC (although any beans passed to or returned from remote calls may need to implement `java.io.Serializable`).

Let's start our exploration of Spring's remoting support by looking at RMI, the original remoting technology for Java.

10.2 Working with RMI

If you've been working in Java for any length of time, you've no doubt heard of (and probably used) Remote Method Invocation (RMI). RMI—first introduced into the Java platform in JDK 1.1—gives Java programmers a powerful way to communicate between Java programs. Before RMI, the only remoting options available to Java programmers were CORBA (which at the time required the purchase of a third-party *Object Request Broker*, or *ORB*) or handwritten socket programming.

But developing and accessing RMI services is tedious, involving several steps, both programmatic and manual. Spring simplifies the RMI model by providing a proxy factory bean that enables you to wire RMI services into your Spring application is if they were local JavaBeans. Spring also provides a remote exporter that makes short work of converting your Spring-managed beans into RMI services.

For the Spitter application, I'll show you how to wire an RMI service into a client application's Spring application context. But first, let's see how to use the RMI exporter to publish the `SpitterService` implementation as an RMI service.

10.2.1 Exporting an RMI service

If you've ever created an RMI service before, you know that it involves the following steps:

1. Write the service implementation class with methods that throw `java.rmi.RemoteException`.
2. Create the service interface to extend `java.rmi.Remote`.
3. Run the RMI compiler (`rmic`) to produce client stub and server skeleton classes.
4. Start an RMI registry to host the services.
5. Register the service in the RMI registry.

Wow! That's a lot of work just to publish a simple RMI service. What's perhaps worse than all the steps required, you may have noticed that `RemoteExceptions` and `MalformedURLExceptions` are thrown around a lot. These exceptions usually indicate a fatal error that can't be recovered from in a catch block, but you're still expected to write boilerplate code that catches and handles those exceptions—even if there's not much you can do to fix them.

Clearly a lot of code and manual work is involved to publish an RMI service. Is there anything Spring can do to make this situation less knotty?

CONFIGURING AN RMI SERVICE IN SPRING

Fortunately, Spring provides an easier way to publish RMI services. Instead of writing RMI-specific classes with methods that throw `RemoteException`, you simply write a POJO that performs the functionality of your service. Spring handles the rest.

The RMI service that we'll create exposes the methods from the `SpitterService` interface. As a reminder, the following shows what that interface looks like.

Listing 10.1 `SpitterService` defines the service layer of the Spitter application.

```
package com.habuma.spitter.service;

import java.util.List;

import com.habuma.spitter.domain.Spitter;
import com.habuma.spitter.domain.Spittle;

public interface SpitterService {
  List<Spittle> getRecentSpittles(int count);
  void saveSpittle(Spittle spittle);

  void saveSpitter(Spitter spitter);
  Spitter getSpitter(long id);
  void startFollowing(Spitter follower, Spitter followee);

  List<Spittle> getSpittlesForSpitter(Spitter spitter);
  List<Spittle> getSpittlesForSpitter(String username);
  Spitter getSpitter(String username);

  Spittle getSpittleById(long id);
  void deleteSpittle(long id);

  List<Spitter> getAllSpitters();
}
```

If we were using traditional RMI to expose this service, all of those methods in `SpitterService` and in `SpitterServiceImpl` would need to throw `java.rmi.RemoteException`. But we're going to turn it into an RMI service using Spring's `RmiServiceExporter`, so the existing implementations will do fine.

`RmiServiceExporter` exports any Spring-managed bean as an RMI service. As depicted in figure 10.4, `RmiServiceExporter` works by wrapping the bean in an adapter class. The adapter class is then bound to the RMI registry and proxies requests to the service class—`SpitterServiceImpl` in this case.

The simplest way to use `RmiServiceExporter` to expose `SpitterServiceImpl` as an RMI service is to configure it in Spring with the following XML:

```
<bean class="org.springframework.remoting.rmi.RmiServiceExporter"
      p:service-ref="spitterService"
      p:serviceName="SpitterService"
      p:serviceInterface="com.habuma.spitter.service.SpitterService" />
```

Here the `spitterService` bean is wired into the `service` property to indicate that the `RmiServiceExporter` is to export the bean as an RMI service. The `serviceName` property names the RMI service. And the `serviceInterface` property specifies the interface that the service implements.

By default `RmiServiceExporter` attempts to bind to an RMI registry on port 1099 of the local machine. If no RMI registry is found at that port, `RmiServiceExporter` will start one. If you'd rather bind to an RMI registry at a different port or host, you can specify so with the `registryPort` and `registryHost` properties. For example, the following `RmiServiceExporter` will attempt to bind to an RMI registry on port 1199 on the host rmi.spitter.com:

```
<bean class="org.springframework.remoting.rmi.RmiServiceExporter"
      p:service-ref="spitterService"
      p:serviceName="SpitterService"
      p:serviceInterface="com.habuma.spitter.service.SpitterService"
      p:registryHost="rmi.spitter.com"
      p:registryPort="1199"/>
```

That's all you need to do to have Spring turn a bean into an RMI service. Now that the Spitter service has been exposed as an RMI service, we may create alternative user interfaces or invite third parties to create new clients for Spitter that use the RMI service. The developers of those clients will have an easy time connecting to the Spitter

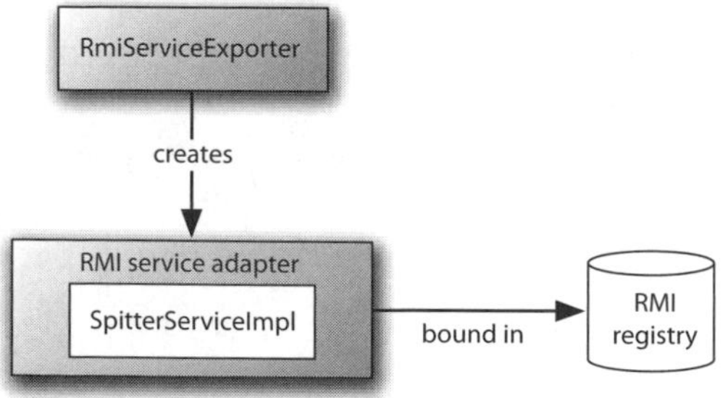

Figure 10.4 `RmiServiceExporter` turns POJOs into RMI services by wrapping them in a service adapter and binding the service adapter to the RMI registry.

RMI service if they're using Spring. Let's switch gears and see how to write a client of the Spitter RMI service.

10.2.2 Wiring an RMI service

Traditionally, RMI clients must use the RMI API's `Naming` class to look up a service from the RMI registry. For example, the following snippet of code might be used to retrieve the RMI Spitter service:

```
try {
  String serviceUrl = "rmi:/spitter/SpitterService";
  SpitterService spitterService =
          (SpitterService) Naming.lookup(serviceUrl);
  ...
}
catch (RemoteException e) { ... }
catch (NotBoundException e) { ... }
catch (MalformedURLException e) { ... }
```

Though this snippet of code would certainly retrieve a reference to the RMI spitter service, it presents two problems:

- Conventional RMI lookups could result in any one of three checked exceptions (`RemoteException`, `NotBoundException`, and `MalformedURLException`) that must be caught or rethrown.
- Any code that needs the spitter service is responsible for retrieving the service itself. That's plumbing code and is probably not directly cohesive with the client's functionality.

The exceptions thrown in the course of an RMI lookup are the kinds that typically signal a fatal and unrecoverable condition in the application. `MalformedURLException`, for instance, indicates that the address given for the service isn't valid. To recover from this exception, the application will at a minimum need to be reconfigured and may have to be recompiled. No try/catch block will be able to recover gracefully, so why should your code be forced to catch and handle it?

But perhaps more sinister is the fact that this code is in direct opposition to the principles of dependency injection. Because the client code is responsible for looking up the Spitter service *and* that the service is an RMI service, there's no opportunity to provide a different implementation of `SpitterService` from some other source. Ideally, you should be able to inject a `SpitterService` object into any bean that needs one instead of having the bean look up the service itself. Using DI, any client of `SpitterService` can be ignorant of where that service comes from.

Spring's `RmiProxyFactoryBean` is a factory bean that creates a proxy to an RMI service. Using `RmiProxyFactoryBean` to reference an RMI `SpitterService` is as simple as adding the following <bean> to the client's Spring configuration file:

```
<bean id="spitterService"
      class="org.springframework.remoting.rmi.RmiProxyFactoryBean"
      p:serviceUrl="rmi://localhost/SpitterService"
      p:serviceInterface="com.habuma.spitter.service.SpitterService" />
```

The URL of the service is set through RmiProxyFactoryBean's serviceUrl property. Here, the service is named SpitterService and is hosted on the local machine. Meanwhile, the interface that the service provides is specified with the serviceInterface property. The interaction between the client and the RMI proxy is illustrated in figure 10.5.

Now that we've declared the RMI service as a Spring-managed bean, we can wire it as a dependency into another bean just as you would a regular non-remote bean. For example, suppose the client needs to use the Spitter service to retrieve a list of Spittles for a given user. You might use @Autowired to wire the service proxy into the client:

```
@Autowired
  SpitterService spitterService;
```

Then you can invoke methods on it as if it were a local bean:

```
public List<Spittle> getSpittles(String userName) {
  Spitter spitter = spitterService.getSpitter(userName);
  return spitterService.getSpittlesForSpitter(spitter);
}
```

What's great about accessing an RMI service in this way is that the client code doesn't even know that it's dealing with an RMI service. It's given a SpitterService object via injection, without any concern for where it comes from.

Furthermore, the proxy catches any RemoteExceptions that may be thrown by the service and rethrows them as unchecked exceptions that you may safely ignore. This makes it possible to easily swap out the remote service bean with another implementation of the service—perhaps a different remote service or maybe a mock implementation used when unit testing the client code.

Even though the client code isn't aware that the SpitterService that it was given is a remote service, you may want to take care designing the service's interface. Note

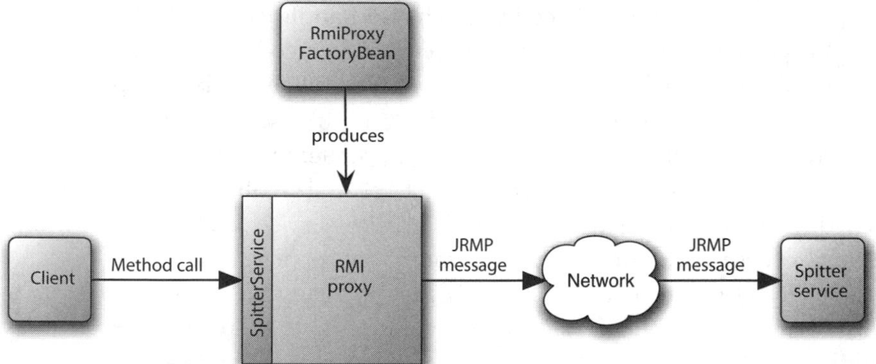

Figure 10.5 RmiProxyFactoryBean produces a proxy object that talks to remote RMI services on behalf of the client. The client talks to the proxy through the service's interface as if the remote service were just a local POJO.

that the client had to make two calls to the service: one to look up the `Spitter` by their username and another to retrieve the list of `Spittle` objects. That's two remote calls that are affected by network latency and will impact the performance of the client. Knowing that this is how the service will be used, it may be worthwhile to revisit the service's interface to consolidate those two calls into a single method. But for now we'll accept the service as is.

RMI is an excellent way to communicate with remote services, but it has some limitations. First, RMI has difficulty working across firewalls. That's because RMI uses arbitrary ports for communication—something that firewalls typically won't allow. In an intranet environment, this usually isn't a concern. But if you're working on the "evil internet," you'll probably run into trouble with RMI. Even through RMI has support for tunneling over HTTP (which is usually allowed by firewalls), setting up RMI tunneling can be tricky.

Another thing to consider is that RMI is Java-based. That means that both the client and the service must be written in Java. And since RMI uses Java serialization, the types of the objects being sent across the network must have the exact same version on both sides of the call. These may or may not be issues for your application, but bear them in mind when choosing RMI for remoting.

Caucho Technology (the same people behind the Resin application server) has developed a remoting solution that addresses the limitations of RMI. Actually, they've come up with two solutions: Hessian and Burlap. Let's see how to use Hessian and Burlap to work with remote services in Spring.

10.3 Exposing remote services with Hessian and Burlap

Hessian and Burlap are two solutions provided by Caucho Technology[1] that enable lightweight remote services over HTTP. They each aim to simplify web services by keeping both their API and their communication protocols as simple as possible.

You may be wondering why Caucho has two solutions to the same problem. Hessian and Burlap are two sides of the same coin, but each serves slightly different purposes. Hessian, like RMI, uses binary messages to communicate between client and service. But unlike other binary remoting technologies (such as RMI), the binary message is portable to languages other than Java, including PHP, Python, C++, and C#.

Burlap is an XML-based remoting technology, which automatically makes it portable to any language that can parse XML. And because it's XML, it's more easily human-readable than Hessian's binary format. Unlike other XML-based remoting technologies (such as SOAP or XML-RPC), Burlap's message structure is as simple as possible and doesn't require an external definition language (such as WSDL or IDL).

You may be wondering how to choose between Hessian and Burlap. For the most part, they're identical. The only difference is that Hessian messages are binary and Burlap messages are XML. Because Hessian messages are binary, they're more

---

[1] http://www.caucho.com

bandwidth friendly. If human readability is important to you (for debugging purposes) or if your application will be communicating with a language for which there's no Hessian implementation, Burlap's XML messages may be preferable.

To demonstrate Hessian and Burlap services in Spring, let's revisit the Spitter service example that we addressed with RMI in the previous section. But this time we'll look at how to solve the problem using Hessian and Burlap as the remoting models.

10.3.1 Exposing bean functionality with Hessian/Burlap

As before, suppose that we want to expose the functionality of the `SpitterServiceImpl` class as a service—a Hessian service this time around. Even without Spring, this would be fairly trivial. You'd write a service class that extends `com.caucho.hessian.server.HessianServlet` and make sure that all of the service methods are `public` (all public methods are considered service methods to Hessian).

Because Hessian services are already easy to implement, Spring doesn't do much to simplify the Hessian model any further. But when used with Spring, a Hessian service can take full advantage of the Spring Framework in ways that a pure Hessian service can't. This includes using Spring AOP to advise a Hessian service with system-wide services such as declarative transactions.

EXPORTING A HESSIAN SERVICE

Exporting a Hessian service in Spring is remarkably similar to implementing an RMI service in Spring. To expose the Spitter service bean as an RMI service, we had to configure an `RmiServiceExporter` bean in the Spring configuration file. In a similar way, to expose the Spitter service as a Hessian service, we'll need to configure another exporter bean. This time it'll be a `HessianServiceExporter`.

`HessianServiceExporter` performs the same function for a Hessian service as `RmiServiceExporter` does for an RMI service: it exposes the public methods of a POJO as methods of a Hessian service. But, as shown in figure 10.6, how it pulls off this feat is different from how `RmiServiceExporter` exports POJOs as RMI services.

`HessianServiceExporter` is a Spring MVC controller (more on that in a moment) that receives Hessian requests and translates them into method calls on the exported POJO.

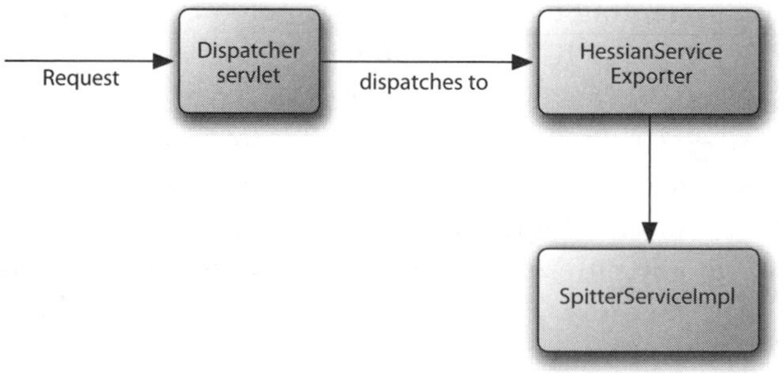

Figure 10.6 `HessianServiceExporter` is a Spring MVC controller that exports a POJO as a Hessian service by receiving Hessian requests and translating them into calls to the POJO.

The following declaration of `HessianServiceExporter` in Spring exports the `spitterService` bean as a Hessian service:

```
<bean id="hessianSpitterService"
      class="org.springframework.remoting.caucho.HessianServiceExporter"
      p:service-ref="spitterService"
      p:serviceInterface="com.habuma.spitter.service.SpitterService" />
```

Just as with `RmiServiceExporter`, the `service` property is wired with a reference to the bean that implements the service. Here, that's a reference to the `spitterService` bean. The `serviceInterface` is set to indicate that `SpitterService` is the interface that the service implements.

Unlike `RmiServiceExporter`, we don't need to get a `serviceName` property. With RMI, the `serviceName` property is used to register a service in the RMI registry. Hessian doesn't have a registry and, therefore, there's no need to name a Hessian service.

CONFIGURING THE HESSIAN CONTROLLER

Another major difference between `RmiServiceExporter` and `HessianServiceExporter` is that because Hessian is HTTP-based, `HessianServiceExporter` is implemented as a Spring MVC Controller. This means that in order to use exported Hessian services, you'll need to perform two additional configuration steps:

- Configure a Spring `DispatcherServlet` in web.xml and deploy your application as a web application.
- Configure a URL handler in your Spring configuration file to dispatch Hessian service URLs to the appropriate Hessian service bean.

We saw how to configure Spring's `DispatcherServlet` and URL handlers in chapter 7. So these steps should be somewhat familiar by now. First, you'll need a `DispatcherServlet`. Fortunately, you have one already configured in the Spitter application's web.xml file. But for the purposes of handling Hessian services, that `DispatcherServlet` will need a servlet mapping that catches `*.service` URLs:

```
<servlet-mapping>
  <servlet-name>spitter</servlet-name>
  <url-pattern>*.service</url-pattern>
</servlet-mapping>
```

Configured this way, any request whose URL ends with `.service` will be given to `DispatcherServlet`, which will in turn hand off the request to the `Controller` that's mapped to the URL. Thus requests to `/spitter.service` will ultimately be handled by the `hessianSpitterService` bean (which is just a proxy to `SpitterServiceImpl`).

How do I know that the request will go to `hessianSpitterService`? Because we're also going to configure a URL mapping to have `DispatcherServlet` send it to `hessianSpitterService`. The following `SimpleUrlHandlerMapping` will make that happen:

```
<bean id="urlMapping" class=
    "org.springframework.web.servlet.handler.SimpleUrlHandlerMapping">
  <property name="mappings">
    <value>
```

```
      /spitter.service=hessianSpitterService
    </value>
  </property>
</bean>
```

An alternative to Hessian's binary protocol is Burlap's XML-based protocol. Let's see how to export a service as a Burlap service.

EXPORTING A BURLAP SERVICE

BurlapServiceExorter is virtually identical to HessianServiceExporter in every way, except that it uses an XML-based protocol instead of a binary protocol. The following bean definition shows how to expose the Spitter service as a Burlap service using BurlapServiceExporter:

```
<bean id="burlapSpitterService"
      class="org.springframework.remoting.caucho.BurlapServiceExporter"
      p:service-ref="spitterService"
      p:serviceInterface="com.habuma.spitter.service.SpitterService" />
```

As you can see, the only thing different between this bean and its Hessian counterpart are the bean's ID and its class. Configuring a Burlap service is otherwise the same as configuring a Hessian service. This includes the need to set up a URL handler and a DispatcherServlet.

Now let's look at the other side of the conversation and consume the service that we published using Hessian (or Burlap).

10.3.2 Accessing Hessian/Burlap services

As you'll recall from section 10.2.2, client code that consumed the Spitter service using RmiProxyFactoryBean had no idea that the service was an RMI service. In fact, it had no clue that it was a remote service at all. It only dealt with the SpitterService interface—all of the RMI details were completely contained in the configuration of the beans in Spring's configuration file. The good news is that because of the client's ignorance of the service's implementation, switching from an RMI client to a Hessian client is extremely easy, requiring no changes to the client's Java code.

The bad news is that if you love writing Java code, this section may be a letdown. That's because the only difference between wiring the client side of an RMI-based service and wiring the client side of a Hessian-based service is that you'll use Spring's HessianProxyFactoryBean instead of RmiProxyFactoryBean. A Hessian-based spitter service can be declared in the client code like this:

```
<bean id="spitterService"
      class="org.springframework.remoting.caucho.HessianProxyFactoryBean"
      p:serviceUrl="http://localhost:8080/Spitter/spitter.service"
      p:serviceInterface="com.habuma.spitter.service.SpitterService" />
```

Just as with an RMI-based service, the serviceInterface property specifies the interface that the service implements. And, as with RmiProxyFactoryBean, serviceUrl indicates the URL of the service. Since Hessian is HTTP-based, it's been set to an HTTP

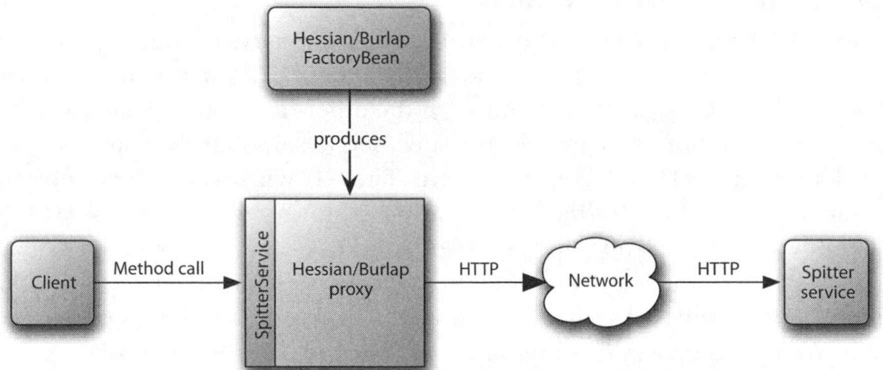

Figure 10.7 `HessianProxyFactoryBean` and `BurlapProxyFactoryBean` produce proxy objects that talk to a remote service over HTTP (Hessian in binary, Burlap in XML).

URL here (determined in part by the URL mapping we defined earlier). Figure 10.7 shows the interaction between a client and the proxy produced by `HessianProxyFactoryBean`.

As it turns out, wiring a Burlap service into the client is equally uninteresting. The only difference is that you'll use `BurlapProxyFactoryBean` instead of `HessianProxyFactoryBean`:

```
<bean id="spitterService"
      class="org.springframework.remoting.caucho.BurlapProxyFactoryBean"
      p:serviceUrl="http://localhost:8080/Spitter/spitter.service"
      p:serviceInterface="com.habuma.spitter.service.SpitterService" />
```

Although I've made light of how uninteresting the configuration differences are among RMI, Hessian, and Burlap, this tedium is a benefit. It demonstrates that you can switch effortlessly between the various remoting technologies supported by Spring without having to learn a completely new model. Once you've configured a reference to an RMI service, it's short work to reconfigure it as a Hessian or Burlap service.

Because both Hessian and Burlap are based on HTTP, they don't suffer from the same firewall issues as RMI. But RMI has both Hessian and Burlap beat when it comes to serializing objects that are sent in RPC messages. Whereas Hessian and Burlap both use a proprietary serialization mechanism, RMI uses Java's own serialization mechanism. If your data model is complex, the Hessian/Burlap serialization model may not be sufficient.

There is a best-of-both-worlds solution. Let's look at Spring's HTTP invoker, which offers RPC over HTTP (like Hessian/Burlap) while at the same time using Java serialization of objects (like RMI).

10.4 Using Spring's HttpInvoker

The Spring team recognized a void between RMI services and HTTP-based services such as Hessian and Burlap. On one side, RMI uses Java's standard object serialization but is difficult to use across firewalls. On the other side, Hessian and Burlap work well across firewalls but use a proprietary object serialization mechanism.

Thus Spring's HTTP invoker was born. The HTTP invoker is a new remoting model created as part of the Spring Framework to perform remoting across HTTP (to make the firewalls happy) and using Java's serialization (to make programmers happy).

Working with HTTP invoker-based services is similar to working with Hessian/Burlap-based services. To get started with the HTTP invoker, let's take another look at the Spitter service—this time implemented as an HTTP invoker service.

10.4.1 Exposing beans as HTTP services

To export a bean as an RMI service, we used `RmiServiceExporter`. To export it as a Hessian service, we used `HessianServiceExporter`. And to export it as a Burlap service, we used `BurlapServiceExporter`. Continuing this monotony over to Spring's HTTP invoker, it shouldn't surprise you that to export an HTTP invoker service, we'll need to use `HttpInvokerServiceExporter`.

To export the Spitter service as an HTTP invoker–based service, you need to configure an `HttpInvokerServiceExporter` bean like this:

```
<bean class=
    "org.springframework.remoting.httpinvoker.HttpInvokerServiceExporter"
    p:service-ref="spitterService"
    p:serviceInterface="com.habuma.spitter.service.SpitterService" />
```

Feeling a sense of déjà vu? You may have a hard time spotting the difference between this bean declaration and the ones in section 10.3.2. The only material difference is the class name: `HttpInvokerServiceExporter`. Otherwise, this exporter isn't much different from the other remote service exporters.

As illustrated in figure 10.8, `HttpInvokerServiceExporter` works much like `HessianServiceExporter` and `BurlapServiceExporter`. It's a Spring MVC controller that receives requests from a client through `DispatcherServlet` and translates those requests into method calls on the service implementation POJO.

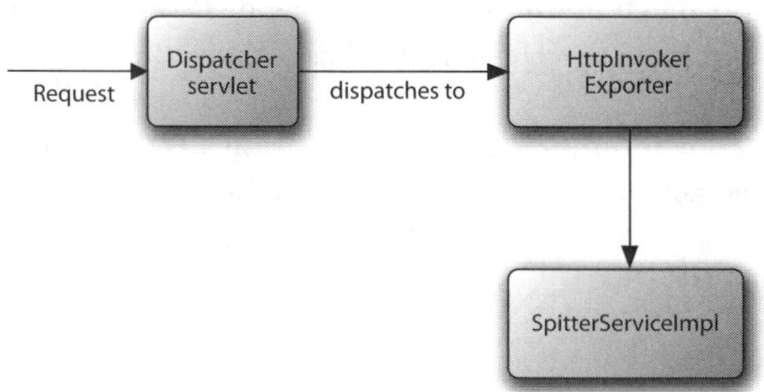

Figure 10.8 `HttpInvokerServiceExporter` works much like its Hessian and Burlap cousins, receiving requests from a Spring MVC `DispatcherServlet` and translating them into method calls on a Spring-managed bean.

Because `HttpInvokerServiceExporter` is a Spring MVC controller, you'll need to set up a URL handler to map an HTTP URL to the service, just like with the Hessian and Burlap exporters:

```
<bean id="urlMapping" class=
    "org.springframework.web.servlet.handler.SimpleUrlHandlerMapping">
  <property name="mappings">
    <value>
      /spitter.service=httpInvokerSpitterService
    </value>
  </property>
</bean>
```

Also, as before, you'll need to make sure you have a `DispatcherServlet` declared in web.xml with the following `<servlet-mapping>`:

```
<servlet-mapping>
  <servlet-name>spitter</servlet-name>
  <url-pattern>*.service</url-pattern>
</servlet-mapping>
```

Configured this way, the Spitter service will be available at /spitter.service, the same URL you used to expose the service through Hessian and Burlap.

We've already seen how to consume services made remote through RMI, Hessian, and Burlap. Now let's rework the Spitter client to use the service that you just exposed with HTTP invoker.

10.4.2 Accessing services via HTTP

At the risk of sounding like a broken record, I must tell you that consuming an HTTP invoker-based service is much like what we've already seen with the other remote service proxies. It's virtually identical. As you can see from figure 10.9, `HttpInvokerProxyFactoryBean` fills the same hole as the other remote service proxy factory beans that we've seen in this chapter.

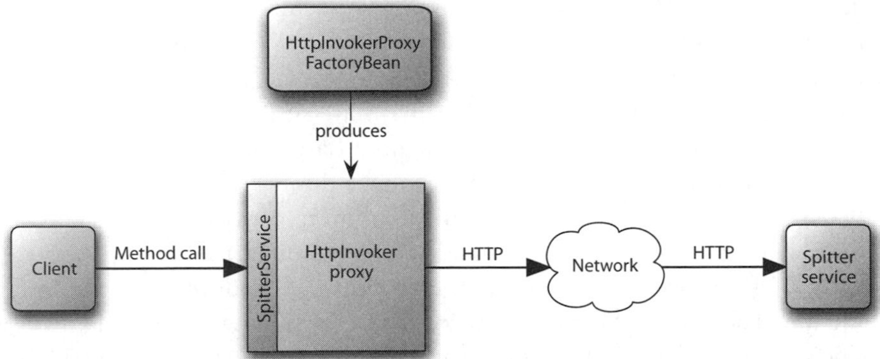

Figure 10.9 `HttpInvokerProxyFactoryBean` is a proxy factory bean that produces a proxy for remoting with a Spring-specific HTTP-based protocol.

To wire the HTTP invoker–based service into our client's Spring application context, we must configure a bean that proxies it using `HttpInvokerProxyFactoryBean` as follows:

```
<bean id="spitterService" class=
     "org.springframework.remoting.httpinvoker.HttpInvokerProxyFactoryBean"
      p:serviceUrl="http://localhost:8080/Spitter/spitter.service"
      p:serviceInterface="com.habuma.spitter.service.SpitterService" />
```

Comparing this bean definition to those in sections 10.2.2 and 10.3.2, you'll find that little has changed. The `serviceInterface` property is still used to indicate the interface implemented by the Spitter service. And the `serviceUrl` property is still used to indicate the location of the remote service. Because HTTP invoker is HTTP-based like Hessian and Burlap, the `serviceUrl` can contain the same URL as with the Hessian and Burlap versions of the bean.

Don't you love the symmetry?

Spring's HTTP invoker presents a best-of-both-worlds remoting solution combining the simplicity of HTTP communication with Java's built-in object serialization. This makes HTTP invoker services an appealing alternative to either RMI or Hessian/Burlap.

`HttpInvoker` has one significant limitation that you should keep in mind: it's a remoting solution offered by the Spring Framework only. This means that both the client and the service must be Spring-enabled applications. This also implies, at least for now, that both the client and the service must be Java-based. And because Java serialization is being used, both sides must have the same version of the classes (much like RMI).

RMI, Hessian, Burlap, and HTTP invoker are great remoting options. But when it comes to ubiquitous remoting, none hold a candle to web services. Next up, we'll look at how Spring supports remoting through SOAP-based web services.

10.5 Publishing and consuming web services

One of the most hyped TLAs (three-letter acronyms) in recent years is SOA (which stands for *service-oriented architecture*). SOA means many things to different people. But at the center of SOA is the idea that applications can and should be designed to lean on a common set of core services instead of reimplementing the same functionality for each application.

For example, a financial institution may have several applications, many of which need access to borrower account information. Rather than build account access logic into each application (much of which would be duplicated), the applications could all rely on a common service to retrieve the account information.

Java and web services have a long history together and several options are available for working with web services in Java. Many of those options integrate with Spring in some way. Though it'd be impossible for me to cover every Spring-enabled web service framework and toolkit in this book, Spring itself comes with some capable support for publishing and consuming SOAP web services using the Java API for XML Web Services, or JAX-WS as it's commonly known.

> **What about JAX-RPC and XFire?**
>
> In previous editions of this book, I wrote about developing web services using XFire (http://xfire.codehaus.org) and Spring's support for JAX-RPC. Those were great topics back then, but both are fading technologies.
>
> JAX-RPC was supplanted by JAX-WS as the web service standard for Java. Spring followed suit and has now deprecated its support for JAX-RPC in favor of the new JAX-WS support. Fortunately, the JAX-WS support in Spring closely mirrors the JAX-RPC support. Spring's `JaxWsPortProxyFactoryBean`, for instance, works much like the old `JaxRpcPortProxyFactoryBean`.
>
> XFire was my favorite way of working with web services in Spring. But development of XFire stopped with the 1.2.6 release. The Apache CXF (http://cxf.apache.org) project is considered by many to be XFire 2; so if you liked XFire, then you should check out Apache CXF. Apache CXF is far more ambitious than XFire and to cover it adequately would be well outside of the scope of this book.
>
> Since one of my objectives for this edition was to remain as current as possible, I chose to leave JAX-RPC and XFire behind. If either of those topics interest you, I encourage you to find a copy of *Spring in Action, Second Edition*. Both topics are covered there and little has changed with regard to JAX-RPC or XFire since that time.

In this section, we'll revisit the Spitter service example one more time. This time, we'll expose and consume the Spitter service as a web service using Spring's JAX-WS support. Let's start by seeing what it takes to create a JAX-WS web service in Spring.

10.5.1 Creating Spring-enabled JAX-WS endpoints

Earlier in this chapter, we created remote services using Spring's service exporters. These service exporters magically turn Spring-configured POJOs into remote services. We saw how to create RMI services using `RmiServiceExporter`, Hessian services using `HessianServiceExporter`, Burlap services using `BurlapServiceExporter`, and HTTP invoker services using `HttpInvokerServiceExporter`. Now you probably expect me to show you how to create web services using a JAX-WS service exporter in this section.

Spring does provide a JAX-WS service exporter, `SimpleJaxWsServiceExporter`, and we'll see it soon enough. But before we get there, you should know that it may not be the best choice in all situations. You see, `SimpleJaxWsServiceExporter` requires that the JAX-WS runtime support publishing of endpoints to a specified address.[2] The JAX-WS runtime that ships with Sun's JDK 1.6 fits the bill, but other JAX-WS implementations, including the reference implementation of JAX-WS, may not.

If you'll be deploying to a JAX-WS runtime that doesn't support publishing to a specified address, then you'll have write your JAX-WS endpoints in a more conventional way. That means that the lifecycle of the endpoints will be managed by the JAX-

[2] More specifically, this means that the JAX-WS provider must come with its own HTTP server that it can use to build up the necessary infrastructure for publishing the service to a requested address.

WS runtime and not by Spring. But that doesn't mean that they can't be wired with beans from a Spring application context.

AUTOWIRING JAX-WS ENDPOINTS IN SPRING

The JAX-WS programming model involves using annotations to declare a class and its methods as web service operations. A class that's annotated with `@WebService` is considered a web service endpoint and its methods, annotated with `@WebMethod`, are the operations.

Just as with any other object in a sizable application, a JAX-WS endpoint will likely depend on other objects to do its work. That means that JAX-WS endpoints could benefit from dependency injection. But if the endpoint's lifecycle is managed by the JAX-WS runtime and not by Spring, it would seem to be impossible to wire Spring-managed beans into a JAX-WS managed endpoint instance.

The secret to wiring JAX-WS endpoints is to extend `SpringBeanAutowiringSupport`. By extending `SpringBeanAutowiringSupport`, you can annotate an endpoint's properties with `@Autowired` and its dependencies will be met.[3] `SpitterServiceEndpoint` shows how this works.

Listing 10.2 `SpringBeanAutowiringSupport` on JAX-WS endpoints

```
package com.habuma.spitter.remoting.jaxws;
import java.util.List;

import javax.jws.WebMethod;
import javax.jws.WebService;

import org.springframework.beans.factory.annotation.Autowired;
import org.springframework.web.context.support.SpringBeanAutowiringSupport;

import com.habuma.spitter.domain.Spitter;
import com.habuma.spitter.domain.Spittle;
import com.habuma.spitter.service.SpitterService;

@WebService(serviceName="SpitterService")
public class SpitterServiceEndpoint
    extends SpringBeanAutowiringSupport {          <-- Enable autowiring

  @Autowired
  SpitterService spitterService;                   <-- Autowire SpitterService

  @WebMethod
  public void addSpittle(Spittle spittle) {
    spitterService.saveSpittle(spittle);           <-- Delegate to SpitterService
  }

  @WebMethod
  public void deleteSpittle(long spittleId) {
    spitterService.deleteSpittle(spittleId);
```

[3] Although we're using `SpringBeanAutowiringSupport` to enable autowiring for JAX-WS endpoints, it's useful to enable autowiring support anywhere an object's lifecycle is managed outside of Spring. The only requirement is that the Spring application context and the non-Spring runtime reside in the same web application.

```
  }

  @WebMethod
  public List<Spittle> getRecentSpittles(int spittleCount) {
    return spitterService.getRecentSpittles(spittleCount);
  }

  @WebMethod
  public List<Spittle> getSpittlesForSpitter(Spitter spitter) {
    return spitterService.getSpittlesForSpitter(spitter);
  }
}
```

Delegate to SpitterService

We've annotated the `spitterService` property with `@Autowired` to indicate that it should be automatically injected with a bean from the Spring application context. From there, this endpoint delegates to the injected `SpitterService` to do the real work.

EXPORTING STANDALONE JAX-WS ENDPOINTS

As I said, `SpringBeanAutowiringSupport` is useful when the object whose properties are being injected doesn't have its lifecycle managed by Spring. But under the right circumstances, it's possible to export a Spring-managed bean as a JAX-WS endpoint.

Spring's `SimpleJaxWsServiceExporter` works in a way similar to the other service exporters that we saw earlier in this chapter, in that it publishes Spring-managed beans as service endpoints in a JAX-WS runtime. Unlike those other service exporters, `SimpleJaxWsServiceExporter` doesn't need to be given a reference to the bean it's supposed to export. Instead, it publishes all beans that are annotated with JAX-WS annotations as JAX-WS services.

`SimpleJaxWsServiceExporter` can be configured using the following `<bean>` declaration:

```
<bean class=
    "org.springframework.remoting.jaxws.SimpleJaxWsServiceExporter"/>
```

As you can see, `SimpleJaxWsServiceExporter` needs nothing else to do its job. When it gets started, it'll dig through the Spring application context looking for beans that are annotated with `@WebService`. When it finds one, it'll publish it as a JAX-WS endpoint with a base address of http://localhost:8080/.

One such bean that it may find is `SpitterServiceEndpoint`.

Listing 10.3 `SimpleJaxWsServiceExporter` turns beans into JAX-WS endpoints.

```
package com.habuma.spitter.remoting.jaxws;
import java.util.List;

import javax.jws.WebMethod;
import javax.jws.WebService;

import org.springframework.beans.factory.annotation.Autowired;
import org.springframework.stereotype.Component;

import com.habuma.spitter.domain.Spitter;
import com.habuma.spitter.domain.Spittle;
```

```
import com.habuma.spitter.service.SpitterService;

@Component
@WebService(serviceName="SpitterService")
public class SpitterServiceEndpoint {
  @Autowired
  SpitterService spitterService;                               Autowire
                                                               SpitterService
  @WebMethod
  public void addSpittle(Spittle spittle) {
    spitterService.saveSpittle(spittle);
  }
                                                               Delegate to
  @WebMethod                                                   SpitterService
  public void deleteSpittle(long spittleId) {
    spitterService.deleteSpittle(spittleId);
  }

  @WebMethod
  public List<Spittle> getRecentSpittles(int spittleCount) {
    return spitterService.getRecentSpittles(spittleCount);
  }

  @WebMethod
  public List<Spittle> getSpittlesForSpitter(Spitter spitter) {
    return spitterService.getSpittlesForSpitter(spitter);
  }
}
```

You'll notice that this new implementation of `SpitterServiceEndpoint` no longer extends `SpringBeanAutowiringSupport`. As a full-fledged Spring bean, it'll qualify for autowiring without extending any special support class.

Since `SimpleJaxWsServiceEndpoint`'s base address defaults to http://localhost:8080/ and since `SpitterServiceEndpoint` is annotated with `@WebService(serviceName="SpitterService")`, the matchup of these two beans will result in a web service at http://localhost:8080/SpitterService. But you're in total control of the service URL, so if you'd like, you can set the base address to something else. For example, the following configuration of `SimpleJaxWsServiceEndpoint` publishes the same service endpoint to http://localhost:8888/services/SpitterService.

```
<bean class=
  "org.springframework.remoting.jaxws.SimpleJaxWsServiceExporter"
      p:baseAddress="http://localhost:8888/services/"/>
```

As simple as `SimpleJaxWsServiceEndpoint` seems, you should be aware that it only works with a JAX-WS runtime that supports publication of endpoints with an address. That includes the JAX-WS runtime that comes with Sun's 1.6 JDK. Other JAX-WS runtimes, such as the JAX-WS 2.1 reference implementation, don't support this type of endpoint publication and thus can't be used with `SimpleJaxWsServiceEndpoint`.

10.5.2 Proxying JAX-WS services on the client side

Publishing web services with Spring turned out to be quite different from how we published services in RMI, Hessian, Burlap, and Http invoker. But as you'll soon see,

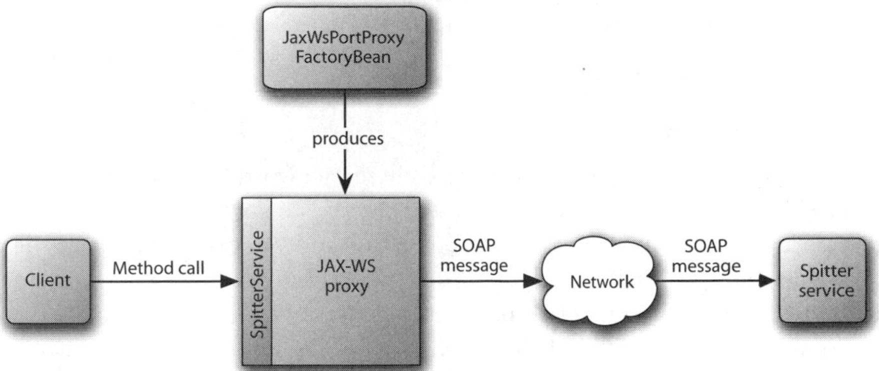

Figure 10.10 `JaxWsPortProxyFactoryBean` **produces proxies that talk to remote web services. These proxies can then be wired into other beans as if they were local POJOs.**

consuming web services with Spring involves client-side proxies in much the same way that Spring-based clients consume those other remoting technologies.

Using `JaxWsPortProxyFactoryBean`, we can wire the Spitter web service in Spring as if it were any other bean. `JaxWsPortProxyFactoryBean` is a Spring FactoryBean that produces a proxy that knows how to talk to a SOAP web service. The proxy itself is created to implement the service's interface (see figure 10.10). Consequently, `JaxWsPortProxyFactoryBean` makes it possible to wire and use a remote web service as if it were just any other local POJO.

We'll configure `JaxWsPortProxyFactoryBean` to reference the Spitter service web service like this:

```
<bean id="spitterService"
      class="org.springframework.remoting.jaxws.JaxWsPortProxyFactoryBean"
      p:wsdlDocumentUrl="http://localhost:8080/services/SpitterService?wsdl"
      p:serviceName="spitterService"
      p:portName="spitterServiceHttpPort"
      p:serviceInterface="com.habuma.spitter.service.SpitterService"
      p:namespaceUri="http://spitter.com"/>
```

As you can see, several properties must be set for `JaxWsPortProxyFactoryBean` to work. The `wsdlDocumentUrl` property identifies the location of the remote web service's definition file. `JaxWsPortProxyFactoryBean` will use the WSDL available at that URL to construct a proxy to the service. The proxy that's produced by `JaxWsPortProxyFactoryBean` will implement the `SpitterService` interface, as specified by the `serviceInterface` property.

The values for the remaining three properties can usually be determined by looking at the service's WSDL. For illustration's sake, suppose that the WSDL for the Spitter service looked like this:

```
<wsdl:definitions targetNamespace="http://spitter.com">
...
  <wsdl:service name="spitterService">
```

```
    <wsdl:port name="spitterServiceHttpPort"
            binding="tns:spitterServiceHttpBinding">
...
    </wsdl:port>
  </wsdl:service>
</wsdl:definitions>
```

Though not likely, it's possible for multiple services and/or ports to be defined in the service's WSDL. For that reason, JaxWsPortProxyFactoryBean requires that we specify the port and service names in the portName and serviceName properties. A quick glance at the name attributes of the <wsdl:port> and <wsdl:service> elements in the WSDL will help you figure out what these properties should be set to.

Finally, the namespaceUri property specifies the namespace of the service. Among other things, the namespace will help JaxWsPortProxyFactoryBean locate the service definition in the WSDL. As with the port and service names, you can find the correct value for this property by looking in the WSDL. It's usually available in the targetNamespace attribute of the <wsdl:definitions> element.

10.6 Summary

Working with remote services is usually a tedious chore. But Spring provides remoting support that makes working with remote services as simple as working with any regular JavaBeans.

On the client side, Spring provides proxy factory beans that enable you to configure remote services in your Spring application. Regardless of whether you're using RMI, Hessian, Burlap, Spring's own HTTP invoker, or web services for remoting, you can wire remote services into your application as if they were POJOs. Spring even catches any RemoteExceptions that are thrown and rethrows runtime RemoteAccessExceptions in their place, freeing your code from having to deal with an exception that it probably can't recover from.

Even though Spring hides many of the details of remote services, making them appear as though they're local JavaBeans, you should bear in mind the consequences of remote services. Remote services, by their nature, are typically less efficient than local services. You should consider this when writing code that accesses remote services, limiting remote calls to avoid performance bottlenecks.

In this chapter, you saw how Spring can be used to expose and consume services based on some basic remoting technologies. Although these remoting options are useful in distributing applications, this was just a taste of what's involved in working within a service-oriented architecture (SOA).

We also looked at how to export beans as SOAP-based web services. Though this is an easy way to develop web services, it may not be the best choice from an architectural standpoint. In the next chapter, we'll look at a different approach to building distributed applications by exposing portions of the application as RESTful resources.

11 Giving Spring some REST

This chapter covers

- Writing controllers that serve REST resources
- Representing resources in XML, JSON, and other formats
- Writing REST clients
- Submitting RESTful forms

Data is king.

As developers, we're often focused on building great software to solve business problems. Data is just the raw materials that our software processes need to get their job done. But if you were to ask most business people which is most valuable to them, data or software, they're likely to choose data. Data is the life's blood of many businesses. Software is often replaceable. But the data gathered over the years can never be replaced.[1]

[1] That's not to say that software has no value. Most businesses would be severely handicapped without their software. But they'd be dead without their data.

Don't you think it's odd that, given the importance of data, the way we develop software often treats data as an afterthought? Take the remote services from the previous chapter as an example. Those services were centered on actions and processes, not information and resources.

In recent years, *Representational State Transfer (REST)* has emerged as a popular information-centric alternative to traditional SOAP-based web services. To help Spring developers take advantage of the REST architectural model, Spring 3.0 came packed with first-class support for working with REST.

The good news is that Spring's REST support builds upon Spring MVC, so we've already covered much of what we'll need for working with REST in Spring. In this chapter, we'll build upon what we already know about Spring MVC to develop controllers that handle requests for RESTful resources. We'll also see what Spring has to offer on the client side of a REST conversation.

But before we get too carried away, let's examine what working with REST is all about.

11.1 Getting REST

I'll wager that this isn't the first time you've heard or read about REST. There's been a lot of talk about REST in recent years and you'll find that it's fashionable in software development to speak ill of SOAP-based web services while promoting REST as an alternative.

Certainly, SOAP can be overkill for many applications and REST brings a simpler alternative. The problem is that not everybody has a solid grasp of what REST really is. As a result, a lot of misinformation is floating about. Before we can talk about how Spring supports REST, we need to establish a common understanding of what REST is all about.

11.1.1 The fundamentals of REST

A mistake that's often made when approaching REST is to think of it as "web services with URLs"—to think of REST as another remote procedure call (RPC) mechanism, like SOAP, but invoked through plain HTTP URLs and without SOAP's hefty XML namespaces.

On the contrary, REST has little to do with RPC. Whereas RPC is service-oriented and focused on actions and verbs, REST is resource-oriented, emphasizing the things and nouns that describe an application.

Also, although URLs play a key role in REST, they're only a part of the story.

To understand what REST is all about, it helps to break down the acronym into its constituent parts:

- *Representational*—REST resources can be represented in virtually any form, including XML, JavaScript Object Notation (JSON), or even HTML—whatever form best suits the consumer of those resources.

- *State*—When working with REST, we're more concerned with the state of a resource than with the actions we can take against resources.
- *Transfer*—REST involves transferring resource data, in some representational form, from one application to another.

Put more succinctly, REST is about transferring the state of resources—in whatever form is most appropriate—from a server to a client (or vice versa).

Given this view of REST, I try to avoid terms such as *REST service*, or *RESTful web service*, or any similar term that incorrectly gives prominence to actions. Instead, I prefer to emphasize the resource-oriented nature of REST and speak of *RESTful resources*.

11.1.2 How Spring supports REST

Spring has long had some of the ingredients needed for exposing REST resources. But with Spring 3 came several enhancements to Spring MVC providing first-class REST support. Now Spring supports development of REST resources in the following ways:

- Controllers can handle requests for all HTTP methods, including the four primary REST methods: `GET`, `PUT`, `DELETE`, and `POST`.
- The new `@PathVariable` annotation enables controllers to handle requests for parameterized URLs (URLs that have variable input as part of their path).
- The `<form:form>` JSP tag from Spring's form-binding JSP tag library, along with the new `HiddenHttpMethodFilter`, make it possible to submit `PUT` and `DELETE` requests from HTML forms, even in browsers that don't support those HTTP methods.
- Resources can be represented in a variety of ways using Spring's view and view resolvers, including new view implementations for rendering model data as XML, JSON, Atom, and RSS.
- The representation best suited for the client can be chosen using the new `ContentNegotiatingViewResolver`.
- View-based rendering can be bypassed altogether using the new `@ResponseBody` annotation and various `HttpMethodConverter` implementations.
- Similarly, the new `@RequestBody` annotation, along with `HttpMethodConverter` implementations, can convert inbound HTTP data into Java objects passed into a controller's handler methods.
- `RestTemplate` simplifies client-side consumption of REST resources.

Throughout this chapter we're going to explore all of these features that make Spring more RESTful and see how to both produce and consume REST resources. We'll start by looking at what goes into a resource-oriented Spring MVC controller.

11.2 Writing resource-oriented controllers

As we saw in chapter 7, Spring MVC's model for writing controller classes is extremely flexible. Almost any method with almost any signature can be annotated to handle a web request. But a side effect of such flexibility is that Spring MVC allows you to develop controllers that aren't ideal in terms of RESTful resources. It's too easy to write *RESTless* controllers.

11.2.1 Dissecting a RESTless controller

To help understand what a RESTful controller looks like, it helps to first know what a RESTless controller looks like. `DisplaySpittleController` is an example of a RESTless controller.

Listing 11.1 `DisplaySpittleController` is a RESTless Spring MVC controller.

```
package com.habuma.spitter.mvc.restless;

import javax.inject.Inject;

import org.springframework.stereotype.Controller;
import org.springframework.ui.Model;
import org.springframework.web.bind.annotation.RequestMapping;
import org.springframework.web.bind.annotation.RequestMethod;
import org.springframework.web.bind.annotation.RequestParam;

import com.habuma.spitter.service.SpitterService;

@Controller
@RequestMapping("/displaySpittle.htm")                    <-- RESTless URL mapping
public class DisplaySpittleController {
  private final SpitterService spitterService;

  @Inject
  public DisplaySpittleController(SpitterService spitterService) {
    this.spitterService = spitterService;
  }

  @RequestMapping(method=RequestMethod.GET)
  public String showSpittle(@RequestParam("id") long id, Model model) {
    model.addAttribute(spitterService.getSpittleById(id));
    return "spittles/view";
  }
}
```

The first thing to notice about the controller in listing 11.1 is its name. Sure, it's just a name. But it accurately describes what the controller does. The first word is *Display*—a verb. This is indicative of the fact that this controller is action-oriented, not resource-oriented.

Take note of the `@RequestMapping` annotation at the class level. It says that this controller will handle requests for /displaySpittle.htm. That seems to imply that this controller is focused on the specific use case of displaying spittles (which is corroborated by the name of the class). What's more, the extension implies that it's only capable of displaying that list in HTML form.

Nothing is terribly wrong with how `DisplaySpittleController` is written. But it isn't a RESTful controller. It's action-oriented and focused on a specific use case: displaying a `Spittle` object's details in HTML form. Even the controller's class name agrees.

Now that you know what a RESTless controller looks like, let's see what goes into writing a RESTful controller. We'll start by looking at how to handle requests for resource-oriented URLs.

11.2.2 Handling RESTful URLs

URLs are one of the first things that most people think about when starting to work with REST. After all, everything that's done in REST is done through a URL. The funny thing about many URLs is that they usually don't do what a URL is supposed to do.

URL is an acronym that stands for *uniform resource locator*. Given that name, it seems that a URL is intended to locate a resource. What's more, all URLs are also URIs, or *uniform resource identifiers*. If that's true, then we should expect that any given URL would not only locate a resource, but should also serve to identify a resource.

The fact that a URL locates a resource should seem natural. After all, for years we've been typing URLs into our web browser's address field to find content on the internet. But it's not a stretch to think of that URL as a means of uniquely identifying a resource. No two resources could share the same URL, so the URL could also be a means of identifying a resource.[2]

Many URLs don't locate or identify anything—they make demands. Rather than identify a thing, they insist that some action be taken. For instance, figure 11.1 illustrates the kind of URL handled by the `DisplaySpittleController`'s `displaySpittle()` method.

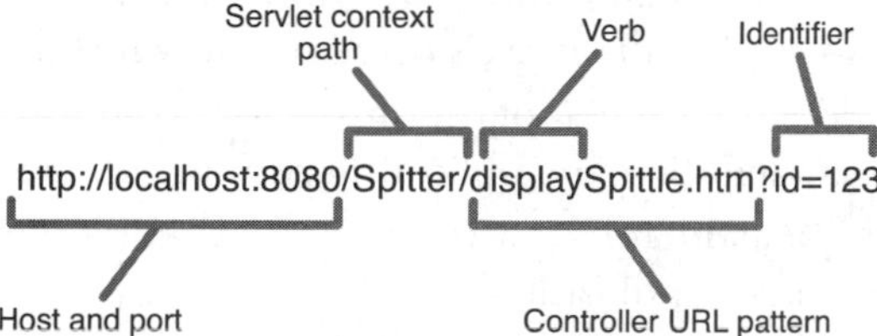

Figure 11.1 A RESTless URL is action-oriented and doesn't identify or locate a resource.

As you can see, this URL doesn't locate or identify a resource. It demands that the server display a `Spittle`. The only part of the URL that identifies anything is the `id` query parameter. The base portion of the URL is verb-oriented. That is to say that it's a RESTless URL.

If we're going to write controllers that properly handle RESTful URLs, we should first get to know what a RESTful URL looks like.

CHARACTERISTICS OF A RESTFUL URL

In contrast to their RESTless cousins, RESTful URLs fully acknowledge that HTTP is all about resources. For example, figure 11.2 shows how we might restructure the RESTless URL to be more resource-oriented.

---

[2] Although outside of the scope of this book, the semantic web takes advantage of the identifying nature of URLs in creating a linked web of resources.

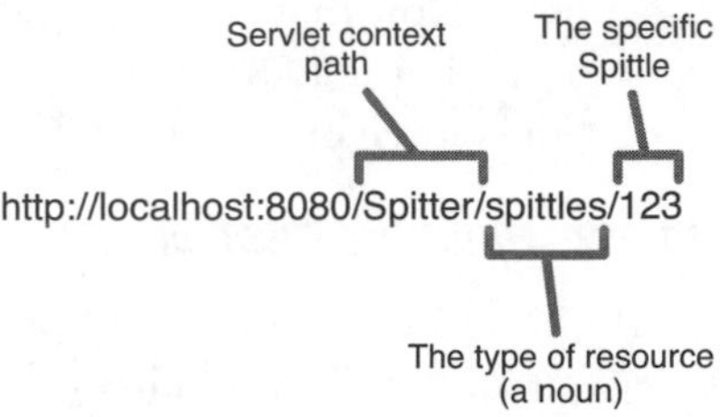

Figure 11.2 A RESTful URL is resource-oriented, both identifying and locating a resource.

One thing that's not clear about this URL is what it does. That's because the URL doesn't *do* anything. Rather, it identifies a resource. Specifically, it locates the resource that represents a `Spittle` object. What will be done with that resource is a separate matter—one for HTTP methods to decide (which we'll look at in section 11.2.3).

This URL not only locates a resource, but it also uniquely identifies that resource—it serves equally well as a URI as it does as a URL. Instead of using a query parameter to identify the resource, the entire base URL identifies the resource.

In fact, the new URL has no query parameters at all. Although query parameters are still a legitimate way to send information to the server, they're intended to provide guidance to the server in producing the resource. They shouldn't be used to help identify a resource.

One final observation should be made about RESTful URLs: they tend to be hierarchical. As you read them from left to right, you move from a broad concept to something more precise. In our example, the URL has several levels, any of which could identify a resource:

- *http://localhost:8080* identifies a domain and port. Although our application won't associate a resource with this URL, there's no reason why it couldn't.
- *http://localhost:8080/Spitter* identifies the application's servlet context. This URL is more specific in that it has identified an application running on the server.
- *http://localhost:8080/Spitter/spittles* identifies a resource that represents a list of `Spittle` objects within the Spitter application.
- *http://localhost:8080/Spitter/spittles/123* is the most precise URL, identifying a specific `Spittle` resource.

What makes the RESTful URL interesting is that its path is parameterized. Whereas the RESTless URL took its input from query parameters, the RESTful URL's input is part of the URL's path. To be able to handle requests for that kind of URL, we'll need a way to write a controller's handler method so that it can take input from the URL's path.

EMBEDDING PARAMETERS IN URLS

To enable parameterized URL paths, Spring 3 introduced a new `@PathVariable` annotation. To see how this works, look at `SpittleController`, a new Spring MVC controller that takes a resource-oriented approach to handling requests for `Spittles`.

Listing 11.2 `SpittleController` is a RESTful Spring MVC controller.

```
package com.habuma.spitter.mvc;
import javax.inject.Inject;
import javax.validation.Valid;
```

```
import org.springframework.stereotype.Controller;
import org.springframework.ui.Model;
import org.springframework.web.bind.annotation.PathVariable;
import org.springframework.web.bind.annotation.RequestMapping;
import org.springframework.web.bind.annotation.RequestMethod;
import com.habuma.spitter.domain.Spittle;
import com.habuma.spitter.service.SpitterService;

@Controller
@RequestMapping("/spittles")                              Handle requests for /spittles
public class SpittleController {
  private SpitterService spitterService;

  @Inject
  public SpittleController(SpitterService spitterService) {
    this.spitterService = spitterService;
  }

  @RequestMapping(value="/{id}",
                  method=RequestMethod.GET)                Use placeholder variable in path
  public String getSpittle(@PathVariable("id") long id,
          Model model) {
    model.addAttribute(spitterService.getSpittleById(id));
    return "spittles/view";
  }
}
```

We've annotated `SpittleController` with `@RequestMapping` at the class level to indicate that this controller will handle requests for `Spittle` resources—requests whose URLs start with */spittles*.

For now, there's only one handler method—the `getSpittle()` method. When this method's `@RequestMapping` annotation is coupled with the class-level `@RequestMapping`, this method is set to handle `GET` requests for URLs that take the form */spittles/{id}*.

You're probably wondering about those weird curly-braces in the URL pattern. The part that says *{id}* is a placeholder through which variable data will be pass into the method. It corresponds to the `@PathVariable` annotation on the `id` method parameter.

So, if a `GET` request comes in for http://localhost:8080/Spitter/spittles/123, then the `getSpittle()` method will be called with `123` passed in for the `id` parameter. The method then uses that value to look up the requested `Spittle` object and place it into the model.

At this point you may have noticed that the phrase `id` is used three times in this method's signature. Not only is it used as the URL path placeholder and as the value of the `@PathVariable` annotation, it's also used as the actual name of the method parameter. That's only a coincidence in this case. But if the method parameter name happens to be the same as the path variable name (and I can think of no reason why it shouldn't be), then you can take advantage of a simple convention and leave out `@PathVariable`'s value. For example:

```
@RequestMapping(value="/{id}", method=RequestMethod.GET)
public String getSpittle(@PathVariable long id, Model model) {
```

```
    model.addAttribute(spitterService.getSpittleById(id));
    return "spittles/view";
}
```

With no value given to `@PathVariable`, the method parameter name serves as the name of the path variable.[3]

Regardless of whether you explicitly identify the path variable by name, `@PathVariable` makes it possible to write controller handler methods that handle requests for URLs that identify a resource instead of describing some action to be taken. The other side of RESTful requests are the HTTP methods that will be applied to the URLs. Let's see how HTTP methods provide the verbs in a REST request.

11.2.3 Performing the REST verbs

As I mentioned before, REST is about the transfer of resource state. Therefore, we really only need a handful of verbs to be able to act upon those resources—verbs to transfer the state of a resource. For any given resource, the most common operations will be to create a resource on the server, retrieve it from the server, update it on the server, or delete it from the server.

The verbs we're interested in (*post*, *get*, *put*, and *delete*) correspond directly to four of the methods as defined by the HTTP specification and as summarized in table 11.1.[4]

Each of the HTTP methods is characterized by two traits: safety and idempotency. A method is considered *safe* if it doesn't change the state of the resource. *Idempotent* methods may or may not change state, but repeated requests should have no further side effects after the first request. By definition, all safe methods are also idempotent, but not all idempotent methods are safe.

Table 11.1 HTTP offers several methods for manipulating resources.

Method	Description	Safe?	Idempotent?
`GET`	Retrieves resource data from the server. The resource is identified by the request's URL.	Yes	Yes
`POST`	Posts data to the server to be handled by a processor listening at the request's URL.	No	No
`PUT`	Puts resource data to the server, at the URL of the request.	No	Yes
`DELETE`	Deletes the resource on the server identified by the request's URL.	No	Yes
`OPTIONS`	Requests available options for communication with the server.	Yes	Yes

[3] This assumes that you've compiled your controller classes with debugging information compiled into the class files. Otherwise, the method parameter names won't be available at runtime to match against path variable names.

[4] The HTTP specification defines four other methods: TRACE, OPTIONS, HEAD, and CONNECT. But we'll focus on the four core methods.

Table 11.1 HTTP offers several methods for manipulating resources. *(continued)*

Method	Description	Safe?	Idempotent?
`HEAD`	Like `GET`, except that only the headers should be returned—no content should be returned in the response body.	Yes	Yes
`TRACE`	Echoes the request body back to the client.	Yes	Yes

It's important to realize that although Spring supports all of HTTP's methods, it's still up to you, the developer, to be sure that the implementation of those methods follows the semantics of those methods. In other words, a `GET`-handling method should only return a resource—it shouldn't update or delete a resource.

The four HTTP methods described in table 11.1 are often mapped to CRUD (create/read/update/delete) operations. Certainly the GET method performs a read operation and the DELETE method performs a delete operation. And, even though PUT and POST can be used in ways other than update and create operations, that's commonly how they're used.

We've already seen an example of how to handle `GET` requests. The `SpittleController`'s `getSpittle()` method is annotated with `@RequestMapping`, with the `method` attribute set to handle `GET` requests. The `method` attribute is the key to detailing the HTTP method that will be handled by a controller method.

UPDATING RESOURCES WITH PUT

When it comes to understanding the `PUT` method's purpose, it helps to know that it's the semantic opposite of `GET`. Whereas a `GET` request transfers the state of a resource from the server to the client, `PUT` transfers the resource state from the client to the server.

For example, the following `putSpittle()` method is annotated to receive a `Spittle` object from a `PUT` request:

```
@RequestMapping(value="/{id}", method=RequestMethod.PUT)
@ResponseStatus(HttpStatus.NO_CONTENT)
public void putSpittle(@PathVariable("id") long id,
        @Valid Spittle spittle) {
  spitterService.saveSpittle(spittle);
}
```

The `putSpittle()` method is annotated with `@RequestMapping`, like any other handler method. In fact, the `@RequestMapping` annotation here is almost the same as the one used with the `getSpittle()` method. The only difference is that the `method` attribute is set to handle HTTP `PUT` requests instead of `GET` requests.

If that's the only difference, then that must mean that the `putSpittle()` method will handle requests with URLs that take the form */spittles/{id}*—the same URLs that are handled by the `getSpittle()` method. Again, the URL identifies a resource, not what'll be done with it. So the URL that identifies a `Spittle` will be the same whether we're `GET`ting it or `PUT`ting it.

The putSpittle() method is also tagged with an annotation we haven't seen before. The @ResponseStatus annotation defines the HTTP status that should be set on the response to the client. In this case, HttpStatus.NO_CONTENT indicates that the response status should be set to the HTTP status code 204. That status code means that the request was processed successfully, but nothing is returned in the body of the response.

HANDLING DELETE REQUESTS

Rather than simply update a resource, we may want to get rid of it altogether. In the case of the Spitter application, for example, we may want to enable clients to delete an embarrassing Spittle that was written in haste or while the user was impaired. When you don't want a resource around anymore, that's what the HTTP DELETE method is for.

As a sample of handling a DELETE request in Spring MVC, let's add a new handler method to SpittleController that answers DELETE requests to remove a Spittle resource:

```
@RequestMapping(value="/{id}", method=RequestMethod.DELETE)
@ResponseStatus(HttpStatus.NO_CONTENT)
public void deleteSpittle(@PathVariable("id") long id) {
  spitterService.deleteSpittle(id);
}
```

Once again, the @RequestMapping annotation looks a lot like the ones we used on getSpittle() and putSpittle(). It only varies in that this method's @Request-Mapping has its method attribute set to handle DELETE requests. The URL pattern that identifies a Spittle resource remains the same.

Just like putSpittle(), deleteSpittle() is also annotated with @ResponseStatus to let the client know that the request was processed successfully, but that no content will be returned in the response.

CREATING RESOURCES WITH POST

There's one in every bunch: a free spirit… a dissident… a rebel. Among the HTTP methods, POST is that rebel. It doesn't obey the rules. It's unsafe and it is certainly *not* idempotent. This nonconformist HTTP method seems to break all of the rules, but in doing so it can handle the jobs that other HTTP methods can't.

To see this rebel in action, watch POST as it performs a job that it is often called on to do—creating new resources. The createSpittle() method is a POST-handling controller method that creates new Spittle resources.

Listing 11.3 Creating new Spittles with POST

```
@RequestMapping(method=RequestMethod.POST)        <-- Handle POST

@ResponseStatus(HttpStatus.CREATED)               <-- Response with HTTP 201
public @ResponseBody Spittle createSpittle(@Valid Spittle spittle,
                  BindingResult result, HttpServletResponse response)
                  throws BindException {
  if(result.hasErrors()) {
```

```
    throw new BindException(result);
  }

  spitterService.saveSpittle(spittle);

  response.setHeader("Location", "/spittles/" + spittle.getId());
  return spittle;
}
```

Set resource location

Return Spittle resource

The first thing you may notice is that this method's `@RequestMapping` is different from the ones we've seen so far. Unlike the others, this one doesn't have its `value` attribute set. That means that the controller's class-level `@RequestMapping` is solely responsible for determining the URL pattern handled by `createSpittle()`. More specifically, `createSpittle()` will handle requests whose URL pattern matches */spittles*.

Typically, the server determines a resource's identity. Since we're creating a new resource here, there's no way that we could know the URL for that resource. So, whereas `GET`, `PUT`, and `DELETE` requests operate directly on the resource identified by their URL, `POST` has to operate against a URL that isn't the same as the resource it's creating (because that URL won't exist until the resource is created).

Once again, this method is annotated with `@ResponseStatus` to set the HTTP status code in the request. This time, the status will be set to 201 (Created) to indicate that a resource was successfully created. When an HTTP 201 response is returned to the client, the URL of the new resource should be sent along with it. So one of the last things that `createSpittle()` does is set the `Location` header to contain the resource's URL.

Although it's not strictly required with an HTTP 201 response, it's possible to return the full entity representation in the body of the response. So, much like the `GET`-handling `getSpittle()` method from before, this method concludes by returning the new `Spittle` object. This object will be transformed into some representation that the client can use.

What's not clear yet is how that transformation will take place. Or what the representation will look like. Let's have a look at the *R* in the REST acronym: representation.

11.3 Representing resources

Representation is an important facet of REST. It's how a client and a server communicate about a resource. Any given resource could be represented in virtually any form. If the consumer of the resource prefers JSON, then the resource could be presented in JSON format. Or if the consumer has a fondness for angle brackets, then the same resource could be presented in XML. Meanwhile, a human user viewing the resource in a web browser will likely prefer seeing it in HTML (or possibly PDF, Excel, or some other human-readable form). The resource doesn't change—only how it's represented.

It's important to know that controllers usually don't concern themselves with how resources will be represented. Controllers will deal with resources in terms of the Java objects that define them. But it's not until after the controller has finished its works that the resource will be transformed into a form that best suits the client.

Spring provides two ways to transform a resource's Java representation into the representation that will be shipped to the client:

- Negotiated view-based rendering
- HTTP message converters

Since we discussed view resolvers in chapter 7 and are already familiar with view-based rendering (also from chapter 7), we'll start by looking at how to use content negotiation to select a view or view resolver that can render a resource into a form that's acceptable to the client.

11.3.1 Negotiating resource representation

As you'll recall from chapter 7, when a controller's handler method finishes, a logical view name is usually returned. Even if the method doesn't directly return a logical view name (if the method returns `void`, for example), then the logical view name is derived from the request's URL. `DispatcherServlet` then passes the view name to a view resolver, asking it to help determine which view should render the results of the request.

In a human-facing web application, the view chosen is almost always rendered as HTML. View resolution is a one-dimensional activity. If the view name matches a view, then that's the view we'll go with.

When it comes to resolving view names into views that can produce resource representations, there's an additional dimension to consider. Not only does the view need to match the view name, but also the view needs to be chosen to suit the client. If the client wants XML, then an HTML-rendering view won't do—even if the view name matches.

Spring's `ContentNegotiatingViewResolver` is a special view resolver that takes the content type that the client wants into consideration. Just like any other view resolver, it's configured as a <bean> in the Spring application context, as shown next.

Listing 11.4 `ContentNegotiatingViewResolver` chooses the best view.

```
<bean class="org.springframework.web.servlet.view.
    ➥ContentNegotiatingViewResolver">
  <property name="mediaTypes">
    <map>
      <entry key="json" value="application/json" />
      <entry key="xml" value="text/xml" />
      <entry key="htm" value="text/html" />
    </map>
  </property>
  <property name="defaultContentType" value="text/html" />
</bean>
```

Understanding how `ContentNegotiatingViewResolver` works involves getting to know the content-negotiation two-step:

1. Determine the requested media type(s)
2. Find the best view for the requested media type(s)

Let's dig deeper into each of these steps to see what makes ContentNegotiatingViewResolver tick. We'll start by figuring out what kind of content the client wants.

DETERMINING THE REQUESTED MEDIA TYPES

The first step in the content-negotiation two-step is determining what kind of resource representation the client wants. On the surface, that seems like a simple job. Shouldn't the request's Accept header give a clear indication of what representation should be sent to the client?

Unfortunately, the Accept header can't always be deemed reliable. If the client in question is a web browser, there's no guarantee that what the client wants is what the browser sends in the Accept header. Web browsers typically only accept human-friendly content types (such as text/html) and there's no way (short of developer-oriented browser plug-ins) to specify a different content type.

ContentNegotiatingViewResolver will consider the Accept header and use whatever media types it asks for; but only after it first looks at the URL's file extension. If the URL has a file extension on the end, it'll match that extension against the entries in the mediaTypes property. mediaTypes is a Map whose keys are file extensions and whose values are media types. If a match is found, then the media type will be used. In this way, the file extension can override any media types in the Accept header.

If the file extension doesn't produce any media types to work with, then the Accept header in the request will be considered. But if the request header doesn't have an Accept header, then it'll fall back to the media type set in the defaultContentType property.

As an example of how this might play out, suppose that ContentNegotiatingViewResolver configured in listing 11.4 is asked to figure out what the desired media types are for a request whose extension is .json. In that case, the file extension matches the json entry in the mediaTypes property. Therefore, the chosen media type will be application/json.

But suppose that a request comes along whose extension is .huh. That extension doesn't match any of the entries in the mediaTypes property. In the absence of a matching extension in the mediaTypes property, ContentNegotiatingViewResolver will look to the request's Accept header for the media types. If the request came from Firefox, then the media types are text/html, application/xhtml+xml, application/xml, and */*. If the request doesn't have an Accept header, then text/html will be chosen from defaultContentType.

INFLUENCING HOW MEDIA TYPES ARE CHOSEN

The media type selection process, as described so far, outlines the default strategy for determining the requested media types. But there are several options that can influence that behavior:

- Setting the favorPathExtension property to false will cause ContentNegotiatingViewResolver to ignore the URL's path extension.
- Adding the Java Activation Framework (JAF) to the classpath will cause ContentNegotiatingViewResolver to ask JAF for help in determining the

media type for the path extension in addition to entries in the `mediaTypes` property.

- If you set the `favorParameter` property to `true` and if the request has a `format` parameter, then the value of the `format` parameter will be matched against the `mediaTypes` property. (Additionally, the name of the parameter can be chosen by setting the `parameterName` property.)
- Setting the `ignoreAcceptHeader` to `true` will remove the `Accept` from consideration.

For example, suppose that you set the `favorParameter` property to `true`:

```
<property name="favorParameter" value="true" />
```

Now a request whose URL doesn't have a file extension could still be matched up with the `application/json` media type as long as the request's `format` parameter is set to `json`.

Once `ContentNegotiatingViewResolver` knows what media types the client wants, it's time to find a view that can render that kind of content.

FINDING A VIEW

Unlike other view resolvers, `ContentNegotiatingViewResolver` doesn't directly resolve views. Instead, it delegates to other view resolvers to find a view that best suits the client. Unless otherwise specified, it'll use any view resolver in the application context. But you can explicitly list the view resolvers it should delegate to by setting the `viewResolvers` property.

`ContentNegotiatingViewResolver` asks all of its view resolvers to resolve the logical view name into a view. Every view that's resolved is added to a list of candidate views. In addition, if a view is specified in the `defaultView` property, it'll be added to the end of the candidate view list.

With the candidate view list assembled, `ContentNegotiatingViewResolver` cycles through all of the requested media types, trying to find a view from among the candidate views that produces a matching content type. The first match found is the one that's used.

In the end, if `ContentNegotiatingViewResolver` fails to find a suitable view, then it returns a `null` view. Or, if `useNotAcceptableStatusCode` is set to `true`, then a view with an HTTP status code of 406 (Not Acceptable) will be returned.

Content negotiation is a way of rendering resource representations to a client that fits right in with how we developed the web front end of our application in chapter 7. It's perfect for adding additional representations on top of the HTML representations that a Spring MVC web application already provides.

When defining machine-consumed RESTful resources, it may make more sense to develop the controller in a way that acknowledges that the data it produces will be represented as a resource consumed by another application. That's where Spring's HTTP message converters and the `@ResponseBody` annotation come into play.

11.3.2 Working with HTTP message converters

As we've seen in chapter 7 and in the previous section, a typical Spring MVC controller method ends by placing one or more pieces of information into the model and designating a view to render that data to the user. Although there are several ways of populating the model with data and many ways of identifying the view, every controller handler method we've seen up until now has followed that basic pattern.

But when a controller's job is to produce a representation of some resource, another more direct option is available that bypasses the model and view. In this style of handler method, the object returned from the controller is automatically converted into a representation appropriate for the client.

Employing this new technique starts with applying the @ResponseBody annotation to a controller's handler method.

RETURNING RESOURCE STATE IN THE RESPONSE BODY

Normally when a handler method returns a Java object (anything other than String), that object ends up in the model for rendering in the view. But if that handler method is annotated with @ResponseBody, then it indicates that the HTTP message converter mechanism should take over and transform the returned object into whatever form the client needs.

For example, consider the following getSpitter() method from SpitterController:

```
@RequestMapping(value = "/{username}", method = RequestMethod.GET,
                headers = {"Accept=text/xml, application/json"})
public @ResponseBody
Spitter getSpitter(@PathVariable String username) {
  return spitterService.getSpitter(username);
}
```

The @ResponseBody annotation tells Spring that we want to send the returned object as a resource to the client, converted into some representational form that the client can accept. More specifically, the resource should take a form that satisfies the request's Accept header. If the request has no Accept header, then it's assumed that the client can accept any representation form.

Speaking of the Accept header, take note of getSpitter()'s @RequestMapping. The headers attribute indicates that this method will only handle requests whose Accept header includes text/xml or application/json. Any other kind of request, even if it's a GET request whose URL matches the path specified, won't be handled by this method. It'll either be handled by some other handler method (if an appropriate one exists) or the client will be sent an HTTP 406 (Not Acceptable) response.

Taking an arbitrary Java object returned from a handler method and converting it into a client-pleasing representation is a job for one of Spring's HTTP message converters. Spring comes with a variety of message converters, as listed in table 11.2, to handle the most common object-to-representation conversion needs.

Table 11.2 Spring provides several HTTP message converters that marshal resource representations to and from various Java types.

Message converter	Description
`AtomFeedHttpMessageConverter`	Converts Rome[a] `Feed` objects to/from Atom feeds (media type `application/atom+xml`). *Registered if Rome library is present on the classpath.*
`BufferedImageHttpMessageConverter`	Converts `BufferedImages` to/from image binary data.
`ByteArrayHttpMessageConverter`	Reads/writes byte arrays. Reads from all media types (`*/*`) and writes as `application/octet-stream`. *Registered by default.*
`FormHttpMessageConverter`	Reads content as `application/x-www-form-urlencoded` into a `MultiValueMap<String, String>`. Also writes `MultiValueMap<String, String>` as `application/x-www-form-urlencoded` and `MultiValueMap<String, Object>` as `multipart/form-data`.
`Jaxb2RootElementHttpMessageConverter`	Reads and writes XML (`text/xml or application/xml`) from/to JAXB2-annotated objects. *Registered if JAXB v2 libraries are present on the classpath.*
`MappingJacksonHttpMessageConverter`	Reads and writes JSON from/to typed objects or untyped `HashMaps`. *Registered if Jackson JSON library is present on the classpath.*
`MarshallingHttpMessageConverter`	Reads and writes XML using an injected marshaller and unmarshaller. Supported (un)marshallers include Castor, JAXB2, JIBX, XMLBeans, and XStream.
`ResourceHttpMessageConverter`	Reads and writes `Resources`. *Registered by default.*
`RssChannelHttpMessageConverter`	Reads and writes RSS feeds from/to Rome `Channel` objects. *Registered if Rome library is present on the classpath.*
`SourceHttpMessageConverter`	Reads and writes XML from/to `javax.xml.transform.Source` objects. *Registered by default.*
`StringHttpMessageConverter`	Reads all media types (`*/*`) into a `String`. Writes Strings to `text/plain`. *Registered by default.*
`XmlAwareFormHttpMessageConverter`	An extension of `FormHttpMessageConverter` that adds support for XML-based parts using a `SourceHttpMessageConverter`. *Registered by default.*

a. https://rome.dev.java.net

For example, suppose the client has indicated via the request's `Accept` header that it can accept `application/json`. Assuming that the Jackson JSON library is in the application's classpath, the object returned from the handler method will be given to the `MappingJacksonHttpMessageConverter` for conversion into a JSON representation to be returned to the client. On the other hand, if the request header indicates that the client prefers `text/xml`, then `Jaxb2RootElementHttpMessageConverter` will be tasked with producing an XML response to the client.

Note that all but three of the HTTP message converters in table 11.2 are registered by default, so no Spring configuration is required to use them. But you may need to add additional libraries to your application's classpath to support them. For instance, if you want to use the `MappingJacksonHttpMessageConverter` to convert JSON messages to and from Java objects, you'll need to add the Jackson JSON Processor[5] library to the classpath.

RECEIVING RESOURCE STATE IN THE REQUEST BODY

On the other side of a RESTful conversation, a client may send us an object in the form of JSON, XML, or some other content type. It'd be inconvenient for our controller's handler methods to receive those objects in their raw form and convert them ourselves. Fortunately, the `@RequestBody` annotation does the same thing for objects sent from the client as `@ResponseBody` does for objects returned to the client.

Let's say that the client submits a `PUT` request with the data for a `Spitter` object represented as JSON in the request's body. To receive that message as a `Spitter` object, we only need to annotate a handler method's `Spitter` parameter with `@RequestBody`:

```
@RequestMapping(value = "/{username}", method = RequestMethod.PUT,
                headers = "Content-Type=application/json")
@ResponseStatus(HttpStatus.NO_CONTENT)
public void updateSpitter(@PathVariable String username,
                          @RequestBody Spitter spitter) {
  spitterService.saveSpitter(spitter);
}
```

When the request arrives, Spring MVC will see that the `updateSpitter()` is able to handle the request. But the message arrives as an XML document, and this method asks for a `Spitter` object. In this case, the `MappingJacksonHttpMessageConverter` may be chosen to convert the JSON message into a `Spitter` object. For that to work, the following criteria must be met:

- The request's `Content-Type` header must be set to `application/json`.
- The Jackson JSON library must be available on the application's classpath.

You may have also noticed that the `updateSpitter()` method is annotated with `@ResponseStatus`. After a PUT request, there's not much to do and no need to return

---

5 http://jackson.codehaus.org

anything to the client. By annotating `updateSpitter()` this way, we're saying that HTTP response to the client should have a status code of 204, also known as No Content.

At this point, we've written some Spring MVC controllers with handler methods to handle requests for resources. There are a few more things to talk about with regard to defining a RESTful API using Spring MVC—and we'll get back to that part of the discussion in section 11.5. But first, let's switch gears and see how to use Spring's `RestTemplate` to write client code that consumes those resources.

11.4 Writing REST clients

When we build web applications, we often think of them as having a user interface that resides in a web browser. But with web applications that are made up of RESTful resources, there's no reason that has to be the case. Just because a resource's data is transmitted across the web, that doesn't mean that it'll necessarily be rendered in a web browser. You may even find yourself writing a web application that interacts with another web application through a RESTful API.

Writing code that interacts with a REST resource as a client can involve some tedium and boilerplate. For example, let's say that we need to write some client-side code to consume the Spittles-for-Spitter REST API we developed earlier. The following listing shows one way of getting the job done.

Listing 11.5 REST clients can involve boilerplate code and exception handling.

```
public Spittle[] retrieveSpittlesForSpitter(String username) {
  try {
    HttpClient httpClient = new DefaultHttpClient();              <- Create HttpClient

    String spittleUrl = "http://localhost:8080/Spitter/spitters/" +
                        username + "/spittles";             <- Assemble URL

    HttpGet getRequest = new HttpGet(spittleUrl);              <- Create request from URL

    getRequest.setHeader(
            new BasicHeader("Accept", "application/json"));

    HttpResponse response = httpClient.execute(getRequest);    <- Execute request

    HttpEntity entity = response.getEntity();    <- Parse result
    ObjectMapper mapper = new ObjectMapper();
    return mapper.readValue(entity.getContent(), Spittle[].class);
  } catch (IOException e) {
    throw new SpitterClientException("Unable to retrieve Spittles", e);
  }
}
```

As you can see, a lot goes into consuming a REST resource. And I'm even cheating by using Jakarta Commons HTTP Client[6] to make the request and the Jackson JSON processor[7] to parse the response.

---

[6] http://hc.apache.org/httpcomponents-client/index.html

[7] http://jackson.codehaus.org/

Looking closely at the `retrieveSpittlesForSpitter()` method, you'll realize that little in that method is directly associated with this specific bit of functionality. If you were to write another method that consumed some other REST resource, it'd probably look a lot like this one, with only a few minor differences.

What's more, there are a few places along the way where an `IOException` could've been thrown. Since `IOException` is a checked exception, I'm forced to either catch it or throw it. In this case, I've chosen to catch it and throw an unchecked `SpitterClientException` in its place.

With so much boilerplate involved in resource consumption, you'd think it'd be wise to encapsulate the common code and parameterize the variations. That's precisely what Spring's `RestTemplate` does. Just as `JdbcTemplate` handles the ugly parts of working with JDBC data access, `RestTemplate` frees us from the tedium of consuming RESTful resources.

In a moment, we'll see how we can rewrite the `retrieveSpittlesForSpitter()` method, using `RestTemplate` to dramatically simplify it and eliminate the boilerplate. But first, let's take a high-level survey of all of the REST operations that `RestTemplate` offers.

11.4.1 Exploring RestTemplate's operations

You'll recall from table 11.1 that the HTTP specification defines seven method types for interacting with RESTful resources. These method types provide the verbs in a RESTful conversation.

`RestTemplate` defines 33 methods for interacting with REST resources using all of HTTP's verbs in a variety of ways. Unfortunately, I don't have enough space to go over all 33 methods in this chapter. As it turns out, there are really only 11 unique operations, each of which is overloaded into three method variants. Table 11.3 describes the 11 unique operations provided by `RestTemplate`.

Table 11.3 `RestTemplate` defines 11 unique operations, each of which is overloaded to a total of 33 methods.

Method	Description
`delete()`	Performs an HTTP DELETE on a resource at a specified URL.
`exchange()`	Executes a specified HTTP method against the URL, returning a `ResponseEntity` containing an object mapped from the response body.
`execute()`	Executes a specified HTTP method against the URL, returning an object mapped from the response body.
`getForEntity()`	Sends an HTTP GET request, returning a `ResponseEntity` containing the response body as mapped to an object.
`getForObject()`	GETs a resource, returning the response body as mapped to an object.
`headForHeaders()`	Sends an HTTP HEAD request, returning the HTTP headers for the specified resource URL.

Table 11.3 `RestTemplate` defines 11 unique operations, each of which is overloaded to a total of 33 methods. *(continued)*

Method	Description
`optionsForAllow()`	Sends an HTTP OPTIONS request, returning the `Allow` header for the specified URL.
`postForEntity()`	POSTs data, returning a `ResponseEntity` that contains an object mapped from the response body.
`postForLocation()`	POSTs data, returning the URL of the new resource.
`postForObject()`	POSTs data, returning the response body as mapped to an object.
`put()`	PUTs a resource to the specified URL.

With the exception of `TRACE`, `RestTemplate` covers all of the HTTP verbs. In addition, `execute()` and `exchange()` offer lower-level general-purpose methods for using any of the HTTP methods.

Each of the operations in table 11.3 is overloaded into three method forms:

- One that takes a `java.net.URI` as the URL specification with no support for parameterized URLs
- One that takes a `String` URL specification with URL parameters specified as a `Map`
- One that takes a `String` URL specification with URL parameters specified as a variable argument list

Once you get to know the 11 operations provided by `RestTemplate` and how each of the variant forms work, you'll be well on your way to writing resource-consuming REST clients. Let's survey `RestTemplate`'s operations by looking at those that support the four primary HTTP methods: `GET`, `PUT`, `DELETE`, and `POST`. We'll start with `getForObject()` and `getForEntity()`, the `GET` methods.

11.4.2 *GETting resources*

You may have noticed that table 11.3 lists two kinds of methods for performing `GET` requests: `getForObject()` and `getForEntity()`. As described earlier, each of these methods are overloaded into three forms. The signatures of the three `getForObject()` methods look like this:

```
<T> T getForObject(URI url, Class<T> responseType)
                                      throws RestClientException;

<T> T getForObject(String url, Class<T> responseType,
                 Object... uriVariables)  throws RestClientException;

<T> T getForObject(String url, Class<T> responseType,
        Map<String, ?> uriVariables) throws RestClientException;
```

Similarly, the signatures of the `getForEntity()` methods are as follows:

```
<T> ResponseEntity<T> getForEntity(URI url, Class<T> responseType)
        throws RestClientException;

<T> ResponseEntity<T> getForEntity(String url, Class<T> responseType,
        Object... uriVariables) throws RestClientException;

<T> ResponseEntity<T> getForEntity(String url, Class<T> responseType,
        Map<String, ?> uriVariables) throws RestClientException;
```

Except for the return type, the `getForObject()` methods are mirror images of the `getForEntity()` methods. And, in fact, they work much the same way. They both perform a GET request, retrieving a resource given a URL. And they both map that resource to some type specified by the `responseType` parameter. The only difference is that `getForObject()` simply returns an object of the type requested, whereas `getForEntity()` returns that object along with extra information about the response.

Let's first have a look at the simpler `getForObject()` method. Then we'll see how to get more information from a GET response by using the `getForEntity()` method.

RETRIEVING RESOURCES

The `getForObject()` method is a no-nonsense option for retrieving a resource. You ask for a resource and you shall receive that resource mapped to a Java type of your choosing. As a simple example of what `getForObject()` can do, let's take another stab at implementing the `retrieveSpittlesForSpitter()`:

```
public Spittle[] retrieveSpittlesForSpitter(String username) {
  return new RestTemplate().getForObject(
     "http://localhost:8080/Spitter/spitters/{spitter}/spittles",
     Spittle[].class, username);
}
```

Back in listing 11.5, `retrieveSpittlesForSpitter()` involved more than a dozen lines of code. Using `RestTemplate`, it's now reduced to a handful of lines (and could be even less if I didn't have to wrap lines to fit within the margins of this book).

`retrieveSpittlesForSpitter()` starts by constructing an instance of `RestTemplate` (an alternate implementation might've used an injected instance instead). Then it invokes the `getForObject()` method to retrieve the list of `Spittles`. In doing so, it asks for the results as an array of `Spittle` objects. Upon receiving that array, it returns it to the caller.

Note that in this new version of `retrieveSpittlesForSpitter()` we don't use `String` concatenation to produce the URL. Instead, we take advantage of the fact that `RestTemplate` accepts parameterized URLs. The *{spitter}* placeholder in the URL will ultimately be filled by the `username` parameter of the method. The last argument of `getForObject()` is a variable-sized list of arguments, where each argument is inserted into a placeholder in the specified URL in the order it appears.

Alternatively, we could've placed the `username` parameter into a `Map` with a key of `spitter` and passed that `Map` in as the last parameter to `getForObject()`:

```
public Spittle[] retrieveSpittlesForSpitter(String username) {
    Map<String, String> urlVariables = new HashMap<String, String();
```

```
    urlVariables.put("spitter", username);
    return new RestTemplate().getForObject(
        "http://localhost:8080/Spitter/spitters/{spitter}/spittles",
        Spittle[].class, urlVariables);
}
```

One thing that's absent here is any sort of JSON parsing or object mapping. Under the covers, `getForObject()` converts the response body into an object for us. It does this by relying on the same set of HTTP message converters from table 11.2 that Spring MVC uses for handler methods that are annotated with `@ResponseBody`.

What's also missing from this method is any sort of exception handling. That's not because `getForObject()` couldn't throw an exception, but because any exception it throws is unchecked. If anything goes wrong in `getForObject()`, an unchecked `RestClientException` will be thrown. You can catch it if you'd like—but you're not forced by the compiler to catch it.

EXTRACTING RESPONSE METADATA

As an alternative to `getForObject()`, `RestTemplate` also offers `getForEntity()`. The `getForEntity()` methods work much the same as the `getForObject()` methods. But where `getForObject()` returns only the resource (converted into a Java object by an HTTP message converter), `getForEntity()` returns that same object carried within a `ResponseEntity`. The `ResponseEntity` also carries extra information about the response, such as the HTTP status code and response headers.

One thing you might want to do with a `ResponseEntity` is to retrieve the value of one of the response headers. For example, suppose that in addition to retrieving the resource, you want to know when that resource was last modified. Assuming that the server provides that information in the `Last-Modified` header, you can use the `getHeaders()` method like this:

```
Date lastModified = new Date(response.getHeaders().getLastModified());
```

The `getHeaders()` method returns an `HttpHeaders` object that provides several convenience methods for retrieving response headers, including `getLastModified()`, which returns the number of milliseconds since January 1, 1970.

In addition to `getLastModified()`, `HttpHeaders` includes the following methods for retrieving header information:

```
public List<MediaType> getAccept() { ... }
public List<Charset> getAcceptCharset() { ... }
public Set<HttpMethod> getAllow() { ... }
public String getCacheControl() { ... }
public long getContentLength() { ... }
public MediaType getContentType() { ... }
public long getDate() { ... }
public String getETag() { ... }
public long getExpires() { ... }
public long getIfNotModifiedSince() { ... }
public List<String> getIfNoneMatch() { ... }
public long getLastModified() { ... }
```

```
public URI getLocation() { ... }
public String getPragma() { ... }
```

For more general-purpose HTTP header access, `HttpHeaders` includes a `get()` method and the `getFirst()` method. Both take a `String` argument that identifies the header. The `get()` method returns a list of `String` values, one for each value assigned to the header. The `getFirst()` method returns only the first header value.

If you're interested in the response's HTTP status code, then you'll want to call the `getStatusCode()` method. For example, look at the implementation of `retrieveSpittlesForSpitter()`.

Listing 11.6 A `ResponseEntity` includes the HTTP status code.

```
public Spittle[] retrieveSpittlesForSpitter(String username) {
  ResponseEntity<Spittle[]> response = new RestTemplate().getForEntity(
      "http://localhost:8080/Spitter/spitters/{spitter}/spittles",
      Spittle[].class, username);

  if(response.getStatusCode() == HttpStatus.NOT_MODIFIED) {
    throw new NotModifiedException();
  }

  return response.getBody();
}
```

Here, if the server responds with a status of 304, it indicates that the content on the server hasn't been modified since the client previously requested it. In that event, a custom `NotModifiedException` is thrown to indicate that the client should check its cache for the resource data.

11.4.3 PUTting resources

For performing `PUT` operations on a resource, `RestTemplate` offers a simple set of three `put()` methods. As with all of `RestTemplate`'s methods, the `put()` method comes in three forms:

```
void put(URI url, Object request) throws RestClientException;

void put(String url, Object request, Object... uriVariables)
        throws RestClientException;

void put(String url, Object request, Map<String, ?> uriVariables)
        throws RestClientException;
```

In its simplest form, the `put()` method takes a `java.net.URI` that identifies (and locates) the resource being sent to the server and an object that's the Java representation of that resource.

For example, here's how you might use the `URI`-based version of `put()` to update a `Spittle` resource on the server:

```
public void updateSpittle(Spittle spittle) throws SpitterException {
  try {
    String url = "http://localhost:8080/Spitter/spittles/" + spittle.getId();
    new RestTemplate().put(new URI(url), spittle);
```

```
  } catch (URISyntaxException e) {
    throw new SpitterUpdateException("Unable to update Spittle", e);
  }
}
```

Here, although the method signature was simple, the implication of using a `java.net.URI` argument is evident. First, in order to create the URL for the `Spittle` object to be updated, we had to do `String` concatenation. Then, because it's possible for a non-URI to be given to the constructor of `URI`, we're forced to catch a `URISyntaxException` (even if we're pretty sure that the given URI is legitimate).

Using one of the other `String`-based `put()` methods alleviates most of the discomfort associated with creating a `URI`, including the need to handle any exceptions. What's more, these methods enable us to specify the URI as a template, plugging in values for the variable parts. Here's a new `updateSpittle()` method rewritten to use one of the `String`-based `put()` methods:

```
public void updateSpittle(Spittle spittle) throws SpitterException {
    restTemplate.put("http://localhost:8080/Spitter/spittles/{id}",
                     spittle, spittle.getId());
}
```

The URI is now expressed as a simple `String` template. When `RestTemplate` sends the `PUT` request, the URI template will be expanded to replace the *{id}* portion with the value returned from `spittle.getId()`. Just like `getForObject()` and `getForEntity()`, the last argument to this version of `put()` is a variable-sized list of arguments, each of which is assigned to the placeholder variables in the order they appear.

Optionally, you could've passed in the template variables as a `Map`:

```
public void updateSpittle(Spittle spittle) throws SpitterException {
    Map<String, String> params = new HashMap<String, String>();
    params.put("id", spittle.getId());
    restTemplate.put("http://localhost:8080/Spitter/spittles/{id}",
                     spittle, params);
}
```

When using a `Map` to send the template variables, the key of each entry in the `Map` corresponds to the placeholder variable of the same name in the URI template.

In all versions of `put()`, the second argument is the Java object that represents the resource being `PUT` to the server at the given URI. In this case, it's a `Spittle` object. `RestTemplate` will use one of the message converters from table 11.2 to convert the `Spittle` into a representation to send to the server in the request body.

The content type that the object will be converted into depends largely on the type being passed into `put()`. If given a `String` value, the `StringHttpMessageConverter` kicks in: the value is written directly to the body of the request and the content type is set to `text/plain`. When given a `MultiValueMap<String,String>`, the values in the map will be written to the request body in `application/x-www-form-urlencoded` form by the `FormHttpMessageConverter`.

Since we're passing in a Spittle object, we'll need a message converter that can work with arbitrary objects. If the Jackson JSON library is in the classpath, then the MappingJacksonHttpMessageConverter will write the Spittle to the request as application/json. Optionally, if the Spittle class were annotated for JAXB serialization and if a JAXB library were on the classpath, then the Spittle would be sent as application/xml and be written to the request body in XML format.

11.4.4 DELETE-ing resources

When you don't want a resource to be kept around on the server anymore, then you'll want to call RestTemplate's delete() methods. Much like the put() methods, the delete() methods keep it simple with only three versions, whose signatures are as follows:

```
void delete(String url, Object... uriVariables)
        throws RestClientException;

void delete(String url, Map<String, ?> uriVariables)
        throws RestClientException;

void delete(URI url) throws RestClientException;
```

Hands down, the delete() methods are the simplest of all of the RestTemplate methods. The only thing you need to supply them with is the URI of the resource to be deleted. For example, to get rid of a Spittle whose ID is given, you might call delete() like this:

```
public void deleteSpittle(long id) {
  try {
    restTemplate.delete(
                 new URI("http://localhost:8080/Spitter/spittles/" + id));
  } catch (URISyntaxException wontHappen) { }
}
```

That's simple enough, but here again we've relied on String concatenation to create a URI object that defensively throws a checked URISyntaxException, which we're forced to catch. So let's turn to one of the simpler versions of delete() to get out of that mess:

```
public void deleteSpittle(long id) {
  restTemplate.delete("http://localhost:8080/Spitter/spittles/{id}", id));
}
```

There. I feel better about that. Don't you?

Now that I've shown you the simplest set of RestTemplate methods, let's look at RestTemplate's most diverse set of methods—those that support HTTP POST requests.

11.4.5 POSTing resource data

Looking back at table 11.3, you see that RestTemplate comes with three different kinds of methods for sending POST requests. When you multiply that by the three variants that each is overridden into, that's a total of nine methods for POSTing data to the server.

Two of those methods have names that look familiar. The postForObject() and postForEntity() methods work with POST requests in a way that's similar to how getForObject() and getForEntity() work for sending GET requests. The other method, getForLocation(), is unique for POST requests.

RECEIVING OBJECT RESPONSES FROM POST REQUESTS

Let's say that you're using RestTemplate to POST a new Spitter object to the Spitter application's REST API. Since it's a brand-new Spitter, the server doesn't know about it (yet). Therefore, it's not officially a REST resource yet and doesn't have a URL. Also, the client won't know the ID of the Spitter until it's created on the server.

One way of POSTing a resource to the server is to use RestTemplate's postForObject() method. The three varieties of postForObject() have the following signatures:

```
<T> T postForObject(URI url, Object request, Class<T> responseType)
        throws RestClientException;

<T> T postForObject(String url, Object request, Class<T> responseType,
        Object... uriVariables) throws RestClientException;

<T> T postForObject(String url, Object request, Class<T> responseType,
        Map<String, ?> uriVariables) throws RestClientException;
```

In all cases, the first parameter is the URL to which the resource should be POSTed, the second parameter is the object to post, and the third parameter is the Java type expected to be given in return. In the case of the two versions that take the URL as a String, a fourth parameter identifies the URL variables (as either a variable arguments list or a Map).

When POSTing new Spitter resources to the Spitter REST API, they should be posted to http://localhost:8080/Spitter/spitters, where a POST-handling controller handler method is waiting to save the object. Since this URL requires no URL variables, we could use any version of postForObject(). But, in the interest of keeping it simple and to avoid catching any exceptions that may be thrown while constructing a new URI, we'll make the call like this:

```
public Spitter postSpitterForObject(Spitter spitter) {
  RestTemplate rest = new RestTemplate();
  return rest.postForObject("http://localhost:8080/Spitter/spitters",
          spitter, Spitter.class);
}
```

The postSpitterForObject() method is given a newly created Spitter object and uses postForObject() to send it to the server. In response, it receives a Spitter object and returns it to the caller.

As with the getForObject() methods, we may want to examine some of the metadata that comes back with the request. In that case, postForEntity() is the preferred method. postForEntity() comes with a set of signatures that mirror those of postForObject():

```
<T> ResponseEntity<T> postForEntity(URI url, Object request,
        Class<T> responseType) throws RestClientException;

<T> ResponseEntity<T> postForEntity(String url, Object request,
        Class<T> responseType, Object... uriVariables)
        throws RestClientException;

<T> ResponseEntity<T> postForEntity(String url, Object request,
        Class<T> responseType, Map<String, ?> uriVariables)
        throws RestClientException;
```

So let's say that, in addition to receiving the `Spitter` resource in return, you'd also like to see the value of the `Location` header in the response. In that case you can call `postForEntity()` like this:

```
RestTemplate rest = new RestTemplate();
ResponseEntity<Spitter> response = rest.postForEntity(
    "http://localhost:8080/Spitter/spitters", spitter, Spitter.class);

Spitter spitter = response.getBody();
URI url = response.getHeaders().getLocation();
```

Just like the `getForEntity()` method, `postForEntity()` returns a `ResponseEntity<T>` object. From that object you can call `getBody()` to get the resource object (a `Spitter` in this case). And the `getHeaders()` method gives you an `HttpHeaders` from which you can access the various HTTP headers returned in the response. Here, we're calling the `getLocation()` to retrieve the `Location` header as a `java.net.URI`.

RECEIVING A RESOURCE LOCATION AFTER A POST REQUEST

The `postForEntity()` method is handy for receiving both the resource posted and any response headers. But often you don't need the resource to be sent back to you (after all, you sent it to the server in the first place). If the value of the `Location` header is all you really need to know, then it's even easier to use `RestTemplate`'s `postForLocation()` method.

Like the other `POST` methods, `postForLocation()` sends a resource to the server in the body of a `POST` request. But, instead of responding with that same resource object, `postForLocation()` responds with the location of the newly created resource. It has the following three method signatures:

```
URI postForLocation(String url, Object request, Object... uriVariables)
        throws RestClientException;

URI postForLocation(
        String url, Object request, Map<String, ?> uriVariables)
        throws RestClientException;

URI postForLocation(URI url, Object request) throws RestClientException;
```

To demonstrate `postForLocation()`, let's try `POST`ing a `Spitter` again. This time, we want the resource's URL in return:

```
public String postSpitter(Spitter spitter) {
  RestTemplate rest = new RestTemplate();
  return rest.postForLocation("http://localhost:8080/Spitter/spitters",
          spitter).toString();
}
```

Here, we're passing in the target URL as a String, along with the Spitter object to be POSTed (there are no URL variables in this case). If, after creating the resource, the server responds with the new resource URL in the response's Location header, then postForLocation() will return that URL as a String.

11.4.6 Exchanging resources

Up to this point, we've seen all manner of RestTemplate methods for GETting, PUTting, DELETE-ing, and POSTing resources. Among those we saw two special methods, getForEntity() and postForEntity(), that gave us the resulting resource wrapped in a RequestEntity from which we could retrieve response headers and status codes.

Being able to read headers from the response is useful. But what if we want to set headers on the request sent to the server? That's what RestTemplate's exchange() methods are good for.

Like all of the other methods in RestTemplate, exchange() is overloaded into three signature forms as shown here:

```
<T> ResponseEntity<T> exchange(URI url, HttpMethod method,
        HttpEntity<?> requestEntity, Class<T> responseType)
        throws RestClientException;

<T> ResponseEntity<T> exchange(String url, HttpMethod method,
        HttpEntity<?> requestEntity, Class<T> responseType,
        Object... uriVariables) throws RestClientException;

<T> ResponseEntity<T> exchange(String url, HttpMethod method,
        HttpEntity<?> requestEntity, Class<T> responseType,
        Map<String, ?> uriVariables) throws RestClientException;
```

As you can see, the three exchange() signatures are overloaded to match the same pattern as the other RestTemplate methods. One takes a java.net.URI to identify the target URL, whereas the other two take the URL in String form with URL variables.

The exchange() method also takes an HttpMethod parameter to indicate the HTTP verb that should be used. Depending on the value given to this parameter, the exchange() method can perform the same jobs as any of the other RestTemplate methods.

For example, one way to retrieve a Spitter resource from the server is to use RestTemplate's getForEntity() method like this:

```
ResponseEntity<Spitter> response = rest.getForEntity(
          "http://localhost:8080/Spitter/spitters/{spitter}",
          Spitter.class, spitterId);
Spitter spitter = response.getBody();
```

As you can see here, exchange() is also up to the task:

```
ResponseEntity<Spitter> response = rest.exchange(
          "http://localhost:8080/Spitter/spitters/{spitter}",
          HttpMethod.GET, null, Spitter.class, spitterId);
Spitter spitter = response.getBody();
```

By passing in `HttpMethod.GET` as the HTTP verb, we're asking `exchange()` to send a `GET` request. The third argument is for sending a resource on the request, but since this is a `GET` request, it can be `null`. The next argument indicates that we want the response converted into a `Spitter` object. And the final argument is the value to place into the {spitter} placeholder in the specified URL template.

Used this way, the `exchange()` method is virtually identical to the previously used `getForEntity()`. But unlike `getForEntity()`—or `getForObject()`—`exchange()` will let us set headers on the request sent. Instead of passing `null` to `exchange()`, we'll pass in an `HttpEntity` created with the request headers we want.

Without specifying the headers, `exchange()` will send the `GET` request for a `Spitter` with the following headers:

```
GET /Spitter/spitters/habuma HTTP/1.1
Accept: application/xml, text/xml, application/*+xml, application/json
Content-Length: 0
User-Agent: Java/1.6.0_20
Host: localhost:8080
Connection: keep-alive
```

Take a look at the `Accept` header. It says that it can accept several different XML content types as well as `application/json`. The leaves a lot of room for the server to decide which format to send the resource back as. Suppose that we want to demand that the server send the response back as JSON. In that case, we need to specify `application/json` as the only value in the `Accept` header.

Setting request headers is a simple matter of constructing the `HttpEntity` sent to `exchange()` with a `MultiValueMap` loaded with the desired headers:

```
MultiValueMap<String, String> headers =
    new LinkedMultiValueMap<String, String>();
headers.add("Accept", "application/json");
HttpEntity<Object> requestEntity = new HttpEntity<Object>(headers);
```

Here, we create a `LinkedMultiValueMap` and add an `Accept` header set to `application/json`. Then we construct an `HttpEntity` (with a generic type of `Object`), passing the `MultiValueMap` as a constructor argument. If this were a `PUT` or a `POST` request, we would've also given the `HttpEntity` an object to send in the body of the request—for a `GET` request, this isn't necessary.

Now we can call `exchange()` passing in the `HttpEntity`:

```
ResponseEntity<Spitter> response = rest.exchange(
          "http://localhost:8080/Spitter/spitters/{spitter}",
          HttpMethod.GET, requestEntity, Spitter.class, spitterId);
Spitter spitter = response.getBody();
```

On the surface, the results should be the same. We should receive the `Spitter` object that we asked for. Under the surface, the request will be sent with the following headers:

```
GET /Spitter/spitters/habuma HTTP/1.1
Accept: application/json
Content-Length: 0
```

```
User-Agent: Java/1.6.0_20
Host: localhost:8080
Connection: keep-alive
```

And, assuming that the server can serialize the `Spitter` response into JSON, the response body should be represented in JSON format.

In this section we've seen how using the various methods that `RestTemplate` provides, you can write Java-based clients that interact with RESTful resources on the server. But what if the client is browser-based? When a web browser is calling on REST resources, there are some limitations to be accounted for—specifically the range of HTTP methods supported in the browser. To wrap up this chapter, let's see how Spring can help overcome those limitations.

11.5 Submitting RESTful forms

We've seen how the four primary HTTP methods—`GET`, `POST`, `PUT`, and `DELETE`—define the basic operations that can be performed on a resource. And by setting the `method` attribute of the `@RequestMapping` annotation appropriately, we can cause `DispatcherServlet` to direct requests for those HTTP verbs to specific controller methods. Spring MVC can handle requests for any of the HTTP methods—assuming the client sends the requests in the form of the desired HTTP method.

The gotchas in that plan are HTML and the web browser. Non-browser clients, such as those that use `RestTemplate`, should have no trouble sending requests to perform any of the HTTP verbs. But HTML 4 only officially supports `GET` and `POST` in forms, leaving `PUT`, `DELETE`, and all other HTTP methods in the cold. Even though HTML 5 and newer browsers will support all of the HTTP methods, you probably can't count on the users of your application to be using a modern browser.

A common trick used to get around the shortcomings of HTML 4 and older browsers is to masquerade a `PUT` or `DELETE` request in the form of a `POST` request. The way it works is to submit a browser-pleasing `POST` request with a hidden field that carries the name of the actual HTTP method. When the request arrives at the server, it's rewritten to be whatever type of request was specified in the hidden field.

Spring supports `POST` masquerading through two features:

- Request transformation with `HiddenHttpMethodFilter`
- Hidden field rendering with the `<sf:form>` JSP tag

Let's first look at how Spring's `<sf:form>` tag can help render a hidden field for `POST` masquerading.

11.5.1 Rendering hidden method fields in JSP

In section 7.4.1, we saw how to use Spring's form-binding library to render HTML forms. The core element of that JSP tag library is the `<sf:form>` tag. As you'll recall, that tag sets the content for the other form-binding tags, associating the rendered form and its fields with a model attribute.

At that time, we used <sf:form> to define a form that was used to create a new Spitter object. In that case, a POST request was appropriate, as POST is often used to create new resources. But what if we wanted to update or delete a resource? In those situations, a PUT or DELETE request seems more fitting.

But as I've already mentioned, HTML's <form> tag can't be trusted to send anything other than a GET or POST request. Though some newer browsers won't have any trouble with a <form> tag whose method attribute is set to PUT or DELETE, accounting for older browsers will require sneaking the request to the server as a POST.

Within an HTML form, the key to masquerading a PUT or DELETE request as a POST is to create a form whose method is POST, along with a hidden field. For example, the following snippet of HTML shows how you might create a form that submits a DELETE request:

```
<form method="post">
    <input type="hidden" name="_method" value="delete"/>

    ...

</form>
```

As you can see, it's not a big deal to create a form with the hidden field that specifies the real HTTP method. All you need to do is to add a hidden field with a name that the form and the server can agree upon, and set that field to the desired HTTP method name. When this form is submitted, a POST request will be sent to the server. Presumably, the server will interpret the _method field to be the actual type of method to process (we'll see how to configure the server to do that in a moment).

When using Spring's form-binding library the <sf:form> can make this even easier. You set the method attribute to the desired HTTP method and <sf:form> will take care of the hidden field for you:

```
<sf:form method="delete" modelAttribute="spitter">
    ...
</sf:form>
```

When <sf:form> is rendered into HTML, the result will be quite similar to the HTML <form> shown before. Using <sf:form> frees you from having to deal with the hidden field, letting you work with PUT and DELETE forms in a more natural way, as if they were supported by the browser.

The <sf:form> tag only tells the browser's side of the POST-masquerade story. How does the server know what to do with those POST requests that should be handled as PUT and DELETE requests?

11.5.2 Unmasking the real request

When the browser submits a PUT or DELETE request from a form rendered by <sf:form>, it's in every way a POST request. It travels across the network as a POST request, arrives at the server as a POST request, and unless something on the server bothers to look at the hidden _method field, it'll be processed as a POST request.

Meanwhile, our controller's handler methods are annotated with `@RequestMapping`, ready to process `PUT` and `DELETE` requests. Somehow, this HTTP method mismatch must be resolved before `DispatcherServlet` tries to find a controller handler method to route them to. That's the job that Spring's `HiddenHttpMethodFilter` was born to do.

`HiddenHttpMethodFilter` is a servlet filter and is configured in web.xml:

```
<filter>
    <filter-name>httpMethodFilter</filter-name>
    <filter-class>
        org.springframework.web.filter.HiddenHttpMethodFilter
    </filter-class>
</filter>
...
<filter-mapping>
    <filter-name>httpMethodFilter</filter-name>
    <url-pattern>/*</url-pattern>
</filter-mapping>
```

Here, we've mapped `HiddenHttpMethodFilter` to the `/*` URL pattern. This is so requests for all URLs can pass through `HiddenHttpMethodFilter` on their way to `DispatcherServlet`.

As illustrated in figure 11.3, `HiddenHttpMethodFilter` transforms `PUT` and `DELETE` requests that are masquerading as `POST` requests into their true form. When a `POST` request arrives at the server, `HiddenHttpMethodFilter` sees that the `_hidden` field prescribes a different request type and rewrites it in its destined HTTP method type.

By the time `DispatcherServlet` and your controller methods see the request, it'll have been transformed. Nobody will be the wiser that the request actually started its life as a `POST` request. Between `<sf:form>`'s automatic rendering of the hidden field and `HiddenHttpMethodFilter`'s ability to transform requests based on the value of that hidden field, your JSP forms and your Spring MVC controllers needn't concern themselves with how the browser-unsupported HTTP methods are handled.

Before we leave the topic of `POST`-masquerading requests, I should remind you that this technique exists only as a workaround for lack of support for `PUT` and `DELETE` requests in HTML 4 and older browsers. Requests sent from non-browser clients,

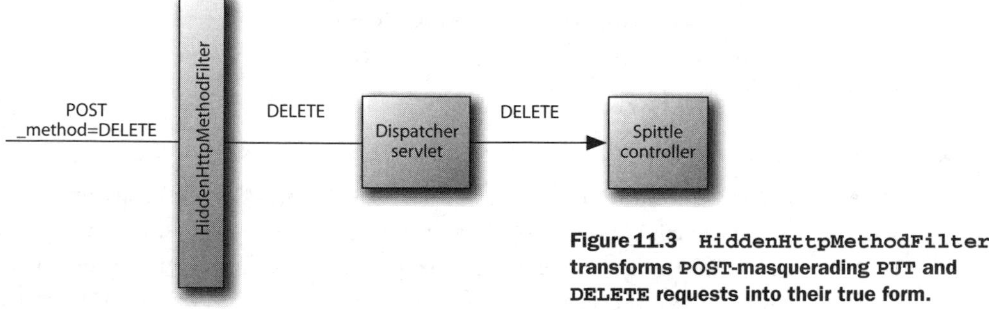

Figure 11.3 `HiddenHttpMethodFilter` transforms `POST`-masquerading `PUT` and `DELETE` requests into their true form.

including those sent from `RestTemplate`, can be sent as whatever HTTP verb is appropriate and don't need to be carried along in a `POST` request. Thus, if you won't be handling any `PUT` and `DELETE` requests from a browser form, then you won't need the services of `HiddenHttpMethodFilter`.

11.6 Summary

RESTful architecture leverages web standards to integrate applications, keeping the interactions simple and natural. Resources in a system are identified by URLs, manipulated with HTTP methods, and represented in one or more forms suitable for the client.

In this chapter, we've seen how to write Spring MVC controllers that respond to requests to manipulate RESTful resources. By utilizing parameterized URL patterns and associating controller handler methods with specific HTTP methods, controllers can respond to `GET`, `POST`, `PUT`, and `DELETE` requests for the resources in an application.

In response to those requests, Spring can represent the data behind those resources in a format that's best for the client. For view-based responses, `ContentNegotiatingViewResolver` can select the best view produced from several view resolvers to satisfy the client's desired content type. Or a controller handler method can be annotated with `@ResponseBody` to completely bypass view resolution and have one of several message converters convert the returned value into a response for the client.

On the client side of REST conversations, Spring provides `RestTemplate`, a template-based approach to consuming RESTful resources from Java. And when the client is browser-based, Spring's `HiddenHttpMethodFilter` can make up for the lack of support for `PUT` and `DELETE` methods in web browsers.

Although the RESTful interactions we've seen in this chapter and the RPC conversations that we covered in the previous chapter are quite different, they share a common trait: they're synchronous in nature. When the client sends a message, the server is expected to be ready to answer immediately. In contrast, asynchronous communication allows the server to react to a message as opportunity allows and not necessarily right away. In the next chapter, we're going to see how to use Spring to integrate applications asynchronously.

12 Messaging in Spring

This chapter covers

- Introduction to the Java Message Service (JMS)
- Sending and receiving asynchronous messages
- Message-driven POJOs

It's 4:55 p.m. on Friday. You're minutes away from starting a much-anticipated vacation. You have just enough time to drive to the airport and catch your flight. But before you pack up and head out, you need to be sure that your boss and colleagues know the status of the work you've been doing so that they can pick up where you left off on Monday. Unfortunately, some of your colleagues have already skipped out for an early weekend departure… and your boss is tied up in a meeting. What do you do?

You could call your boss's cell phone… but it's not necessary to interrupt his meeting for a mere status report. Maybe you could stick around and wait until he returns from the meeting. But it's anyone's guess how long the meeting will last and you have a plane to catch. Perhaps you could leave a sticky note on his monitor… right next to 100 other sticky notes that it'll blend in with.

The most practical way to communicate your status and still catch your plane is to send a quick email to your boss and your colleagues, detailing your progress and promising to send a postcard. You don't know where they are or when they'll read the email, but you do know that they'll eventually return to their desks and read it. Meanwhile, you're on your way to the airport.

Sometimes it's necessary to talk to someone directly. If you injure yourself and need an ambulance, you're probably going to pick up the phone—emailing the hospital just won't do. But often, sending a message is sufficient and offers some advantages over direct communication, such as letting you get on with your vacation.

A couple of chapters back, you saw how to use RMI, Hessian, Burlap, HTTP invoker, and web services to enable communication between applications. All of these communication mechanisms employ synchronous communication in which a client application directly contacts a remote service and waits for the remote procedure to complete before continuing.

Synchronous communication has its place, but it's not the only style of inter-application communication available to developers. Asynchronous messaging is a way of indirectly sending messages from one application to another without waiting for a response. Asynchronous messaging has several advantages over synchronous messaging, as you'll soon see.

The Java Message Service (JMS) is a standard API for asynchronous messaging. In this chapter, we'll look at how Spring simplifies sending and receiving messages with JMS. In addition to basic sending and receiving of messages, we'll look at Spring's support for message-driven POJOs, a way to receive messages that resembles EJB's message-driven beans (MDBs).

12.1 A brief introduction to JMS

Much like the remoting mechanisms and REST interfaces we've covered so far in this part of the book, JMS is all about applications communicating with one another. JMS differs from those other mechanisms in how information is transferred between systems.

Remoting options such as RMI and Hessian/Burlap are synchronous. As illustrated in figure 12.1, when the client invokes a remote method, the client must wait for the method to complete before moving on. Even if the remote method doesn't return anything back to the client, the client will be put on hold until the service is done.

JMS, on the other hand, provides asynchronous communication between applications. When messages are sent asynchronously, as shown in figure 12.2, the client doesn't have to wait for the service to process the message or even for the message to be delivered. The client sends its message and then moves along with the assumption that the service will eventually receive and process the message.

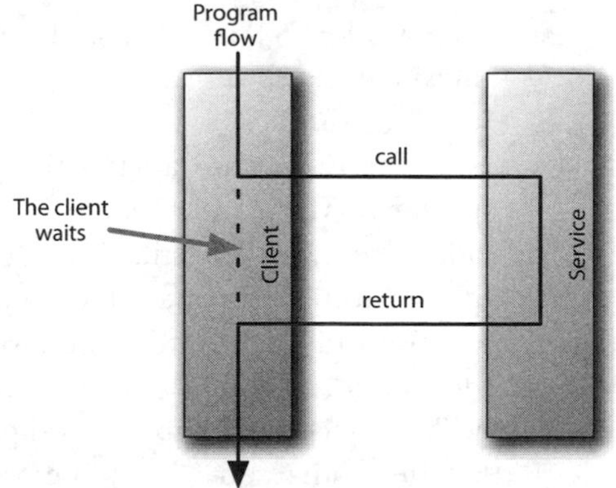

Figure 12.1 When communicating synchronously, the client must wait for the operation to complete.

Asynchronous communication through JMS offers several advantages over synchronous communication. We'll take a closer look at these advantages in a moment. But first, let's see how messages are sent using JMS.

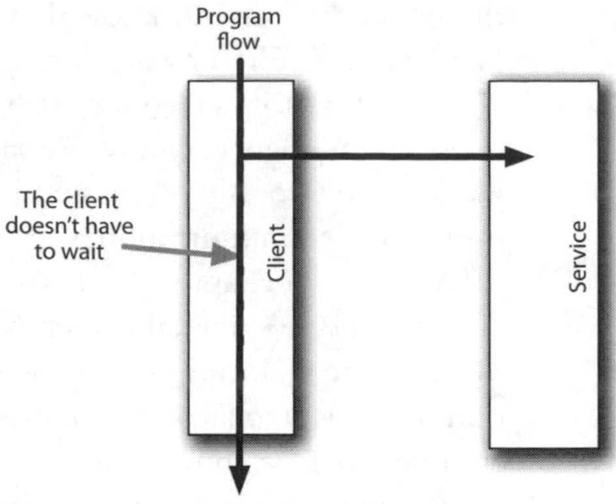

Figure 12.2 Asynchronous communication is a no-wait form of communication.

12.1.1 Architecting JMS

Most of us take the postal service for granted. Millions of times every day, people place letters, cards, and packages in the hands of postal workers, trusting that they'll get to the desired destination. The world's too big of a place for us to hand-deliver these things ourselves, so we rely on the postal system to handle it for us. We address them, place the necessary postage on them, and then drop them in the mail to be delivered without giving a second thought to how they might get there.

The key to the postal service is indirection. When Grandma's birthday comes around, it'd be inconvenient if we had to deliver a card directly to her. Depending on where she lives, we'd have to set aside anywhere from a few hours to a few days to deliver a birthday card. Fortunately, the postal service will deliver the card to her while we go about our lives.

Similarly, indirection is the key to JMS. When one application sends information to another through JMS, there's no direct link between the two applications. Instead, the sending application places the message in the hands of a service that will ensure delivery to the receiving application.

There are two main actors in JMS: *message brokers* and *destinations.*

When an application sends a message, it hands it off to a message broker. A message broker is JMS's analog of the post office. The message broker will ensure that the message is delivered to the specified destination, leaving the sender free to go about other business.

When you send a letter through the mail, it's important to address it so that the postal service knows where it should be delivered. Likewise, in JMS, messages are addressed with a destination. Destinations are like mailboxes where the messages are placed until someone comes to pick them up.

But unlike mail addresses, which may indicate a specific person or street address, destinations are less specific. Destinations are only concerned about *where* the message will be picked up—not *who* will pick them up. In this way, destinations are like sending a letter addressed, "To current resident."

In JMS, there are two types of destination: queues and topics. Each of these is associated with a specific messaging model, either point-to-point (for queues) or publish-subscribe (for topics).

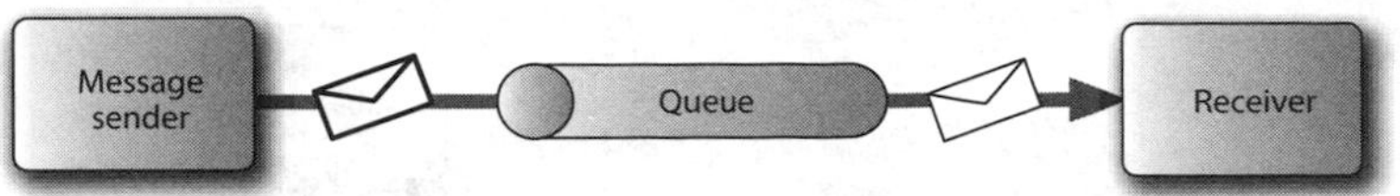

Figure 12.3 A message queue decouples a message sender from the message receiver. Though a queue may have several receivers, each message is picked up by exactly one receiver.

POINT-TO-POINT MESSAGING

In the point-to-point model, each message has exactly one sender and one receiver, as illustrated in figure 12.3. When the message broker is given a message, it places the message in a queue. When a receiver comes along and asks for the next message in the queue, the message is pulled from the queue and delivered to the receiver. Because the message is removed from the queue as it's delivered, it's guaranteed that the message will be delivered to only one receiver.

Although each message in a message queue is delivered to only one receiver, this doesn't imply that only one receiver is pulling messages from the queue. In fact, it's likely that several receivers are processing messages from the queue. But they'll each be given their own messages to process.

This is analogous to waiting in line at the bank. As you wait, you may notice that multiple tellers are available to help you with your financial transaction. After each customer is helped and a teller is freed up, she will call for the next person in line. When it's your turn at the front of the line, you'll be called to the counter and helped by one teller. The other tellers will help other banking customers.

Another observation to be made at the bank is that when you get in line, you probably won't know which teller will eventually help you. You could count how many people are in line, match that up with the number of available tellers, note which teller is fastest, and then come up with a guess as to which teller will call you to their window. But chances are you'll be wrong and end up at a different teller's window.

Likewise, in JMS, if multiple receivers are listening to a queue, there's no way of knowing which one will actually process a specific message. This uncertainty is a good thing because it enables an application to scale up message processing by simply adding another listener to the queue.

PUBLISH-SUBSCRIBE MESSAGING

In the publish-subscribe messaging model, messages are sent to a topic. As with queues, many receivers may be listening to a topic. But unlike queues, where a message is delivered to exactly one receiver, all subscribers to a topic will receive a copy of the message, as shown in figure 12.4.

As you may have guessed from its name, the publish-subscribe message model is much like the model of a magazine publisher and its subscribers. The magazine (a message) is published, sent to the postal service, and then all subscribers receive their own copy.

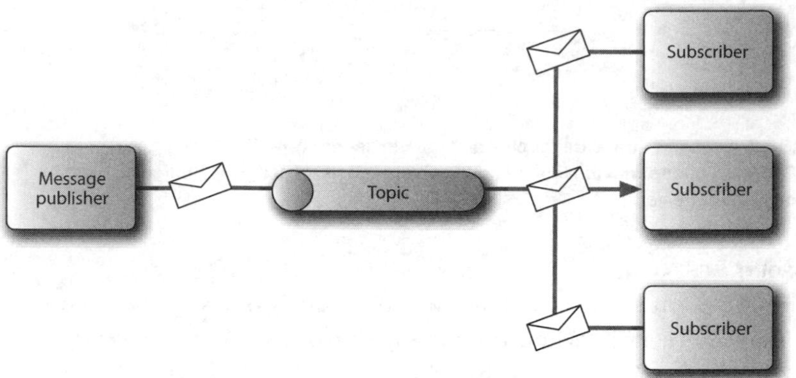

Figure 12.4 Like queues, topics decouple message senders from message receivers. Unlike queues, a topic message could be delivered to many topic subscribers.

The magazine analogy breaks down when you realize that in JMS, the publisher has no idea of who its subscribers are. The publisher only knows that its message will be published to a particular topic—not who's listening to that topic. This also implies that the publisher has no idea of how the message will be processed.

Now that we've covered the basics of JMS, let's see how JMS messaging compares to synchronous RPC.

12.1.2 Assessing the benefits of JMS

Even though it's intuitive and simple to set up, synchronous communication imposes several limitations on the client of a remote service. Most significantly:

- Synchronous communication implies waiting. When a client invokes a method on a remote service, it must wait for the remote method to complete before the client can continue. If the client communicates frequently with the remote service and/or the remote service is slow to respond, this could negatively impact performance of the client application.
- The client is coupled to the service through the service's interface. If the interface of the service changes, all of the service's clients will also need to change accordingly.
- The client is coupled to the service's location. A client must be configured with the service's network location so that it knows how to contact the service. If the network topology changes, the client will need to be reconfigured with the new location.
- The client is coupled to the service's availability. If the service becomes unavailable, the client is effectively crippled.

Though synchronous communication has its place, these shortcomings should be taken into account when deciding what communication mechanism is a best fit for your application's needs. If these constraints are a concern for you, you may want to consider how asynchronous communication with JMS addresses these issues.

NO WAITING

When a message is sent with JMS, the client doesn't need to wait around for it to be processed or even delivered. The client drops the message off with the message broker and moves along with faith that the message will make it to the appropriate destination.

Since it doesn't have to wait, the client will be freed up to perform other activities. With all of this free time, the client's performance can be dramatically improved.

MESSAGE ORIENTATION AND DECOUPLING

Unlike RPC communication that's typically oriented around a method call, messages sent with JMS are data-centric. This means that the client isn't fixed to a specific method signature. Any queue or topic subscriber that can process the data sent by the client can process the message. The client doesn't need to be aware of any service specifics.

LOCATION INDEPENDENCE

Synchronous RPC services are typically located by their network address. The implication of this is that clients aren't resilient to changes in network topology. If a service's IP address changes or if it's configured to listen on a different port, the client must be changed accordingly or the client will be unable to access the service.

In contrast, JMS clients have no idea who will process their messages or where the service is located. The client only knows the queue or topic through which the messages will be sent. As a result, it doesn't matter where the service is located, as long as it can retrieve messages from the queue or topic.

In the point-to-point model, it's possible to take advantage of location independence to create a cluster of services. If the client is unaware of the service's location and if the service's only requirement is that it must be able to access the message broker, there's no reason why multiple services can't be configured to pull messages from the same queue. If the service is being overburdened and falling behind in its processing, all we need to do is turn up a few more instances of the service to listen to the same queue.

Location independence takes on another interesting side effect in the publish-subscribe model. Multiple services could all subscribe to a single topic, receiving duplicate copies of the same message. But each service could process that message differently. For example, let's say you have a set of services which together process a message that details the new hire of an employee. One service might add the employee to the payroll system, another to the HR portal, and yet another makes sure that the employee is given access to the systems they'll need to do their job. Each service works independently on the same data that they each received from a topic.

GUARANTEED DELIVERY

In order for a client to communicate with a synchronous service, the service must be listening at the IP address and port specified. If the service were to go down or otherwise become unavailable, the client wouldn't be able to proceed.

But when sending messages with JMS, the client can rest assured that its messages will be delivered. Even if the service is unavailable when a message is sent, it'll be stored until the service is available again.

Now that you have a feel for the basics of JMS and asynchronous messaging, let's set up a JMS message broker that we'll use in our examples. Although you're free to use any JMS message broker you'd like, we'll use the popular ActiveMQ message broker.

12.2 Setting up a message broker in Spring

ActiveMQ is a great open source message broker and a wonderful option for asynchronous messaging with JMS. As I'm writing this, the current version of ActiveMQ is 5.4.2. To get started with ActiveMQ, you'll need to download the binary distribution from http://activemq.apache.org. Once you've downloaded ActiveMQ, unzip it to your local hard drive. In the lib directory of the unzipped distribution, you'll find activemq-core-5.4.2.jar. This is the JAR file you'll need to add to the application's classpath to be able to use ActiveMQ's API.

Under the bin directory, you'll find several subdirectories for various operating systems. Within those, you'll find scripts that you can use to start ActiveMQ. For example, to start ActiveMQ on Mac OS X, run `activemq start` from the bin/macosx directory. Within moments ActiveMQ will be ready and waiting to broker your messages.

12.2.1 Creating a connection factory

Throughout this chapter, we're going to see different ways that Spring can be used to both send and receive messages through JMS. In all cases, we'll need a JMS connection factory to be able to send messages through the message broker. Since we're using ActiveMQ as our message broker, we'll have to configure the JMS connection factory so that it knows how to connect to ActiveMQ. `ActiveMQConnectionFactory` is the JMS connection factory that comes with ActiveMQ, and it's configured in Spring like this:

```
<bean id="connectionFactory"
      class="org.apache.activemq.spring.ActiveMQConnectionFactory">
  <property name="brokerURL" value="tcp://localhost:61616"/>
</bean>
```

Optionally, since we know that we're dealing with ActiveMQ, we can use ActiveMQ's own Spring configuration namespace (available with all versions of ActiveMQ since version 4.1) to declare the connection factory. First, be sure to declare the `amq` namespace in the Spring configuration XML file:

```
<?xml version="1.0" encoding="UTF-8"?>
<beans xmlns="http://www.springframework.org/schema/beans"
 xmlns:xsi="http://www.w3.org/2001/XMLSchema-instance"
 xmlns:jms="http://www.springframework.org/schema/jms"
 xmlns:amq="http://activemq.apache.org/schema/core"
 xsi:schemaLocation="http://activemq.apache.org/schema/core
   http://activemq.apache.org/schema/core/activemq-core-5.5.0.xsd
   http://www.springframework.org/schema/jms
   http://www.springframework.org/schema/jms/spring-jms-3.0.xsd
   http://www.springframework.org/schema/beans
   http://www.springframework.org/schema/beans/spring-beans-3.0.xsd">
 ...
</beans>
```

Then we can use the <amq:connectionFactory> element to declare the connection factory:

```
<amq:connectionFactory id="connectionFactory"
      brokerURL="tcp://localhost:61616"/>
```

Note that the <amq:connectionFactory> element is clearly specific to ActiveMQ. If you're using a different message broker implementation, there may or may not be a Spring configuration namespace available. If not, then you'll need to wire the connection factory as a <bean>.

Later in this chapter we'll use this connectionFactory bean a lot. But for now, suffice it to say that the brokerURL tells the connection factory where the message broker is located. In this case, the URL given to brokerURL tells the connection factory to connect to ActiveMQ on the local machine at port 61616 (which is the port that ActiveMQ listens to by default).

12.2.2 Declaring an ActiveMQ message destination

In addition to a connection factory, we'll need a destination for the messages to be passed along to. The destination can be either a queue or a topic, depending on the needs of the application.

Regardless of whether you're using a queue or a topic, you must configure the destination bean in Spring using a message broker–specific implementation class. For example, the following <bean> declaration declares an ActiveMQ queue:

```
<bean id="queue" class="org.apache.activemq.command.ActiveMQQueue">
  <constructor-arg value="spitter.queue"/>
</bean>
```

Similarly, the following <bean> declares a topic for ActiveMQ:

```
<bean id="topic" class="org.apache.activemq.command.ActiveMQTopic">
  <constructor-arg value="spitter.topic"/>
</bean>
```

In either case, the <constructor-arg> specifies the name of the queue, as it's known to the message broker—spitter.topic in this case.

As with the connection factory, the ActiveMQ namespace offers an alternative way to declare queues and topics. For queues, we could also use the <amq:queue> element:

```
<amq:queue id="queue" physicalName="spitter.queue" />
```

Or, if it's a JMS topic that's in order, use the <amq:topic>:

```
<amq:topic id="topic" physicalName="spitter.topic" />
```

Either way, the physicalName attribute sets the name of the message channel.

At this point we've seen how to declare the essential components of working with JMS, whether you're sending or receiving messages. Now we're ready to start sending and receiving messages. For that, we'll use Spring's JmsTemplate, the centerpiece of Spring's JMS support. But first, let's gain an appreciation for what JmsTemplate provides by looking at what JMS is like without JmsTemplate.

12.3 Using Spring's JMS template

As you've seen, JMS gives Java developers a standard API for interacting with message brokers and for sending and receiving messages. Furthermore, virtually every message broker implementation out there supports JMS. So there's no reason to learn a proprietary messaging API for every message broker you deal with.

But though JMS offers a universal interface to all message brokers, its convenience comes at a cost. Sending and receiving messages with JMS isn't a simple matter of licking a stamp and placing it on an envelope. As you'll see, JMS demands that you also (figuratively) fuel up the mail carrier's truck.

12.3.1 Tackling runaway JMS code

In section 5.3.1 I showed you how conventional JDBC code can be an unwieldy mess of code to handle connections, statements, result sets, and exceptions. Unfortunately, conventional JMS follows a similar model, as you'll observe in the following listing.

Listing 12.1 Sending a message using conventional (non-Spring) JMS

```
ConnectionFactory cf =
    new ActiveMQConnectionFactory("tcp://localhost:61616");
Connection conn = null;
Session session = null;
try {
  conn = cf.createConnection();
  session = conn.createSession(false, Session.AUTO_ACKNOWLEDGE);
  Destination destination = new ActiveMQQueue("spitter.queue");
  MessageProducer producer = session.createProducer(destination);
  TextMessage message = session.createTextMessage();

  message.setText("Hello world!");
  producer.send(message);                            <-- Send message
} catch (JMSException e) {
  // handle exception?
} finally {
  try {
    if (session != null) {
      session.close();
    }
    if (conn != null) {
      conn.close();
    }
  } catch (JMSException ex) {
  }
}
```

At the risk of sounding repetitive—holy runaway code, Batman! As with the JDBC example, there are almost 20 lines of code here just to send a simple "Hello world!" message. Only a few of those actually send the message; the rest are merely setting the stage for sending the message.

It isn't much better on the receiving end, as you can see in the following listing.

Listing 12.2 Receiving a message using conventional (non-Spring) JMS

```
ConnectionFactory cf =
    new ActiveMQConnectionFactory("tcp://localhost:61616");
Connection conn = null;
Session session = null;
try {
  conn = cf.createConnection();
  conn.start();
  session = conn.createSession(false, Session.AUTO_ACKNOWLEDGE);
  Destination destination =
      new ActiveMQQueue("spitter.queue");
  MessageConsumer consumer = session.createConsumer(destination);
  Message message = consumer.receive();
  TextMessage textMessage = (TextMessage) message;
  System.out.println("GOT A MESSAGE: " + textMessage.getText());
  conn.start();
} catch (JMSException e) {
  // handle exception?
} finally {
  try {
    if (session != null) {
      session.close();
    }
    if (conn != null) {
      conn.close();
    }
  } catch (JMSException ex) {
  }
}
```

Again, just as in listing 12.1, that's a lot of code to do something so darn simple. If you take a line-by-line comparison, you'll find that they're almost identical. And if you were to look at a thousand other JMS examples, you'd find them all to be strikingly similar. Some may retrieve their connection factories from JNDI and some may use a topic instead of a queue. Nevertheless, they all follow roughly the same pattern.

A consequence of all of this boilerplate code is that you'll find that you repeat yourself every time you work with JMS. Worse still, you'll find yourself repeating other developers' JMS code.

We've already seen in chapter 5 how Spring's `JdbcTemplate` handles runaway JDBC boilerplate. Now let's look at how Spring's `JmsTemplate` can do the same thing for JMS boilerplate code.

12.3.2 Working with JMS templates

`JmsTemplate` is Spring's answer to verbose and repetitive JMS code. `JmsTemplate` takes care of creating a connection, obtaining a session, and ultimately sending or receiving messages. This leaves you to focus your development efforts on constructing the message to send or processing the messages that are received.

What's more, `JmsTemplate` can handle any clumsy `JMSException` that may be thrown along the way. If a `JMSException` is thrown in the course of working with

JmsTemplate, JmsTemplate will catch it and rethrow it as one of the unchecked subclasses of Spring's own JmsException.

Table 12.1 shows how Spring maps standard JMSExceptions to Spring's unchecked JmsExceptions.

In fairness to the JMS API, JMSException does come with a rich and descriptive set of subclasses that give you a better sense of what went wrong. Nevertheless, all of these subclasses of JMSException are checked exceptions and thus must be caught. JmsTemplate will attend to that for you by catching those exceptions and rethrowing an appropriate unchecked subclass of JmsException.

Table 12.1 Spring's JmsTemplate catches standard JMSExceptions and rethrows them as unchecked subclasses of Spring's own JmsException.

Spring (org.springframework.jms.*)	Standard JMS (javax.jms.*)
DestinationResolutionException	Spring-specific—thrown when Spring can't resolve a destination name
IllegalStateException	IllegalStateException
InvalidClientIDException	InvalidClientIDException
InvalidDestinationException	InvalidDestinationException
InvalidSelectorException	InvalidSelectorException
JmsSecurityException	JmsSecurityException
ListenerExecutionFailedException	Spring-specific—thrown when execution of a listener method fails
MessageConversionException	Spring-specific—thrown when message conversion fails
MessageEOFException	MessageEOFException
MessageFormatException	MessageFormatException
MessageNotReadableException	MessageNotReadableException
MessageNotWriteableException	MessageNotWriteableException
ResourceAllocationException	ResourceAllocationException
SynchedLocalTransactionFailedException	Spring-specific—thrown when a synchronized local transaction fails to complete
TransactionInProgressException	TransactionInProgressException
TransactionRolledBackException	TransactionRolledBackException
UncategorizedJmsException	Spring-specific—thrown when no other exception applies

A tale of two `JmsTemplate`s

Spring actually comes with two JMS template classes: `JmsTemplate` and `JmsTemplate102`. `JmsTemplate102` is a special version of `JmsTemplate` for JMS 1.0.2 providers. In JMS 1.0.2, topics and queues are treated as completely different concepts known as *domains*. In JMS 1.1+, topics and queues are unified under a domain-independent API. Because topics and queues are treated so differently in JMS 1.0.2, there has to be a special `JmsTemplate102` for interacting with older JMS implementations. In this chapter, we'll assume a modern JMS provider and therefore will focus our attention on `JmsTemplate`.

WIRING A JMS TEMPLATE

To use `JmsTemplate`, we'll need to declare it as a bean in the Spring configuration file. The following XML should do the trick:

```
<bean id="jmsTemplate"
      class="org.springframework.jms.core.JmsTemplate">
  <property name="connectionFactory" ref="connectionFactory" />
</bean>
```

Because `JmsTemplate` needs to know how to get connections to the message broker, we must set the `connectionFactory` property with a reference to the bean that implements JMS's `ConnectionFactory` interface. Here, we've wired it with a reference to the `connectionFactory` bean that we declared earlier in section 12.2.1.

That's all you need to do to configure `JmsTemplate`—it's now ready to go. Let's start sending messages!

SENDING MESSAGES

One of the features we'd like to build into the Spitter application is the option of alerting (perhaps by email) other users whenever a spittle has been created. We could build that feature directly into the application at the point where a spittle is added. But figuring out who to send alerts to and actually sending those alerts may take a while and it could hurt the perceived performance of the application. When a new spittle is added, we want the application to be snappy and respond quickly with a response.

Rather than taking the time to send those messages at the moment when the spittle is added, it makes more sense to queue up that work and deal with it later, after the response has gone back to the user. The time it takes to send a message to a message queue or a topic is negligible, especially compared to the time it may take to send the alerts to other users.

To support sending spittle alerts asynchronously with the creation of spittles, let's introduce `AlertService` to the Spittle application:

```
package com.habuma.spitter.alerts;
import com.habuma.spitter.domain.Spittle;

public interface AlertService {
  void sendSpittleAlert(Spittle spittle);
}
```

As you can see, `AlertService` is a interface that defines a single operation, `sendSpittleAlert()`. `AlertServiceImpl` is an implementation of the `AlertService` interface that uses `JmsTemplate` to send `Spittle` objects to a message queue to be processed at some later time.

Listing 12.3 Sending a Spittle using `JmsTemplate`

```
package com.habuma.spitter.alerts;

import javax.jms.JMSException;
import javax.jms.Message;
import javax.jms.Session;

import org.springframework.beans.factory.annotation.Autowired;
import org.springframework.jms.core.JmsTemplate;
import org.springframework.jms.core.MessageCreator;

import com.habuma.spitter.domain.Spittle;

public class AlertServiceImpl implements AlertService {
  public void sendSpittleAlert(final Spittle spittle) {
    jmsTemplate.send(                                          <-- Sends message
      "spittle.alert.queue",                 <-- Specifies destination
      new MessageCreator() {
        public Message createMessage(Session session)
                throws JMSException {
          return session.createObjectMessage(spittle);      <-- Creates message
        }
      }
    );
  }

  @Autowired                                   Inject JMS
  JmsTemplate jmsTemplate;                 <-- template
}
```

The first parameter to the `JmsTemplate`'s `send()` method is the name of the JMS destination that the message will be sent to. When the `send()` method is called, `JmsTemplate` will deal with obtaining a JMS connection and session and will send the message on behalf of the sender (see figure 12.5).

As for the message itself, it's constructed using a `MessageCreator`, implemented here as an anonymous inner class. In `MessageCreator`'s `createMessage()` method, we simply ask for an object message from the session, giving it the `Spittle` object to build the object message from.

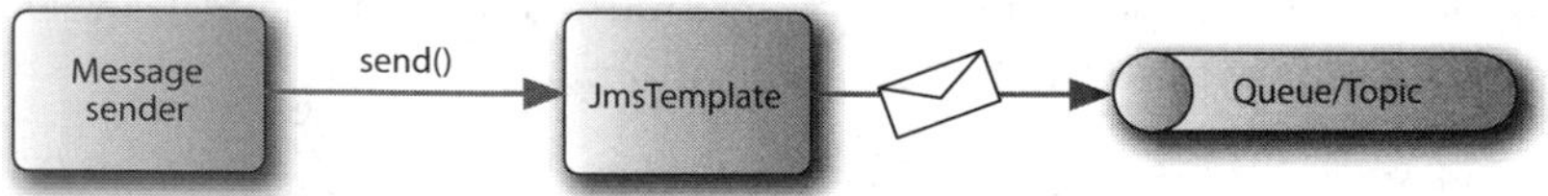

Figure 12.5 `JmsTemplate` deals with the complexities of sending a message on behalf of the sender.

And that's it! Note that the `sendSpittleAlert()` method is focused entirely on assembling and sending a message. There's no connection or session management code; `JmsTemplate` handles all of that for us. And there's no need to catch `JMSException`; `JmsTemplate` will catch any `JMSException` that's thrown and then rethrow it as one of Spring's unchecked exceptions from table 12.1.

SETTING A DEFAULT DESTINATION

In listing 12.3, we explicitly specified a specific destination that the spittle message would be sent to in the `send()` method. That form of `send()` method comes in handy when we want to programmatically choose a destination. But in the case of `AlertServiceImpl`, we'll always be sending the spittle message to the same destination, so the benefits of that form of `send()` aren't as clear.

Instead of explicitly specifying a destination each time we send a message, we could opt for wiring a default destination into `JmsTemplate`:

```
<bean id="jmsTemplate"
      class="org.springframework.jms.core.JmsTemplate">
  <property name="connectionFactory" ref="connectionFactory" />
  <property name="defaultDestinationName"
            value="spittle.alert.queue"/>
</bean>
```

Now the call to `JmsTemplate`'s `send()` method can be simplified slightly by removing the first parameter:

```
jmsTemplate.send(
  new MessageCreator() {
  ...
  }
);
```

This form of the `send()` method only takes a `MessageCreator`. There's no need to specify a destination because the default destination is the one we want to send messages to.

CONSUMING MESSAGES

Now you've seen how to send a message using `JmsTemplate`. But what if you're on the receiving end? Can `JmsTemplate` be used to receive messages too?

Yes, it can. In fact, it's even easier to receive messages with `JmsTemplate`. All you need to do is call `JmsTemplate`'s `receive()` method, as shown.

Listing 12.4 Receiving a message using `JmsTemplate`

```
public Spittle getAlert() {
  try {
    ObjectMessage receivedMessage =
        (ObjectMessage) jmsTemplate.receive();          <-- Receive message

    return (Spittle) receivedMessage.getObject();       <-- Get object
  } catch (JMSException jmsException) {
```

```
    throw JmsUtils.convertJmsAccessException(jmsException);
  }
}
```

Throw converted exception

When the JmsTemplate's receive() method is called, it'll attempt to retrieve a message from the message broker. If no message is available, the receive() method will wait until a message becomes available. This interaction is illustrated in figure 12.6.

Since we know that the spittle message was sent as an object message, it can be cast to ObjectMessage upon arrival. After that, we call getObject() to extract the Spittle object from the ObjectMessage and return it.

The one gotcha here is that we have to do something about the JMSException that may be thrown. As I already mentioned, JmsTemplate is good about handling any checked JMSExceptions that are thrown and then rethrowing them as one of Spring's unchecked JmsExceptions. But that's only applicable when calling one of JmsTemplate's methods. JmsTemplate can't do much about the JMSException that may be thrown by the call to ObjectMessage's getObject() method.

Therefore, we must either catch that JMSException or declare that the method throws it. In keeping with Spring's philosophy of avoiding checked exceptions, we don't want to let the JMSException escape this method, so we'll catch it instead. In the catch block, we can use the convertJmsAccessException() method from Spring's JmsUtils class to convert the checked JMSException to an unchecked JmsException. This is effectively the same thing that JmsTemplate does for us in other cases.

The big downside of consuming messages with JmsTemplate is that the receive() method is synchronous. This means that the receiver must wait patiently for the message to arrive, as the receive() message will block until a message is available (or until a timeout condition occurs). Doesn't it seem odd to synchronously consume a message that was asynchronously sent?

That's where message-driven POJOs come in handy. Let's see how to receive messages asynchronously using components that react to messages rather than waiting on them.

The big downside of consuming messages with JmsTemplate is that the receive() method is synchronous. This means that the receiver must wait patiently for the message to arrive, as the receive() method will block until a message is available (or until a timeout condition occurs). Doesn't it seem odd to synchronously consume a message that was asynchronously sent?

Figure 12.6 Receiving messages from a topic or queue using JmsTemplate is as simple as calling the receive() method. JmsTemplate takes care of the rest.

12.4 Creating message-driven POJOs

During one summer in college, I had the privilege of working in Yellowstone National Park. The job wasn't one of the high-profile jobs like park ranger or the guy who turns Old Faithful on and off. Instead, I held a position in housekeeping at Old Faithful Inn, changing sheets, cleaning bathrooms, and vacuuming floors. Not glamorous, but at least I was working in one of the most beautiful places on Earth.

Every day after work, I'd head over to the local post office to see if I had any mail. I was away from home for several weeks, so it was nice to receive a letter or card from my friends back at school. I didn't have my own post box, so I'd walk up and ask the man sitting on the stool behind the counter if I had received any mail. That's when the wait would begin.

You see, the man behind the counter was approximately 195 years old. And like most people that age he had a difficult time getting around. He'd drag his keister off the stool, slowly scoot his feet across the floor, and then disappear behind a partition. After a few moments, he'd emerge, shuffle his way back to the counter, and lift himself back up onto the stool. Then he'd look at me and say, "No mail today."

`JmsTemplate`'s `receive()` method is a lot like that aged postal employee. When you call `receive()`, it goes away and looks for a message in the queue or topic and doesn't return until a message arrives or until the timeout has passed. Meanwhile, your application is sitting there doing nothing, waiting to see if there's a message. Wouldn't it be better if your application could go about its business and be notified when a message arrives?

One of the highlights of the EJB 2 specification was the inclusion of the *message-driven bean (MDB)*. MDBs are EJBs that process messages asynchronously. In other words, MDBs react to messages in a JMS destination as events and respond to those events. This is in contrast to synchronous message receivers, which block until a message is available.

MDBs were a bright spot in the EJB landscape. Even many of EJB's most rabid detractors would concede that MDBs were an elegant way of handling messages. The only blemish to be found in EJB 2 MDBs was that they had to implement `javax.ejb.MessageDrivenBean`. In doing so, they also had to implement a few EJB lifecycle callback methods. Put simply, EJB 2 MDBs were very un-POJO.

With the EJB 3 specification, MDBs were cleaned up to have a slightly more POJO feel to them. No longer must you implement the `MessageDrivenBean` interface. Instead, you implement the more generic `javax.jms.MessageListener` interface and annotate MDBs with `@MessageDriven`.

Spring 2.0 addresses the need for asynchronous consumption of messages by providing its own form of message-driven bean that's quite similar to EJB 3's MDBs. In this section, you'll learn how Spring supports asynchronous message consumption using message-driven POJOs (we'll call them *MDPs*, for short).

12.4.1 Creating a message listener

If we were to build our spittle alert handler using EJB's message-driven model, it'd need to be annotated with @MessageDriven. And, although it's not strictly required, it's recommended that the MDB implement the MessageListener interface. The result would look something like this:

```
@MessageDriven(mappedName="jms/spittle.alert.queue")
public class SpittleAlertHandler implements MessageListener {
  @Resource
  private MessageDrivenContext mdc;

  public void onMessage(Message message) {
     ...
  }
}
```

For a moment, try to imagine a simpler world where message-driven components don't have to implement the MessageListener interface. In such a happy place, the sky would be the brightest of blues, the birds would always whistle your favorite song, and you wouldn't have to implement the onMessage() method or have a MessageDrivenContext injected.

Okay, maybe the demands placed on an MDB by the EJB 3 specification aren't that arduous. But the fact is that the EJB 3 implementation of SpittleAlertHandler is too tied to EJB's message-driven APIs and isn't as POJO-ish as we'd like. Ideally, we'd like the alert handler to be capable of handling messages, but not coded as if it knows that's what it'll be doing.

Spring offers the ability for a method on a POJO to handle messages from a JMS queue or topic. For example, the following POJO implementation of SpittleAlertHandler is perfectly sufficient.

Listing 12.5 A Spring MDP asynchronously receives and processes messages.

```
package com.habuma.spitter.alerts;
import com.habuma.spitter.domain.Spittle;

public class SpittleAlertHandler {

  public void processSpittle(Spittle spittle) {      <-- Handler method
    // ... implementation goes here...
  }

}
```

Although the color of the sky and training birds to sing are out of scope for Spring, listing 12.5 shows that the dream world I described is much closer to reality. We'll fill in the details of the processSpittle() method later. For now, consider that nothing in SpittleAlertHandler shows any hint of JMS. It's a POJO in every sense of the term. It can nevertheless handle messages just like its EJB cousin. All it needs is some special Spring configuration.

Figure 12.7 A message listener container listens to a queue/topic. When a message arrives, it's forwarded to a message listener (such as a message-driven POJO).

12.4.2 Configuring message listeners

The trick to empowering a POJO with message-receiving abilities is to configure it as a message listener in Spring. Spring's `jms` namespace provides everything we need to do that. First, we must declare the handler as a `<bean>`:

```
<bean id="spittleHandler"
      class="com.habuma.spitter.alerts.SpittleAlertHandler" />
```

Then, to turn `SpittleAlertHandler` into a message-driven POJO, we can declare the bean to be a message listener:

```
<jms:listener-container connection-factory="connectionFactory">
  <jms:listener destination="spitter.alert.queue"
       ref="spittleHandler" method="processSpittle" />
</jms:listener-container>
```

Here we have a message listener that's contained within a message listener container. A *message listener container* is a special bean that watches a JMS destination, waiting for a message to arrive. Once a message arrives, it retrieves the message and then passes it on to any message listeners that are interested. Figure 12.7 illustrates this interaction.

To configure the message listener container and message listener in Spring, we're using two elements from Spring's `jms` namespace. The `<jms:listener-container>` is used to contain `<jms:listener>` elements. Here its `connectionFactory` attribute is configured with a reference to the `connectionFactory` that's to be used by each of the child `<jms:listener>`s as they listen for messages. In this case, the `connectionFactory` attribute could've been left off because it defaults to `connectionFactory`.

Regarding the `<jms:listener>` element, it's used to identify a bean and a method that should handle incoming messages. For the purposes of handling spittle alert messages, the `ref` element refers to our `spittleHandler` bean. When a message arrives on spitter.alert.queue (as designated by the `destination` attribute), the `spittleHandler` bean's `processSpittle()` method gets the call (per the `method` attribute).

12.5 Using message-based RPC

In chapter 10, we explored several of Spring's options for exposing bean methods as remote services and for making calls on those services from clients. In this chapter, we've seen how to send messages between applications over message queues and topics. Now we're going to bring those two concepts together and see how to make remote calls that use JMS as a transport.

There are two options for message-based RPC in Spring:

- Spring itself offers `JmsInvokerServiceExporter` for exporting beans as message-based services and `JmsInvokerProxyFactoryBean` for clients to consume those services.
- Lingo provides a similar approach to message-based remoting with its `JmsServiceExporter` and `JmsProxyFactoryBean`.

As you'll see, these two options are very similar to each other, but each has advantages and disadvantages. I'll show you both approaches and let you decide which works best for you. Let's start by looking at how to work with Spring's own support for JMS-backed services.

12.5.1 Working with Spring message-based RPC

As you'll recall from chapter 10, Spring provides several options for exporting beans as remote services. We used `RmiServiceExporter` to export beans as RMI services over JRMP, `HessianExporter` and `BurlapExporter` for Hessian and Burlap services over HTTP, and `HttpInvokerServiceExporter` to create HTTP invoker services over HTTP. But Spring has one more service exporter that we didn't talk about in chapter 10.

CONSUMING JMS-BASED SERVICES

`JmsInvokerServiceExporter` is much like those other service exporters. In fact, note that there's some symmetry in the names of `JmsInvokerServiceExporter` and `HttpInvokerServiceExporter`. If `HttpInvokerServiceExporter` exports services that communicate over HTTP, then `JmsInvokerServiceExporter` must export services that converse over JMS.

To demonstrate how `JmsInvokerServiceExporter` works, consider `AlertServiceImpl`.

Listing 12.6 `AlertServiceImpl` is a JMS-free POJO that will handle JMS messages.

```
package com.habuma.spitter.alerts;

import org.springframework.mail.SimpleMailMessage;
import org.springframework.mail.javamail.JavaMailSender;
import org.springframework.stereotype.Component;

import com.habuma.spitter.domain.Spittle;

@Component("alertService")
public class AlertServiceImpl implements AlertService {
  private JavaMailSender mailSender;
  private String alertEmailAddress;
  public AlertServiceImpl(JavaMailSender mailSender,
                          String alertEmailAddress) {
    this.mailSender = mailSender;
    this.alertEmailAddress = alertEmailAddress;
  }

  public void sendSpittleAlert(final Spittle spittle) {      // Send Spittle alert
    SimpleMailMessage message = new SimpleMailMessage();
    String spitterName = spittle.getSpitter().getFullName();
```

```
    message.setFrom("noreply@spitter.com");
    message.setTo(alertEmailAddress);
    message.setSubject("New spittle from " + spitterName);
    message.setText(spitterName + " says: " + spittle.getText());
    mailSender.send(message);
  }
}
```

Don't concern yourself too much with the inner details of the `sendSpittleAlert()` method at this point. We'll talk more about how to send emails with Spring later, in section 14.3. The important thing to notice is that `AlertServiceImpl` is a simple POJO and has nothing that indicates that it'll be used to handle JMS messages. It does implement the simple `AlertService` interface, as shown here:

```
package com.habuma.spitter.alerts;
import com.habuma.spitter.domain.Spittle;

public interface AlertService {
  void sendSpittleAlert(Spittle spittle);
}
```

As you can see, `AlertServiceImpl` is annotated with `@Component` so that it'll be automatically discovered and registered as a bean in the Spring application context with an ID of `alertService`. We'll refer to this bean as we configure a `JmsInvokerServiceExporter`:

```
<bean id="alertServiceExporter"
      class="org.springframework.jms.remoting.JmsInvokerServiceExporter"
      p:service-ref="alertService"
      p:serviceInterface="com.habuma.spitter.alerts.AlertService" />
```

This bean's properties describe what the exported service should look like. The `service` property is wired to refer to the `alertService` bean, which is the implementation of the remote service. Meanwhile, the `serviceInterface` property is set to the fully-qualified class name of the interface that the service provides.

The exporter's properties don't describe the specifics of how the service will be carried over JMS. But the good news is that `JmsInvokerServiceExporter` qualifies as a JMS listener. Therefore, we can configure it as such within a `<jms:listener-container>` element:

```
<jms:listener-container connection-factory="connectionFactory">
  <jms:listener destination="spitter.alert.queue"
       ref="alertServiceExporter" />
</jms:listener-container>
```

The JMS listener container is given the connection factory so that it can know how to connect to the message broker. Meanwhile, the `<jms:listener>` declaration is given the destination that the remote message will be carried on.

CONSUMING JMS-BASED SERVICES

At this point, the JMS-based alert service should be ready and waiting for RPC messages to arrive on the queue whose name is spitter.alert.queue. On the client side, `JmsInvokerProxyFactoryBean` will be used to access the service.

JmsInvokerProxyFactoryBean is a lot like the other remoting proxy factory beans that we looked at in chapter 10. It hides the details of accessing a remote service behind a convenient interface, through which the client interacts with the service. The big difference is that instead of proxying RMI- or HTTP-based services, JmsInvokerProxyFactoryBean proxies a JMS-based service that was exported by JmsInvokerServiceExporter.

To consume the alert service, we can wire the JmsInvokerProxyFactoryBean like this:

```
<bean id="alertService"
    class="org.springframework.jms.remoting.JmsInvokerProxyFactoryBean">
  <property name="connectionFactory" ref="connectionFactory" />
  <property name="queueName" value="spitter.alert.queue" />
  <property name="serviceInterface"
          value="com.habuma.spitter.alerts.AlertService" />
</bean>
```

The connectionFactory and queueName properties specify how RPC messages should be delivered—here, on the queue named spitter.alert.queue at the message broker configured in the given connection factory. As for the serviceInterface, this specifies that the proxy should be exposed through the AlertService interface.

JmsInvokerServiceExporter and JmsInvokerProxyFactoryBean offer an JMS-based alternative to Spring's other remoting options. But it's not the only way to export beans and consume JMS-based services. It may not even be the best way. Let's look at Lingo and see how it offers something that the JMS invoker doesn't.

12.5.2 Asynchronous RPC with Lingo

Lingo[1] is a Spring-based remoting option that's similar to Spring's own JMS invoker support. In fact, the Javadoc for Spring's JMS invoker classes even indirectly gives credit to Lingo as their inspiration.[2]

What makes Lingo different is that, unlike the JMS invoker, it can truly take advantage of the asynchronous nature of JMS to invoke services asynchronously. That means that the server doesn't have to even be available when the client makes the call. Furthermore, if the service is long-running, then the client won't have to wait for it to finish.

Unlike the other remoting option we discussed in chapter 10 or even Spring's own JMS invoker classes, Lingo isn't part of the Spring Framework. It's a separate project that builds upon Spring Remoting, offering a JMS-based service exporter and client proxy.

We'll start our exploration of Lingo by seeing how to export services with Lingo's JmsServiceExporter. Then we'll consume that service using Lingo's JmsServiceProxy.

---

1 http://lingo.codehaus.org

2 The Javadoc doesn't mention Lingo, but it does give credit to James Strachan, Lingo's creator.

EXPORTING THE ASYNCHRONOUS SERVICE

As you can see from the following <bean> declaration, `JmsServiceExporter` and `JmsInvokerServiceExporter` are configured in much the same way:

```
<bean id="alertServiceExporter"
      class="org.logicblaze.lingo.jms.JmsServiceExporter"
      p:connectionFactory-ref="connectionFactory"
      p:destination-ref="alertServiceQueue"
      p:service-ref="alertService"
      p:serviceInterface="com.habuma.spitter.alerts.AlertService" />
```

The `service` and `serviceInterface` properties are exactly the same as with `JmsInvokerServiceExporter`. But a new property is injected on the `JmsServiceExporter` bean. `JmsServiceExporter` can't be used as a message listener in a Spring listener container, so we must tell it about the JMS connection factory and the message destination in the `connectionFactory` and `destination` properties so that it knows how to send the message.

Note that the `destination` property is of `javax.jms.Destination`. So we'll need to wire in a reference to a destination bean. The following `alertServiceQueue` bean will make sure that JMS RPC messages are transported over the queue named spittle .alert.queue:

```
<amq:queue id="alertServiceQueue"
           physicalName="spitter.alert.queue" />
```

At this point, Lingo hasn't given us anything that Spring's own JMS invoker didn't provide. So you may be wondering why I'd bother telling you about Lingo if Spring's own JMS RPC mechanism provides effectively the same capabilities.

As you're about to see, the client side of Lingo offers something that the JMS invoker doesn't: asynchronous invocation.

PROXYING ASYNCHRONOUS SERVICES

When we called methods on a proxy created by Spring's `JmsInvokerServiceProxy`, we had to wait. Even though the underlying transport was JMS, the proxy would wait until it received a response.

Lingo's `JmsProxyFactoryBean`, on the other hand, can be configured to treat `void` methods as one-way asynchronous methods. For example, the client side of a Lingo-based alert service, might be configured something like this:

```
<bean id="alertService"
      class="org.logicblaze.lingo.jms.JmsProxyFactoryBean"
  p:connectionFactory-ref="connectionFactory"
  p:destination-ref="queue"
  p:serviceInterface="com.habuma.spitter.alerts.AlertService">
   <property name="metadataStrategy">
     <bean id="metadataStrategy"
           class="org.logicblaze.lingo.SimpleMetadataStrategy">
       <constructor-arg value="true"/>
     </bean>
   </property>
</bean>
```

The connectionFactory, destination, and serviceInterface properties serve the same purpose as in previous examples. What's new here is the metadataStrategy property, which we've set using an inner-bean declaration of type SimpleMetadataStrategy.

Among other things, a metadata strategy is Lingo's way of determining which methods should be asynchronous one-way operations. The only implementation available is SimpleMetadataStrategy, whose constructor can take a single argument Boolean value to indicate whether void methods should be asynchronous. Here, we've declared the constructor argument as true, indicating that any void methods on the service should be considered one-way methods and thus should be asynchronous and immediately return.

Had we declared the constructor argument as false or not injected JmsProxyFactoryBean's metadataStrategy property at all, all service methods would be treated synchronously and JmsProxyFactoryBean would be roughly equivalent in power to Spring's JmsInvokerServiceProxy.

12.6 Summary

Asynchronous messaging presents several advantages over synchronous RPC. Indirect communication results in applications that are loosely coupled with respect to one another, and thus reduces the impact of any one system going down. Additionally, because messages are forwarded to their recipients, there's no need for a sender to wait for a response. In many circumstances, this can be a boost to application performance.

Although JMS provides a standard API for all Java applications wishing to participate in asynchronous communication, it can be cumbersome to use. Spring eliminates the need for JMS boilerplate code and exception-handling code and makes asynchronous messaging easier to use.

In this chapter, we've seen several ways that Spring can help establish asynchronous communication between two applications by way of message brokers and JMS. Spring's JMS template eliminates the boilerplate that's commonly required by the traditional JMS programming model. And Spring-enabled message-driven beans make it possible to declare bean methods which react to messages that arrive in a queue or topic.

We also looked at using Spring's JMS invoker as well as Lingo to provide message-based RPC with Spring beans. Although Spring's JMS invoker drew inspiration from Lingo and may be considered its replacement, it only offers synchronous communication. Meanwhile Lingo offers something that Spring's JMS invoker doesn't: the ability to invoke remote methods asynchronously.

Now that we've seen how Spring simplifies JMS, let's look at how Spring works with a similarly named Java standard. In the next chapter, we'll explore Spring's ability to export beans as managed beans using JMX.

13 Managing Spring beans with JMX

This chapter covers

- Exposing Spring beans as managed beans
- Remotely managing Spring beans
- Handling JMX notifications

Spring's support for DI is a great way to configure bean properties in an application. But once the application has been deployed and is running, DI alone can't do much to help you change that configuration. Suppose that you want to dig into a running application and change its configuration on the fly. That's where *Java Management Extensions (JMX)* comes in.

JMX is a technology that enables you to instrument applications for management, monitoring, and configuration. Originally available as a separate extension to Java, JMX is now a standard part of the Java 5 distribution.

The key component of an application that's instrumented for management with JMX is the *MBean (managed bean)*. An MBean is a JavaBean that exposes certain methods which define the management interface. The JMX specification defines four types of MBeans:

- *Standard MBeans*—Standard MBeans are MBeans whose management interface is determined by reflection on a fixed Java interface that's implemented by the bean class.
- *Dynamic MBeans*—Dynamic MBeans are MBeans whose management interface is determined at runtime by invoking methods of the `DynamicMBean` interface. Because the management interface isn't defined by a static interface, it can vary at runtime.
- *Open MBeans*—Open MBeans are a special kind of dynamic MBean whose attributes and operations are limited to primitive types, class wrappers for primitive types, and any type that can be decomposed into primitives or primitive wrappers.
- *Model MBeans*—A model MBean is a special kind of dynamic MBean that bridges a management interface to the managed resource. Model MBeans aren't written as much as they are declared. They're typically produced by a factory that uses some metainformation to assemble the management interface.

Spring's JMX module enables you to export Spring beans as Model MBeans so that you can see inside your application and tweak the configuration—even while the application is running. Let's see how to JMX-enable our Spring application so that we can manage the beans in the Spring application context.

13.1 Exporting Spring beans as MBeans

There are several ways that we could use JMX to manage the beans within the Spitter application. In the interest of keeping things simple, let's start with a modest change to the `HomeController` to add a new `spittlesPerPage` property:

```
public static final int DEFAULT_SPITTLES_PER_PAGE = 25;

private int spittlesPerPage = DEFAULT_SPITTLES_PER_PAGE;

public void setSpittlesPerPage(int spittlesPerPage) {
  this.spittlesPerPage = spittlesPerPage;
}

public int getSpittlesPerPage() {
  return spittlesPerPage;
}
```

Previously, when `HomeController` called `getRecentSpittles()` on the `SpitterService`, it passed in `DEFAULT_SPITTLES_PER_PAGE`, which would result in at most 25 spittles being displayed on the home page. Now, rather than commit to that decision at build time, we're going to use JMX to leave that decision open to change at runtime. The new `spittlesPerPage` property is the first step to enabling that.

But on its own, the `spittlesPerPage` property can't enable external configuration of the number of spittles displayed on the home page. It's just a property on a bean, like any other property. What we'll need to do next is to expose the `HomeController` bean as an MBean. Then, the spittlesPerPage property will be exposed as the MBean's *managed attribute* and we'll be able to change its value at runtime.

Spring's MBeanExporter is the key to JMX-ifying beans in Spring. MBeanExporter is a bean that exports one or more Spring-managed beans as Model MBeans in an *MBean server.* An MBean server (sometimes called an *MBean agent*) is a container where MBeans live and through which the MBeans are accessed.

As illustrated in figure 13.1, exporting Spring beans as JMX MBeans makes it possible for a JMX-based management tool such as JConsole or VisualVM to peer inside a running application to view the beans' properties and invoke their methods.

The following <bean> declares an MBeanExporter in Spring to export the homeController bean as a Model MBean:

```
<bean id="mbeanExporter"
  class="org.springframework.jmx.export.MBeanExporter">
  <property name="beans">
    <map>
      <entry key="spitter:name=HomeController"
             value-ref="homeController"/>
    </map>
  </property>
</bean>
```

In its most straightforward form, MBeanExporter can be configured through its beans property by injecting a Map of one or more beans that you'd like to expose as model MBeans in JMX. The key of each <entry> is the name to be given to the MBean (composed of a management domain name and a key-value pair—spitter:name=HomeController in the case of the HomeController MBean). The value of the entry is a

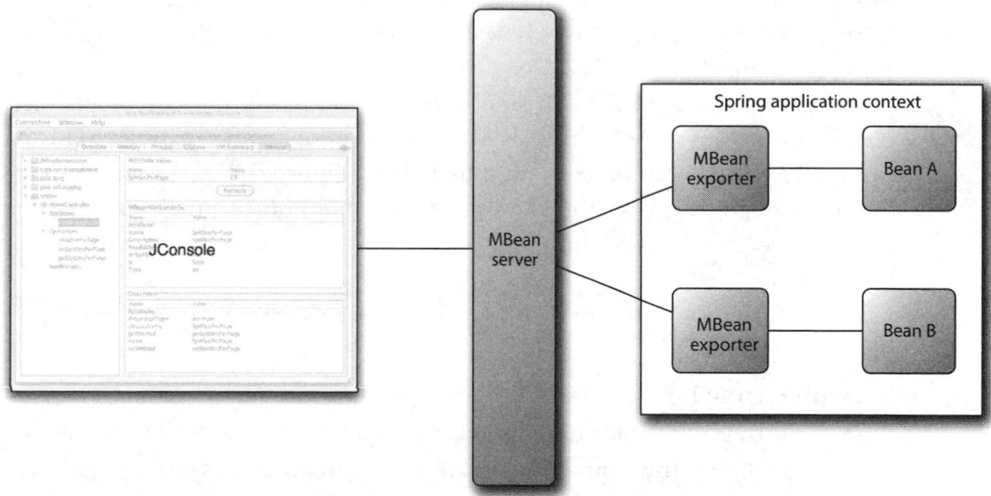

Figure 13.1 Spring's MBeanExporter exports the properties and methods of Spring beans as JMX attributes and operations in an MBean server. From there, a JMX management tool such as JConsole can look inside the running application.

From whence the MBean server?

As configured, `MBeanExporter` assumes that it's running within an application server (such as Tomcat) or some other context that provides an MBean server. But if your Spring application will be running standalone or in a container that doesn't provide an MBean server, you'll want to configure an MBean server in the Spring context. The `<context:mbean-server>` element can handle that for you:

```
<context:mbean-server />
```

`<context:mbean-server>` will create an MBean server as a bean within the Spring application context. By default, that bean's ID is `mbeanServer`. Knowing this, you can then wire it into `MBeanExporter`'s `server` property to specify which MBean server an MBean should be exposed through:

```
<bean id="mbeanExporter"
      class="org.springframework.jmx.export.MBeanExporter">
  <property name="beans">
    <map>
      <entry key="spitter:name=HomeController"
             value-ref="homeController"/>
    </map>
  </property>

  <property name="server" ref="mbeanServer" />
</bean>
```

reference to the Spring-managed bean that's to be exported. Here, we're exporting the `homeController` bean so that its properties can be managed at runtime through JMX.

With the `MBeanExporter` in place, the `homeController` bean will be exported as a Model MBean to the MBean server for management under the name `HomeController`. Figure 13.2 shows how the `homeController` MBean appears when viewed through JConsole.

As you can see on the left side of figure 13.2, all public members of the `homeController` bean are exported as MBean operations and attributes. This is probably not what we want. All we really want to do is configure the `spittlesPerPage` property. We don't need to invoke the `showHomePage()` method or muck about with any other part of `HomeController`. Thus, we need a way to select which attributes and operations are available.

To gain finer control on an MBean's attributes and operations, Spring offers a few options, including

- Declaring bean methods to expose/ignore by name
- Fronting the bean with an interface to select the exposed methods
- Annotating the bean to designate managed attributes and operations

Let's try out each of these options to see which best suits our `HomeController` MBean. We'll start with selecting the bean methods to expose by name.

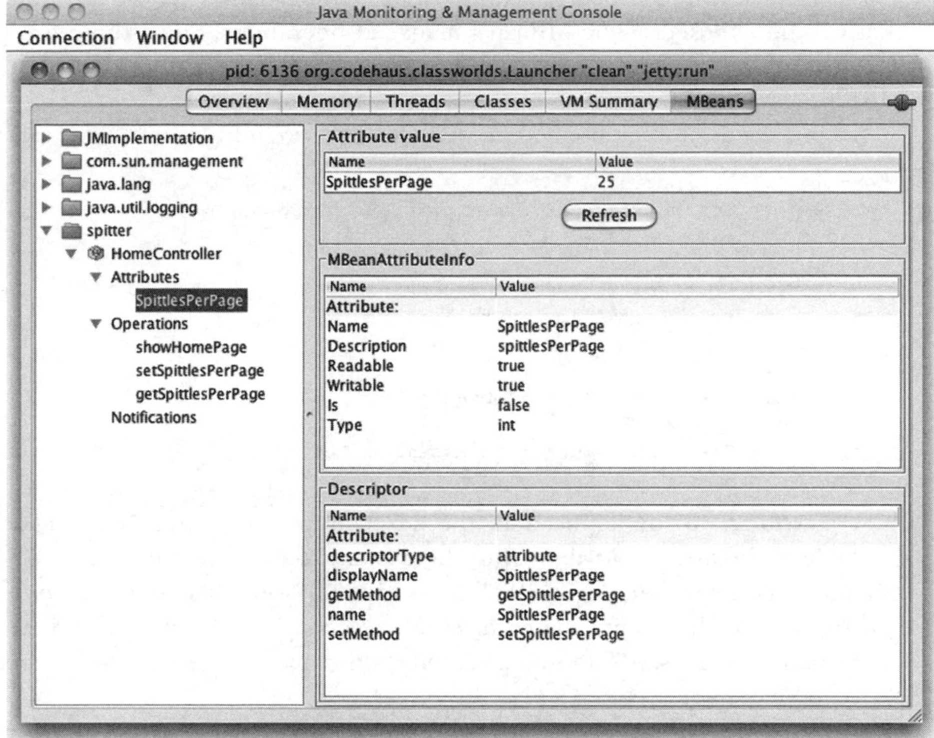

Figure 13.2 `HomeController` **exported as an MBean and seen through the eyes of JConsole**

13.1.1 Exposing methods by name

An *MBean info assembler* is the key to constraining which operations and attributes are exported in an MBean. One such MBean info assembler is `MethodNameBasedMBeanInfoAssembler`. This assembler is given a list of names of methods to export as MBean operations. For the `HomeController` bean, what we want to do is export `spittlesPerPage` as a managed attribute. How can a method name–based assembler help us export a managed attribute?

Recall that per JavaBean rules (not necessarily Spring bean rules), what makes `spittlesPerPage` a property is that it has corresponding accessor methods names `setSpittlesPerPage()` and `getSpittlesPerPage()`. To limit our MBean's exposure, we'll need to tell `MethodNameBasedMBeanInfoAssembler` to only include those methods in the MBean's interface. The following declaration of a `MethodNameBasedMBeanInfoAssembler` bean singles out those methods:

```
<bean id="assembler"
        class="org.springframework.jmx.export.assembler.
        ➥MethodNameBasedMBeanInfoAssembler"
        p:managedMethods="getSpittlesPerPage,setSpittlesPerPage" />
```

The managedMethods property takes a list of method names. Those are the methods that will be exposed as the MBean's managed operations. Since those are property accessor methods, they'll also result in a spittlesPerPage managed attribute on the MBean.

To put the assembler into action, we'll need to wire it into the MBeanExporter:

```
<bean id="mbeanExporter"
  class="org.springframework.jmx.export.MBeanExporter">
  <property name="beans">
    <map>
      <entry key="spitter:name=HomeController"
             value-ref="homeController"/>
    </map>
  </property>
  <property name="server" ref="mbeanServer" />

  <property name="assembler" ref="assembler"/>
</bean>
```

Now if we fire up the application, the HomeController's spittlesPerPage will be available as a managed attribute, but the showHomePage() method won't be exposed as a managed operation. Figure 13.3 shows what this looks like in JConsole.

Another method name–based assembler to consider is MethodExclusionMBean-InfoAssembler. This MBean info assembler is the inverse of MethodNameBasedMBean-

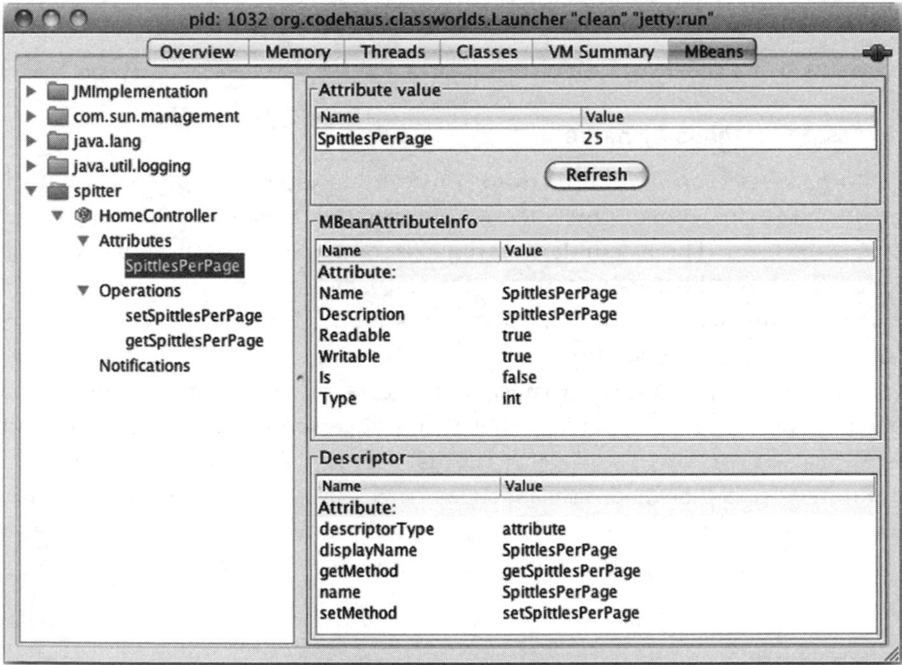

Figure 13.3 After specifying which methods are exported in the HomeController MBean, the showHomePage() method is no longer a managed operation.

InfoAssembler. Rather than specifying which methods to expose as managed operations, MethodExclusionMBeanInfoAssembler is given a list of methods to *not* reveal as managed operations. For example, here's how to use MethodExclusion-MBeanInfoAssembler to keep showHomePage() out of consideration as a managed operation:

```
<bean id="assembler"
    class="org.springframework.jmx.export.assembler.
    ➥MethodExclusionMBeanInfoAssembler"
p:ignoredMethods="showHomePage" />
```

Method name–based assemblers are straightforward and easy to use. But can you imagine what would happen if we were to export several Spring beans as MBeans? After a while the list of method names given to the assembler would be huge. And there's also a possibility that we may want to export a method from one bean while another bean has a same-named method that we don't want to export.

Clearly, in terms of Spring configuration, the method name approach doesn't scale well when exporting multiple MBeans. Let's see if using interfaces to expose MBean operations and attributes would be any better.

13.1.2 Using interfaces to define MBean operations and attributes

Spring's InterfaceBasedMBeanInfoAssembler is another MBean info assembler that lets you use interfaces to pick and choose which methods on a bean get exported as MBean-managed operations. It's similar to the method name–based assemblers, except that instead of listing method names to be exported, you list interfaces that define the methods to be exported.

For example, suppose that you were to define an interface named HomeController-ManagedOperations like this:

```
package com.habuma.spitter.jmx;

public interface HomeControllerManagedOperations {
  int getSpittlesPerPage();
  void setSpittlesPerPage(int spittlesPerPage);
}
```

Here you've selected the setSpittlesPerPage() and getSpittlesPerPage methods as the operations that you want to export. Again, these accessor methods will indirectly export the spittlesPerPage property as a managed attribute. To use this assembler, you just need to use the following assembler bean instead of the method name–based assemblers from before:

```
<bean id="assembler"
      class="org.springframework.jmx.export.assembler.
      ➥InterfaceBasedMBeanInfoAssembler"
  p:managedInterfaces=
                 "com.habuma.spitter.jmx.HomeControllerManagedOperations"
/>
```

The managedInterfaces property takes a list of one or more interfaces that serve as the MBean-managed operation interfaces—in this case, the HomeControllerManagedOperations interface.

What may not be apparent, but is certainly interesting, is that HomeController doesn't have to explicitly implement HomeControllerManagedOperations. The interface is there for the sake of the exporter, but we don't need to implement it directly in any of our code.

The nice thing about using interfaces to select managed operations is that we could collect dozens of methods into a few interfaces and keep the configuration of InterfaceBasedMBeanInfoAssembler clean. This goes a long way toward keeping the Spring configuration tidy even when exporting multiple MBeans.

Ultimately, those managed operations must be declared somewhere, whether in Spring configuration or in some interface. Moreover, the declaration of the managed operations represents a duplication in code—method names declared in an interface or Spring context and method names in the implementation. This duplication exists for no other reason than to satisfy the MBeanExporter.

One of the things that Java annotations are good at is helping to eliminate such duplication. Let's see how to annotate a Spring-managed bean so that it can be exported as an MBean.

13.1.3 Working with annotation-driven MBeans

In addition to the MBean info assemblers I've shown you thus far, Spring provides another assembler known as MetadataMBeanInfoAssembler that can be configured to use annotations to appoint bean methods as managed operations and attributes. I could show you how to use that assembler, but I won't. That's because wiring it up manually is burdensome and not worth the trouble just to be able to use annotations.

Instead, I'm going to show you how to use the <context:mbean-export> element from Spring's context configuration namespace. This handy element wires up an MBean exporter and all of the appropriate assemblers to turn on annotation-driven MBeans in Spring. All you have to do is use it instead of the MBeanExporter bean that we've been using:

```
<context:mbean-export server="mbeanServer" />
```

Now, to turn any Spring bean into an MBean, all we must do is annotate it with @ManagedResource and annotate its methods with @ManagedOperation or @ManagedAttribute. For example, here's how to alter HomeController to be exported as an MBean using annotations.

Listing 13.1 Annotating HomeController to be an MBean

```
package com.habuma.spitter.mvc;
import java.util.Map;
import org.springframework.beans.factory.annotation.Autowired;
import org.springframework.jmx.export.annotation.ManagedAttribute;
```

```
import org.springframework.jmx.export.annotation.ManagedResource;
import org.springframework.stereotype.Controller;
import org.springframework.web.bind.annotation.RequestMapping;
import com.habuma.spitter.service.SpitterService;

@Controller
@ManagedResource(objectName="spitter:name=HomeController") //  <-- Export HomeController as MBean

public class HomeController {

  ...

  @ManagedAttribute   //   <-- Expose spittlesPerPage as managed attribute

  public void setSpittlesPerPage(int spittlesPerPage) {
    this.spittlesPerPage = spittlesPerPage;
  }

  @ManagedAttribute   //

  public int getSpittlesPerPage() {
    return spittlesPerPage;
  }
}
```

The `@ManagedResource` annotation is applied at the class level to indicate that this bean should be exported as an MBean. The `objectName` attribute indicates the domain (`spitter`) and name (`HomeController`) of the MBean.

The accessor methods for the `spittlesPerPage` property are both annotated with `@ManagedAttribute` to indicate that it should be exposed as a managed attribute. Note that it's not strictly necessary to annotate both accessor methods. If you choose to only annotate the `setSpittlesPerPage()` method, then you'll still be able to set the property through JMX, but you won't be able to see what its value is. Conversely, annotating `getSpittlesPerPage()` will enable the property's value to be viewed as read-only via JMX.

Also note that it's possible to annotate the accessor methods with `@ManagedOperation` instead of `@ManagedAttribute`. For example:

```
@ManagedOperation
public void setSpittlesPerPage(int spittlesPerPage) {
  this.spittlesPerPage = spittlesPerPage;
}

@ManagedOperation
public int getSpittlesPerPage() {
  return spittlesPerPage;
}
```

This will expose those methods through JMX, but it won't expose the `spittlesPerPage` property as a managed attribute. That's because methods annotated with `@ManagedOperation` are treated strictly as methods and not as JavaBean accessors when it comes to exposing MBean functionality. Thus, `@ManagedOperation` should be reserved for exposing methods as MBean operations and `@ManagedAttribute` should be used when exposing managed attributes.

13.1.4 Handing MBean collisions

So far you've seen how to publish an MBean into an MBean server using several approaches. In all cases, we've given the MBean an object name that's made up of a management domain name and a key-value pair. Assuming that there's not already an MBean published with the name we've given our MBean, we should have no trouble publishing our MBean. But what happens if there's a name collision?

By default, `MBeanExporter` will throw an `InstanceAlreadyExistsException` should you try to export an MBean that's named the same as an MBean that's already in the MBean server. But you can change that behavior by specifying how the collision should be handled via the `MBeanExporter`'s `registrationBehaviorName` property or through `<context:mbean-export>`'s `registration` attribute.

There are three ways that an MBean name collision can be handled:

- Fail if an existing MBean has the same name (this is the default behavior)
- Ignore the collision and don't register the new MBean
- Replace the existing MBean with the new MBean

For example, if you're using `MBeanExporter`, you can configure it to ignore collisions by setting the `registrationBehaviorName` property to `REGISTRATION_IGNORE_EXISTING` like this:

```
<bean id="mbeanExporter"
  class="org.springframework.jmx.export.MBeanExporter">
  <property name="beans">
    <map>
      <entry key="spitter:name=HomeController"
             value-ref="homeController"/>
    </map>
  </property>
  <property name="server" ref="mbeanServer" />

  <property name="assembler" ref="assembler"/>
  <property name="registrationBehaviorName"
            value="REGISTRATION_IGNORE_EXISTING" />
</bean>
```

The `registrationBehaviorName` property accepts `REGISTRATION_FAIL_ON_EXISTING`, `REGISTRATION_IGNORE_EXISTING`, or `REGISTRATION_REPLACING_EXISTING`, each representing one of the three collision-handling behaviors available.

If you're using `<context:mbean-export>` to export annotated MBeans, then you'll use the `registration` attribute to specify collision-handling behavior. For example:

```
<context:mbean-export server="mbeanServer"
    registration="replaceExisting"/>
```

The `registration` attribute accepts `failOnExisting`, `ignoreExisting`, or `replaceExisting`.

Now that we've registered our MBeans using MBeanExporter, we'll need a way to access them for management. As you've seen already, we can use tools like JConsole to access a local MBean server to view and manipulate MBeans. But a tool such as JConsole doesn't lend itself to programmatic management of MBeans. How can we manipulate MBeans in one application from within another application? Fortunately, there's another way to access MBeans as remote objects. Let's explore how Spring's support for remote MBeans will enable us to access our MBeans in a standard way through a remote interface.

13.2 Remoting MBeans

Although the original JMX specification referred to remote management of applications through MBeans, it didn't define the actual remoting protocol or API. Consequently, it fell to JMX vendors to define their own, often proprietary, remoting solutions for JMX.

In response to the need for a standard for remote JMX, the Java Community Process produced *JSR-160*, the Java Management Extensions Remote API Specification. This specification defines a standard for JMX remoting, which at a minimum requires an RMI binding and optionally the *JMX Messaging Protocol (JMXMP)*.

In this section, we'll see how Spring enables remote MBeans. We'll start by configuring Spring to export our `HomeController` MBean as a remote MBean. Then we'll see how to use Spring to manipulate that MBean remotely.

13.2.1 Exposing remote MBeans

The simplest thing we can do to make our MBeans available as remote objects is to configure Spring's `ConnectorServerFactoryBean`:

```
<bean class=
    "org.springframework.jmx.support.ConnectorServerFactoryBean" />
```

`ConnectorServerFactoryBean` creates and starts a JSR-160 `JMXConnectorServer`. By default, the server listens for the JMXMP protocol on port 9875—thus, it's bound to `service:jmx:jmxmp://localhost:9875`. But we're not limited to exporting MBeans using only JMXMP.

Depending on the JMX implementation, you may have several remoting protocol options to choose from, including RMI, SOAP, Hessian/Burlap, and even IIOP. To specify a different remote binding for our MBeans, we just need to set the `serviceUrl` property of `ConnectorServerFactoryBean`. For example, if we wanted to use RMI for MBean remoting, we'd set `serviceUrl` like this:

```
<bean class="org.springframework.jmx.support.ConnectorServerFactoryBean"
    p:serviceUrl=
        "service:jmx:rmi://localhost/jndi/rmi://localhost:1099/spitter" />
```

Here, we're binding it to an RMI registry listening on port 1099 of the localhost. That means that we'll also need an RMI registry running and listening at that port. As you'll recall from chapter 10, `RmiServiceExporter` can start an RMI registry automatically for you. But in this case we're not using `RmiServiceExporter`, so we'll need to start an

RMI registry by declaring an RmiRegistryFactoryBean in Spring with the following <bean> declaration:

```
<bean class="org.springframework.remoting.rmi.RmiRegistryFactoryBean"
      p:port="1099" />
```

And that's it! Now our MBeans are available through RMI. But there's little point to doing this if nobody will ever access the MBeans over RMI. So let's now turn our attention to the client side of JMX remoting and see how to wire up a remote MBean in Spring.

13.2.2 Accessing remote MBeans

Accessing a remote MBean server involves configuring an MBeanServerConnectionFactoryBean in the Spring context. The following bean declaration sets up an MBeanServerConnectionFactoryBean that can be used to access the RMI-based remote server we created in the previous section:

```
<bean id="mBeanServerClient"
    class=
        "org.springframework.jmx.support.MBeanServerConnectionFactoryBean"
    p:serviceUrl=
        "service:jmx:rmi://localhost/jndi/rmi://localhost:1099/spitter"/>
```

As its name implies, MBeanServerConnectionFactoryBean is a factory bean that creates an MBeanServerConnection. The MBeanServerConnection produced by MBeanServerConnectionFactoryBean acts as a local proxy to the remote MBean server. It can be wired into a bean property just as if it were any other bean:

```
<bean id="jmxClient" class="com.springinaction.jmx.JmxClient">
  <property name="mbeanServerConnection" ref="mBeanServerClient" />
</bean>
```

MBeanServerConnection provides several methods that let us query the remote MBean server and invoke methods on the MBeans contained therein. For example, say that we'd like to know how many MBeans are registered in the remote MBean server. The following code snippet will print that information:

```
int mbeanCount = mbeanServerConnection.getMBeanCount();
System.out.println("There are " + mbeanCount + " MBeans");
```

And we may also query the remote server for the names of all of the MBeans using the queryNames() method:

```
java.util.Set mbeanNames = mbeanServerConnection.queryNames(null, null);
```

The two parameters passed to queryNames() are used to refine the results. Passing in null for both parameters indicates that we're asking for the names of all of the registered MBeans.

Querying the remote MBean server for bean counts and names is fun, but doesn't get much work done. The real value of accessing an MBean server remotely is found in accessing attributes and invoking operations on the MBeans that are registered in the remote server.

For accessing MBean attributes, you'll want to use the `getAttribute()` and `setAttribute()` methods. For example, to retrieve the value of an MBean attribute, you'd call the `getAttribute()` method like so:

```
String cronExpression = mbeanServerConnection.getAttribute(
    new ObjectName("spitter:name=HomeController"), "spittlesPerPage");
```

Similarly, changing the value of an MBean attribute can be done using the `setAttribute()` method:

```
mbeanServerConnection.setAttribute(
    new ObjectName("spitter:name=HomeController"),
    new Attribute("spittlesPerPage", 10));
```

If you'd like to invoke an MBean's operation, then the `invoke()` method is what you're looking for. Here's how you might invoke the `setSpittlesPerPage()` method on the `HomeController` MBean:

```
mbeanServerConnection.invoke(
    new ObjectName("spitter:name=HomeController"),
    "setSpittlesPerPage",
    new Object[] { 100 },
    new String[] {"int"});
```

And you can do dozens of other things with remote MBeans by using the methods available through `MBeanServerConnection`. I'll leave it to you to explore the possibilities.

But invoking methods and setting attributes on remote MBeans is awkward when done through `MBeanServerConnection`. Doing something as simple as calling the `setSpittlesPerPage()` method involves creating an `ObjectName` instance and passing several other parameters to the `invoke()` method. This isn't nearly as intuitive as a normal method invocation would be. For a more direct approach, we'll need to proxy the remote MBean.

13.2.3 Proxying MBeans

Spring's `MBeanProxyFactoryBean` is a proxy factory bean in the same vein as the remoting proxy factory beans we examined in chapter 10. But instead of providing proxy-based access to remote Spring-managed beans, `MBeanProxyFactoryBean` lets you access remote MBeans directly (as if they were any other locally configured bean). Figure 13.4 illustrates how this works.

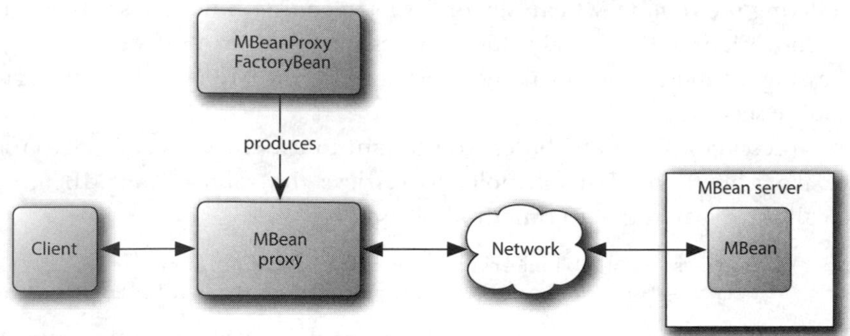

Figure 13.4 `MBeanProxyFactoryBean` **produces a proxy to a remote MBean. The proxy's client can then interact with the remote MBean as if it were a locally configured POJO.**

For example, consider the following declaration of `MBeanProxyFactoryBean`:

```
<bean id="remoteHomeControllerMBean"
      class="org.springframework.jmx.access.MBeanProxyFactoryBean"
      p:objectName="spitter:name=HomeController"
      p:server-ref="mBeanServerClient"
      p:proxyInterface=
        "com.habuma.spitter.jmx.HomeControllerManagedOperations" />
```

The `objectName` property specifies the object name of the remote MBean that's to be proxied locally. Here it's referring to the `HomeController` MBean that we exported earlier.

The `server` property refers to an `MBeanServerConnection` through which all communication with the MBean is routed. Here we've wired in the `MBeanServerConnectionFactoryBean` that we configured earlier.

Finally, the `proxyInterface` property specifies the interface that will be implemented by the proxy. In this case, we're using the same `HomeControllerManagedOperations` interface that we defined in section 13.1.2.

With the `remoteHomeControllerMBean` bean declared, we can now wire it into any bean property whose type is `HomeControllerManagedOperations` and use it to access the remote MBean. From there, we'll be able to invoke the `setSpittlesPerPage()` and `getSpittlesPerPage()` methods.

We've now seen several ways that we can communicate with MBeans, and can now view and tweak our Spring bean configuration while the application is running. But thus far it's been a one-sided conversation. We've talked to the MBeans, but the MBeans haven't been able to get a word in edgewise. It's now time for us to hear what they have to say by listening for notifications.

13.3 Handling notifications

Querying an MBean for information is only one way of keeping an eye on the state of an application. But it's not the most efficient way to be informed of significant events within the application.

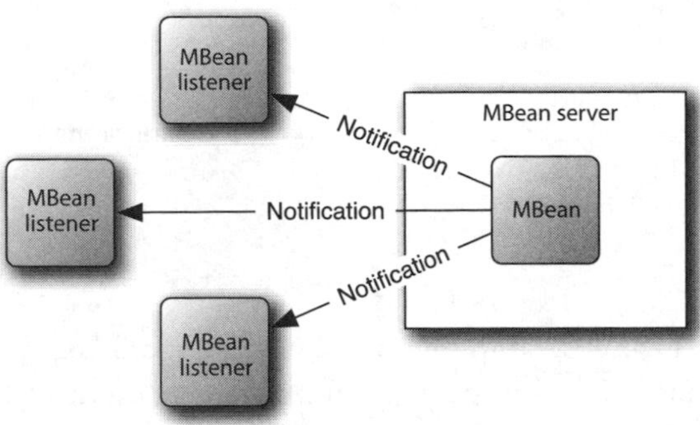

Figure 13.5 JMX notifications enable MBeans to communicate proactively with the outside world.

For example, suppose that the Spitter application were to keep a count of how many spittles have been posted. And suppose that you want to know every time the count has increased by one million spittles (for the 1,000,000th, 2,000,000th, 3,000,000th spittle, and so on). One way to handle this is to write some code that periodically queries the database, counting the number of spittles. But the process that performs that query would keep itself and the database busy as it constantly checks for the spittle count.

Instead of repeatedly querying the database to get that information, a better approach may be to have an MBean notify you when the momentous occasion takes place. JMX notifications, as illustrated in figure 13.5, are a way that MBeans can communicate with the outside world proactively, instead of waiting for some external application to query them for information.

Spring's support for sending notifications comes in the form of the `NotificationPublisherAware` interface. Any bean-turned-MBean that wishes to send notifications should implement this interface. For example, consider `SpittleNotifierImpl`.

Listing 13.2 Using a `NotificationPublisher` to send JMX notifications

```
package com.habuma.spitter.jmx;

import javax.management.Notification;
import org.springframework.jmx.export.annotation.ManagedNotification;
import org.springframework.jmx.export.annotation.ManagedResource;
import org.springframework.jmx.export.notification.NotificationPublisher;
import org.springframework.jmx.export.notification.NotificationPublisherAware;
import org.springframework.stereotype.Component;

@Component
@ManagedResource("spitter:name=SpitterNotifier")
@ManagedNotification(
        notificationTypes="SpittleNotifier.OneMillionSpittles",
        name="TODO")
public class SpittleNotifierImpl
    implements NotificationPublisherAware, SpittleNotifier {    // Implement NotificationPublisherAware

  private NotificationPublisher notificationPublisher;

  public void setNotificationPublisher(                           // Inject notification publisher
          NotificationPublisher notificationPublisher) {
```

```
    this.notificationPublisher = notificationPublisher;
  }

  public void millionthSpittlePosted() {
    notificationPublisher.sendNotification(       <-- Send notification
            new Notification(
                    "SpittleNotifier.OneMillionSpittles", this, 0));
  }
}
```

As you can see, `SpittleNotifierImpl` implements `NotificationPublisherAware`. This isn't a demanding interface. It requires only that a single method be implemented: `setNotificationPublisher`.

`SpittleNotifierImpl` also implements a single method from the `SpittleNotifier` interface,[1] `millionthSpittlePosted()`. This method uses the `NotificationPublisher` that's automatically injected via the `setNotificationPublisher()` method to send a notification that another million spittles have been posted.

Once the `sendNotification()` method has been called, the notification is on its way to… hmm… it seems that we haven't decided who'll receive the notification yet. Let's set up a notification listener to listen to and react to the notification.

13.3.1 Listening for notifications

The standard way to receive MBean notifications is to implement the `javax.management.NotificationListener` interface. For example, consider `PagingNotificationListener`:

```
package com.habuma.spitter.jmx;
import javax.management.Notification;
import javax.management.NotificationListener;

public class PagingNotificationListener implements NotificationListener {
  public void handleNotification(Notification notification,
                                  Object handback) {
     // ...
  }
}
```

`PagingNotificationListener` is a typical JMX notification listener. When a notification is received, its `handleNotification()` method will be invoked to react to the notification. Presumably, `PagingNotificationListener's handleNotification()` method will send a message to a pager or cell phone about the fact that another million spittles have been posted. (I've left the actual implementation to the reader's imagination.)

The only thing left to do is register `PagingNotificationListener` with the `MBeanExporter`:

[1] For brevity's sake, I'm not showing the `SpittleNotifier` interface. But as you can imagine, its only method is `millionthSpittlePosted`.

```
<bean class="org.springframework.jmx.export.MBeanExporter">
  ...
  <property name="notificationListenerMappings">
    <map>
      <entry key="Spitter:name=PagingNotificationListener">
        <bean class="com.habuma.spitter.jmx.PagingNotificationListener" />
      </entry>
    </map>
  </property>
</bean>
```

`MBeanExporter`'s `notificationListenerMappings` property is used to map notification listeners to the MBeans that they'll be listening to. In this case, we've set up `PagingNotificationListener` to listen to any notifications published by the `SpittleNotifier` MBean.

13.4 Summary

With JMX, you can open a window into the inner workings of your application. In this chapter, we saw how to configure Spring to automatically export Spring beans as JMX MBeans so that their details could be viewed and manipulated through JMX-ready management tools. We also saw how to create and use remote MBeans for times when those MBeans and tools are distant from each other. Finally, we saw how to use Spring to publish and listen for JMX notifications.

By now you've probably noticed that the number of remaining pages in this book is dwindling fast. Our journey through Spring is almost complete. But before we conclude, we have a few more quick stops to make along the way. In the next chapter, we'll explore a handful of Spring features that, although useful, haven't appeared in any chapter up until now, including how to use Spring to access objects in JNDI, send email, and schedule tasks.

14 Odds and ends

This chapter covers

- Externalizing configuration
- Wiring JNDI resources in Spring
- Sending email messages
- Scheduling tasks
- Asynchronous methods

I don't know about your house, but many houses (including mine) have a so-called junk drawer. Despite its name, the contents of a junk drawer are often handy or even necessary. Things such as screwdrivers, ballpoint pens, paper clips, and extra keys often call the junk drawer their home. It's not that they're truly junk and have no value—it's that they don't have a place otherwise.

We've covered a lot of ground so far in this book and have explored several corners of working with Spring. Each topic has had a chapter of its own. But there are a few more Spring tricks that I'd like to show you, and none of them were big enough to justify a chapter of their own.

This is the junk drawer of the book. But don't think that the topics here are useless. You'll find valuable techniques here. We'll see how to externalize Spring configuration, encrypt property values, work with JNDI objects, send emails, and configure methods to run in the background—all using Spring.

First up, let's look at how to move property value configuration out of Spring configuration and into external properties files that can be managed without repackaging and redeploying your applications.

14.1 Externalizing configuration

For the most part, it's possible to configure your entire application in a single bean-wiring file. But sometimes you may find it beneficial to extract certain pieces of that configuration into a separate property file. For example, a configuration concern that's common to many applications is configuring a data source. In Spring, you could configure a data source with the following XML in the bean-wiring file:

```
<bean id="dataSource"
      class="org.springframework.jdbc.datasource.DriverManagerDataSource"
      p:driverClassName="org.hsqldb.jdbcDriver"
      p:url="jdbc:hsqldb:hsql://localhost/spitter/spitter"
      p:username="spitterAdmin"
      p:password="t0ps3cr3t" />
```

As you can see, everything you need to do to connect to the database is available in this bean declaration. This has two implications:

- If you need to change the database URL or the username and password, you'll have to edit the Spring configuration file; then recompile and redeploy the application.
- The username and password are sensitive details that you wouldn't want to fall into the wrong hands.

In situations like this, it might be better to not directly configure these details in the Spring application context. Spring comes with a couple of options for externalizing Spring configuration details into property files that can be managed outside of the deployed application:

- *Property placeholder configurers* replace placeholder variables placed in property values with values from an external properties file.
- *Property overriders* override bean property values with values from an external properties file.

In addition, the open source Jasypt project[1] offers alternative implementations of Spring's property placeholder configurer and overrider that can pull those values from encrypted properties files.

We'll look at all of these options, starting with the basic property placeholder configurer that comes with Spring.

---

1 http://www.jasypt.org

14.1.1 Replacing property placeholders

In versions of Spring prior to version 2.5, configuring a property placeholder configurer in Spring involved declaring PropertyPlaceholderConfigurer as a <bean> in the Spring context definition. Although that wasn't terribly complex, Spring 2.5 made it even easier with a new <context:property-placeholder> element in the context configuration namespace. Now a placeholder configurer can be configured like this:

```
<context:property-placeholder
    location="classpath:/db.properties" />
```

Here, the placeholder configurer is configured to pull property values from a file named db.properties that resides at the root of the classpath. But it could just as easily pull configuration data from a properties file on the file system:

```
<context:property-placeholder
    location="file:///etc/db.properties" />
```

As for the contents of the db.properties file, it would contain (at a minimum) the properties needed by the DriverManagerDataSource:

```
jdbc.driverClassName=org.hsqldb.jdbcDriver
jdbc.url=jdbc:hsqldb:hsql://localhost/spitter/spitter
jdbc.username=spitterAdmin
jdbc.password=t0ps3cr3t
```

Now we can replace the hardcoded values in the Spring configuration with placeholder variables based on the properties in db.properties:

```
<bean id="dataSource"
      class="org.springframework.jdbc.datasource.DriverManagerDataSource"
      p:driverClassName="${jdbc.driverClassName}"
      p:url="${jdbc.url}"
      p:username="${jdbc.username}"
      p:password="${jdbc.password}" />
```

For what it's worth, a property placeholder configurer's power isn't limited to bean property configuration in XML. You can also use it to configure @Value-annotated properties. For example, if you have a bean that needs the JDBC URL, you can use the ${jdbc.url} placeholder with @Value like this:

```
@Value("${jdbc.url}")
String databaseUrl;
```

What's more, you can even use placeholder variables in the properties file itself. For example, you could define the jdbc.url property using placeholder variables to break its configuration into multiple parts:

```
jdbc.protocol=hsqldb:hsql
db.server=localhost
db.name=spitter
jdbc.url=jdbc:${jdbc.protocol}://${db.server}/${db.name}/${db.name}
```

Here I've defined three properties, `jdbc.protocol`, `db.server`, and `db.name`. And I've also defined a fourth property that uses the other properties to construct the database URL.

That describes the essentials of property placeholder replacement in Spring. But we can do a few more things with a property placeholder configurer. First, let's see how to cope with property placeholder variables for which no property is defined.

REPLACING MISSING PROPERTIES

What would happen if a property placeholder variable referred to a property that hasn't been defined? Or worse, what if the `location` attribute pointed to a properties file that doesn't exist?

Well, what happens by default is that an exception will be thrown as the Spring context is being loaded and the beans are being created. But you can configure it to fail silently, without incident, by setting the `<context:property-placeholder>`'s `ignore-resource-not-found` and `ignore-unresolvable` attributes:

```
<context:property-placeholder
  location="file:///etc/myconfig.properties"
  ignore-resource-not-found="true"
  ignore-unresolvable="true"
  properties-ref="defaultConfiguration"/>
```

By setting these properties to `true`, the property placeholder configurer will withhold exceptions when the placeholder variable can't be resolved or if the properties file doesn't exist. Instead, the placeholders will remain unresolved.

Okay, but if the placeholders are unresolved, isn't that a bad thing? After all, `${jdbc.url}` can't be used to access a database. It's not a valid JDBC URL.

Instead of wiring useless placeholder variables, it'd be better to wire in default values. That's where the `properties-ref` attribute comes in handy. This attribute is set to the ID of a `java.util.Properties` bean that contains the properties to use by default. For our database properties, the following `<util:properties>` will hold the default database configuration values:

```
<util:properties id="defaultConfiguration">
  <prop key="jdbc.url">jdbc:hsqldb:hsql://localhost/spitter/spitter</prop>
  <prop key="jdbc.driverClassName">org.hsqldb.jdbcDriver</prop>
  <prop key="jdbc.username">spitterAdmin</prop>
  <prop key="jdbc.password">t0ps3cr3t</prop>
</util:properties>
```

Now, if any of the placeholder variables can't be found in the db.properties file, then the default values in the `defaultConfiguration` bean will be used.

RESOLVING PLACEHOLDER VARIABLES FROM SYSTEM PROPERTIES

At this point, we've seen how to resolve placeholder variables from a properties file and from a `<util:properties>` definition. But it's also possible to resolve them from system properties. All we must do is set the `system-properties-mode` attribute of `<component:property-placeholder>`. For example:

```
<context:property-placeholder
  location="file:///etc/myconfig.properties"
  ignore-resource-not-found="true"
  ignore-unresolvable="true"
  properties-ref="defaultConfiguration"
  system-properties-mode="OVERRIDE"/>
```

Here, the `system-properties-mode` has been set to `OVERRIDE` to indicate that `<component:property-placeholder>` should prefer system properties over those in db.properties or in the `defaultConfiguration` bean. `OVERRIDE` is just one of three values that the `system-properties-mode` attribute accepts:

- `FALLBACK`—Resolve placeholder variables from system properties if they can't be resolved from the properties file.
- `NEVER`—Never resolve placeholder variables from system properties.
- `OVERRIDE`—Prefer system properties over those in a properties file.

The default behavior of `<component:property-placeholder>` is to try to resolve placeholder variables from a properties file, but to fall back to system properties, if available—using the `FALLBACK` value of the `system-properties-mode` attribute.

14.1.2 Overriding properties

Another approach to external configuration in Spring is to override bean properties with those from a property file. In this case, no placeholders are required. Instead, the bean properties are either wired with default values or are left unwired altogether. If an external property matches a bean property, then the external value will be used instead of the one explicitly wired in Spring.

For example, consider the `dataSource` bean as it was before we learned about property placeholders. As a reminder, this is what it looked like with hardcoded values:

```
<bean id="dataSource"
      class="org.springframework.jdbc.datasource.DriverManagerDataSource"
      p:driverClassName="org.hsqldb.jdbcDriver"
      p:url="jdbc:hsqldb:hsql://localhost/spitter/spitter"
      p:username="spitterAdmin"
      p:password="t0ps3cr3t" />
```

In the previous section, I showed you how to declare default values using `<util :properties>` along with a property placeholder configurer. But with a property overrider, you can leave the default values in the bean properties—the overrider will take care of the rest.

Configuring a property overrider is much the same as configuring a property placeholder configurer. The difference is that instead of using `<component :property-placeholder>`, we'll use `<component:property-override>`:

```
<context:property-override
    location="classpath:/db.properties" />
```

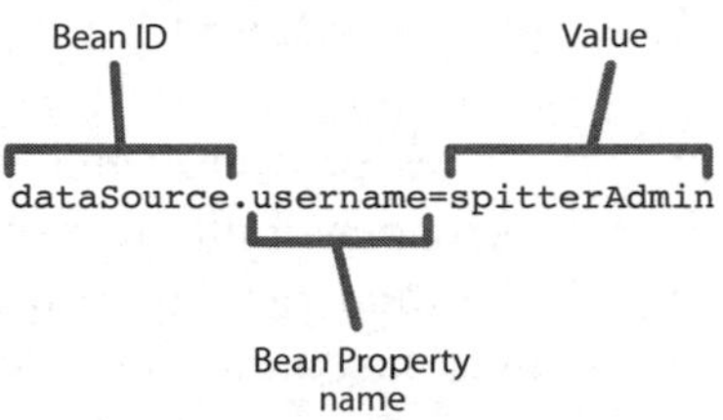

Figure 14.1 A property overrider determines which bean properties to override by mapping keys from a properties file to a bean ID and a property name.

In order for a property overrider to know which property in db.properties goes to which bean property in the Spring application context, you must map the bean and property name to the property name in the properties file. Figure 14.1 breaks down how this works.

As you can see, the property key in the external properties file is made up of a bean ID and a property name, separate by a period. If you flip back to the beginning of section 14.1, you'll see that the properties defined in db.properties were close, but not quite right. The properties all began with *jdbc.*. which would only work if our data source bean were given an ID of `jdbc`. But its ID is `dataSource`, so we'll need to make some adjustments to the db.properties file:

```
dataSource.driverClassName=org.hsqldb.jdbcDriver
dataSource.url=jdbc:hsqldb:hsql://localhost/spitter/spitter
dataSource.username=spitterAdmin
dataSource.password=t0ps3cr3t
```

Now the keys in db.properties match up with the `dataSource` bean and its properties. In the absence of the db.properties file, the explicitly wired values in the Spring configuration will be in play. But if the db.properties file exists and contains the properties we just defined, those properties will take precedence over those in the Spring XML configuration.

You may be interested to know that `<context:property-override>` can be configured with the same set of attributes as `<context:property-placeholder>`. You can set it up to resolve properties from a `<util:properties>` or from system properties.

At this point we've seen two options for externalizing property values. It should be easy to change the database URL or password without having to rebuild and redeploy the application. But one thing still isn't quite right. Even though the database password is no longer in the Spring context definition, it's still laying out in the open in some properties file somewhere. Let's see how to use Jasypt's property placeholder configurer and overrider to be able to encrypt the password stored in the external properties file.

14.1.3 Encrypting external properties

The *Jasypt project* is a wonderful library that simplifies encryption in Java. It does many things that are beyond the scope of this book. But germane to the topic of externalizing bean property configuration, Jasypt comes with special implementations of Spring's property placeholder configurer and property overrider that can read properties that are encrypted in the external property file.

As I mentioned earlier, Spring 2.5 introduced the `context` namespace and, in doing so, the `<context:property-placeholder>` and `<context:property-overrider>`

elements. Prior to that, you would have to configure PropertyPlaceholderConfigurer and PropertyOverrideConfigurer as <bean>s to get the same functionality.

Jasypt's implementations of the property placeholder configurer and property overrider don't currently have a special configuration namespace. Therefore, much like their pre-2.5 Spring counterparts, Jasypt's placeholder configurer and overrider must be configured as <bean> elements.

For example, the following <bean> configures a Jasypt property placeholder configurer:

```
<bean class=
   "org.jasypt.spring.properties.EncryptablePropertyPlaceholderConfigurer"
   p:location="file:///etc/db.properties">
  <constructor-arg ref="stringEncrypter" />
</bean>
```

Or, if a property overrider suits you better, then this <bean> will do the trick:

```
<bean class=
     "org.jasypt.spring.properties.EncryptablePropertyOverrideConfigurer"
    p:location="file:///etc/db.properties">
  <constructor-arg ref="stringEncrypter" />
</bean>
```

Whichever you choose, either will need to be configured with the location of the properties file through its location property. And both require a string encryptor object as a constructor argument.

In Jasypt, a *string encryptor* is a strategy class that handles the chore of encrypting String values. The placeholder configurer/overrider will use the string encryptor to decrypt any encrypted values it finds in the external properties file. For our purposes, the StandardPBEStringEncryptor that comes with Jasypt is perfectly sufficient:

```
<bean id="stringEncrypter"
      class="org.jasypt.encryption.pbe.StandardPBEStringEncryptor"
      p:config-ref="environmentConfig" />
```

The only things that StandardPBEStringEncryptor really needs to do its job are the algorithm and the password used to encrypt the data. If you look at the Javadoc for StandardPBEStringEncryptor, you'll see that it has algorithm and password properties—so we could configure those directly in the stringEncryptor bean.

But if we leave the encryption password in the Spring configuration, then have we really secured access to the database? Figuratively speaking, we'd be locking the keys to the database in a box and leaving the keys to the box on the table next to it. At best we've made it slightly more inconvenient, but certainly not secure.

Instead of configuring the password directly in Spring, I've configured StandardPBEStringEncryptor's config property with an EnvironmentStringPBEConfig. EnvironmentStringPBEConfig will let us configure encryption details, such as the encryption password, in environment variables. The EnvironmentStringPBEConfig is just another bean declared like this:

```
<bean id="environmentConfig" class=
     "org.jasypt.encryption.pbe.config.EnvironmentStringPBEConfig"
      p:algorithm="PBEWithMD5AndDES"
      p:passwordEnvName="DB_ENCRYPTION_PWD" />
```

I didn't mind configuring the algorithm in the Spring configuration—I've configured it as `PBEWithMD5AndDES`. The encryption password is what I want stored outside of Spring in an environment variable. Here, that environment variable is named `DB_ENCRYPTION_PWD`.

So you may be wondering how moving the encryption password to an environment variable makes this arrangement any more secure. Can't a hacker read an environment variable just as easily as they can read a Spring configuration file? The answer to that question is, yes. But the idea here is that the environment variable would be set by a system administrator just before the application is started and then unset once the application is underway. By then the data source properties will have been set and the environment variable will no longer be needed.

Externalizing bean property values is one way to manage configuration details that are sensitive and/or may need to be changed after the application has been deployed. Another way to cope with those situations is to externalize entire objects in JNDI and configure Spring to retrieve those objects into the Spring context. That's what we'll look at next.

14.2 Wiring JNDI objects

The *Java Naming and Directory Interface*, or *JNDI* as it's known to its friends, is a Java API that enables lookup of objects by name in a directory (often but not necessarily an LDAP directory). JNDI provides Java applications with access to a central repository for storing and retrieving applications objects. JNDI is typically used in Java EE applications to store and retrieve JDBC data sources and JTA transaction managers. You'll also find that EJB 3 session beans frequently find their home in JNDI.

But if some of our application objects are configured in JNDI, external to Spring, how can we inject them into the Spring-managed objects that need them?

In this section, we'll look at how Spring supports JNDI by providing a simplified abstraction layer above the standard JNDI API. Spring's JNDI abstraction makes it possible to declare JNDI lookup information in your Spring context definition file. Then you can wire a JNDI-managed object into the properties of other Spring beans as though the JNDI object were just another bean in the Spring application context.

To gain a deeper appreciation of what Spring's JNDI abstraction provides, let's look up an object from JNDI without Spring.

14.2.1 Working with conventional JNDI

Looking up objects in JNDI can be a tedious chore. For example, suppose you need to perform the common task of retrieving a `javax.sql.DataSource` from JNDI. Using the conventional JNDI APIs, you might write some code that looks like this:

```
InitialContext ctx = null;
try {
  ctx = new InitialContext();

  DataSource ds =
      (DataSource) ctx.lookup("java:comp/env/jdbc/SpitterDatasource");
} catch (NamingException ne) {
  // handle naming exception ...
} finally {
  if(ctx != null) {
      try {
        ctx.close();
      } catch (NamingException ne) {}
  }
}
```

If you've ever written JNDI lookup code before, you're probably familiar with what's going on in this code snippet. You may have written a similar incantation dozens of times before to raise an object out of JNDI. Before you repeat it again, take a closer look at what is going on:

- You must create and close an initial context for no other reason than to look up a `DataSource`. This may not seem like a lot of extra code, but it's extra plumbing that's not directly in line with the goal of retrieving a data source.
- You must catch or, at the least, rethrow a `javax.naming.NamingException`. If you choose to catch it, you must also deal with it appropriately. If you choose to rethrow it, the calling code will be forced to deal with it. Ultimately, someone somewhere will have to handle this exception.
- Your code is tightly coupled with a JNDI lookup. All your code needs is a `DataSource`. It doesn't matter whether it comes from JNDI or somewhere else. But if your code contains code like this, then you're stuck retrieving the `DataSource` from JNDI.
- Your code is tightly coupled with a specific JNDI name—in this case `java:comp/env/jdbc/SpitterDatasource`. Sure, you could extract that name into a properties file, but then you'll have to add even more plumbing code to look up the JNDI name from the properties file.

Upon closer inspection we find that most of the code is boilerplate JNDI lookup that looks much the same for all JNDI lookups. Only one line is directly responsible for retrieving the data source:

```
DataSource ds =
    (DataSource) ctx.lookup("java:comp/env/jdbc/SpitterDatasource");
```

Even more disquieting than boilerplate JNDI code is the fact that the application knows where the data source comes from. It's coded to *always* retrieve a data source from JNDI. As illustrated in figure 14.2, the DAO that uses the data source will be coupled to JNDI. This makes it almost impossible to use this code in a setting where JNDI isn't available or desirable.

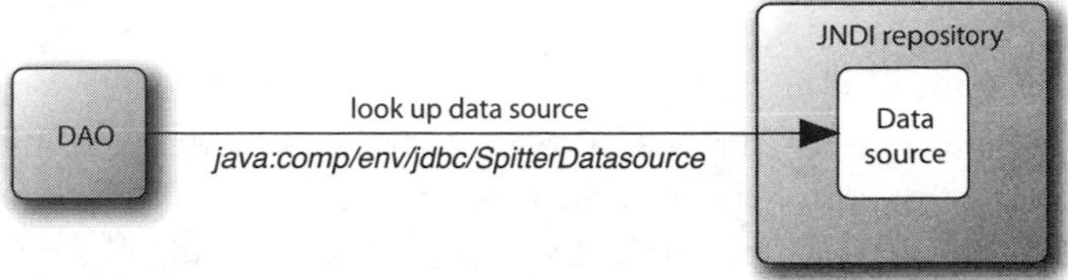

Figure 14.2 Using conventional JNDI to retrieve dependencies means that an object is coupled to JNDI, making it difficult to use the object anywhere that JNDI isn't available.

For instance, imagine that the data source lookup code is embedded in a class that's being unit tested. In an ideal unit test, we're testing an object in isolation without any direct dependence on specific objects. Although the class is decoupled from the data source through JNDI, it's coupled to JNDI itself. Therefore, our unit test has a direct dependence on JNDI and a JNDI server must be available for the unit test to run.

Regardless, this doesn't change the fact that sometimes you need to be able to look up objects in JNDI. DataSources are often configured in an application server to take advantage of the application server's connection pooling and then retrieved by the application code to access the database. How can your code get an object from JNDI without being dependent on JNDI?

The answer is found in dependency injection. Instead of asking for a data source from JNDI, you should write your code to accept a data source from anywhere—your code should have a DataSource property that's injected. Where the object comes from is of no concern to the class that needs it.

The data source object still lives in JNDI. So how can we configure Spring to inject an object that's stored in JNDI?

14.2.2 Injecting JNDI objects

Spring's jee configuration namespace holds the answer to working with JNDI in a loosely coupled manner. Within that namespace you'll find the <jee:jndi-lookup> element, which makes simple work of wiring a JNDI object into Spring.

To illustrate how this works, let's revisit an example from chapter 5. There, we used <jee:jndi-lookup> to retrieve a DataSource from JNDI:

```
<jee:jndi-lookup id="dataSource"
                 jndi-name="/jdbc/SpitterDS"
                 resource-ref="true" />
```

The jndi-name attribute specifies the name of the object in JNDI. By default, this is the name used to look up the object in JNDI. But if the lookup is occurring in a Java EE container, then a java:comp/env/ prefix may need to be added. You could manually add the prefix when specifying the value in jndi-name. But setting resource-ref to true will tell <jee:jndi-lookup> to do it for you.

With the dataSource bean declared, you may now wire it into a dataSource property. For instance, you may use it to configure a Hibernate session factory:

```
<bean id="sessionFactory"
  class="org.springframework.orm.hibernate3.annotation.
                                    ➥ AnnotationSessionFactoryBean">
```

```
  <property name="dataSource" ref="dataSource" />
  ...
</bean>
```

As shown in figure 14.3, when Spring wires the `sessionFactory` bean, it'll inject the `DataSource` object retrieved from JNDI into the session factory's `dataSource` property.

The great thing about using `<jee:jndi-lookup>` to look up an object in JNDI is that the only part of the code that knows that the `DataSource` is retrieved from JNDI is the XML declaration of the `dataSource` bean. The `sessionFactory` bean doesn't know (or care) where the `DataSource` came from. This means that if you decide that you'd rather get your `DataSource` from a JDBC driver manager, all you need to do is redefine the `dataSource` bean to be a `DriverManagerDataSource`.

Now our data source is retrieved from JNDI and then injected into the session factory. No more explicit JNDI lookup code! Whenever we need it, the data source is always handy in the Spring application context as the `dataSource` bean.

As you've seen, wiring a JNDI-managed bean in Spring is fairly simple. Now let's explore a few ways that we can influence when and how the object is retrieved from JNDI, starting with caching.

CACHING JNDI OBJECTS

Often, the objects retrieved from JNDI will be used more than once. A data source, for example, will be needed every time you access the database. It'd be inefficient to repeatedly retrieve the data source from JNDI every time that it's needed. For that reason, `<jee:jndi-lookup>` caches the object that it retrieves from JNDI by default.

Caching is good in most circumstances. But it precludes hot redeployment of objects in JNDI. If you were to change the object in JNDI, the Spring application would need to be restarted so that the new object can be retrieved.

If your application is retrieving an object from JNDI that will change frequently, you'll want to turn caching off for `<jee:jndi-lookup>`. To turn caching off, you'll need to set the `cache` attribute to `false`:

```
<jee:jndi-lookup id="dataSource"
    jndi-name="/jdbc/SpitterDS"
    resource-ref="true"
    cache="false"
    proxy-interface="javax.sql.DataSource" />
```

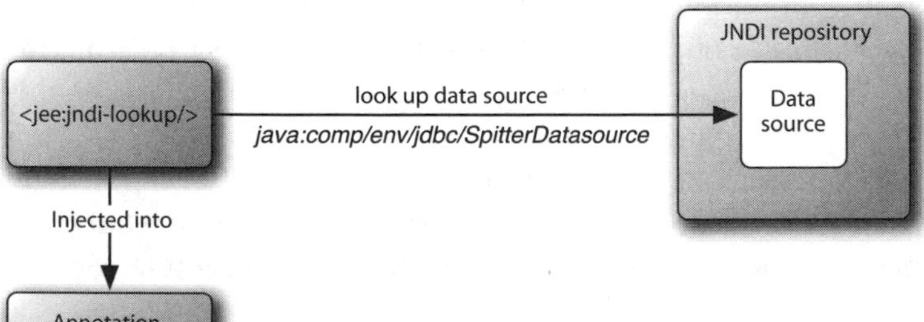

Figure 14.3 `<jee:jndi-lookup>` looks up an object from JNDI, making it available as a bean in the Spring application context. From there, it can be wired into any other object that depends on it.

Setting the `cache` attribute to `false` tells `<jee:jndi-lookup>` to always fetch the object from JNDI. Note that the `proxy-interface` attribute has also been set. Since the JNDI object can be changed at any time, there's no way for `<jee:jndi-lookup>` to know the actual type of the object. The `proxy-interface` attribute specifies a type that's expected for the object retrieved from JNDI.

LAZILY LOADING JNDI OBJECTS

Sometimes your application won't need to retrieve the JNDI object right away. For instance, suppose that a JNDI object is only used in an obscure branch of your application's code. In that situation, it may not be desirable to load the object until it's actually needed.

By default, `<jee:jndi-lookup>` fetches objects from JNDI when the application context is started. Nevertheless, you can configure it to wait to retrieve the object until it's needed by setting the `lookup-on-startup` attribute to `false`:

```
<jee:jndi-lookup id="dataSource"
    jndi-name="/jdbc/SpitterDS"
    resource-ref="true"
    lookup-on-startup="false"
    proxy-interface="javax.sql.DataSource" />
```

As with the `cache` attribute, you'll need to set the `lookup-on-startup` attribute when setting `lookup-on-startup` to `false`. That's because `<jee:jndi-lookup>` won't know the type of the object being retrieved until it's actually retrieved. The `proxy-interface` attribute tells it what type to expect from the fetched object.

FALLBACK OBJECTS

You now know how to wire JNDI objects in Spring and have a JNDI-loaded data source to show for it. Life is good. But what if the object can't be found in JNDI?

For instance, maybe your application can count on a data source being available in JNDI when running in a production environment. But that arrangement may not be practical in a development environment. If Spring is configured to retrieve its data source from JNDI for production, the lookup will fail in development. How can we make sure that a data source bean is always available from JNDI in production and explicitly configured in development?

As you've seen, `<jee:jndi-lookup>` is great for retrieving objects from JNDI and wiring them in a Spring application context. But it also has a fallback mechanism that can account for situations where the requested object can't be found in JNDI. All you must do is configure its `default-ref` attribute.

For example, suppose that you've declared a data source in Spring using `DriverManagerDataSource` as follows:

```
<bean id="devDataSource"
      class="org.springframework.jdbc.datasource.DriverManagerDataSource"
      lazy-init="true">
  <property name="driverClassName"
            value="org.hsqldb.jdbcDriver" />
  <property name="url"
```

```
        value="jdbc:hsqldb:hsql://localhost/spitter/spitter" />
  <property name="username" value="sa" />
  <property name="password" value="" />
</bean>
```

This is the data source that you'll use in development. But in production, you'd rather use a data source configured in JNDI by the system administrators. If that's the case, you'll configure the `<jee:jndi-lookup>` element like this:

```
<jee:jndi-lookup id="dataSource"
    jndi-name="/jdbc/SpitterDS"
    resource-ref="true"
    default-ref="devDataSource" />
```

Here, we've wired the `default-ref` attribute with a reference to the `devDataSource` bean. If `<jee:jndi-lookup>` can't find an object in JNDI at `jdbc/SpitterDS`, it'll use the `devDataSource` bean as its object. And because the fallback datasource bean has `lazy-init` set to `true`, it won't be created unless it's needed.

As you can see, it's reasonably simple to use `<jee:jndi-lookup>` to wire JNDI-managed objects into a Spring application context. As it turns out, `<jee:jndi-lookup>` can also be used to wire EJB session beans into a Spring application context. Let's see how to do that.

14.2.3 Wiring EJBs in Spring

In EJB 3, session beans are just objects stored away in JNDI, much like any other object in JNDI. Therefore, `<jee:jndi-lookup>` is perfectly sufficient for retrieving EJB 3 session beans. But what if you want to wire an EJB 2 session bean into the Spring application context?

To access an EJB 2 stateless session bean, you start by retrieving an object from JNDI. But that object is an implementation of the EJB's home interface, not the EJB itself. To get a handle to the EJB, you have to call the `create()` method on the home interface.

Fortunately, you don't need to deal with those details when using Spring to access EJB 2 session beans. Instead of using `<jee:jndi-lookup>`, Spring offers two other elements in the `jee` namespace that are expressly for accessing EJBs:

- `<jee:local-slsb>` to access local stateless session beans
- `<jee:remote-slsb>` to access remote stateless session beans

Both of these elements work in a way very similar to `<jee:jndi-lookup>`. For example, to declare a reference to a remote stateless session bean in Spring, use `<jee:remote-slsb>` like this:

```
<jee:remote-slsb id="myEJB"
    jndi-name="my.ejb"
    business-interface="com.habuma.ejb.MyEJB" />
```

The `jndi-name` attribute is the JNDI name used to lookup the EJB's home interface. Meanwhile, the `business-interface` specifies the business interface the EJB implements. With an EJB reference declared like this, the `myEJB` bean can then be wired into any other bean's property that is of the type `com.habuma.ejb.MyEJB`.

Similarly, a reference to a local stateless session bean can be declared with the `<jee:local-slsb>` element like this:

```
<jee:local-slsb id="myEJB"
    jndi-name="my.ejb"
    business-interface="com.habuma.ejb.MyEJB" />
```

Here, we've discussed using the `<jee:local-slsb>` and `<jee:remote-slsb>` elements to declare EJB 2 session beans in Spring. But what's especially interesting about these elements is that they can also be used to wire EJB 3 session beans. They're smart enough to retrieve the object requested from JNDI and determine whether they're dealing with an EJB 2 home interface or an EJB 3 session bean. If it's an EJB 2 home interface, they'll call `create()` for you. Otherwise, they'll assume that they're dealing with an EJB 3 bean and make that object available in the Spring context.

Looking up objects in JNDI comes in handy when you need access to objects that are configured external to Spring. As you've seen, data sources may be configured through an application server and accessed through JNDI. And as you'll see next, Spring's JNDI lookup capability can be useful when sending email. Let's take a look at Spring's email abstraction layer next.

14.3 Sending email

In chapter 12, we used Spring messaging support to asynchronously queue up jobs to send spittle alerts to other Spitter application users. Now we're ready to use Spring's email support to send the emails.

Spring comes with an email abstraction API that makes simple work of sending emails.

14.3.1 Configuring a mail sender

At the heart of Spring's email abstraction is the `MailSender` interface. As its name implies and as illustrated in figure 14.4, a `MailSender` implementation sends email. Spring comes with one implementation of the `MailSender` interface, `JavaMailSenderImpl`.

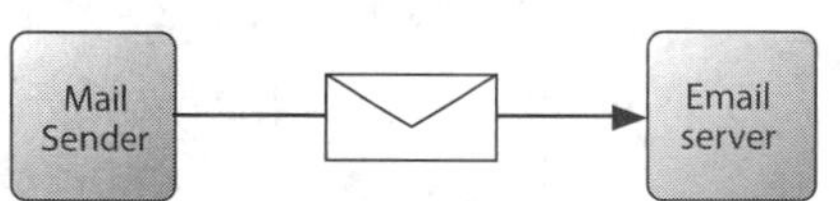

Figure 14.4 Spring's `MailSender` interface is the primary component of Spring's email abstraction API. It sends an email to a mail server for delivery.

> **WHAT ABOUT COSMAILSENDERIMPL?** Older versions of Spring, up to and including Spring 2.0, included another implementation of `MailSender` called `CosMailSenderImpl`. That implementation was removed in Spring 2.5. If you're still using it, you'll need to switch to `JavaMailSenderImpl` before moving up to Spring 2.5 or Spring 3.0.

To use JavaMailSenderImpl, we'll declare it as a <bean> in the Spring application context:

```
<bean id="mailSender"
      class="org.springframework.mail.javamail.JavaMailSenderImpl"
      p:host="${mailserver.host}" />
```

The host property specifies the hostname for the mail server that we'll use to send the email. Here it's configured with a placeholder variable so that we can manage the mail server configuration outside of Spring. By default, JavaMailSenderImpl assumes that the mail server is listening on port 25 (the standard SMTP port). If your mail server is listening on a different port, specify the correct port number using the port property. For example:

```
<bean id="mailSender"
      class="org.springframework.mail.javamail.JavaMailSenderImpl"
      p:host="${mailserver.host}"
      p:port="${mailserver.port}"/>
```

Likewise, if the mail server requires authentication, you'll also want to set values for the username and password properties:

```
<bean id="mailSender"
      class="org.springframework.mail.javamail.JavaMailSenderImpl"
      p:host="${mailserver.host}"
      p:port="${mailserver.port}"
      p:username="${mailserver.username}"
      p:password="${mailserver.password}" />
```

This shows how to fully configure the mail sender in Spring with all of the details it'll need to access the mail server. Optionally, you may prefer to use an existing mail session configured in JNDI. Let's see how to configure JavaMailSenderImpl to use a mail session that's resident in JNDI.

USING A JNDI MAIL SESSION

You may already have a javax.mail.MailSession configured in JNDI (or perhaps one was placed there by your application server). If so then Spring's JavaMailSenderImpl offers you an option to use the MailSender that you already have ready to use from JNDI.

We've seen how to retrieve objects from JNDI using Spring's <jee:jndi-lookup> element. So let's use that to reference a mail session from JNDI:

```
<jee:jndi-lookup id="mailSession"
    jndi-name="mail/Session" resource-ref="true" />
```

With the mail sender in hand, we can now wire it into the mailSender bean like this:

```
<bean id="mailSender"
      class="org.springframework.mail.javamail.JavaMailSenderImpl"
      p:session-ref="mailSession" />
```

By wiring the mail session into the `session` property of `JavaMailSenderImpl`, we've completely replaced the explicit server (and username/password) configuration from before. Now the mail session is completely configured and managed in JNDI. `JavaMailSenderImpl` can focus on sending emails and not dealing with the mail server itself.

WIRING THE MAIL SENDER INTO A SERVICE BEAN

Now that the mail sender has been configured, it's time to wire it into the bean that will use it. In the Spitter application, the `SpitterEmailServiceImpl` class is the most appropriate place to send the email from. This class has a `mailSender` property that's annotated with `@Autowired`:

```
@Autowired
JavaMailSender mailSender;
```

When Spring creates `SpitterEmailServiceImpl` as a bean, it'll try to find a bean that implements `MailSender` that it can wire into the `mailSender` property. It should find our `mailSender` bean and use that. With the `mailSender` bean wired in, we're ready to construct and send emails.

14.3.2 Constructing the email

Since we want to send an email to a Spitter user to alert them of new spittles that their friends may have written, we'll need a method that, given an email address and a `Spittle` object, will send that email. The `sendSimpleSpittleEmail()` method uses the mail sender to do just that.

Listing 14.1 Sending an email with Spring using a `MailSender`

```
public void sendSimpleSpittleEmail(String to, Spittle spittle) {
  SimpleMailMessage message = new SimpleMailMessage();        <- Construct message

  String spitterName = spittle.getSpitter().getFullName();
  message.setFrom("noreply@spitter.com");                     <- Address email
  message.setTo(to);
  message.setSubject("New spittle from " + spitterName);

  message.setText(spitterName + " says: " +                   <- Set message text

          spittle.getText());

  mailSender.send(message);                                   <- Send email
}
```

The first thing that `sendSimpleSpittleEmail()` does is construct an instance of a `SimpleMailMessage`. This mail message object, as its name implies, is perfect for sending no-nonsense email messages.

Next, the details of the message are set. The sender and recipient of the email are specified via the `setFrom()` and `setTo()` methods on the mail message. After setting the subject with `setSubject()`, the virtual "envelope" has been addressed. All that's left is to call `setText()` to set the message's content.

The last step is to pass the message to the mail sender's `send()` method and the email is on its way.

Simple emails are a fine start. But what if you want to add an attachment? Or what if you want the body of the email to have a polished look? Let's see how to dress up our emails sent by Spring, starting with simply adding an attachment.

ADDING ATTACHMENTS

The trick to sending emails with attachments is to create multipart messages—emails composed of multiple parts, one of which is the body of the email and the other parts being the attachments.

The `SimpleMailMessage` class is too… well… simple for sending attachments. To send multipart emails, you need to create a *MIME (Multipurpose Internet Mail Extensions)* message. The mail sender object's `createMimeMessage()` method can get you started:

```
MimeMessage message = mailSender.createMimeMessage();
```

There you go. We now have a MIME message to work with. It seems that all we need to do is give it to and from addresses, a subject, some text, and an attachment. Though that's true, it's not as straightforward as you might think. The `javax.mail.internet.MimeMessage` class has an API that's too cumbersome to use on its own. Fortunately, Spring provides `MimeMessageHelper` to lend a hand.

To use `MimeMessageHelper`, instantiate an instance of it, passing in the `MimeMessage` to its constructor:

```
MimeMessageHelper helper = new MimeMessageHelper(message, true);
```

The second parameter to the constructor, a Boolean `true` as shown here, indicates that this message is to be a multipart message.

From the `MimeMessageHelper` instance, we're ready to assemble our email message. The only major difference here is that you'll provide the email specifics through methods on the helper instead of on the message itself:

```
String spitterName = spittle.getSpitter().getFullName();
helper.setFrom("noreply@spitter.com");
helper.setTo(to);
helper.setSubject("New spittle from " + spitterName);
helper.setText(spitterName + " says: " + spittle.getText());
```

The only thing needed before you can send the email is to attach the coupon image. To do that, you'll need to load the image as a resource and then pass that resource in as you call the helper's `addAttachment()` method:

```
FileSystemResource couponImage =
      new FileSystemResource("/collateral/coupon.png");
helper.addAttachment("Coupon.png", couponImage);
```

Here, you're using Spring's `FileSystemResource` to load coupon.png from within the application's classpath. From there, you call `addAttachment()`. The first parameter is the name to be given to the attachment in the email. The second parameter is the image's resource.

The multipart email has been constructed. Now you're ready to send it. The complete sendSpittleEmailWithAttachment() method is shown next.

Listing 14.2 MimeMessageHelper simplifies sending emails with attachments.

```
public void sendSpittleEmailWithAttachment(
        String to, Spittle spittle) throws MessagingException {
  MimeMessage message = mailSender.createMimeMessage();
  MimeMessageHelper helper =
      new MimeMessageHelper(message, true);                 // Construct message helper

  String spitterName = spittle.getSpitter().getFullName();
  helper.setFrom("noreply@spitter.com");
  helper.setTo(to);
  helper.setSubject("New spittle from " + spitterName);

  helper.setText(spitterName + " says: " + spittle.getText());

  FileSystemResource couponImage =
      new FileSystemResource("/collateral/coupon.png");
  helper.addAttachment("Coupon.png", couponImage);         // Add attachment

  mailSender.send(message);
}
```

Adding attachments to an email is only one thing you can do with multipart emails. In addition, by specifying that the body of the email is HTML, you can produce polished emails that look much nicer than flat text. Let's see how to send attractive-looking emails using Spring's MimeMessageHelper.

SENDING EMAILS WITH RICH CONTENT

Sending a rich email isn't much different than sending plain-text emails. The key is to set the message's text as HTML. Doing that is as simple as passing in an HTML string to the helper's setText() method and true as the second parameter:

```
helper.setText("<html><body><img src='cid:spitterLogo'>" +
    "<h4>" + spittle.getSpitter().getFullName() + " says...</h4>" +
    "<i>" + spittle.getText() + "</i>" +
        "</body></html>", true);
```

The second parameter indicates that the text passed into the first parameter is HTML, so that the message part's content type will be set accordingly.

Note that the HTML passed in has an <img> tag to display the Spitter application's logo as part of the email. The src attribute could be set to a standard http: URL to pull the Spitter logo from the web. But here, we've embedded the logo image in the email itself. The value cid:spitterLogo indicates that there will be an image in one of the message's parts identified as spitterLogo.

Adding the embedded image to the message is much like adding an attachment. Instead of calling the helper's addAttachment() method, you must call the addInline() method:

```
ClassPathResource image = new ClassPathResource("spitter_logo_50.png");
helper.addInline("spitterLogo", image);
```

The first parameter to addInline specifies the identity of the inline image—which is the same as was specified by the <img>'s src attribute. The second parameter is the resource reference for the image, created here using Spring's ClassPathResource to retrieve the image from the application's classpath.

Aside from the slightly different call to setText() and the use of the addInline() method, sending an email with rich content is much like how you sent a plain-text message with attachments. For sake of comparison, here's the new sendRichSpitterEmail() method.

```
public void sendRichSpitterEmail(String to, Spittle spittle) throws Messaging
  Exception {
  MimeMessage message = mailSender.createMimeMessage();
  MimeMessageHelper helper = new MimeMessageHelper(message, true);
  helper.setFrom("noreply@spitter.com");
  helper.setTo("craig@habuma.com");
  helper.setSubject("New spittle from " +
          spittle.getSpitter().getFullName());
                                                                    Set
  helper.setText("<html><body><img src='cid:spitterLogo'>" +    <-- HTML body

      "<h4>" + spittle.getSpitter().getFullName() + " says...</h4>" +
      "<i>" + spittle.getText() + "</i>" +
          "</body></html>", true);

  ClassPathResource image = new ClassPathResource("spitter_logo_50.png");
  helper.addInline("spitterLogo", image);   <-- Add
  mailSender.send(message);                     inline image
}
```

And now you're sending emails with rich content and embedded images! You could stop here and call your email code complete. But it bugs me that the email's body was created by using string concatenation to construct an HTML message. Before we put the email topic to rest, let's see how to replace that string-concatenated message with a template.

CREATING EMAIL TEMPLATES

The problem with constructing an email message using string concatenation is that it's not clear what the resulting email will look like. It's hard enough to mentally parse HTML markup to imagine how it might appear when rendered. But mixing that HTML up within Java code compounds the issue. Moreover, it might be nice to extract the email layout into a template that a graphic designer (who has an aversion to Java code) can produce.

What we need is a way to express the email layout in something close to what the resulting HTML will look like and then transform that template into a String to be passed into the setText() method on the message helper. When it comes to transforming templates into strings, Apache Velocity[2] is one of the best options available.

---

[2] http://velocity.apache.org

To use Velocity to lay out our email messages, we'll first need to wire a `VelocityEngine` into `SpitterEmailServiceImpl`. Spring provides a handy factory bean called `VelocityEngineFactoryBean` that will produce a `VelocityEngine` in the Spring application context. The declaration for `VelocityEngineFactoryBean` looks like this:

```
<bean id="velocityEngine"
      class="org.springframework.ui.velocity.VelocityEngineFactoryBean">
  <property name="velocityProperties">
    <value>
resource.loader=class
class.resource.loader.class=org.apache.velocity.runtime.resource.loader.Class
     pathResourceLoader
    </value>
  </property>
</bean>
```

The only property that needs to be set on `VelocityEngineFactoryBean` is `velocityProperties`. In this case, we're configuring it to load Velocity templates from the classpath (see the Velocity documentation for more details on how to configure Velocity).

Now we can wire the Velocity engine into `SpitterEmailServiceImpl`. Since `SpitterEmailServiceImpl` is automatically registered with the component scanner, we can use `@Autowired` to automatically wire a `velocityEngine` property:

```
@Autowired
  VelocityEngine velocityEngine;
```

Now that the `velocityEngine` property is available, we can use it to transform a Velocity template into a `String` to send as our email text. To help out with that, Spring comes with `VelocityEngineUtils` to make simple work of merging a Velocity template and some model data into a `String`. Here's how we might use it:

```
Map<String, String> model = new HashMap<String, String>();
    model.put("spitterName", spitterName);
    model.put("spittleText", spittle.getText());
    String emailText = VelocityEngineUtils.mergeTemplateIntoString(
            velocityEngine, "emailTemplate.vm", model );
```

In preparation for processing the template, we start by creating a `Map` to hold the model data used by the template. In our previous string-concatenated code, we needed the full name of the spitter and the text of their spittle, so we'll need that here as well. To produce the merged email text, we then just need to call `VelocityEngineUtils`'s `mergeTemplateIntoString()` method, passing in the Velocity engine, the path to the template (relative to the root of the classpath), and the model map.

All that's left to be done in the Java code is to hand off the merged email text to the message helper's `setText()` method:

```
helper.setText(emailText, true);
```

As for the template itself, that's sitting at the root of the classpath in a file called emailTemplate.vm, which looks like this:

```
<html>
  <body>
    <img src='cid:spitterLogo'>
    <h4>${spitterName} says...</h4>
    <i>${spittleText}</i>
  </body>
</html>
```

As you can see, the template file is a lot easier to read than the string-concatenated version from before. Consequently, it's also easier to maintain and edit. Figure 14.5 gives a sample of the kind of email it might produce.

After looking at figure 14.5, I see a lot of opportunity left to dress up the template so that the email appears much nicer. But, as they say, I'll leave that as an exercise for the reader.

But for now, we have one more Spring attraction to look at. And I've saved one of the best for last! Let's see how to make short work of running jobs in the background using Spring.

14.4 Scheduling and background tasks

The better part of the functionality in most applications happens in response to something that the application's users have done. A user fills in a form and then clicks a button, and the application reacts by processing the data, persisting it to a database, and producing some output.

But sometimes applications have work of their own to do, without the user being involved. While the users click the buttons, the application can be handling background jobs that don't involve user interaction.

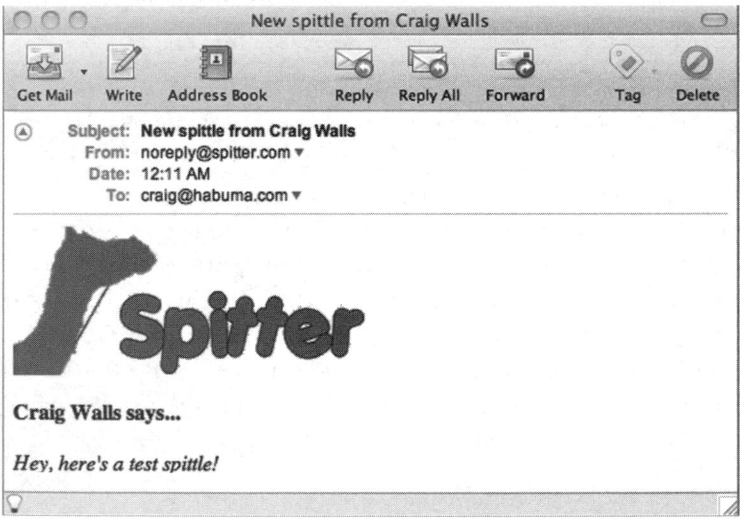

Figure 14.5 A Velocity template and some embedded images can dress up an otherwise ho-hum email.

There are two kinds of background jobs to choose from:

- Scheduled jobs
- Asynchronous methods

Scheduled jobs involve functionality that takes place every so often, either at some specified period or at some specific time. Asynchronous methods, on the other hand, are methods that are called, but that return immediately so that the caller can proceed—while the asynchronous method continues running in the background.

Regardless of which kind of background job you need, you'll need to add a single line of configuration to the Spring application context:

```
<task:annotation-driven/>
```

The `<task:annotation-driven/>` element sets Spring up to automatically support scheduled and asynchronous methods. These methods are identified with the `@Scheduled` and `@Async` methods, respectively.

Let's see how to use these annotations, starting with using the `@Scheduled` annotation to fire off methods on a schedule.

14.4.1 Declaring scheduled methods

If you've been working with Spring for awhile, then you know that Spring has supported scheduling of method invocations for a long time. But until recently, the Spring configuration required to schedule methods was involved. In the second edition of this book, I spent 10 pages showing how to invoke methods periodically.

Spring 3 changes that with the new `@Scheduled` annotation. What used to take several lines of XML and a handful of beans now can be done with the `<task:annotation-driven>` element and a single annotation. I definitely won't need 10 pages to show you how it works.

To schedule a method, all you have to do is to annotate it with `@Scheduled`. For example, to have Spring automatically invoke a method every 24 hours (86,400,000 milliseconds):

```
@Scheduled(fixedRate=86400000)
public void archiveOldSpittles() {
  // ...
}
```

The `fixedRate` attribute indicates that the method should be invoked periodically, every so many milliseconds. In this case, 86,400,000 milliseconds will pass between the start of each invocation. If you'd rather specify the time that passes in between invocations (between the completion of one invocation and the start of the next), then use the `fixedDelay` attribute instead:

```
@Scheduled(fixedDelay=86400000)
public void archiveOldSpittles() {
  // ...
}
```

Running a task at a given interval can be handy. But you may want more precise control over when a method is invoked. With fixedRate and fixedDelay, you can only control how often a method is invoked, but not *when* it happens. To be specific about the times a method should be called, use the cron attribute:

```
@Scheduled(cron="0 0 0 * * SAT")
public void archiveOldSpittles() {
  // ...
}
```

The value given to the cron attribute is a Cron expression. For those who aren't so well-versed in Cron expressions, let's break down the cron attribute. The Cron expression is made up of six (or possibly seven) time elements, separated by spaces. In order from left to right, the elements are defined as follows:

1. Seconds (0-59)
2. Minutes (0-59)
3. Hours (0-23)
4. Day of month (1-31)
5. Month (1-12 or JAN-DEC)
6. Day of week (1-7 or SUN-SAT)
7. Year (1970-2099)

Each of these elements can be specified with an explicit value (6), a range (9-12), a list (9,11,13), or a wildcard (for example, *). The day of the month and day of the week elements are mutually exclusive, so you should also indicate which one of the fields you don't want to set by specifying it with a question mark (?). Table 14.1 shows some example Cron expressions that could be used with the cron attribute.

In the example, I've specified that old Spittles should be archived every Saturday at midnight. But since this method is scheduled using a Cron expression, the scheduling options are virtually limitless. Where fixedRate and fixedDelay are limited to fixed time periods, a Cron-scheduled method could be scheduled to run at odd times. I'm sure you can dream up some interesting Cron expressions to schedule methods with.

Table 14.1 Some sample Cron expressions

Cron expression	What it means
`0 0 10,14,16 * * ?`	Every day at 10 a.m., 2 p.m., and 4 p.m.
`0 0,15,30,45 * 1-30 * ?`	Every 15 minutes on the first 30 days of the month
`30 0 0 1 1 ? 2012`	30 seconds after midnight on January 1, 2012
`0 0 8-17 ? * MON-FRI`	Every working hour of every business day

14.4.2 Declaring asynchronous methods

When it comes to dealing with the human users of an application, there are two kinds of application performance: actual and perceived. The *actual performance* of an application (the discrete measurement of how long it takes to perform an operation) is certainly important. But even if the actual performance is less than ideal, its effect on the users can be mitigated with the perceived performance.

Perceived performance is exactly what it sounds like. Who cares how long it takes to do something, as long as the user sees something happening immediately? For example, let's suppose that the act of adding a `Spittle` is a costly operation. If handled synchronously, the perceived performance would be a function of the actual performance. The user would have to wait while the `Spittle` is saved.

But if there were only some way for the `SpitterService`'s `saveSpittle()` method to be handled asynchronously, then the application could be presenting a new page to the user while the persistence logic is handled in the background. That's what the `@Async` annotation is for.

`@Async` is a simple annotation and has no attributes to set. All you need to do is use it to annotate a bean method and that method becomes asynchronous. It couldn't be any simpler than that.

For example, here's roughly what the `SpittleServiceImpl`'s `saveSpittle()` method might look like as an asynchronous method:

```
@Async
public void addSpittle(Spittle spittle) {
    ...
}
```

That's really all there is to it. When the `saveSpittle()` method is called, control will return to the caller immediately. Meanwhile, the `saveSpittle()` method will continue running in the background.

You might be wondering what would happen if an asynchronous method needs to return something to the caller. If the method returns immediately, then how can it possibly pass results back to the caller?

Since Spring asynchronous methods are based on Java's concurrency API, they can return an object that implements `java.util.concurrent.Future`. This interface represents a holder for some value that will eventually be available at some point after the method returns, but not necessarily at the point that the method returns. Spring comes with a convenient implementation of `Future` called `AsyncResult` that makes it easy to work with future values.

For example, suppose that you have an asynchronous method that attempts to perform some complex and long-running calculation. You want the method to run in the background, but once it's finished you want to be able to see what the results were. In that case, you might write the method something like this:

```
@Async
public Future<Long> performSomeReallyHairyMath(long input) {
    // ...

    return new AsyncResult<Long>(result);
}
```

This method can take as long as it needs to produce the result, while the caller can go about any other business that needs to be done. The caller will receive a `Future` object (actually, an `AsyncResult`) to hold on to while the result is calculated.

Once the result is ready, the caller can retrieve it by calling the `get()` method on the `Future` object. Until then, the caller can check in on the status of the result by calling `isDone()` and `isCancelled()`.

14.5 Summary

In this chapter, we've covered a mixed bag of topics—Spring features that, by themselves, didn't have a home in any other chapter.

We started by looking at how to externalize bean property values using property placeholder configurers and overriders. We also learned how to not only externalize properties, but to encrypt them so that prying eyes won't gain access to the sensitive configuration details of our application.

We then took externalization up a notch by pushing entire objects into JNDI and then configuring Spring to pull those objects into the Spring context where they can be wired into other beans as if they were beans themselves.

Then we looked at sending emails with Spring. Although Spring's email abstraction is hardly the most exciting thing that Spring can do, it beats writing code to send email without Spring. We saw how to send simple emails, HTML-based emails, and emails with attachments and embedded content.

Finally, we tinkered with background jobs in Spring. We started by annotating methods to run on a specific schedule. Then we annotated methods to run asynchronously with our application so that the perceived performance of the application could be improved.

14.6 The end...?

I hate to admit it, but we've come to the end of the book. That's not to say that there's nothing else to learn about Spring. As I stated in the preface, I could literally write *volumes* about Spring. But if I did that, this book would never have made it into your hands and I'd never know the satisfaction of a full night's sleep.

Although some tough decisions had to be made with regard to the scope of this book, I think we've covered the most important topics that you'll need to build applications with Spring. And now you're equipped to explore those other topics on your own.

So, although this chapter ends *Spring in Action*, your journey in Spring is just beginning. I encourage you to leverage what you've learned here to dig more into the other areas of Spring such as Spring Integration, Spring Batch, Spring Dynamic Modules, and (my personal favorite) Spring Roo. Fortunately, Manning has *in Action* books on each of these topics to help you explore further:

- *Spring Integration in Action* by Mark Fisher, Jonas Partner, Marius Bogoevici, and Iwein Fuld
- *Spring Batch in Action* by Thierry Templier and Arnaud Cogoluègnes
- *Spring Dynamic Modules in Action* by Arnaud Cogoluègnes, Thierry Templier, and Andy Piper
- *Roo in Action* by Gordon Dickens and Ken Rimple

And you can always hang out at the Spring forums—http://forum.springframework.org—to learn about these and other Spring-related projects.

It's been fun for me. I hope it's been fun for you.

index

Symbols

^ operator 56
- operator 56
! operator 58
?: operator 58
* operator 56
/ operator 56
&& operator 92
% operator 56
+ operator 56
== operator 57
> and < operators 57
>= and <= operators 57
|| operator 92

A

Accept header 289, 291, 305
access attribute 233, 237
Acegi Security. *See* Spring Security
ACID, defined 148
action states 203–204
<action-state> element 204
ActiveMQ 316–317
actual performance 373
addAttachment() method 366
addInline() method 367
ADO.NET 26
Adobe AIR 26
Adobe Flex 26
advice 86–87
  after advice 87
  after-returning advice 87, 95
  after-throwing 87
  <aop:advisor> element 93
  around advice 87
  before advice 87
  method before advice 95
  passing parameters to 98, 100
  <tx:advice> element 160
  written in Java 89
after advice 14, 87
  <aop:after> element 93
  declaring 95, 97
afterPropertiesSet() method 20, 40
after-returning advice 87, 93, 95, 108
after-throwing advice 87, 93, 95
algorithm property 356
Amazon S3 196–197
Amazon Simple Storage. *See* Amazon S3
ambiguous dependencies 72–73
<amq:queue> element 317
<amq:topic> element 317
and operator 58
annotatedClasses property 136
@annotation pointcut designator 91
AnnotationAwareAspectJAutoProxyCreator class 104
annotations
  and autodiscovery 78–79
  and introduction 106–107
  and Spring Expression Language 76–77
  and Spring MVC 170
  annotation-driven MBeans 340–341
  annotation-driven transactions 162–163
  AnnotationSessionFactoryBean 135
  @Around 104
  @AspectJ 32, 102, 107
  @Async 373–374
  @Autowired 27, 71, 74, 137, 262, 272, 365

annotations *(continued)*
@Bean 81
@Before 103
@Component 27, 78, 171, 329
@Configuration 81
@Controller 78, 171, 182
@CookieValue 28
@DeclareParents 106
enabling autowiring with 70
@Entity 136
@Inject 74, 76, 171
JSR-303 28
@ManagedAttribute 340
@ManagedOperation 340
@ManagedResource 340
@MappedSuperclass 136
@MessageDriven 326
@Named 75
@PathVariable 188, 282, 284
@Pattern 190
@Pointcut 103
@PostAuthorize 248
@PostConstruct 27
@PostFilter 248–249, 251
@PreAuthorize 248
@PreFilter 248
@Qualifier 27, 72
@Repository 78, 137, 144
@RequestBody 293–294
@RequestHeader 28
@RequestMapping 170, 185, 280, 283, 285, 291
@RequestParam 182, 195
@Resource 27
@ResponseBody 291, 293
@ResponseStatus 286–287
@RolesAllowed 247
@Scheduled 371–372
@Secured 246
@Service 78
@Size 190
@Transactional 144, 156, 162
@Valid 189, 195
@Validation 188
@Value 76, 352
wiring with 70, 77
AnnotationSessionFactoryBean class 135
aop namespace 14, 32, 104, 160
<aop:advisor> element 93
<aop:after> element 14, 93
<aop:after-returning> element 93, 95
<aop:after-throwing> element 93, 95
<aop:around> element 93, 98
<aop:aspect> element 14, 93, 96, 104
<aop:aspectj-autoproxy> element 93, 104, 107
<aop:before> element 14, 94–95
<aop:config> element 94–95
<aop:declare-parents> element 94, 101
<aop:pointcut> element 94, 96
AOP. *See* aspect-oriented programming
Apache CXF 271
Apache Struts 23
Apache Tiles 176–177, 183
<definition> element 186
tile definitions 177
Apache Velocity 369
application context 9–10, 18–19, 22
ApplicationContext interface 18, 90
ApplicationContextAware interface 20
application-managed entity managers 139–141
arg-names attribute 100
@args() pointcut designator 91
args() pointcut designator 91
arithmetic operators 56–57
around advice 87
advantages over before and after advice 97
<aop:around> element 93, 98
@Around annotation 104
declaring 97–98
@Around annotation 104
ASP.NET 26
@AspectJ 102, 107
<aop:aspectj-autoproxy> element 93
compared to <aop:aspect> 104
parameters 105
AspectJ 14, 27, 89, 107, 110
aop namespace 32
@AspectJ 102, 107
compared to Spring AOP 90, 107
filtering 80
writing pointcuts 91
@AspectJ annotation 32
aspect-oriented programming 10, 15
advice 86–87
and Spring Security 225
AspectJ 107, 110
aspects 87
declaring aspects 93, 102
defined 85
example 12, 15
frameworks 89
introductions 88
join points 87
method join points 90
pointcuts 87
securing methods 246, 252
Spring AOP module 22
support in Spring 88, 91
weaving 88

aspects 10, 15, 87
  advice 86
  after advice 14
  <aop:advisor> element 93
  <aop:after> element 93
  <aop:after-returning> element 93
  <aop:after-throwing> element 93
  <aop:around> element 93
  <aop:aspect> element 93, 96
  <aop:aspectj-autoproxy> element 93, 104, 107
  <aop:before> element 94
  <aop:config> element 94–95
  <aop:declare-parents> element 94, 101
  <aop:pointcut> element 94
  as blankets 11
  AspectJ 107, 110
  before advice 14
  compared to inheritance and delegation 86
  cross-cutting concerns 11
  declaring in XML 93, 102
  defined 86
  example 12, 15
  introduction 100, 102
  join points 87
  pointcuts 87
  proxy class 90
  weaving 88
@Async annotation 373–374
asynchronous communication 311
  benefits of 314, 316
  decoupling 315
  guaranteed delivery 315
  JmsProxyFactoryBean 331–332
  Lingo 330, 332
  location independence 315
  no waiting 315
asynchronous methods 371, 373–374
AsyncResult class 373
at inject. *See* @Inject annotation
AtomFeedHttpMessageConverter 292
atomicity. *See* transactions
attachments 366–367
attributes
  access 233, 237
  arg-names 100
  attributes 223
  authentication-failure-url 230
  authorities 239
  authorities-by-username-query 241
  auto-config 229, 231
  base-package 78, 81
  base-path 201
  business-interface 363
  cache 361
  class 34
  connectionFactory 327
  content 186
  cron 372
  cssClass 192
  data-source-ref 240
  defaultImpl 107
  default-impl 102
  default-init-method 41
  default-ref 361
  defining with interfaces 339–340
  delegate-ref 102
  destroy-method 40
  else 205
  expression 79, 204
  factory-method 37, 109
  fixedDelay 371
  fixedRate 371
  flow-registry 201
  group-authorities-by-username-query 241
  group-search-base 242
  group-search-filter 242
  hash 243
  header 291
  id 34, 46
  ignore-resource-not-found 353
  ignore-unresolvable 353
  implement-interface 102
  init-method 40
  jndi-name 121, 359, 362
  jsr250-annotations attribute 247
  key 50, 335
  key-ref 50
  lazy-init 362
  ldif 244
  login 230
  login-processing-url 230
  logout-url 232
  lookup-on-startup 361
  managed 335
  mapping 168
  model 204
  name 160, 239
  objectName 341
  on 206
  on-attribute 207
  params 185
  password 239, 243
  path 192, 202
  path-type 232
  pattern 229, 232
  physicalName 317
  pointcut 95
  pointcut-ref 97
  pre-post-annotations 247
  primary 67

attributes *(continued)*
properties-ref 353
property 235
proxy-interface 361
ref 37, 95
registration 342
required 72
requires-channel 234
resource-ref 121, 359
scope 38, 236
secured-annotations 246
start-state 211
String attributes 82
system-properties-mode 353
targetNamespace 276
then 205
to 206
transactionmanager 162
<tx:attributes> element 160
type 79
types-matching 102
url 237
use-expressions 233
userPassword 243
users-by-username-query 241
user-search-base 242
user-search-filter 242
user-service-ref 239–240
value 37, 43, 50, 53, 106, 287
value-ref 50
view 204, 206
audience example 94, 98, 102, 105
authentication 235–236, 238, 246
LDAP authentication providers 242
Lightweight Directory Access Protocol 241, 245
remember-me feature 245–246
with database 240–241
with in-memory user repository 239–240
authentication providers 242
authentication-failure-url attribute 230
<authentication-manager> element 239, 242
<authentication-provider> element 240, 242
authorities 236, 238
authorities attribute 239
authorities property 236
authorities-by-username-query attribute 241
auto-config attribute 229, 231
autodetect autowiring 65, 68
autodiscovery 77–80
autowire property 65, 70
autodetect 65, 68
byName 65–66
byType 65, 67–68
constructor 65, 68
@Autowired annotation 27, 71, 74, 137, 262, 272, 365
ambiguous dependencies 72–73
and constructors 71
and private keyword 71
and setter methods 71
annotating properties with 71
custom qualifiers 73–74
@Inject 74
optional autowiring with 71
@Qualifier annotation 72
required attribute 72
autowiring
ambiguous dependencies 72–73
autodetect 65, 68
@Autowired annotation 71, 74
best-fit 65, 68
by constructor 65, 68
by name 65–66
byType 65, 67–68
default-autowire property 68
enabling with annotations 70
@Inject annotation 74, 76
JAX-WS endpoints 272–273
mixing with explicit wiring 69–70
null 69
optional 71
@Qualifier annotation 72
standards-based 74, 76
with annotations 70, 77

B

background tasks 370, 374
base-package attribute 78, 81
base-path attribute 201
Basic authentication 231
BasicDataSource
driverClassName property 122
initialSize property 122
maxActive property 122
maxIdle property 122
maxOpenPreparedStatements property 122
maxWait property 122
minEvictableIdleTimeMillis property 123
minIdle property 123
password property 122
pool-configuration properties 122
poolPreparedStatements property 123
url property 122
username property 122
@Bean annotation 81
<bean> element
ActiveMQ configuring 317
and AspectJ injection 109

<bean> element *(continued)*
- class attribute 34
- dataSource property 151
- destroy-method attribute 40
- entityManagerFactory property 152
- factory-method attribute 37, 109
- id attribute 34
- init-method attribute 40
- inner beans 46
- inside <list> 49
- and Jasypt encryption 356
- LocalContainerEntityManagerFactoryBean 141
- LocalEntityManagerFactoryBean 140
- and MBeans 335
- p namespace 46
- primary attribute 67
- scope attribute 38
- sessionFactory property 151
- and SimpleJaxWsServiceExporter 273
- TilesViewResolver 176
- transactionManagerName property 153

bean factories 18, 22, 90
bean scoping 38–39
bean() pointcut designator 93
BeanFactory interface 18
BeanFactoryAware interface 19
bean-managed persistence 138
BeanNameAware interface 19
BeanNameUrlHandlerMapping 170
BeanNameViewResolver 174
BeanPostProcessor interface 20
beans
- autodiscovery 77, 80
- autowiring 65, 70
- bean-managed persistence 138
- <constructor-arg> element 35
- creating through factory methods 37–38
- declaring 31, 41
- entity beans 138
- exporting as HTTP services 268–269
- exporting as JAX-WS endpoints 273–274
- exporting as MBeans 334, 343
- exposing functionality with Hessian and Burlap 264, 266
- Hibernate session factories 135
- initializing and destroying 39, 41
- injecting inner beans 45–46
- injecting into properties 41, 52
- injecting through constructors 34, 38
- lifecycle 19–20
- LocalContainerEntityManagerFactoryBean 139–140
- LocalEntityManagerFactoryBean 139
- referencing by ID 54–55
- referencing other beans 43, 46
- retrieving from application contexts 18
- scoping 38–39
- singletons 38
- wiring 30, 63
- *See also* JavaBeans

<beans> element 32
- default-autowire property 68
- default-destroy-method 41
- default-init-method attribute 41

beans namespace 32
BeanShell, with lang namespace 32
before advice 14, 87
- <aop:before> element 94
- declaring 95, 97
- method before advice 95

@Before annotation 103
best-fit autowiring 65, 68
BMP. *See* bean-managed persistence
boilerplate code, eliminating 15, 17
BufferedImageHttpMessageConverter 292
Burlap 23, 257
- accessing services 266–267
- compared to Hessian 263
- exporting services 266
- exposing bean functionality 264, 266

BurlapServiceExporter class 266
business-interface attribute 363
byName autowiring 65–66
ByteArrayHttpMessageConverter 292
byType autowiring 65, 67–68

C

<c:forEach> element 184
cache attribute 361
caching, JNDI objects 360
callback methods 6
callbacks 118
cascading 133
catch blocks 115, 117
Caucho. *See* Hessian
CCI. *See* Common Client Interface
CciDaoSupport class 120
CciLocalTransactionManager 150
CciTemplate 119
Central Authentication Service, and Spring Security 226
city example 59
class attribute 34
classes
- AnnotationAwareAspectJAutoProxyCreator 104
- AnnotationSessionFactoryBcan 135
- aspect proxy class 90
- AsyncResult 373
- BurlapServiceExporter 266

classes *(continued)*
CciDaoSupport 120
CommonsMultipartResolver 197
configuration class 81
CosMailSenderImpl 363
DAO support classes 119, 121
DefaultMethodSecurityExpressionHandler 251
DelegatingFilterProxy 228
DriverManagerDataSource 123, 361
FileSystemResource 366
FilterChainProxy 228
FlowHandlerAdapter 202
FlowHandlerMapping 202
HessianServiceExporter 264
HibernateDaoSupport 120
HibernateTemplate 134
java.io.File 195
JavaMailSenderImpl 363
JdbcDaoSupport 120, 131
JdbcTemplate 128
JdoDaoSupport 120
JmsUtils class 324
JpaDaoSupport 120
LinkedMultiValueMap 305
LocalSessionFactoryBean 135
Math 55
MBeanExporter 335, 338
MimeMessageHelper 366
MultiValueMap 305
NamedParameterJdbcDaoSupport 120, 131
NamedParameterJdbcTemplate class 128, 130
Naming 261
ParameterizedRowMapper 130
PersistenceAnnotationBeanPostProcessor 144
PersistenceExceptionTranslationPostProcessor 138
ProviderManager 239
RmiProxyFactoryBean 261
RmiServiceExporter 260
SimpleJdbcDaoSupport 120, 131
SimpleJdbcTemplate 128, 130–131
SimpleMetadataStrategy 332
SingleConnectionDataSource 123
SqlMapClientDaoSupport 120
TransactionTemplate 154
VelocityEngineUtils 369
classload-time weaving 88
ClassPathXmlApplicationContext 10, 18
clients, REST 294, 306
cloud storage, Amazon S3 196–197
CMP. *See* container-managed persistence
CMTs. *See* container-managed transactions
Cogoluègnes, Arnaud 24
collections
accessing members with SpEL 60–61
and Spring Expression Language 59, 63
<list> element 47
map collections 49–50
<map> element 47
projection 62–63
properties collections 51
<props> element 47
selecting members 61
selection and projection 62
<set> element 47
wiring 47, 51
collisions, MBean collisions 342–343
commit() method 151–153
Common Client Interface 150
CommonsMultipartResolver class 197
comparison operators 56–57
compile-time weaving 88
@Component annotation 27, 78, 171, 329
<component:property-override> element 354
components 10–11, 15
conditional operators 56, 58–59
@Configuration annotation 81
configuration classes 81
configuring
data sources 121, 124
embedded LDAP servers 244
entity manager factories 139, 142
externalizing configuration 351, 357
flow registries 201–202
Hessian controllers 265–266
mail senders 363, 365
message listeners 327
minimal web security 228
property overriders 351, 354–355
property placeholder configurers 351–352, 354
RMI services 259, 261
Spring 32–33
Spring for file uploads 197
Spring Security 226–227
Spring using XML 32
Spring Web Flow 200, 203
Spring with Java 80
connecting to databases 351
connectionFactory attribute 327
connectionFactory property 321, 330–332
ConnectorServerFactoryBean 343–344
consistency. *See* transactions
constructor autowiring 65, 68
constructor injection 8, 36
constructor pointcuts 107
<constructor-arg> element 35, 317
eliminating with constructor autowiring 68
ref attribute 37
value attribute 37
constructors
autowiring 65, 68
constructor injection 8

constructors *(continued)*
  constructor pointcuts 107
  injecting object references 35, 37
  injecting through 34, 38
container-managed entity managers 139, 141–142
container-managed persistence 138
container-managed transactions 149, 156
containers 20, 32
  bean lifecycle within 19
  container-managed entity managers 139
  container-managed persistence 138
  core container 22
  dependency injection 17
content attribute 186
ContentNegotiatingViewResolver 174, 288–290
  finding views 290
  influencing media types 289
contestant example 101, 106
context namespace 27, 32, 70, 340
  element 353
  <context:property-placeholder> element 352–353
<context:annotation-config> element 70
<context:component-scan> element 77, 137, 171
  base-package attribute 78
  filtering 79–80
<context:exclude-filter> element 79
<context:include-filter> element 79
<context:mbean-export> element 340, 342
<context:mbean-server> element 336
<context:property-placeholder> element 352–353
contextConfigLocation parameter 180
ContextLoaderListener interface 179–180
contextual sessions 134
@Controller annotation 78, 171, 182
ControllerBeanNameHandlerMapping 170
ControllerClassNameHandlerMapping 170
controllers
  @Controller annotation 171
  front controller 166
  handler mappings 170
  handling input 181, 185
  Hessian controllers 265–266
  message converters 291, 294
  RESTful 279, 287
  RESTless 280–281
  Spitter home page controller 170, 173
  testing 172
  writing controllers in Spring MVC 169, 180
conversation scope 208
convertJmsAccessException() method 324
@CookieValue annotation 28
core container 22
CosMailSenderImpl class 363
coupling 7
create() method 363
createContainerEntityManagerFactory() method 139
createEntityManagerFactory() method 139
createMessage() method 322
createMimeMessage() method 366
credentials property 236
cron attribute 372
Cron expressions 372
cross-cutting concerns 11, 85
CRUD operations 285
cssClass attribute 192

D

DAO support classes 119, 121
  and JDBC 131–132
  CciDaoSupport 120
  JdbcDaoSupport 120
  JdoDaoSupport 120
  JpaDaoSupport 120
  NamedParameterJdbcDaoSupport 120
  SimpleJdbcDaoSupport 120
  SqlMapClientDaoSupport 120
DAO. *See* data access objects
data access 144–145
  callbacks 118
  data sources 121, 124
  exception hierarchy 115, 117
  JDBC 124, 132
  JDBC driver-based data source 123–124
  overview 113
  runaway code 124, 127
  templates 118
  templating 117, 119
  tiers 114, 117
  with SimpleJdbcTemplate 128, 130
data access objects 22, 114
  JPA-based 143
  support classes 119, 121
  support classes with JDBC 131–132
  wiring Hibernate to DAO classes 137–138
data access tiers 114
data sources
  BasicDataSource 122
  JDBC driver-based 123–124
  JNDI 121
  pooled 122–123
  with SimpleJdbcTemplate 128
DataAccessException 117
database property 142
databases 113, 145
  authentication 240–241
  connecting to 351
  querying rows with JDBC 126
  updating rows with JDBC 125

DataSource interface 151
dataSource property 132, 135, 141, 151, 359
DataSource, retrieving from JNDI 357, 359
data-source-ref attribute 240
DataSourceTransactionManager 150–151
decision states 203, 205
<decision-state> element 205, 215
@DeclareParents annotation
  defaultImpl attribute 107
  value attribute 106
declaring
  around advice 97–98
  aspects 93, 102
  beans 31, 41
  before and after advice 95, 97
  transactions 155, 163
  transactions in XML 160, 162
  variables in flows 208
DefaultAnnotationHandlerMapping 170
default-autowire property 68
default-destroy-method attribute 41
defaultImpl attribute 107
default-impl attribute 102
DefaultMethodSecurityExpressionHandler class 251
default-ref attribute 361
defaultView property 290
<definition> element 186
definitions property 176
delegate-ref attribute 102
DelegatingFilterProxy class 228
delegation, compared to aspects 86
DELETE method 284, 286, 307
delete() method 295, 301
dependency injection 6, 10, 17
  and AspectJ 107, 110
  and JNDI 359, 362
  and Spring Security 225
  constructor injection 8
  @Resource annotation 27
  with Java configuration 82
Dependency Injection for Java specification. *See* JSR-330;@Inject annotation
design patterns, Template Method 118
destination property 331–332
destinations 312
  queues 313
  setting a default 323
  topics 313–314
destroy() method 20
destroying beans 39, 41
details property 236
dirty reads 158
DispatcherServlet 166, 173
  and HessianServlet 265
  and HTTP invoker 268
  configuring 167
  configuring for file uploads 197
  handler mappings 170
  HiddenHttpMethodFilter 308
  loading application context 179
  mapped to URL patterns 167
  mapping to / 167
  with Spring Web Flow 200
DisposableBean interface 20, 40
doInTransaction() method 155
don't repeat yourself 96
driverClassName property 122
DriverManagerDataSource class 123, 352, 361
DRY principle. *See* don't repeat yourself
durability. *See* transactions
Dynamic MBeans 334

E

eager fetching 133
EclipseLinkJpaVendorAdapter 141
EJB. *See* Enterprise JavaBeans
else attribute 205
Elvis operator 59
email
  attachments 366–367
  constructing 365, 370
  mail senders 363, 365
  mail sessions 364
  rich content 367–368
  templates 368, 370
  wiring mail sender into service bean 365
encryption 243, 355–357
end states 203, 205
endpoints
  autowiring JAX-WS endpoints 272–273
  exporting standalone JAX-WS endpoints 273–274
  JAX-WS 271, 274
<end-state> element 205, 220, 222
Enterprise JavaBeans
  and transactions 149
  forcing you to use its classes or interfaces 5
  jee namespace 32
  specification 4
  stateless 362
  versions 138
  wiring 362–363
  See also JavaBeans
@Entity annotations 136
entity beans 138
entity managers
  application-managed 139–141
  container-managed 139, 141–142
EntityManagerFactory interface 139, 142, 152

entityManagerFactory property 152
<entry> element
  key attribute 50, 335
  key-ref attribute 50
  value attribute 50
  value-ref attribute 50
EnvironmentStringPBEConfig 356
<evaluate> element 204, 208, 212, 216
examples
  audience 94, 98, 102, 105
  city example 59
  contestant 101, 106
  instrumentalist 41, 47, 66–67, 69, 71–73, 78
  JDBC 15, 17
  judge 107, 110
  juggler 33, 38, 81–82
  knife juggler 75
  knight 7, 10, 12, 15
  magician 105
  mind reader 99
  one-man band 48, 51
  pizza ordering 209, 223
  poetic juggler 35, 37, 68
  Spring Idol 31, 63
  stage 37
  ticket 39
exceptions 92
  catch blocks 115, 117
  data access exception hierarchy 115, 117
  DataAccessException 117
  Hibernate 116
  ImageUploadException 195
  InstanceAlreadyExistsException 342
  JDBC exception hierarchy versus Spring exception hierarchy 116
  JMSException 320
  JmsException 320
  MalformedURLException 259
  NamingException 358
  NoSuchBeanDefinitionException 72
  NullPointerException 55, 70
  platform-agnostic 116
  RemoteAccessException 258
  RemoteException 258–259
  SQLException 16, 115, 125
  UnsupportedOperationException 251
  URISyntaxException 300
exchange() method 295, 304
execute() method 155, 295
execution() pointcut designator 91
expression attribute 79, 204
expressions 52–54, 63
Extensible Markup Language (XML) 9
  aspects 14
  configuring Spring with 32
  declaring aspects in 93, 102
  declaring transactions 160, 162
  reducing with annotations 71, 74
  reducing with Java-based configuration 80, 83
  REST-style URLs 28
external properties 355, 357
externalizing configuration 351, 357

F

factory methods, creating beans with 37–38
FactoryBean interface 135
factory-method attribute 37, 109
failOnExisting 342
fallback objects 361–362
favorParameter property 290
favorPathExtension property 289
file system, uploading files to 195
files
  configuring Spring for uploads 197
  saving to Amazon S3 196–197
  saving to file system 195
  user uploads 193, 197
FileSystemResource class 366
FileSystemXmlApplicationContext 18
<filter> element 228
Filter interface 228
FilterChainProxy class 228
filtering
  <context:component-scan> element 79–80
  <context:exclude-filter> element 79
  <context:include-filter> element 79
<filter-name> element 228
fixedDelay attribute 371
fixedRate attribute 371
flash scope 208
flow data 207, 209
  collecting 213, 218
  conversation scope 208
  flash scope 208
  flow scope 208
  request scope 208
  scoping 208
  view scope 208
<flow> element, start-state attribute 211
flow executors 201
flow registries 201–202
flow requests 202
flow scope 208
flow states 206
  action states 203–204
  decision states 203, 205
  end states 203, 205
  subflow states 203, 205
  view states 203–204

<flow:flow-executor> element 201
<flow:flow-location-pattern> element 201
<flow:flow-registry> element 201
FlowHandlerAdapter class 202
FlowHandlerMapping class 202
flow-registry attribute 201
flows 199, 223
  collecting information 213, 218
  declaring variables 208
  defining a base flow 209
  flow data 207, 209
  flow executors 201
  flow registries 201–202
  flow requests 202
  scoping data 208
  securing 222
  states 203, 206
  transitions 206–207
<form> element 307
format parameter 290
FormHttpMessageConverter 292, 300
<form-login> element 230
forms
  adding file upload field 193
  content type 193
  defining views 186–187
  hidden method fields 306–307
  path variables 188
  processing 185, 193
  processing input 187, 189
  RESTful 306, 309
  uploading files 193, 197
  validating input 189, 193
  validation errors 190, 193
  validation rules 189–190
Fowler, Martin 149
frameworks, for aspect-oriented programming 89
FreeMarkerViewResolver 174, 176
front controller, DispatcherServlet 166
Future interface 373

G

Gemini Blueprint 25
GET method 284, 296, 299
get() method 299
getAttribute() method 345
getConnection() method 120
getFirst() method 299
getForEntity() method 295, 298–299
getForObject() method 295, 297–298
getHeaders() method 298
getInstance() method 38
getJdbcTemplate() method 120
getLastModified() method 298
getObject() method 324
getSimpleJdbcTemplate() method 131
getStatusCode() method 299
global transitions 207
<global-method-security> element 246, 251
  jsr250-annotations attribute 247
  pre-post-annotations attribute 247
  secured-annotations attribute 246
<global-transition> element 207
Grails 26
Groovy, with lang namespace 32
group-authorities-by-username-query 241
group-search-base attribute 242
group-search-filter attribute 242

H

hasAnyRole() expression 233
hash attribute 243
hasIpAddress() expression 233
hasPermission() method 250
hasRole() expression 233, 237
HEAD method 285
headers attribute 291
headers, Accept 289, 291, 305
headForHeaders() method 295
Hessian 23, 257
  accessing services 266–267
  compared to Burlap 263
  configuring controllers 265–266
  exporting services 264–265
  exposing bean functionality 264, 266
HessianProxyFactoryBean 266
HessianServiceExporter class 264
Hibernate 22
  and JNDI 359
  and transactions 150–151
  cascading 133
  contextual sessions 134
  declaring a session factory 134, 136
  eager fetching 133
  eliminating template classes 137–138
  @Entity annotation 136
  exception hierarchy 116
  HibernateTemplate 119
  integrating with Spring 132, 138
  JPA vendor adapter 142
  lazy loading 133
  overview 134
  wiring directly to DAO classes 137–138
Hibernate JPA vendor adapter 142
HibernateDaoSupport class 120
HibernateJpaVendorAdapter 141
hibernateProperties property 135
HibernateTemplate class 119, 134

HibernateTransactionManager 150–151
HiddenHttpMethodFilter 307, 309
host property 364
<http> element 229
  path-type attribute 232
  use-expressions attribute 233
HTTP invoker 257
  accessing services via HTTP 269–270
  exporting beans as HTTP services 268–269
<http-basic> element 232
HttpInvoker. *See* HTTP invoker
HttpInvokerProxyFactoryBean 269
HttpInvokerServiceExporter 268
HttpMethod parameter 304
HTTPS. *See* Hypertext Transfer Protocol Secure
HttpServletRequest 227
Hypertext Transfer Protocol
  message converters 291, 294
  methods 284, 287
Hypertext Transfer Protocol Secure 234

I

iBATIS SQL Maps 22
iBATIS, and transactions 150–151
id attribute 34, 46
idempotency 284
<if> element 205
ignoreAcceptHeader property 290
ignoreExisting 342
ignore-resource-not-found attribute 353
ignore-unresolvable attribute 353
IllegalArgumentException 92
image parameter 195
ImageUploadException 195
implement-interface attribute 102
inheritance, compared to aspects 86
initialization on demand holder 38
initializing beans 39, 41
InitializingBean interface 20, 40
initialSize property 122
init-method 20
@Inject annotations 74–76, 171
injection
  injecting inner beans 45–46
  injecting values 42–43
  into bean properties 41, 52
  setter injection 41
  through constructors 34–35, 37–38
inner beans 45–46
input
  controllers 181, 185
  uploading files 193, 197
<input> element 194, 205, 212, 219, 221
installing Spring Web Flow 200, 203
InstanceAlreadyExistsException 342
instrumentalist example 41, 47, 66–67, 69, 71–73, 78
<intercept-url> element 237
  access attribute 233
  pattern attribute 229, 232
  requires-channel attribute 234
InterfaceBasedMBeanInfoAssembler 339
interfaces
  and loose coupling 44
  ApplicationContext 18, 90
  ApplicationContextAware 20
  BeanFactory 18
  BeanFactoryAware 19
  BeanNameAware 19
  BeanPostProcessor 20
  coding to 44
  ContextLoaderListener 179–180
  DataSource 151
  defining MBean operations and attributes with 339–340
  DisposableBean 20, 40
  EntityManagerFactory 139, 142, 152
  FactoryBean 135
  Filter 228
  Future 373
  hiding persistence layer 115
  InitializingBean 20, 40
  java.util.Collection 47, 49
  java.util.Map 47, 50, 131
  java.util.Properties 47, 51, 61
  java.util.Set 49
  javax.sql.DataSource 128
  JpaDialect 152
  MailSender 363, 365
  MailSession 364
  MessageCreator 322
  MessageListener 326
  MultipartResolver 197
  NotificationListener 348
  NotificationPublisherAware 347
  org.hibernate.Session 134
  PersistenceProvider 139
  Provider 75
  Remote 259
  Serializable 258
  SessionFactory 137
  Transaction 152
  TransactionCallback 154
  TransactionDefinition 156, 158
  TransactionManager 153
  UserTransaction 153
InternalResourceViewResolver 174–176

introduction 88, 100, 102
and annotations 106–107
<aop:declare-parents> element 101
invoke() method 345
isAnonymous() expression 233
isAuthenticated() expression 233, 237
isCancelled() method 374
isDone() method 374
isFullyAuthenticated() expression 233
isolation levels 157–159, 161
isolation. *See* transactions
ISOLATION_DEFAULT isolation level 158
ISOLATION_READ_COMMITTED isolation level 158
ISOLATION_READ_UNCOMMITTED isolation level 158
ISOLATION_REPEATABLE_READ isolation level 158
ISOLATION_SERIALIZABLE isolation level 158
isRememberMe() expression 233

J

J2EE Connector Architecture 150
Jakarta Commons Database Connection Pooling 122–123
Jakarta Commons HTTP Client, REST clients 294
JAR files 20
JasperReportsViewResolver 174, 176
Jasypt 351, 355–357
Java
configuring Spring with 80, 83
dependency injection and Java-based configuration 82
jee namespace 32
jms namespace 32
Math class 55
POJOs 5–6
simplifying development 4, 17
Spring advice 89
Java APIs, boilerplate code 15
Java Community Process, JSR-330 74
Java Data Objects 22, 138, 150
Java Management Extensions 334, 349
and remoting 343, 346
JMX Messaging Protocol 343
JSR-160 343
notifications 346, 349
Java Message Service 23, 311, 332
and remote procedure calls 327, 332
and transactions 150
architecting 312, 314
benefits of 314, 316
destinations 312
introduction to 311, 316
JMS invoker 328, 330
jms namespace 32
JmsTemplate 318, 324
JmsTemplate102 321
message brokers 312
message-driven POJOs 325, 327
queues 313
runaway code 318–319
topics 313–314
Java Naming and Directory Interface 357, 359, 362–363
caching JNDI objects 360
conventional 357, 359
fallback objects 361–362
lazy loading 361
mail sessions 364
wiring EJBs 362–363
Java Persistence API 22, 138, 144
and transactions 150, 152
application-managed entity managers 140–141
container-managed entity managers 141–142
Hibernate JPA vendor adapter 142
JPA-based data access objects 143
Java Transaction API 149–150, 153
java.io.File class 195
java.util.Collection interface 47, 49
java.util.Map interface 47, 50, 131
java.util.Map namespace 60
java.util.Properties interface 47, 51, 61
java.util.Set interface 49
JavaBeans
and autodiscovery 77, 80
aspects 10, 15
containers 17, 20
declaring 31, 41
dependency injection 6, 10
entity beans 138
lifecycle 19
POJOs 5–6
specification 3
See also beans
JavaMailSenderImpl class 363
JavaServer Pages 173
and DispatcherServlet 166
and Spring Security 226
rendering hidden method fields 306–307
Standard Tag Library 175
tags for Spring Security 235
JavaServer Pages Standard Tag Library 175
javax.inject package 75
javax.sql.DataSource interface 128
Jaxb2RootElementHttpMessageConverter 292
JAX-RPC 257, 271
JAX-WS 23, 257
autowiring endpoints 272–273
endpoints 271, 274

JAX-WS *(continued)*
  exporting standalone endpoints 273–274
  proxying services on client side 274, 276
JaxWsPortProxyFactoryBean 275
JBoss 121
JBoss AOP 89
JCA. *See* J2EE Connector Architecture
JConsole, and JMX 335
JDBC 124, 132
  and DAO support classes 131–132
  and transactions 150–151
  boilerplate code 15, 126
  driver-based data sources 123–124
  JDBC exception hierarchy versus Spring exception hierarchy 116
  JdbcTemplate 119
  querying rows from databases 126
  runaway code 124, 127
  SQLException 115
  templates 127
  updating rows in databases 125
jdbc.url property 352
JdbcDaoSupport class 120, 131
JdbcTemplate 16, 119, 128
jdbcTemplate property 132
<jdbc-user-service> element 240–241
JDO. *See* Java Data Objects
JdoDaoSupport class 120
JdoTemplate 119
JdoTransactionManager 150
jee namespace 32, 121
<jee:jndi-lookup> element 121, 142, 359
  caching 360
  default-ref attribute 361
  jndi-name attribute 121
  lookup-on-startup attribute 361
  resource-ref attribute 121
<jee:local-slsb> element 362
<jee:remote-slsb> element 362
JetS3t library 196
JMS invoker 328, 330
jms namespace 27, 32, 327
<jms:listener> element 327
<jms:listener-container> element 327, 329
JMS. *See* Java Messaging Service
JMSException 320
JmsException 320–321
JmsInvokerProxyBean 329–330
JmsInvokerProxyFactoryBean 329
JmsInvokerServiceExporter 328–330
JmsServiceExporter 331
JmsTemplate 318, 324
  consuming messages 323–324
  receive() method 323
  send() method 322–323
  sending messages 321, 323
  setting a default destination 323
  wiring 321
JmsTemplate102 321
JmsTransactionManager 150
JmsUtils class, convertJmsAccessException() method 324
JMX Messaging Protocol 343
JMX. *See* Java Management Extensions
JMXConnectorServer 343
JMXMP. *See* JMX Messaging Protocol
JNDI 357, 363
  and EntityManagerFactory 142
  data sources 121
  <jee:jndi-lookup> element 121
jndi-name attribute 121, 359, 362
Johnson, Rod 4
join points 87
  method join points 90
  selecting with pointcuts 91, 93
JpaDaoSupport class 120
JpaDialect interface 152
JpaTransactionManager 150, 152
jpaVendorAdapter property 141
JRuby, with lang namespace 32
JSF 23
JSON 28
JSR-160 343
JSR-250, @RolesAllowed annotation 247
jsr250-annotations attribute 247
JSTL. *See* JavaServer Pages Standard Tag Library
JTA. *See* Java Transaction API
JtaTransactionManager 150, 153
judge example 107, 110
juggler example 33, 38, 81–82
junk drawers 350

K

key attribute 50, 335
key-ref attribute 50
keywords, new 19
knife juggler example, @Inject 75

L

lang namespace 32
lazy loading 133, 361
lazy-init attribute 362
LDAP. *See* Lightweight Directory Access Protocol
<ldap-authentication-provider> element 242
<ldap-server> element 243–244
ldif attribute 244
le and ge operators 57

Lightweight Directory Access Protocol
and authentication 241, 245
and Spring Security 226
authentication providers 242
configuring embedded servers 244
password comparison 242
remote servers 243
Lingo 330–332
LinkedMultiValueMap class 305
<list> element 47
inside another <list> 49
values 48
<listener> element 180
listeners, for notifications 348–349
load-time weaving. *See* classload-time weaving
LocalContainerEntityManagerFactoryBean 139–140
LocalEntityManagerFactoryBean 139
LocalSessionFactoryBean class 135
location property 356
logging out 232
logical operators 56, 58
login attribute 230
login forms 229, 231
login-processing-url attribute 230
<logout> element 232
logout-url attribute 232
lookup-on-startup attribute 361
loose coupling 6, 10, 44
lt and gt operators 57
LTW. *See* classload-time weaving

M

magician example 105
mail senders 363, 365
mail sessions 364
MailSender interface 363, 365
MailSession interface 364
MalformedURLException 259
managed attributes 335
@ManagedAttribute annotation 340
@ManagedOperation annotation 340
@ManagedResource annotation 340
<map> element 47, 50
@MappedSuperclass annotation 136
mapping attribute 168
MappingJacksonHttpMessageConverter 292
mappingResources property 135
maps 49–50
MarshallingHttpMessageConverter 292
matches operator 59
Math class 55
maxActive property 122
maxIdle property 122
maxOpenPreparedStatements property 122
maxWait property 122
MBean agents. *See* MBean servers
MBean info assemblers 337, 339
InterfaceBasedMBeanInfoAssembler 339
MetadataMBeanInfoAssembler 340
MethodExclusionMBeanInfoAssembler 338
MethodNameBasedMBeanInfoAssembler 337
MBeanExporter class 335, 338
registrationBehaviorName property 342
server property 336
MBeanProxyFactoryBean 345
MBeans
accessing remote MBeans 344–345
annotation-driven 340–341
defining operations and attributes with interfaces 339–340
Dynamic MBeans 334
exporting Spring beans as 334, 343
exposing methods by name 337, 339
exposing remote MBeans 343–344
handling collisions 342–343
MBean servers 335
notifications 346, 349
proxying 345–346
remoting 343, 346
Standard MBeans 334
MBeans servers 335
MBeanServerConnection 344
MBeanServerConnectionFactoryBean 344
MDPs. *See* message-driven POJOs
media types 289
mediaTypes property 289
mergeTemplateIntoString() method 369
message brokers 312
ActiveMQ 316–317
setting up 316–317
message converters 291–292, 294
message listeners
configuring 327
creating 326
message-based POJOs
and remote procedure calls 327, 332
JmsInvokerProxyBean 329
JmsInvokerProxyFactoryBean 329
JmsInvokerServiceExporter 328–330
MessageCreator interface 322
@MessageDriven annotation 326
message-driven POJOs, message listeners 326–327
MessageListener interface 326
messages
consuming with JmsTemplate 323–324
sending with JmsTemplate 321, 323
messaging
ActiveMQ 316–317
asynchronous 311

messaging *(continued)*
  benefits of Java Message Service 314, 316
  destinations 312
  message brokers 312
  message listeners 326–327
  message-driven POJOs 325, 327
  point-to-point 313
  publish-subscribe 313–314
  synchronous 311
  with Java Message Service 311, 332
MetadataMBeanInfoAssembler 340
metadataStrategy property 332
method before advice. *See* before advice
MethodExclusionMBeanInfoAssembler 338
MethodNameBasedMBeanInfoAssembler 337
methods
  addAttachment() 366
  addInline() 367
  afterPropertiesSet() 20, 40
  asynchronous 371, 373–374
  callback methods 6
  commit() 151–153
  convertJmsAccessException() 324
  create() 363
  createContainerEntityManagerFactory() 139
  createEntityManagerFactory() 139
  createMessage() 322
  createMimeMessage() 366
  DELETE 284, 286
  delete() 295, 301
  destroy() 20
  doInTransaction() 155
  exchange() 295, 304
  execute() 155, 295
  exposing by name 337, 339
  factory methods 37–38
  GET 284
  get() 299
  getAttribute() 345
  getConnection() 120
  getForEntity() 295, 298–299
  getForObject() 295, 297–298
  getHeaders() 298
  getInstance() 38
  getJdbcTemplate() 120
  getMethods() 299
  getObject() 324
  getSimpleJdbcTemplate() 131
  getStatusCode 299
  hasPermission() 250
  HEAD 285
  headForHeaders() 295
  hidden method fields in forms 306–307
  HiddenHttpMethodFilter 307, 309
  invoke() 345
  isCancelled() 374
  isDone() 374
  mergeTemplateIntoString() 369
  method join points 90
  method-level security pointcuts 252
  OPTIONS 284
  optionsForAllow() 296
  POST 284, 286
  post-authorizing 248
  post-filtering 249, 251
  postForEntity() 296, 302
  postForLocation() 296, 303
  postForObject() 296, 302
  postProcessAfterInitialization() 20
  postProcessBeforeInitialization() 20
  pre-authorizing 248
  PUT 284–285
  put() 296, 299
  queryNames() 344
  receive() 323
  referencing by ID 54
  REST methods 284, 287
  rollback() 151–153
  scheduling 371–372
  securing 246, 252
  securing with SpEL 247, 251
  send() 322–323
  setApplicationContext() 20
  setAttribute() 345
  setBeanFactory() 19
  setBeanName() 19
  setRollbackOnly() 155
  setter methods 42
  setText() 367
  toUpperCase() 55
  TRACE 285
  <tx:methods> element 160
MIME. *See* Multipurpose Internet Mail Extensions
MimeMessageHelper class 366
mind reader example 99
minEvictableIdleTimeMillis property 123
minIdle property 123
mock implementations 8–9, 23
Mockito 9, 173
model attribute 204
Model MBeans 334
Model parameter 183
Model/View/Controller pattern 166
  See also Spring MVC
models 166
Model-View-Controller 23, 32
modules 20, 22–23
MSMQ 26
MultipartResolver interface 197
Multipurpose Internet Mail Extensions 366
MultiValueMap class 305

mvc namespace 32, 168
<mvc:annotation-driven> element 170
<mvc:resources> element 168
MVC. *See* Model-View-Controller

N

name attribute 239
@Named annotation 75
named parameters 130–131
NamedParameterJdbcDaoSupport class 120, 131
NamedParameterJdbcTemplate class 119, 128, 130
namespaces
  aop 14, 32, 104, 160
  beans 32
  context 27, 32, 70, 340, 352
  java.util.Map 60
  jee 32, 121
  jms 27, 32, 327
  lang 32
  mvc 32, 168
  oxm 33
  p 46–47
  Spring Security configuration namespace 226–227
  tx 33, 160
  util 33, 60
namespaceUrl property 276
Naming class 261
NamingException 358
new keyword 19
NHibernate 26
nonrepeatable reads 158
NoSuchBeanDefinitionException 72
NotificationListener interface 348
NotificationPublisherAware interface 347
notifications 346, 348–349
<null/> element
  and autowiring 69
  inside <list> 49
  wiring 52
NullPointerException 55, 70

O

object references, injecting with constructors 35, 37
Object Request Broker 258
objectName attribute 341
objectName property 346
object-relational mapping 22, 133
object-to-XML mapping 28, 33
OC4J container, and transactions 150
OC4JJtaTransactionManager 150
on attribute 206
one-man band example 48, 51
<on-entry> element 220
on-exception attribute 207
Open MBeans 334
OpenID, and Spring Security 226
OpenJpaVendorAdapter 141
operators 60
  - 56
  ^ 56
  ! 58
  ?: 58
  * 56
  / 56
  && 92
  % 56
  + 56
  == 57
  > and < 57
  >= and <= 57
  || 92
  and 58
  arithmetic 56–57
  comparison 56–57
  conditional 56, 58–59
  Elvis operator 59
  le and ge 57
  logical 56, 58
  lt and gt 57
  matches 59
  not 58
  or 58
  regular expressions 56, 59
  relational 56–57
  T() 55
OPTIONS method 284
optionsForAllow() method 296
or operator 58
ORB. *See* Object Request Broker
org.hibernate.Session interface 134
org.springframework.jdbc.datasource package 123
ORM. *See* object-relational mapping
OSGi Blueprint Container 25
oxm namespace 33
OXM. *See* object-to-XML mapping

P

p namespace 46–47
packages, javax.inject 75
packagesToScan property 136
ParameterizedRowMapper class 130
parameters
  contextConfigLocation 180
  format 290

parameters *(continued)*
HttpMethod 304
in @AspectJ 105
Model 183
named 130–131
passing to advice 98, 100
ProceedingJoinPoint 97
params attribute 185
Pareto principle 127
password attribute 239
password property 122, 356, 364
password-attribute attribute 243
<password-compare> element 243
passwords, comparing with LDAP 242
path attribute 192, 202
path-type attribute 232
@PathVariable annotation 188, 282, 284
@Pattern annotation 190
pattern attribute 229, 232
perceived performance 373
performance 373
persistence layer, hiding behind interfaces 115
persistence.xml file 140
PersistenceAnnotationBeanPostProcessor class 144
PersistenceExceptionTranslationPostProcessor class 138
PersistenceProvider interface 139
persistenceUnitName property 140
persisting data 113, 144–145
bean-managed persistence 138
container-managed persistence 138
JDBC 124, 132
JDBC templates 127
overview 113
templating 117, 119
with Hibernate 134, 136
with Java Persistence API 138, 144
phantom reads 158
physicalName attribute 317
pizza delivery example
asking for phone number 215
building an order 218
checking delivery area 217
collecting customer information 213
defining base flow 209
ending flow 218
looking up customer 216
registering new customers 216
storing customer data 218
taking payment 221
pizza ordering example 209, 223
placeholder variables 352–354
plain-old Java objects. *See* POJOs
platform-agnostic exceptions 116
poetic juggler example 35, 37, 68
@Pointcut annotation 103
pointcut attribute 95
pointcut designators 91, 93
<pointcut> element 14
pointcut-ref attribute 97
pointcuts 14, 87, 91, 93
@annotation 91
<aop:pointcut> element 94, 96
@args() 91
args() 91
AspectJ 91
bean() 93
constructor pointcuts 107
execution() 91
method-level 252
pointcut designators 91
@target() 91
target() 91
this() 91
@within() 91
within() 91
writing 92–93
POJOs 5–6, 325, 327
pooled data sources 122–123
poolPreparedStatements property 123
port property 364
portName property 276
POST method 284, 286, 301, 304
HiddenHttpMethodFilter 307–308
receiving object responses 302–303
receiving resource locations 303–304
@PostAuthorize annotation 248
@PostConstruct annotation 27
@PostFilter annotation 248–249, 251
postForEntity() method 296, 302
postForLocation() method 296, 303
postForObject() method 296, 302
postProcessAfterInitialization() method 20
postProcessBeforeInitialization() method 20
Prasanna, Dhanji R. 10
@PreAuthorize annotation 248
@PreFilter annotation 248
pre-post-annotations attribute 247
primary attribute 67
principal expression 237
principal property 236
private keyword, and @Autowired annotation 71
ProceedingJoinPoint parameter 97
processing forms 185, 193
input 187, 189
path variables 188
uploading files 193, 197
validating input 189, 193
validation errors 190, 193
validation rules 189–190

projection 62–63
<prop> element 51
propagation behavior 156–157, 161
PROPAGATION_MANDATORY behavior 157
PROPAGATION_NESTED behavior 157
PROPAGATION_NEVER behavior 157
PROPAGATION_NOT_SUPPORTED behavior 157
PROPAGATION_REQUIRED behavior 157
PROPAGATION_REQUIRES_NEW behavior 157
PROPAGATION_SUPPORTS behavior 157
properties
  algorithm 356
  annotatedClasses 136
  annotating with @Autowired 71
  autowire 65, 70
  collections 47
  connectionFactory 321, 330–332
  database 142
  dataSource 132, 135, 141, 359
  default-autowire property 68
  defaultView 290
  definitions 176
  destination 331–332
  different meanings of term 51
  external 355, 357
  favorParameter 290
  favorPathExtension 289
  hibernateProperties 135
  host 364
  ignoreAcceptHeader 290
  injecting 37
  injecting into 41, 52
  injecting values 42–43
  jdbc.url 352
  jdbcTemplate 132
  jpaVendorAdapter 141
  location 356
  mappingResources 135
  mediaTypes 289
  metadataStrategy 332
  missing 353
  namespaceUrl 276
  objectName 346
  p namespace 46–47
  packagesToScan 136
  password 356
  persistenceUnitName 140
  port 364
  portName 276
  properties collections 51
  property overriders 351, 354–355
  property placeholder configurers 351–352, 354
  proxyInterface 346
  qualifying with @Named 75
  queueName property 330
  referencing by ID 54
  registrationBehaviorName 342
  registryHost 260
  registryPort 260
  server 336, 346
  service 331
  serviceInterface 262, 270, 331–332
  serviceName 276
  serviceUrl 262, 270, 343
  session 365
  system properties 353–354
  systemEnvironment 61
  systemProperties 61
  useNotAcceptableStatusCode 290
  username 364
  velocityProperties 369
  wiring null into 52
  wsdlDocumentUrl 275
properties-ref attribute 353
property attribute 235
<property> element 69
  injecting values 42–43
  inner beans 46
  ref attribute 54
  referencing beans 44
  value attribute 43, 53
property overriders 351, 354–355
property placeholder configurers 351–354
  missing properties 353
<props> element 47, 51
<protect-pointcut> element 252
Provider interface, and @Inject annotation 75
ProviderManager class 239
proxying, MBeans 345–346
proxy-interface attribute 361
proxyInterface property 346
PUT method 284–285
  hidden form fields 307
  HiddenHttpMethodFilter 308
put() method 296, 299, 301

Q

@Qualifier annotation 27, 72–74
<qualifier> element 73
qualifiers, custom 73–75
queryNames() method 344
queueName property 330
queues 313

R

read-only transactions 159
receive() method 323

redirect, prefix 188
ref attribute 37, 95
referencing beans 43, 46
registration attribute 342
registration forms 185, 193
registrationBehaviorName property 342
REGISTRATION_FAIL_ON_EXISTING 342
REGISTRATION_IGNORE_EXISTING 342
REGISTRATION_REPLACING_EXISTING 342
registryHost property 260
registryPort property 260
regular expression operators 56, 59
relational operators 56–57
<remember-me> element 245
remember-me functionality 245–246
Remote interface 259
Remote Method Invocation 23, 257–259, 261, 263, 343
remote procedure calls 256
  Burlap 257, 263, 267
  Hessian 257, 263, 267
  HTTP invoker 257, 268, 270
  JAX-RPC and JAX-WS 257
  JMS invoker 328, 330
  JmsInvokerProxyBean 329–330
  JmsInvokerProxyFactoryBean 329
  JmsInvokerServiceExporter 328–330
  JmsProxyFactoryBean 331–332
  JmsServiceExporter 331
  Lingo 330, 332
  message-based 327, 332
  models 257
  Remote Method Invocation 257–258, 263
remote services 256, 276
  Hessian and Burlap 263, 267
  HTTP invoker 268, 270
  overview 256, 258
  Remote Method Invocation 257–258, 263
RemoteAccessException 258
RemoteException 258–259
remoting. *See* remote services
replaceExisting 342
repositories. *See* data access objects
@Repository annotation 78, 137, 144
representation 278
  negotiating 288, 290
  REST resources 287, 294
request scope 208
@RequestBody annotation 293–294
@RequestHeader annotation 28
@RequestMapping annotation 170–171, 182, 185, 280, 283, 285–287, 291
@RequestParam annotation 182, 195
requests
  determining media type 289
  extracting response metadata 298
  finding views 290
  forcing HTTPS 234
  HiddenHttpMethodFilter 307, 309
  HttpServletRequest 227
  in Spring MVC 165, 167
  influencing media types 289
  intercepting 232, 234
  receiving object responses 302–303
  receiving resource locations 303
  receiving resource state in request body 293–294
  securing 227, 234
required attribute 72
requires-channel attribute 234
resolving views 173, 176–177
@Resource annotation 27
ResourceBundleViewResolver 174
ResourceHttpMessageConverter 292
resource-ref attribute 121, 359
resources
  DELETE requests 301
  exchanging 304, 306
  GET requests 296, 299
  negotiating representation 288, 290
  POST requests 301, 304
  PUT requests 299, 301
  receiving locations 303–304
  receiving state in request body 293–294
  representing 287, 294
  resource-oriented URLs 282
  REST 278, 309
  REST clients 294, 306
  RESTful controllers 279, 287
  retrieving 297–298
  returning state in response body 291, 293
@ResponseBody annotation 291, 293
ResponseEntity 298
responses
  extracting metadata 298–299
  returning resource state in response body 291, 293
@ResponseStatus annotation 286–287
REST 28, 278, 309
  controllers 279, 287
  exchanging resources 304, 306
  forms 306, 309
  introduction 278
  methods 284, 287
  negotiating representation 288, 290
  representing resources 287, 294
  RESTful URLs 281, 284
  RESTless controllers 280–281
  RestTemplate 295–296
  Spring support for 279
  verbs 284, 287
  writing clients 294, 306

REST clients
  GET requests 296, 299
  PUT requests 299, 301
  writing 294, 306
RESTful resources 279
RESTful URLs 281–282, 284
RestTemplate 294–296, 306
-rex suffix 47
rich text email 367–368
RMI 23, 257
RmiProxyFactoryBean class 261
RmiRegistryFactoryBean 343
RmiServiceExporter class 260, 343
@RolesAllowed annotation 247
rollback rules 159, 161
rollback() method 151–153
RPC. *See* remote procedure calls
RssChannelHttpMessageConverter 292
Ruby on Rails 26
runaway code 124, 127, 318–319
runtime weaving 88

S

<s:url> element 178
safety 284
@Scheduled annotation 371–372
scheduled jobs 371
scheduling 370–372, 374
scope 38–39, 208
scope attribute 38–39, 236
@Secured annotation 246
secured-annotations attribute 246
<security:authentication> element, credentials property 236
security
  minimal 228
  securing flows 222
  See also Spring Security
<security:accesscontrollist> element 235
<security:authentication> element 235–236
<security:authorize> element 235–238
send() method 322–323
sending email 363, 370
Serializable interface 258
server property 336, 346
<server-name> element 167
servers, MBean servers 335
@Service annotation 78
service property 331
serviceInterface property 262, 270, 331–332
serviceName property 276
service-oriented architecture 270, 276
services
  accessing Burlap and Hessian services 266–267
  accessing via HTTP 269–270
  configuring RMI services 259, 261
  exporting beans as HTTP services 268–269
  exporting Burlap services 266
  exporting Hessian services 264–265
  exporting RMI services 259, 261
  JAX-WS on client side 274, 276
  publishing and consuming web services 270, 276
  remote 256, 276
  wiring RMI services 261, 263
serviceUrl property 262, 270, 343
<servlet> element 167
servlet filters 228
<servlet-mapping> element 269
servlets
  DispatcherServlet 166
  servlet filters 228
session beans 5
session factories 134, 136
session property 365
SessionFactory interface 137
sessionFactory property 151
<set> element 47, 208
setApplicationContext() method 20
setAttribute() method 345
setBeanFactory() method 19
setBeanName() method 19
setRollbackOnly() method 155
setter injection 41
  inner beans 45
  versus constructor injection 36
setter methods 42, 71
setText() method 367
<sf:checkbox> element 187
<sf:errors> element 191–192
<sf:form> element 193, 306–307
<sf:input> element 187
<sf:password> element 187
<sf:form> element 187
SimpleJaxWsServiceExporter 271, 273–274
SimpleJdbcDaoSupport class 120, 131
SimpleJdbcTemplate 16, 119, 128, 130–131
SimpleMetadataStrategy class 332
SimpleUrlHandlerMapping 170
SingleConnectionDataSource class 123
singleton beans 18, 38
@Size annotation 190
SOA. *See* service-oriented architecture
SourceHttpMessageConverter 292
SpEL. *See* Spring Expression Language
Spitter example 128, 144, 154–155, 160, 163
  and email 365
  and JmsInvokerServiceExporter 328
  and MBeans 334, 349
  and REST 280, 309

Spitter example *(continued)*
  controllers 181, 185
  home page controller 170, 173
  home page view 177, 179
  messaging with JMS 321
  registration form 185, 193
  remote services 256, 259, 276
  Spring MVC controller 169, 197
  uploading files from users 194, 197
  with message-driven POJO 326
Spring
  and POJOs 5–6
  application context 9, 18–19, 179–180
  aspect-oriented programming 10, 15
  configuring 32–33
  configuring for file uploads 197
  configuring with Java 80, 83
  containers 17, 20
  core container 22
  data access exception hierarchy 115, 117
  data access objects module 22
  data access tiers 114
  declaring beans 31, 41
  declaring transactions 155, 163
  dependency injection 6, 10
  eliminating boilerplate code 15, 17
  exception hierarchy versus JDBC exception hierarchy 116
  flexibility 6
  history 3
  integrating with Hibernate 132, 138
  integration with Java Persistence API 138, 144
  JmsTemplate 318, 324
  messaging with JMS 311, 332
  modules 20, 23
  MVC framework 23
  ORM module 22
  portfolio 23
  programming transactions 153, 155
  runtime AOP 90
  simplifying Java development 4, 17
  Spring AOP 89
  Spring Batch 24
  Spring Dynamic Modules 25
  Spring Faces 28
  Spring Framework 20, 23
  Spring Integration 24
  Spring JavaScript 28
  Spring LDAP 25
  Spring Rich Client 25
  Spring Roo 26
  Spring Security 24, 225, 252
  Spring Social 25
  Spring Web Flow 24, 199, 223
  Spring Web Services 24
  Spring.NET 26
  Spring-Flex 26
  support for aspect-oriented programming 88, 91
  support for REST 279
  testing module 23
  transaction support 149
  what's new in Spring 2.5 27
  what's new in Spring 3.0 28
  wiring beans 30, 63
  working with databases 113, 145
  XML configuration 32
Spring AOP 89
  classic 89
  compared to AspectJ 90, 107
  method join points 90
Spring Batch 24
Spring Dynamic Modules 25
Spring Expression Language 52, 63, 205
  - operator 56
  ^ operator 56
  ! operator 58
  ?: operator 58
  * operator 56
  / operator 56
  % operator 56
  + operator 56
  == operator 57
  > and < 57
  >= and <= 57
  accessing collection members 60–61
  and annotations 76–77
  and operator 58
  and Spring Security 233–234
  and types 55
  and @Value annotation 77
  collections 59, 63
  le and ge operators 57
  literal values 53–54
  lt and gt operators 57
  not operator 58
  operations on values 59
  operators 56
  or operator 58
  referencing beans by ID 54–55
  securing methods 247, 251
  security-specific expressions 233
  selecting collection members 61
  systemEnvironment property 61
  systemProperties property 61
  T() operator 55
Spring Faces 28
Spring Framework 20, 22–23, 89
Spring Integration 24
Spring JavaScript 28

Spring LDAP 25
Spring MVC 164, 198
  and annotations 170
  basics 165, 168
  DispatcherServlet 166
  handling controller input 181, 185
  processing forms 185, 193
  requests 165, 167
  REST support 28
  setting up 167–168
  Spring Web Flow 200
  with Apache Tiles 176–177
  writing controllers 169, 180
Spring portfolio 23, 28
Spring Rich Client 25
Spring Roo 26
Spring Security 24, 225, 252
  Acegi Security 225
  and Spring Expression Language 233–234
  and view-level elements 235, 238
  aspect-oriented programming 225
  authentication 235–236, 238–240, 246
  authentication with database 240–241
  authentication with in-memory user repository 239–240
  authorities 236, 238
  Basic authentication 231
  configuration namespace 226–227
  configuring 226–227
  dependency injection 225
  encryption 243
  forcing HTTPS 234
  intercepting requests 232, 234
  Lightweight Directory Access Protocol 241, 245
  logging out 232
  login forms 229, 231
  method-level pointcuts 252
  methods 246, 252
  minimal web security 228
  modules 226
  password comparison with LDAP 242
  remember-me functionality 245–246
  securing web requests 227, 234
  security-specific expressions 233
  servlet filters 228
Spring Security 2.0 28
Spring Security 3.0 29
Spring Security modules 226
Spring Social 25
Spring Web Flow 24, 199–200, 203, 223
  See also flows
Spring Web Flow 2.0 28
Spring Web Services 24
Spring.NET 26
SpringBeanAutowiringSupport 272
Spring-DM 25
Spring-Flex 26
SQLException 16, 125
SqlMapClientDaoSupport class 120
SqlMapClientTemplate 119
stage example 37
Standard MBeans 334
StandardPBEStringEncryptor 356
start-state attribute 211
state 279
String attributes, downside of 82
string encryptors 356
StringHttpMessageConverter 292
Struts 6
subflow states 203, 205
<subflow-state> element 205, 212
synchronous communication 311, 314–315
  coupling 315
system properties 353–354
systemEnvironment property 61
systemProperties property 61
system-properties-mode attribute 353

T

T() operator 55
Tapestry 6, 23
@target() pointcut designator 91
target() pointcut designator 91
targetNamespace attribute 276
<task:annotation-driven> element 371
template classes, relationship to DAO support classes 120
Template Method pattern 118
templates 15, 17, 118
  CciTemplate 119
  eliminating template classes with Hibernate 137–138
  email templates 368, 370
  HibernateTemplate 119
  JDBC 127
  JdbcTemplate 16, 119
  JdoTemplate 119
  NamedParameterJdbcTemplate 119
  SimpleJdbcTemplate 16, 119
  SqlMapClientTemplate 119
templating, data access 117, 119
Templier, Thierry 24
testing
  controllers 172
  mock implementations 8, 23
  testing module 23
  unit testing 7
then attribute 205
this() pointcut designator 91

ticket example 39
tight coupling 7, 358
tile definitions 177
TilesConfigurer 176
TilesViewResolver 174, 176–177
timeout 159, 161
to attribute 206
Tomcat 121
topics 313–314
TopLinkJpaVendorAdapter 141
toUpperCase() method, referencing by ID 55
TRACE method 285
transaction attributes 156, 160
  isolation levels 157, 159, 161
  propagation behavior 156–157, 161
  read-only 159, 161
  rollback rules 159, 161
  timeout 159, 161
Transaction interface 152
transaction managers 150–153
@Transactional annotation 144, 156, 162
TransactionCallback interface 154
TransactionDefinition interface 156, 158
transactionmanager attribute 162
TransactionManager interface 153
transactionManagerName property 153
TransactionProxyFactoryBean 156, 160
transactions 146
  ACID 148
  annotation-driven 162–163
  atomicity 148
  consistency 148
  container-managed 149
  declaring 155, 163
  declaring in XML 160, 162
  dirty reads 158
  durability 148
  explained 147, 150
  isolation 148
  isolation levels 157, 159, 161
  Java Transaction API 149
  nonrepeatable reads 158
  phantom reads 158
  programming in Spring 153, 155
  propagation behavior 156–157, 161
  read-only 159, 161
  rollback rules 159, 161
  support in Spring 149
  timeout 159, 161
  transaction attributes 156, 160
  transaction managers 150, 153
  tx namespace 33
TransactionTemplate class 154
<transition> element 206
transitions 206–207
tx namespace 33, 156, 160, 162
<tx:advice> element 160
<tx:annotation-driven> element 162
<tx:attributes> element 160
<tx:method> element 160
type attribute 79
types, with Spring Expression Language 55
types-matching attribute 102

U

uniform resource locators
  embedded parameters 282, 284
  pattern matching 167
  RESTful 281, 284
  RESTful URLs explained 281–282
unit testing 7
UnsupportedOperationException 251
URISyntaxException 300
url attribute 237
url property 122
UrlBasedViewResolver 174
URLs. *See* uniform resource locators
use-expressions attribute 233
useNotAcceptableStatusCode property 290
<user> element 239
username property 122, 364
userPassword attribute 243
users-by-username-query attribute 241
user-search-base attribute 242
user-search-filter attribute 242
<user-service> element 239–240
user-service-ref attribute 239–240
UserTransaction interface 153
util namespace 33, 60
<util:properties> element 61, 353–354
<util-list> element 60

V

@Valid annotation 188–189
validation
  errors 190, 193
  form input 189, 193
  rules 189–190
@Value annotation 76, 195, 352
value attribute 37, 43, 50, 53, 106, 287
<value> element, inside <list> 49
value-ref attribute 50
values
  injecting 42–43
  literal 53–54
  operations on SpEL values 59
<var> element 208

variables
  declaring in flows 208
  placeholder variables 352–354
Velocity, and Spring Security 235
VelocityEngine 369
VelocityEngineFactoryBean 369
VelocityEngineUtils class 369
VelocityLayoutViewResolver 174, 176
velocityProperties property 369
VelocityViewResolver 174, 176
view attribute 204, 206
view resolvers 173
  BeanNameViewResolver 174
  ContentNegotiatingViewResolver 174, 288, 290
  FreeMarkerViewResolver 174, 176
  InternalResourceViewResolver 174–176
  JasperReportsViewResolver 174, 176
  ResourceBundleViewResovler 174
  TilesViewResolver 174, 176–177
  UrlBasedViewResolver 174
  VelocityLayoutViewResolver 174, 176
  VelocityViewResolver 174, 176
  XmlViewResolver 174
  XsltViewResolver 174, 176
view scope 208
view states 203–204
views 166
  authorities 236, 238
  finding 290
  form views 186–187
  home page view 177, 179
  internal 175–176
  rendering 183
  resolving 173, 177
  securing view-level elements 235, 238
  with Apache Tiles 176–177
<view-state> element 204
VisualVM, and JMX 335

W

weaving 88
web services
  JAX-WS endpoints 271, 274
  JAX-WS on client side 274, 276
  publishing and consuming 270, 276
WEB-INF directory 167
WebLogic, and transactions 150
WebLogicJtaTransactionManager 150
WebSphere 121
WebSphereUowTransactionManager 150
WebWork 6, 23
wiring 9
  autowiring 65, 70
  beans 30, 37, 63
  collections 47, 51
  defined 30
  Enterprise JavaBeans 362–363
  Hibernate to DAO classes 137–138
  inner beans 46
  JmsTemplate 321
  JNDI objects 357, 363
  mail sender to service bean 365
  map collections 49–50
  mixing autowiring and explicit wiring 69–70
  <null/> element 52
  properties 46–47
  properties collections 51
  -ref suffix 47
  referencing by ID 54–55
  RMI services 261, 263
  with annotations 70, 77
  with Spring Expression Language 52, 63
@within() pointcut designator 91
writing pointcuts 92–93
<wsdl:definitions> element, targetNamespace
    attribute 276
<wsdl:port> element 276
<wsdl:service> element 276
wsdlDocumentUrl property 275

X

XFire 271
XML. *See* Extensible Markup Language
XmlAwareHttpMessageConverter 292
XmlViewResolver 174
XmlWebApplicationContext 18
XsltViewResolver 174, 176